Peace Impossible — War Unlikely

The Cold War Between the United States and the Soviet Union

D0104381

Peace Impossible —

War Unlikely

The Cold War Between the United States and the Soviet Union

Joseph L. Nogee
University of Houston

John Spanier
University of Florida

Scott, Foresman/Little, Brown College Division
Scott, Foresman and Company
Glenview, Illinois   Boston   London

Library of Congress Cataloging-in-Publication Data

Nogee, Joseph L.
  Peace impossible — war unlikely.

  Bibliography: p.
  Includes index.
  1. United States — Foreign relations — Soviet Union.
  2. Soviet Union — Foreign relations — United States.
  3. United States — Foreign relations — 1945–   .
  4. Soviet Union — Foreign relations — 1945–   .
  5. World politics — 1945–   . I. Spanier, John
  II. Title.
  E183.8.S65N64   1988   327.73047   87-26500
  ISBN 0-673-39783-1

1 2 3 4 5 6 7 8 9 10 — VPI — 93 92 91 90 89 88 87

Printed in the United States of America

Question to Radio Armenia:
"Will there be a Third World War?"

Answer:
"There will not be a Third World War. But there will be such a fight for peace that not a single stone will be left unturned!"

Preface

As we enter the fifth decade of the conflict between the Soviet Union and the United States, it seems appropriate to reexamine the nature and causes of the Cold War. Like the war itself, the literature analyzing Soviet-American relations seems endless. Why another interpretation? We believe that as long as the conflict endures it must continuously be examined and reexamined in light of changing events. For while the underlying causes of the conflict might remain constant, the circumstances in which the rivalry is played out are always changing. Neither technology nor politics are static.

Taken from a felicitous phrase of the late French political scientist Raymond Aron, the title "Peace Impossible — War Unlikely" sums up the essence of our interpretation of the Cold War. With Aron we believe that until there is a fundamental change in the Soviet regime the conflict will endure; but because of the existence of nuclear weapons, this conflict will not lead to war. Our interpretation of the Cold War borrows from the investigations of many. We want to mention three works in particular: Voytech Mastny's *Russia's Road to the Cold War,* William Taubman's *Stalin's American Policy* and, more recently, Hugh Thomas's *Armed Truce.* Their scholarship has provided important insights regarding the Soviet perspective. Much of the literature of the Cold War is based upon Western sources for the unavoidable reason that Soviet archives and sources are inaccessible to Western scholars. We have found that the above-mentioned books, which include Soviet and Eastern European sources, useful as a corrective to the curious American habit of writing about the Cold War as if only the United States played a major role in bringing it about.

The variety of Cold War interpretations is extensive. The standard or orthodox school stresses the culpability of the USSR. Within that school, many scholars focus on the aggressiveness of Soviet policy in the 1940s, but differ as to the roots of Soviet expansionism. Some find its roots in the dynamics of Marxist-Leninist ideology, while others see Soviet behavior as following in the Russian imperial tradition. Soviet foreign policy can be the product of both. There are those who stress Soviet expansionism but reject ideology or tradition as the mainspring of Soviet behavior. They see Soviet policy in terms of the concept of the balance of power. Even within this concept, opinions vary. It can be argued that the defeat of Germany and Japan produced power vacuums which the USSR sought to fill, as any great power would. A conflict between the great powers would therefore have been unavoidable no matter what the ideological or political makeup of either regime. Another variant of the balance of power perspective focuses on the legitimate Soviet needs for security in Eastern Europe. Having paid a terrible price to defeat Nazi Germany, Moscow, it is argued, was entitled to expand its power so as never to be vulnerable to the same kind of threat again. But as we argue with our use of the concept of political culture, Soviet expansionism can be the result of both Marxist-Leninist ideology and imperial tradition.

Contrasting with the orthodox — or conservative — interpretations are the "revisionist" writers who hold the United States responsible for both the origins and the perpetuation of the Cold War. Here too there are subschools and varieties of explanations. Operating from a Marxist perspective, some believe American opposition to the Soviet Union was a result of an "imperialistic" economy. The United States could not accept a "socialist" Eastern Europe because it wanted to penetrate the markets of Eastern Europe for its surplus production.

In other words, capitalist imperialism caused the Cold War. Others offer less grandiose explanations and find the roots of American hostility to the Soviet Union in the anti-communist ideology which dominated the Truman administration. One revisionist interpretation argues that Truman used the atomic bomb against Japan to pressure or frighten Stalin into accepting the American vision of a postwar world order. Presumably, if Franklin Roosevelt had lived, the United States would have been more sympathetic to Soviet concerns and there would have been no Cold War.

Besides those schools of thought which apportion blame to one side or the other is that which claims that the conflict is the result of misperception, a disease which afflicted east and west alike. The United States failed to understand Stalin's desire for security or his particular interpretation of democracy, while Stalin, perhaps because of his extreme suspiciousness, saw in every action taken by the Truman administration a hostile maneuver. Misperception has continued unabated, year after year, resulting in the action-reaction phenomenon of each administration.

We have examined these and other interpretations of U.S.-Soviet relations. From some we have borrowed elements to construct our own hypotheses; some we rejected outright as not conforming to the facts. In the end, we conclude that no one factor explains the Cold War; rather, it has a three-fold explanation, whose elements correspond to a major theoretical approach to explaining international politics. The three approaches are: the systemic, the character of the nation-state, and decision-making.

It has been fashionable in the name of fairness or objectivity to apportion equal responsibility for the Cold War to the United States and the USSR. We do not believe that conclusion to be supported by the evidence. We have examined revisionist and post-revisionist arguments and conclude that the Soviet state and its leaders bear primary responsibility for the Cold War, and that until there is a change in the Soviet regime the Cold War will continue in some form. To the charge of undue pessimism, we express the belief that the Soviet system will change in time, though how and when cannot now be forseen.

As is customary and proper we take full responsibility for the interpretations and conclusions contained herein. This book has been made the better by the editorial modifications of John S. Covell, as well as the criticism of Charles Gati, Columbia University and Union College; Patrick Morgan, Washington State University; and David Ziegler, Western Washington University.

Joseph L. Nogee
John Spanier

Contents

Peace Impossible — War Unlikely

The Cold War Between
the United States and
the Soviet Union

From Wartime Allies to Postwar Enemies

Why and How the Cold War Started

Neither War nor Peace

The Cold War between the United States and the Soviet Union has entered its fifth decade. That is a long time for any international conflict; more remarkable is that it shows no signs of termination. There is every reason to expect that it will still be with us in the year 2000. Initially limited to the southern flank of Russia and then western Europe, it has now become a global rivalry. Since the mid-1970s it has been extended to Africa, especially the Horn of Africa, southwest Asia, notably the Persian Gulf, and the Central American–Caribbean area. It is not only the longest rivalry engaged in by either the United States or Russia; it already ranks as history's second most extended conflict. It is almost twice as long as the Peloponnesian War between the city-states of Athens and Sparta for the control of ancient Greece; it almost equals the time span of the three Punic Wars between Rome and Carthage for domination of the Mediterranean world; and it is longer than the Thirty Years War between the forces of Protestantism and Catholicism in the seventeenth century, the almost uninterrupted 25 years of war between revolutionary and Napoleonic France and the rest of Europe for European dominion, and the two efforts by Germany in this century to establish its hegemony over Europe, if not Eurasia and beyond. Indeed, the Cold War already exceeds the length of World Wars I and II plus the interwar period. In addition to length, the American-Soviet rivalry represents two nations whose strength far exceeds those of all preceding great powers in history. Their power so eclipses that of all past contestants that the word "superpower" has been applied to both of them — and would have even if neither had possessed enormous nuclear arsenals.

Defining the Cold War
While the term Cold War has now become commonplace in describing U.S.–Soviet relations for the last forty years, the use of the word "war" in this context is somewhat misleading. After all, neither country has declared war on the other. Nor,

to date, have American and Soviet armed forces been directly engaged in hostilities against each other. Yet the word "war" is apt and not an accident. States do not go to war lightly. While moralists may reject war as immoral, and philosophers and social scientists often regard it as not only inhumane but "socially deviant behavior," statesmen throughout history have regarded war as a rational instrument of statecraft, although it was usually used only as a means of last resort. It was rational because the benefits of securing or defending the issues at stake were calculated as being greater than the costs in lives and money; and it was normally an instrument of last resort because to resolve issues without resorting to force would be less costly.

Nevertheless, when the stakes were believed to be critical and peaceful resolution proved impossible, the sword replaced the pen. In the wars cited above — the major struggles of their time — the stakes were which power and whose values would prevail in the state system.[1] As Hans Morgenthau wrote many years ago:

> All the great wars which decided the course of history and changed the political face of the earth were fought for real stakes, not for imaginary ones. The issue in these great convulsions was invariable: who shall rule and who shall be ruled? Who shall be free, and who, slave?[2]

The stakes in the contemporary Cold War are no less. But this time the outcome will affect not just Greece, the Mediterranean, Europe, or Eurasia — it will affect the entire world.

It is therefore quite correct to say that the United States and the Soviet Union have been engaged in a form of warfare since World War II. Interestingly and somewhat paradoxically, despite the military connotation of the word "warfare," the conventional view is that the period since 1945 has been essentially one of peace. Much like the nineteenth century, it is seen as a period of general peace despite the repeated occurrences of many small wars. A leading historian of the Cold War has in fact described the postwar period as "the long peace," although he acknowledges that it is "arguable whether this can legitimately be called 'peace.'"[3] It is our contention that the nature of the contest between the two superpowers over the past half century is closer to war than peace, even though the U.S. and Soviet military forces have not engaged each other in direct combat. What determines the character of the U.S.–Soviet belligerency is (1) their perception of each other as the principal enemy, (2) the extent of their conflicting interests, and (3) the willingness of both to use all safe means to diminish the power of the adversary. In turn, this reflects the profoundly different world order each seeks to establish. The resulting struggle involves political, military, economic, and psychological weapons and, more than in the two world wars, it is truly a global one.

To be sure, it is a complex struggle, alternating between periods of relative peace and war, between great tensions and détente. But this does not mean that the Cold War has been discontinued. Many analysts and commentators limit the term Cold War to the period of the 1940s and 1950s, ending with the Cuban missile crisis in 1962. Soviet-American relations are generally described as having changed after the nuclear test ban treaty in 1963, and the 1970s are conventionally labeled as a period of détente. Thus when détente collapsed and U.S.–Soviet relations soured after the Soviet invasion of Afghanistan in 1979, a frequent term used to describe the relationship in the 1980s was "Cold War II." While this term is quite an appropriate description of the higher levels of tension after years of détente, we believe that the Cold War never really ended and that it will probably endure for many years to come.

The reason why the noun "war" is preceded by the adjective "cold" is because both sides have nuclear weapons and both sides know that a "hot" war could mean mutual suicide. In the past, the purpose of the military has been to win wars, but since 1945 its task has been to avoid them since an all-out war is now irrational. The superpowers' fear of extinction has compelled them to conduct their rivalry with restraint and discipline, not to initiate military action against each other. While this testifies to the very horror of nuclear weapons and their awesome destructive capabilities, the 40 years that a nuclear war has been avoided is no mean achievement, given the time and intensity of the Soviet-American struggle. It took the great powers of Europe only 20 years from the signing of the peace treaty ending World War I (1919) to begin World War II. But as Winston Churchill, Britain's great World War II leader and orator, remarked 10 years after that conflict, nations have "by a process of sublime irony" reached a stage where "safety will be the sturdy child of terror, and survival the twin brother of annihilation." Since World War II, there has been no war not only between the two superpowers but also between their main allies as well.

Thus the Cold War represents a U.S.–Soviet relationship characterized by continuous mutual enmity in which force is not used to decide who is the winner. Despite the struggle, the tensions do not escalate to the level where violence is actually used by either against the other; military power is used only to intimidate, pressure, or deter. War has been called a continuation of politics by other means; the Cold War may be said to be the continuation of war by other means. Involving on the one hand political conflict and a clash of wills and, on the other, the rejection of force, this relationship may also be called one of "neither war nor peace." The implication is as obvious as it is critical: The rejection of force means the perpetuation of this political conflict. Whereas preceding rivalries were usually decided on the battlefield, the perpetuation of the Cold War means that it becomes a contest of protracted or historical attrition.[4]

The Balance of Power and U.S. Foreign Policy

How did the Cold War start and why? This takes us back to fundamentals and the basis of international conflict. The root of the problem is the "state system."[5] Composed of nation-states, each of whom claims to be the sovereign and has exclusive control over its people and territory, each is also independent of all other states and responsible for protecting itself. Thus the fundamental condition is one of anarchy. This does not mean chaos as much as the absence of worldwide governmental institutions to keep order, mediate conflicts among members-states, and assure peaceful change. States must provide for their own security. Not surprisingly, states therefore arm themselves, for in the final analysis, if one state has designs on another, the latter may be able to defend itself only by force. Military resistance may be the only way of preserving its security, which usually means its territorial integrity and political independence.

In the international environment, states tend to regard one another as potential adversaries.* Insecure, they live in a condition of mutual suspicion and fear. Even the most peace-loving state is likely to be armed, if only because its neighbors are armed and it may suspect that one or more of them may be less peace-loving than itself. A neighbor may claim that its intentions are only the friendliest and it may be sincere. The problem is that tomorrow that neighbor may become unfriendly. Governments may change their minds or a friendly one may be replaced by an unfriendly one. A neighbor may be amicable because it is not strong enough to make demands, but it may increase its strength and become more of a threat. Its ambitions may grow as its power increases. Thus the question is whether the state professing only the most peaceful intentions is genuinely sincere or whether it is pursuing a strategy of deception, trying to lull another state into relaxing its guard as a prelude to a strike. When nations feel that the stakes are high — their security, if not their survival — they prefer to remain on guard and to feel safe rather than sorry.

How in these circumstances do states achieve a degree of security they feel they can live with? (The use of the word

---

*We are presenting here a model of the state system. In the real world, while this is often true (especially for great powers), there are notable exceptions such as the United States and Canada or the contemporary states of western-central Europe, formerly bitter enemies.

"degree" is deliberate since in a system of many states none can be *absolutely* secure. Thus all states must live with a degree of *in*security.) The answer is the "balance of power." If states are to preserve their security and independence, they cannot allow any state or coalition of states to achieve a superiority of power or hegemony because if it does, it may be tempted to impose its will or demands upon other states. States confronting potentially hostile powers will be concerned with their relative power positions and try to be at least as strong as potential adversaries, if not achieve a margin of superiority for extra insurance. Weaker states seek allies in order to pool their strength. The result will be a tendency toward an equilibrium. For the basic idea remains the same: If a state is as powerful as a possible aggressor, it is not likely to be attacked. The cost of victory for the latter, if it were even possible, will be too great. Since an equitable distribution of power among nations tends to guarantee their security and independence — and therefore their specific way of life — the basic rules for states are simple: Protect yourself; do not rely heavily on professions of amicable intentions by other states; ensure your security by being as strong as any potentially hostile state.

The United States Emergence from Isolationism
If the balance of power is so important in preserving a state's security, it follows that it is one of the more critical factors explaining its foreign policies. The United States provides a superb example of this, for it was the shift in the European balance that compelled this nation to come out of its isolationist shell. During much of its existence, this nation had deliberately pursued a policy of nonentanglement in European affairs. Isolationism had meant isolation from Europe. Weak neighbors to the north and south, the Atlantic and Pacific Oceans to the east and west, and the British Navy guarding the approaches to the western hemisphere — all of these factors provided the United States with security for most of the nineteenth century. The reason that Britain, the world's premier

naval power during much of that time, did guard the western hemisphere was to protect its own security. It was Britain's historic policy to preserve a balance among the continental European powers. It opposed any nation that tried to conquer Europe, mobilize the vanquished nations' populations and resources, and sought to achieve a superiority of power that could be used to invade Britain. But as a continental nation, larger in population and industrial strength, arose, Britain's ability to prevent that power from gaining control over Europe declined. Therefore, the United States became increasingly drawn into international politics.

It was Germany that ended America's isolation from European power politics. United under Prussian leadership and having defeated France in 1870, by 1914 it was Europe's most powerful state. It had the largest population, except for Russia, and superseded England as the most advanced in industry.[6] Germany twice tried to establish continental hegemony: the first time as a monarchy, which led to World War I; the second time, as a Fascist power under Hitler, which led to World War II. Even when Britain's power was added to that of France and Russia, it was barely enough to prevent a German victory but insufficient to defeat her. Germany's power was simply too great. It was American power that had to be thrown onto the scales on the allied side to defeat Germany. And by 1914, the United States was "not merely an economic power on the European level; she was a rival continent. Her coal production equalled that of Great Britain and Germany put together; her iron and steel production surpassed that of all Europe." In short, America's economic growth from 1880 to 1913 was "probably the single most decisive shift in the long-term balance of power."[7]

In World War I, the United States, provoked in 1917 by Germany's unrestricted submarine campaign against all shipping to Britain in order to starve her into submission, entered the war at just the right time. Tsarist Russia — defeated by Germany and torn apart by a domestic revolution that eventually brought the Bolsheviks to power — quit. This would allow

Germany to transfer up to 2 million men to the western front in France for a final attempt to defeat the badly mauled British and French armies in the spring of 1918. This thrust was defeated, and Germany had to sue for peace because of the presence of a sizable U.S. Army.

In World War II, America again became involved. After almost a century of isolationism, the United States had attempted to return to that stance after 1918. While American bankers played an important role in the economic recovery and stabilization of Europe in the 1920s, the nation continued to want nothing to do with international politics. But after Nazi Germany began World War II in 1939 and defeated the French Army in the spring of 1940, President Roosevelt increasingly moved to help Britain stay in the war. By December 7, 1941, the United States was engaged in a limited but unofficial naval war with Germany in the Atlantic. It was only a matter of time until Germany, as in World War I, would unleash its submarines against American warships as well as merchant ships, which were finally allowed to carry war supplies to Britain directly.

Thus a pattern clearly established itself in the early twentieth century: Britain used its power to back the weaker states against the state seeking dominance. When Britain's capability to restore Europe's equilibrium declined, the United States intervened. This pattern was to be repeated a third time after World War II as the result of four events. First, the Soviets ended up in the center of Europe. Second, Soviet forces remained huge, between 4,000,000 and 5,000,000, after demobilization; in East Germany, there were about 30 divisions, supported by tactical air power and backed up by large reserves.[8] Third, the United States indulged in a helter-skelter demobilization. A year after the war in Europe ended, American forces overseas totaled only 400,000 with six battalions in reserve in the United States. Fourth, western Europe collapsed, leaving the Soviets as the sole dominant power. A commonly heard quip at the time was that the only thing preventing the Soviet Army's march to the English Channel was a sufficient supply of durable boots. Under these circumstances, there was little choice about what the United States had to do.

The Soviet Union and the Interwar Balance

If the United States had experienced almost a century of isolation and was a novice in the art of power politics, Russia was a long-time "player." Unprotected by an Atlantic Ocean (as the United States), an English Channel (as Britain), or a mountain range (as Spain or Italy), Russia was only too aware of neighbors and near-neighbors as potential enemies and invaders, aware of the need to protect itself by maintaining strong military forces, and aware that it had to rely on itself rather than other states who publicly professed good will.

Russia's Foreign Policy Experiences
By the time the Communist leaders displaced the tsar and abolished the monarchy, Russia had suffered a long history of invasions, defeats, near-defeats, and humiliations by the Mongols, Turks, Poles, Lithuanians, Swedes, French, French and British in the Crimean War (1854–1856), the Japanese (1904–1905), and the Germans (1914 and 1941). They were also almost defeated in World War II. They were saved, however, not only by the onset of winter weather as the German Army stood in the outskirts of Moscow but also by German errors: a delay of six weeks in launching the invasion for a quick campaign against Yugoslavia in order to rescue Mussolini's Italian army from defeat by Greece; Hitler's decision to divide his armies into three for the drive on Leningrad, Moscow, and the Caucasus instead of concentrating them for the capture of Moscow before the bad weather started; and the Nazi's extensive executions and mistreatment of the very people who, like the Ukrainians, welcomed them as liberators from the great Russians! World War II and the Soviet Union's bare survival reinforced the sense of the nation's vulnerability. A country with no geographical barriers to hinder or stop an invasion, its leaders were almost paranoid about their insecurity and the con-

sequences of military weakness. Whereas an isolationist United States took security for granted, Russian leaders were always sensitive to possible dangers and felt vulnerable. They did not assume the good neighborliness of surrounding states; rather their enmity was more or less taken for granted. Thus, feeling highly insecure, Russian leaders expanded outward to keep the foreign threat as far away as possible. Louis Halle has called this expansionism "defensive expansionism."[9]

Russia's lack of geographical barriers, however, also proved to be a boon to the outward thrust of Soviet power as, for instance, in the search for warm water ports. Richard Pipes has said that Russia could no more have become the largest state in the world, covering a sixth of the world's land surface and spanning Eurasia, merely by suffering foreign invasions than an individual could gain wealth by constantly being robbed.[10] Sustained territorial expansion, he claims, has been the "Russian way" since the early fourteenth century, and from the middle of the sixteenth century to the end of the seventeenth century, Russia conquered the territorial equivalent of the modern Netherlands *every year for 150 years* running.[11] It is precisely this lack of clearly definable boundaries which, together with its heartland position, have made territorial expansion an attractive way of achieving security. Russia borders on Europe, the Middle East, and Asia, areas containing most of the world's population and much of its resources. Russia's advantage is precisely that it is able to probe along the periphery for weak spots and expand where opportunities exist. Zbigniew Brzezinski, like Pipes, has also argued that rather than being a victim of aggression, Russia has been a "persistent aggressor" against its neighbors. "Any list of aggressions committed in the last two centuries against Russia would be dwarfed by a parallel list of Russian expansionist moves against her neighbors." Russian leaders may be insecure not because of frequent foreign attacks but rather because of their "territorial acquisitions with its inevitably antagonistic ripple-effects."[12]

Whether Russian expansion is the product of "defensive expansion," or a "will to power," or "manifest destiny," expansion has resulted in new conflicts, new threats, and new experimental drives. "A relentless historical cycle was thus set in motion: insecurity generated expansion; expansion bred insecurity; insecurity, in turn, would fuel further expansion."[13] Whatever the motivation, intense fear or dedication to expansion, Russia's growth in power has posed a threat to the security of its neighbors and aroused a fear in all of western Europe. Soviet annexation of the Baltic states of Lithuania, Latvia, and Estonia just before the Nazi attack, and the postwar establishment of loyal Moscow-trained and supervised Communist regimes in eastern and central Europe, in which the Red Army was also stationed, was consistent with a Russian tradition of extending its power. So was the squashing of resistance to its power.

But Russia's historic foreign policy has been more than expansionism; it was also accompanied by a strong military organization and capability, as well as the centralization of political power and the supremacy of state power. By comparison, the United States, enjoying an unparalleled sense of security, did not give priority to security considerations. It largely ignored them and disclaimed all things military. Indeed, the United States looked optimistically at the future and concentrated on being a democracy (the same has been true for Britain). Nothing could contrast more starkly than the Kremlin's fortresslike mentality, which looked at the world pessimistically, always alert to possible dangers, always maintaining their "garrison state" and strong military forces.

Moscow and Berlin
In the period between the two world wars, the new Soviet Russia was a weak and vulnerable state. It was wracked by defeat and revolution, then by civil war and the consolidation of Communist power, then by the reign of Stalin and the subsequent upheavals of collectivizing the peasantry (which killed millions) and the drive to industrialize, followed by the great purges of the middle-late 1930s (killing several more millions).

Yet a wary eye had to be kept on Russia's neighbors. During the early twenties when Lenin was still alive, Soviet Russia and Germany — the two outcasts of Europe, the former because its ideological goals were hostile to western capitalism, the latter because its former enemies still regarded it as an incurable aggressor — established economic and military links. The rise of Hitler changed the Soviet Union's orientation. In 1935, Stalin, who had succeeded Lenin as the nation's leader, signed an alliance not only with France but also Czechoslovakia, France's more stalwart ally in western Europe (the others were Poland, Yugoslavia, and Rumania). In 1938, however, Britain and France, fearful of war, succumbed to German pressure and surrendered the Sudetenland, a part of Czechoslovakia, to Hitler (to be followed shortly thereafter by the Nazi takeover of the rest of Czechoslovakia), Moscow reversed itself once more. The western appeasement policy was viewed by the Soviet leaders as an attempt by Britain and France to shift the German menace from the west to the east, to precipitate a Soviet-German war in which these two powers would weaken each other while leaving the two western powers sitting on the sidelines, conserving their strength, and waiting to dictate final terms to both Germany and Russia.

So Stalin decided on his own appeasement policy, turning Hitler westward once more. He did so with the Nazi-Soviet pact in 1939, which took the world by surprise. Stalin and Hitler had so often expressed their enmity for each other that an alliance between the two seemed impossible. The Soviet Union's gains were clear: the partition of Poland, which allowed the Soviets to acquire the eastern one-third of Poland; Germany's redirection against France and Britain; and time to strengthen Soviet defenses in case Hitler decided to attack Russia at some future point. Stalin probably did not expect that attack as soon as it came because he did not expect the French armies to collapse as they did in 1940. Stalin knew that his pact with Hitler would start a war but he probably thought he could sit on the sidelines waiting for the western allies and Germany to exhaust each other.

However, after France was defeated and England pushed off the continent, Hitler felt the war in the west was over. No longer confronting a two-front war, he turned eastward. He expected to defeat the Red Army in a few weeks and, then as master of all of Europe and much of Eurasia, he would once more turn westward and invade Britain. Hitler's gamble almost paid off. He attacked his ally in June 1941, and within a short time his army had captured millions of Russian soldiers and most of European Russia. By December, the German Army stood at the gates of Leningrad and Moscow. Then winter struck, giving Stalin and his generals time to recover and plan for the 1942 campaign, which became a turning point in the war as the German Army was finally held and badly mauled at Stalingrad. By early 1943, Germany was beginning the long retreat that brought the Red Army to Berlin.

No group of Russian leaders would have expected international rivalries to cease after the defeat of Nazi Germany. In a system of sovereign states, each concerned with its protection and therefore armed, conflict continues; only enemies and allies change. Nor would any Russian leaders, tsarist or Soviet, have expected a harmonious relationship with the United States, which had emerged as the strongest western power, overshadowing the exhausted and rapidly weakening Britain. One of the repetitive patterns of power in history had been that of former allies becoming adversaries once the former enemy, which had brought them together, had been defeated. This occurred again as Nazi Germany was collapsing and Soviet Russia perceived the United States as its enemy.

The Emergence of the U.S.–Soviet Rivalry

In World War I it had taken the combined power of France, Britain, Russia, and the United States four years to defeat Germany. At the time of the armistice, Germany had exhausted the French Army, almost strangled Britain, and defeated Russia. In World War II, it was to take the collective efforts of France (defeated in 1940), Britain, the Soviet Union, and the

United States six years to bring Germany down. Given Germany's enormous strength, the Soviet Union and the two western allies had little choice but to cooperate. Neither felt it could defeat Germany alone; hence their alliance was truly one of necessity, forced upon both sides by the task of first halting and then defeating Germany's awesome military machine. Stalin was greatly worried that he might have to fight alone and that the unremitting pressure of the German onslaught might rout the Red Army. This was the reason for the continued Russian pressure on Washington and London to open a second front in France. This pressure remained high even after late 1942 when the great Soviet victory at Stalingrad had assured Russia's survival and it was only a question of time until the Red Army would drive the German armies out of the country and pursue them into Germany.

At this point the western allies were faced with a dilemma. On the one hand, they feared that the Soviet Union might perhaps make a separate peace with Hitler before they landed their forces in France. On the other hand, without the Russian front, it is questionable whether they could have established a foothold on the continent; and, if they had, whether they could have defeated the German forces in France as quickly and at such relatively low costs — if they could have defeated them at all. By 1944, the Red Army had broken the offensive spirit and capability of the German Army and also continued to tie down the bulk of the German forces, about 150 divisions. Although there were only a dozen German divisions in France, the Russians were asked to launch an offensive at the time of the allied landings so that the Germans would not transfer divisions to France. Even had the allies somehow managed a successful landing in France, a very bloody war would have ensued if there were no Soviet front and if the Germans concentrated all their forces in the west. Had the two hostile forces faced each other at near full manpower strength, they would probably have become bogged down in a static war, as in World War I.[14]

This is how the war was in fact fought in the east, with enormous casualties on both sides. The Soviets pursued an attrition strategy, wearing the Germans out, forcing them to retreat, which they did to prepared positions; then the Red Army would grind the German forces down again. As in World War I, American costs were, by contrast to the Soviets, modest. Great powers rarely fight other great powers "on the cheap"; fighting a first-class enemy is normally expensive in lives. In the European theater during World War II, the United States did not have to pay that price for defeating Germany — because of the Red Army. The war with Germany cost the Soviets 20 million lives.* In the 138-day battle to hold Moscow in the winter of 1941 one million soldiers and civilians lost their lives.[15]

Bipolarity and Conflict

Thus, in a real sense, the emergence of the Soviet Union and the United States as superpowers wielding primary influence in the world, if not the Cold War itself, was predetermined. To survive and defeat Hitler, Stalin wanted a western front in France. American power, far greater than Britain's, was therefore bound to flow eastward. Similarly, pushing the German armies backward meant that Soviet power would expand into central Europe.[16] Germany, the continent's strongest power, did not organize itself for a long war and did not mobilize itself fully until 1942, after Stalingrad when the illusion of quick victory faded. German tank production rose from 6,200 in 1942 to 19,000 in 1944; artillery production went up from 23,000 to 71,000. Thus, in the year of the allied invasion, German war production reached its peak. But its average production from

---

*Actually, Stalin was responsible for many of these casualties. He dismembered Russia's armored forces — the Russian military were among the first to realize the impact of independently organized armored forces upon war; he purged the officer corps on the eve of World War II, and since he disbelieved all warnings that Hitler would attack, the Russian forces were not ready on June 22, 1941, when the Germans descended on Moscow. Still, whatever the causes, 20 million dead is an enormous price and the fighting in the east was brutal.

1942–1944 of 12,000 tanks and self-propelled guns and 26,000 aircraft was far behind the Russian average of 30,000 and 40,000 respectively. And America's war production was almost unbelievable: From 1940 to 1945, the United States produced 297,000 aircraft, 86,000 tanks, 17,400,000 small arms, 64,500 land ships, and 5,200 larger ships (of approximately 53 million tons).[17] British war production was fourth. In World War I, Britain and the empire had raised 95 divisions, 74 of which were British. In World War II, the goal was to raise 55 divisions, 32 of which were British, the rest from the empire. They reached 49 divisions only in 1945; by 1943, only 19 divisions had been mobilized and by the end of that year that figure rose to just over 20. By 1942, Britain could create more divisions only by mobilizing war-production workers, which could not be done. As it was, Britain's war effort, in which women too were mobilized (unlike Germany), was straining its economy.[18] At that point Britain had to begin relying on America whereby 1944 arms production was six times more than Britain's. America, with its continental size, large population, rich resources, and huge industry, was realizing its superpower status; Britain, once the world's greatest power, became America's junior partner. America and Russia had no rivals.

After World War II, France never recovered from its defeat and occupation, Germany was brought to its knees by allied arms, and Britain was exhausted by its effort. No new balance of power involving them could be arranged; instead of being the principal actors in organizing the postwar balance, they were acted upon. America and Russia were now the only major actors left. By past measurements of population, territory, industry, and possession of natural resources, the two superpowers of World War II outranked all the great powers in history. The key characteristic of this new distribution of power was its bipolar character.

The reason is that, in a two-power structure, if one regards the other as a potential military threat to its security and then takes the necessary measures to bolster its security, the other feels compelled to react. The Soviet Union was determined to establish a buffer or security zone in eastern Europe. (This was hardly surprising; until 1917 tsarist Russia had incorporated Poland, Finland, and the Baltic states of Latvia, Lithuania, and Estonia.) But the powerful Red Army poised in the center of Europe was bound to arouse fear of Russian domination in western Europe, and since the European states could not mobilize sufficient countervailing power, the United States had to fill that position.

However, bipolarity does not make conflict inevitable. After the defeat of Napoleon, Russian power extended as far as Paris. But a new postwar balance was negotiated and conflict with Russia, which had looked likely at times, was avoided. The western powers in fact tried to arrange some sort of *modus vivendi* at Yalta in early 1945 as the war was ending, but unlike in 1815 it failed. Had Britain emerged as the second most powerful state instead of Russia, the ideological and cultural solidarity of the United States and Britain would surely have restrained their rivalry.[19] What made the Cold War unavoidable was Soviet attitudes and behavior. Russia's suspicion, truculence, defiance, and hostility toward the western allies, and the manner in which it imposed its rule on eastern Europe and then sought to expand southward as well, helped create the postwar bipolarity as much as the war itself. In any event, Soviet attitudes and behavior made the Cold War inevitable in the best Marxist sense because, unlike the United States and Britain, the American and Soviet political cultures were complete opposites.

Political Culture, Political Leadership, and the Wartime Alliance

A political culture is a composite of its historical experiences, geographical position, economic resources, political values, and organizational system. And it expresses itself in both thought and action.[20] Nations have distinctive histories; they evaluate their specific experiences and draw certain lessons from them. They apply their conclusions to the present. States develop certain characteristics giving each one of them a unique and distinct "personality," which is reflected in their beliefs and attitudes and therefore in the ways they perceive the world and behave in it. These ways of perception and behavior may of course change over time, but only slowly if they occur at all. Policy makers, born into and socialized by a particular political culture, generally act within its broad parameters. But they also have their own specific views that reflect a president's or prime minister's personality, background, and position as a party or bureaucratic leader. It was the very different American and Soviet ways of viewing the world — as articulated by President Roosevelt and Marshal Stalin — and different ways of behaving that not only thwarted genuine accommodation between the United States and Russia but also helped precipitate the postwar conflict.

American and Soviet Approaches to International Politics
The United States, even though it had been propelled into both world wars by hostile actions, was in fact a novice in international politics and not accustomed to thinking in terms of power. Rather, as an isolationist country, America had not been socialized by the state system; nor, therefore, had it internalized the rules of the balance of power. Thinking of international politics in moral terms, the United States divided nations into either good or bad, moral or immoral, categories. This black-and-white thinking reflected America's experience, domestic character, and the long peace it enjoyed for much of its history after the War of 1812. That peace was not attributed to its distance from Europe or its relationship with Europe. Instead, peace was believed to be the product of the nation's democratic system. The American people believed that their country was a virtuous country. Americans saw a contrast between the United States and Europe, which had frequent wars and was ruled by aristocratic — that is, undemocratic — governments not elected by the people or held accountable by them. The dichotomy was obvious: The people, who suffer during war, do not want to fight; democratic nations were

therefore peaceful as well as moral. Undemocratic countries, in which those who govern — an aristocracy or a dictator — benefit from war, are warlike and immoral.

This type of thinking was natural for a democratic nation that considered itself a society in which the common man could determine his own destiny. The United States was a post-European nation, a model for all nations in the future. American isolationism, therefore, reflected not only geography and the fact that Britain kept a balance in Europe, but also the American desire to abstain from European power politics and preserve its moral purity. Power politics was considered corrupt and "dirty"; and balance of power politics was regarded as something unnatural, something oldfashioned that belonged to the "Old World." It was not therefore something a "New World" nation would want.

If the United States was a moral country, reflecting its democratic principles, an opponent was by the very nature of its opposition immoral. When America was provoked by an enemy and compelled to play power politics, it defined its opponents as evil. Germany made it easy to keep on seeing the world in terms of good and evil. In World War I, German militarism and the unrestricted submarine campaign that sank American ships in violation of the international laws of neutrality left no question that Germany was an aggressor. In World War II, Hitler and his Nazi regime left even less doubt of the wisdom of the American way of viewing the world. Hitler's Germany could hardly be thought of as peace-loving or moral. Thus the stimulus for American participation in international politics came from the outside. The United States, essentially preoccupied domestically, was basically a reactive power.

America's entry into both world wars, although coming at the right time and due to enemy initiatives, were explained in universal and moral terms, not in terms of balance of power and national interest. Once provoked, the United States fought total wars, to compel the aggressor to surrender unconditionally. Since power was evil and corrupting, then the only justification for resorting to it was the nobility of the cause. If war was essentially immoral, it could be justified only if it were used to destroy evil itself, which meant the undemocratic country that had provoked America in the first place. After totally defeating the aggressor the United States could then reform that country by democratizing it. Or to put it another way, American wars were "wars to end all wars," crusades to eliminate power politics itself. And once the evil aggressor had been eliminated and his people sent to democratic reform school, the United States could once more retire from the international arena and concentrate on its first priority — enjoying democracy at home.

The American approach to international politics was one of opposites: Peace was regarded as a natural state of existence; war was the product of evil nations or leaders. States were either peace-loving or aggressors. War was abnormal and temporary; peace and harmony among states could be restored once the aggressors had been defeated, their regime replaced, and their people democratized. War distorted social priorities and therefore represented a malfunction of the international system. Diplomacy, on the other hand, was a means of straightening out conflicts that arose occasionally from misunderstandings. However, diplomacy was regarded with suspicion since its aim was only to *reconcile* differences — instead of eliminating evil, it continued to coexist with it. To the United States, international politics was a morality tale, a conflict between good and evil states. America could thus enter two world wars while denying to itself that these had anything to do with preserving the balance of power.

The *Russian* (pre-Soviet) view of the world was bound to be different if a nation's foreign and military strategy are a reflection of its political culture which, in turn, largely mirrors its historical experience. As already noted, Russia, surrounded by large and potentially powerful states, has not taken security for granted. Its rulers had long ago internalized the rules of the international game. Conflict among sovereign states was assumed; states coexisting were bound to have differences. If conflicts of interest could not be solved by negotiation, war was a legitimate instrument. In the balance of power game, nations often need allies against today's enemy, but that enemy might be tomorrow's ally against another enemy, who might well be yesterday's ally. International politics is neither moral nor immoral; nations are neither innately peace-loving nor aggressors. States must defend their security, and they must rely mainly on their own strength to do so, not on professions of good faith by potential adversaries. They can change partners as they see fit, and while their security interests are permanent their friends are not.

These views with their emphasis on self-help, distrust of other states, and war and diplomacy as instruments of statecraft, were accentuated by Russia's Communist leaders. *Soviet Russia did not consider itself a traditional state but a revolutionary one.* Its (early) leaders believed that their ideology gave them a historic mission to fulfill, namely, to liberate the world's peoples from the chains of capitalism. Like other revolutionary leaders (e.g., the French after their revolution), they asked themselves two questions: Why are most people poor and why do nations go to war? The answer is exploitation. A small class of the privileged — aristocracy for the French, capitalists for the Communists — profit from exploiting their citizens at home, and greed is also their prime motive for conquest and war away from home. Therefore, if people are ever to prosper and achieve social justice domestically and enjoy freedom and peace internationally, this class must be overthrown.

The Marxist-Leninist ideology is characterized by the following:

1. Economic forces are fundamental. The organization of the production and the distribution of wealth is the foundation, or "substructure," upon which society is built.
2. The capitalist "superstructure" consists of the owners of the means of production and wealth and of those who work for them and are exploited by them. Class relations are

essentially based on opposing interests and conflict. According to Marx, all history is the history of class struggle between the rich and the poor — between the slave owners and the slaves, the feudal, land-owning nobility and the peasantry, the capitalist owners of industry (the bourgeoisie) and the working class (the proletariat).

3. The capitalist political system, like the class structure, reflects the nature of the economic system. The owners of wealth control the state and use its instruments — the army, the police, and other levers of governmental power — to keep control. They can also manipulate other means of control, such as the legal and educational systems and religion, to maintain their power.

4. Capitalists cannot be reformed, and the nature of capitalism cannot be changed. Superficial changes may be attempted in order to "buy off" the underprivileged and the exploited, but they cannot save the system. Only the abolition of private property and the profit motive will allow industry to be used for the benefit of the many rather than only for the luxury of the few.

5. The injustices of capitalism, however, will end with the proletarian revolution. This revolution will occur when the proletariat has become the majority and politically conscious of its own exploitation. This day of reckoning is historically inevitable.

6. Lenin explained the failure of this "inevitable" revolution to happen in the western industrial countries as follows: The exploitation was so profitable that some of the profits trickled down to the industrial proletariat, so that its standard of living was improved, its revolutionary consciousness eroded, and its vested interest in capitalism strengthened. Domestic revolution was thus avoided by means of a policy of imperialism.

7. The Marxist class struggle within the capitalist states was thus projected onto the global plane. The rich are now defined as the western industrial states, the poor and exploited as the less developed countries (LDCs). This

worldwide class struggle has become the critical conflict in the world. Only when the industrial states lose the cheap raw materials previously provided by the LDCs and the economic growth rate slows, so that unemployment increases and the standard of living declines, will the domestic proletariat again recognize that its interests clash with those of the bourgeoisie. Then the class conflict will resume and will end in the proletariat revolution.

This general ideological outlook, with its total critique of capitalist society, provided the Soviet leadership with a comprehensive way of perceiving and analyzing the world, defining friend and foe, stating its ultimate aim, and making a commitment to help history along to its predestined fulfillment. That the ideology helped shape the way Stalin and Soviet leaders saw the world and affected their conduct of foreign policy does not mean either an inflexible pursuit of some "master plan" for world conquest or a slavish, mechanistic devotion to Marxism-Leninism's written words. After all, the Soviet leaders have been indoctrinated over their lifetimes. It does mean that daily decisions, while pragmatic in character, reflect this way of viewing the world, or *Weltanschaaung*. Its first premise was that the Soviet Union was in conflict with capitalism. In the words of George Kennan, the American diplomat and historian of American-Russian relations, "This hostility from the Communist side is preconceived, ideological, deductive. In the minds of Soviet leaders, it long predated the Communist seizure of power in Russia. . . . The Communists hated the Western government for what they were regardless of what they did."[21]

Ideology thus reinforced the ideas of *realpolitik* inherent in the traditional view of international politics. For the Soviet leaders, who considered their country as the nucleus of a postcapitalist world order, conflict between states was natural. Their ideology defined capitalist states as enemies and they therefore expected the relationship between capitalist and socialist states to be characterized by hostility and struggle. They also assumed that the capitalist states were equally hostile to them and were determined to do everything they could to destroy them before they themselves were destroyed. "Russian history and Marxist-Leninist philosophy coincide to produce an obsession with power, both political and military, internal and external, which may perhaps legitimately be called national instinct."[22]

In this context, politics was not a means of reconciliation and live-and-let-live. Instead, it was an unending series of "campaigns," the aim of which was to defeat the capitalist enemy.[23] The only question was *kto, kovo*? ("who, whom"?, meaning "Who will destroy whom?"), even though history had already predicted the outcome. If, as has been said, war is the continuation of politics by other means, then to the Soviets peace was the continuation of the last war by other means. This view of politics as a bitter struggle against a ruthless opponent was a basic outlook. Between adversaries, one of whom has been condemned to extinction by history and the other selected to triumph, there could be no final settlement. A lasting peace would come only after the elimination of capitalism and the victory of communism. Until then, agreements were only temporary, only tactical moves in a struggle that must be waged with vigor and persistence.

This Soviet outlook did not reject temporary relaxation of tensions, or détente, when "correlation of forces" — the overall balance of power — was unfavorable and time was needed to recoup the nation's strength, or build greater strength, or recover from a setback; nor did it reject accords with adversaries. Such tactical moves were required by the ebb and flow of circumstances, but the ultimate objectives remained constant. The scope for accommodation was thus clearly limited. The question was not whether ultimate objectives were to be abandoned but only how they could best be realized. The long-run aim was unchangeable; only the methods or tactics to be employed were flexible. When the correlation of forces favors the Soviet Union, it must pressure the enemy and seek to advance Soviet goals; to accept the status quo in these circumstances is unacceptable. When the correlation favors the adversary, then one does not take unnecessary risks or provoke him; rather, one adjusts and, if necessary, knows how to retreat.

This ideological perspective accentuated, to the point of paranoia, the regime's sense of insecurity, its perception of the deep hostility of capitalist states, and its emphasis on constant and long-term struggle. It also made Soviet leaders profoundly suspicious of capitalist words of friendship and peaceful intent and convinced them that such professions were only to deceive and relax the Soviet Union's guard. Furthermore, Soviet leaders have always believed that their ideology has given them a superior insight into the historical process so that they know "what is *really* going on." Since the capitalist states are inherently incapable of showing goodwill or being peace-loving, when they do demonstrate goodwill or make concessions it is only to relax the Soviet Union guard. Translated into policy, this means that the Soviet Union must be self-reliant, vigilant, and militarily strong. It must also exploit any opportunities that can advance the cause of socialism (i.e., Soviet power) and weaken capitalism. The use of force for defensive or coercive purposes is not immoral; it is a matter of circumstances, that is, how risky and costly it might be. There is no special emphasis on the use of force, however. "The Kremlin is under no ideological compulsion to accomplish its purpose in a hurry. Like the Church, it is dealing in ideological concepts which are of long-term validity, and it can afford to be patient. It has no right to risk the existing achievements of the revolution for the sake of vain baubles of the future."[24]

President Roosevelt's Expectations
Thus, the United States and the Soviet Union approached their wartime cooperation against Nazi Germany from quite different perspectives.[25] First of all, the American emphasis was on the military defeat of Germany. The goal was its unconditional surrender. It was by and largely assumed that after the war American troops would be withdrawn quickly from Europe

and, once Japan was defeated as well, that the United States
would demobilize most of its forces. The idea that a sizable
number of troops would be kept in Europe until the two allies
had worked out a mutually acceptable settlement never occurred to American leaders. President Roosevelt commented
at the Yalta Conference of American, Soviet, and British leaders in early 1945 that United States forces would be withdrawn
within two years of the end of the war. Since victory had been
achieved, "normalcy" would return. The American Joint
Chiefs of Staff had no plans for permanent military bases in
Europe because they did not expect a conflict with the Soviet
Union. It was assumed that the cooperation of the wartime
alliance would continue in the postwar era.

The absence of balance of power thinking was notable.
There was no awareness that after the war the allies might become adversaries, even though the United States knew that the
Soviet Union would emerge from the war as the dominant
power on the European continent.[26] The memory that twice
before in this century when Germany threatened the European
balance and almost became the dominant continental power,
the United States had to become involved in European wars,
had apparently no lesson for U.S. leaders during World War
II. Instead, an era of good feeling was expected to emerge.[27]
Franklin Roosevelt, addressing the Congress upon his return
from Yalta, said that that conference should spell the end of
nations resorting to unilateral action, forming exclusive alliances, or establishing spheres of influence and balances of
power, "and all the other expedients that have been tried for
centuries — and have always failed."[28]

To be sure, problems would arise from time to time. But
they were perceived as manageable. The focus of resolving
these difficulties would be a new universal organization, the
United Nations. This organization, whose establishment owes
its existence primarily to the United States, was foreseen as
continuing the wartime great power cooperation after their
joint victory. The United Nations, whose name itself was very
symbolic, was critical to U.S. postwar aims and hopes because

it was expected to reduce the nationalistic and ideological differences among its peace-loving members, temper their rivalries, and resolve their conflicts of interests. The result was that the Americans spent a great deal of time and energy on issues of membership and voting procedures, on eloquent declarations and preambles instead of the key issue that would affect postwar American-Soviet cooperation: Soviet behavior in eastern Europe.

American leaders believed instead that if they could achieve Soviet friendship, the postwar peace would be assured. President Roosevelt, who in many ways embodied the American approach to international politics, was strongly convinced that he could win Stalin's trust. The President, who could say "my friend" in half a dozen languages, had enormous self-confidence in his skills of personal diplomacy and his ability to exude great charm. During one of the early meetings with Churchill and Stalin, Roosevelt called Stalin "Uncle Joe," seemingly suggesting that Stalin was a rather genial member of the wartime family. Characteristically American, Roosevelt felt that to win a friend one had to be a friend; to win trust one had to demonstrate trust rather than suspicion. The President's assumption was also an attempt to transfer the American political experience to the international arena.

At home Roosevelt met with other politicians and struck bargains. He assumed that he could use the same mixture of skill and charm on Stalin. He too was just "another politician." As reasonable men, they could compromise differences and avoid conflict. The difficulty was that the President did not see the critical differences between U.S. domestic and international politics. Domestically, most Americans shared common goals; differences were over how to achieve these aims. But internationally, especially in the midst of a terrible world war, differences were not just over how the war was to be fought, but on how the participating states wanted the world to look after the war was over. Differences, in short, were not only over the means to the end, but the end itself — the polit-

ical objectives of each state.[29] Stalin was not another democratic politician who would be won over by demonstrations of
goodwill; he was the leader of Soviet Russia with specific defensive needs and offensive goals.

In his personal approach to Stalin, Roosevelt was very careful not to arouse any suspicions in Stalin's mind of a special
Anglo-American relationship. The President treated Churchill
as an old imperialist out of touch with the modern world, re-
marking several times that his role was one of mediating between Churchill and Stalin! But in unveiling Anglo-American
differences in front of Stalin on a number of occasions, Roosevelt's tactics backfired. It weakened rather than strengthened
his bargaining power with the Soviet leader. His anticolonialism stance also undercut his strategy. In the process, Roosevelt, whose understanding of history and skepticism about
political leaders lacked Churchill's depth, overlooked the dangers of Russian imperialism and the need for a united Anglo-
American front.

Stalin's Behavior
While Roosevelt and other American leaders were generally
optimistic about the future, Stalin approached Soviet policy on
the basis of the inherent antagonism between capitalism and
communism. Roosevelt may have thought of Stalin as another
Roosevelt but Stalin thought of Roosevelt as another Stalin,
viewing him and Churchill as "adversaries who would do unto
him approximately what he would do unto them, assuming
they got the opportunity."[30] The image can be varied in the
sense that Stalin saw no *essential* difference between Roosevelt and Hitler; both were, in his perception, leaders of major
capitalist states whose goals clashed with those of Soviet Russia. One of the major contributory factors to the outbreak of
the Cold War beyond the emerging bipolar character of the
state system, then, was a gross misperception. But it was not
the usual mirror image, in which each leader sees himself as
the embodiment of virtue, his opponent the symbol of evil, and

his country's behavior only defensive and peaceful, the other's as aggressive and expansionist. Rather, in this instance, each leader saw in his opposite number the image of himself![31]

Obviously, Stalin's suspicions of his western allies were in part those of a statesman of a nation conditioned by the state system — indeed, a Russian leader deeply distrustful of foreigners; in part, a Soviet leader who after years of western efforts to assure him of their friendship after the war could still pause before a map of the Soviet Union colored in red and categorically assert: "They will never accept the idea that so great a space should be red, never, never!"; in part, a dictator constantly suspicious of his colleagues whom he regularly dispatched to their Marxist heaven (or hell); and no doubt, also in part, Stalin's personality. Should it be surprising that Stalin distrusted Roosevelt and Churchill when he distrusted his immediate colleagues, as well as foreign Communist leaders who showed any signs of independence; and when he welcomed back his own soldiers and those shipped to Germany as forced labor by sending them to *Russian* labor camps because they had seen the bourgeois west?[32]

A few examples of Stalin's suspicious perceptions are illuminating. To defeat Germany, the western armies had to be put back on the continent. At some point, the British-American forces had to be landed across the English Channel in France where they could come to grips with the German Army and smash it. The problem was when? British forces in 1942 were stretched thin, from the home islands to North Africa to the Pacific. Britain, with a far smaller population than the United States, could not mount an invasion of Europe by itself. But the large American forces that were needed would first have to be raised, trained, equipped, and transported across the Atlantic to supplement British and other allied forces for the invasion of Europe. This, in turn, required that the Battle of the Atlantic, where German submarines were waging an intense campaign against allied shipping, be won first; and that was not achieved until May 1943. Another of the key problems was landing craft. Thousands would be needed to transport such a

large army across the Channel. Since these were also desperately needed in the Pacific war against Japan, this became —
together with all the other necessary instruments of war — a
production problem. It was a matter of time. Eventually, all
these needs would be met, but in the meantime, British and
American armies (which lacked battle experience) cleared the
German armies out of North Africa, invaded Italy, Germany's
ally, and drove her to surrender, and pushed northward in Italy. The date for the invasion was June 1944.

The two western allies realized that the Red Army was taking the brunt of the German onslaught and that allied operations in North Africa and Italy were providing only slight relief. They knew that a second front in France was necessary
to draw more German troops from the Russian front. But with
the best of intentions and maximum effort there was little they
could do before 1944. To risk an earlier invasion before thorough preparations had been made would not only risk having
the invasion thrown back into the sea with tremendous loss of
life and material, but allied morale would be so lowered that
another invasion might not be attempted again. The Soviets,
however, viewed the second front differently. Given their ideological suspicions of western capitalist statesmen, Stalin and
his colleagues thought that the United States and Britain were
deliberately stalling and delaying the invasion as long as possible so that Germany and Russia could bleed each other
"white" first. Only when they had exhausted each other would
the western allies invade, advance into Germany with few casualties, and dictate the peace terms to Germany *and* the Soviet Union.

In fact, Roosevelt and Churchill, as already noted, could not
afford this strategy, even had it occurred to them. The Soviet
Union had to be kept in the war if Germany were to be defeated. Therefore, from the time of the German invasion, the
British and Americans provided Russia with military aid. They
knew that they would have to relieve the pressure on the Soviet
front by military actions against the Germans, even if this simply meant continuing their operations in the Mediterranean,

climaxing in the invasion of first Sicily and then Italy. That is also a major reason why they devised the unconditional surrender formula for Germany; it was a commitment to Stalin that the United States and Britain would not seek a separate peace, leaving him to face Hitler alone. The hope was, of course, that Stalin would not sign another Nazi-Soviet pact.

Nevertheless, western motives were always suspect. Nothing seemed to reassure the ever-suspicious Soviets. A Soviet general was allowed to participate in the surrender ceremony of German forces in Italy to reassure Stalin, who suspected the Germans were deliberately letting Allied forces through to stop the Soviet advance into Germany. Another example occurred as the Red Army approached Warsaw, the Union of Polish Patriots appealed to the Polish underground resistance to help the Soviet forces in the liberation of the Polish capital. When they did so, the Red Army suddenly stopped, claiming that it needed time for recuperation and repairs after months of heavy fighting. In the meantime, the Polish underground had struck at the German forces in Warsaw; and the Germans proceeded to reinforce their army and destroy the Polish resistance. No appeals by Roosevelt and Churchill moved the Red Army forward even one inch. Stalin would not even permit American and British planes with supplies for the Poles to land behind the Soviet lines for refueling. The reason was blatantly political: to destroy the Polish forces because they were non-Communist and could potentially resist a Soviet move to install a Communist regime in Poland. The Red Army resumed its advance only after the Warsaw resistance had been crushed by the Germans.

The Clash over Eastern Europe

Indeed, the issue of eastern Europe became a critical one as the war was ending. It showed how far apart the western allies and Soviet Union really were. The countries of eastern Europe were obviously significant for Soviet security. They provided the Soviets with a buffer zone. If these nations were in the hands of regimes friendly to the Soviet Union, they would greatly increase Russia's postwar security by pushing her frontier westward. If they were governed by regimes unfriendly to the Soviet Union, they would constitute a threat. Poland was especially critical in this respect because it lay on a direct path from west to east. As Stalin observed, Poland was the "corridor" through which every invader of Russia had passed (correspondingly, and left unsaid, it was a corridor through which the Red Army could support its forward position in what is now East Germany).

The American and British leaders were not unmindful of Soviet Russia's security needs. Indeed they were sympathetic because Russia had suffered devastating losses. They too wanted the postwar regimes throughout eastern Europe to be friendly to the Soviet Union. At the same time, as democratic leaders of countries that had fought a long war and also suffered significantly — especially the British who had fought Hitler from the beginning, as Churchill once reminded Stalin, Hitler's former ally, after the Soviet leader accused the British of cowardice — they could hardly abandon the democratic principles of self-determination. Could Soviet security be reconciled with the democratic insistence on self-government? The western leaders believed so.[33] Their model was Czechoslovakia. Betrayed by Britain and France at Munich in 1938, the Czech government-in-exile moved to Moscow after the German occupation instead of London, where most of the governments-in-exile moved after the Germans occupied their countries. Czech leaders were democratic and had been prowestern before Munich, but they realized after having been sold out that Czechoslovakia's postwar security depended on the Soviet Union. They were therefore determined to establish good relations with Stalin; in turn, he promised to respect Czechoslovakia's independence after the war. To Roosevelt and Churchill, the Czech example demonstrated that the Soviet Union could have a friendly neighbor sensitive to Soviet security interests and that the western democracies would not be betraying their own principles by allowing the Soviets to install Moscow-trained Communist leaders in eastern Europe.

Thus at Yalta in early 1945 they attempted to achieve a settlement of this key issue. They declared that they shared Stalin's desire for friendly regimes in eastern Europe, but they also elicited a promise from Stalin to hold free elections throughout the area. These would soon occur, said Stalin, and all but the Fascist parties, which had cooperated with the Germans, could participate in these elections. The problem was that the two sides understood completely different things by such terms as democracy and free elections. Churchill and Roosevelt understood it in English and American terms, and both leaders felt confident that free elections would produce coalition governments in which the Communist parties in the different countries might, if they won sufficient votes, participate. In any event — whether it had Communist members or not — no government in eastern Europe could be unaware of the overwhelming power of the Soviet Union, and the need to be accommodating. As long as such regimes remained sensitive to Russia's needs in foreign policy issues, the internal character of these countries should not matter too much.

That was the rub. The Soviet leadership did not think of its sphere of influence in eastern Europe in traditional terms. It drew no distinction between the foreign and domestic policies. Only a Communist regime with a monopoly of authority could assure Soviet security needs. Non-Communist parties were by definition anti-Communist parties, reflecting the interests of class enemies. Only the Communist party represented the majority interests of the workers and peasants. And was an election not free if the workers and peasants could vote for their party? What was wrong with preventing the class enemies, representing the privileged, the exploiters, the reactionary forces, from running their parties? To Stalin, a coalition government as defined by western leaders was totally unacceptable. At best such governments would be allowed to exist only temporarily, that is, while Stalin watched to see if the United States and Britain would strongly protest his free elections and establishment of democratic governments Soviet-style.

But principles not backed by power remained unrealized. While the west, especially the United States, was rapidly demobilizing its forces after the surrender of Germany and Japan, the Red Army remained in eastern and central Europe. Stalin had the divisions to impose his will. Seeing western actions limited to verbal protests, Stalin gradually transformed all regimes throughout eastern Europe into Communist ones called People's Republics. Even where he had allowed free elections, as in Czechoslovakia (where the Communist party had in fact gained the largest percentage of the vote) and in Hungary (where no Communist plurality emerged), he finally eliminated the coalition governments. The Czech government, which the western leaders had seen as a model reconciling democratic principles at home with Soviet security interests in foreign policy, was the last to be transformed, and rather brutally, in 1948. But from the very beginning, the Soviets had seen to it that Communists controlled the key ministries of coalition governments: interior (controlling the police) and the military. By the end of 1945, the non-Communist parties were squeezed out in Bulgaria and Romania. By late 1947, they were eliminated in other countries such as Hungary.[34] It was Moscow's belief that Soviet security interests in the area could not be achieved without absolute domination — that is, with the same monopoly of power that the Communist party held within the Soviet Union. Stalin later reportedly expressed regret that he had not also seized Finland!

Stalin's preoccupation with absolute dominion was so profound that even when the western powers bent over backwards they could not persuade him of their friendly and peaceable intentions. In Poland, for example, they recognized the government after the Soviet leader assented to adding a few nondemocratic leaders to the Soviet-trained and Soviet-installed Communist regime. They knew that Poland was an especially sensitive matter to Moscow. But nothing could persuade the Soviet leadership that western intentions were amicable. Moscow was convinced that the west's constant insistence on free elections in which all non-Fascist parties should participate was but an attempt to roll Soviet power back to Russia's frontiers and establish a containment line there.

The quarrel over eastern Europe was a symptom of the opposite natures of Soviet and U.S. societies and political cultures. Could America have stood by quietly after fighting a war to save democracy from totalitarian might while the Soviet Union transformed the states of Europe into satellites? While non-Communist leaders were jailed, executed, or disappeared, and all opposition was crushed? Although the issue for the United States was a one of national self-determination, the basic principle of western democracy, the issue was more than one of principle. For Roosevelt, Stalin's behavior also raised profound issues in domestic politics.[35] For one thing, with the 1944 election coming up, in which he was running for an unprecedented fourth term the President was fearful of being charged with betraying Poland. He might lose much of the 6 to 7 million Polish-American vote, especially in a critical electoral state like Illinois. Roosevelt was also very concerned about how the Senate would react to Soviet behavior. He feared that violations of the principle of self-determination would lead the Senate to reject his most cherished project, the United Nations, as it had rejected the Versailles peace treaty (which included a League of Nations) after World War I because of similar violations by the victors.

Thus, even before the end of the war, the question of Poland and the eastern European nations threatened to arouse controversy in the United States and perhaps even weaken the unity needed to support the war effort. It could also have an effect on America's willingness to play an international role within an international organization after hostilities had ceased. Added to all this was the pressure from the military to "win the war first and leave the politics to after the war," that is, to avoid political issues that might jeopardize Russian military cooperation against the Germans and, after their defeat, against

Japan. Thus Roosevelt pursued a strategy of delay, seeking to postpone critical issues until after the war.

It was on the issue of Poland especially that Roosevelt appealed to Stalin as "one politician to another." He continuously implored Stalin to restrain himself or make some concession or gesture in order not to alienate American public opinion; or he would cite American opinion as the reason for not compromising an issue dear to Stalin. To Stalin, statements such as these were just as insincere as all those western expressions of friendship and hope for a postwar era of good feelings. After all, what credibility could Roosevelt's concern about U.S. opinion have had when Stalin knew that the President had been elected three times (and after 1944, four times) and that he was the leader of a capitalist country in which elections were a sham? Why should Roosevelt, therefore, have any fears of public opinion, except to masquerade behind it in order to do/not do what he wished to do/not do and disguise his hostile intentions? Since Stalin manipulated public opinion, why couldn't Roosevelt do the same thing? Thus the Soviet leader dismissed Roosevelt's pleas as deceitful. Thinking the worst of his western colleagues anyway because of his ideological preconceptions, the Soviet leader's distrust of Roosevelt's actions and appeals only intensified.

But Roosevelt, not really understanding the man he was dealing with, was not to be put off. Just before his death he told Churchill that the Soviet problem was a manageable one. In seeking a reason why the Soviets continued to be so suspicious and truculent, he had throughout the war attributed Soviet behavior to the *west's prewar policies*.[36] Soviet anger and hostility were the product of western actions such as the intervention in Russia after the Soviet seizure of power, French attempts in the interwar period to use its alliance with several east European countries not only to contain German power but to keep Soviet Russia out of Europe, and the British appeasement of Hitler. Roosevelt was determined to demonstrate that the past was past, that whatever had happened earlier the west now sincerely wanted to have good and harmonious postwar relations with the Soviet Union. If the west demonstrated its good faith to Stalin, helped him gain security for his nation, and accepted it as an equal power, the Soviet leadership's paranoia about Russia's security and suspicions about foreign states would decline, and Soviet Russia would take its rightful place as a status quo power in the world. Even Churchill at Yalta talked of the "three policemen" — the United States, Britain, the Soviet Union — who, if they were "satisfied," would be able to get along after the war and preserve the peace. Attempts such as the settlement of the eastern European question were part of this effort to ensure that all the policemen, but especially the Soviet policemen, would be satisfied. Similar agreements were negotiated over the future administration of postwar Germany and other issues.

The Soviet Union was accorded its place as one of the five great powers in the postwar United Nations. Roosevelt also made a special effort to satisfy Soviet demands for the restoration of Russia's former sphere of influence in Manchuria (taken by Japan in its war with Russia in 1904) plus the southern part of Sakhalin Island and adjacent islands. These concessions, as well as the recognition of Outer Mongolia and the Kurile Islands as part of the Soviet sphere, were the main ingredients of Stalin's price for participation in the war against Japan, which the United States military felt would be necessary. At that time the atomic bomb had not yet been tested and the Chinese Nationalists were preoccupied with their civil war against the Communists rather than fighting the Japanese. At the same time, Roosevelt won Stalin's acknowledgment that the Nationalist government was the legitimate government of China, which meant that, hopefully, he would not support the Chinese Communists in the civil war.

Yalta was the last major attempt to resolve outstanding differences with the Soviet Union, to satisfy the principal interests of the three major allies, and thereby avoid postwar conflict. Nonetheless, Soviet power flowed into the power vacuums created by the defeat of Germany and Japan. No doubt, Soviet motives were in part defensive; eastern Europe was to be a buffer zone. But they were also offensive. In China, Stalin played the tsar reclaiming his imperial heritage. The Far Eastern Agreement of Yalta included the following revealing words: "The former rights of Russia violated by the treacherous attack of Japan in 1904 shall be restored."[37] Finally, Stalin was also in part the revolutionary seeking to expand "Socialism in One Country" (the U.S.S.R.) to "Socialism in One Zone" (Russia and eastern Europe). The Soviet Union's isolation would be ended as the base of the world revolution was expanded and the zone of world capitalism shrunk.

Above all, Stalin knew that he had to act quickly. Roosevelt had told him that American forces would be withdrawn from Europe within two years after the war. But America's return to isolationism might not last long. It didn't. The remarkable thing was that the United States tried to return to a hemispheric policy and demobilize its military forces so quickly while at the same time continuing to seek accommodations with Moscow. These acts strongly demonstrated the tenacity of America's national style and the desire to believe that once the war was over, normalcy would be restored.

The Transition from Allies to Adversaries

It was Britain, governed by a Labour government, which once again took the lead in opposing the Soviet Union, as it had done twice earlier against Germany. There was an irony to this anti-Soviet initiative inasmuch as part of the Labour party's slogan before it assumed power after the war was "no enemies to the left." Labour, like many European democratic Socialist parties, had been sympathetic to the Soviet experiment before the war and was aware that after the Great Depression capitalism, with its high unemployment, seemed to have failed. The Soviet experiment with government ownership of the means of production and the abolition of private property and the profit motive promised a better life for the masses of workers and peasants, the lower strata of society. Nevertheless, after World War II the Labour government behaved the same as a Conservative government by pursuing a traditional balance of power policy. The Soviet Union might be on the left, but its enormous power in 1945 despite its heavy losses during the war years constituted a threat to the security and independence of the countries in western Europe. (Churchill, out of office and leader of the Conservative opposition in Britain, was touring the United States in early 1946, warning of the "Iron Curtain" that had come down across Europe and divided it; and he pleaded for an Anglo-American coalition to protect western Europe and contain Soviet power.)

Initially, the American reaction to the British was lukewarm, if not downright critical. The memories of the wartime alliance with the Soviet Union and Russian heroism were too fresh and the American public too eager to focus on its domestic pursuits. The British warnings of the Soviet danger were attributed to British imperialism, historic Anglo-Russian rivalry, Conservative British suspicions of and hostility toward communism, and other such reasons. To be sure, the Soviets were often very difficult and sometimes impossible, too insistent on doing things their own way, and not very sensitive to the interests of their allies. But a threat, no.

In the immediate postwar period American policy initially was to continue the wartime policy of cooperation. When President Truman succeeded Roosevelt after his death, he maintained Roosevelt's policy. When differences arose over eastern Europe, he sent high-level emissaries to Moscow to explain the American position, remind Stalin of Yalta, and then settle for what he could get — as in Poland — in an effort to relieve Soviet anxieties and fears.

Changing Course

The reevaluation of Soviet policy came only after the Soviets began to show signs of expansionism. They tried to break through the perimeter from Turkey to India to her south. The first effort came in Iran, where Moscow refused, contrary to treaty obligations, to withdraw its troops. Iran had served as a transit point for allied war supplies to the Soviet Union, and the Soviets now wanted to detach the northern province of Azerbijan from that country. (A tough American stance did lead to the withdrawal of all Russian troops.) The Soviets also exerted intense and persistent pressure on Turkey, which had remained neutral during the war, to cede territory to Russia and, more importantly, control of the Dardanelles, the gateway from the Black Sea to the Mediterranean. For all practical purposes, this would have converted Turkey into another Soviet satellite (as the eastern European countries were by then generally labeled in the west). And the Soviets were suspected of using the Yugoslavs and Bulgarians to help the Communist forces in the civil war raging in Greece. Britain had backed Turkey and Greece in the eastern Mediterranean which had long been a British sphere of influence since the British Empire's lifeline to India ran through this area. But after the two long and very costly world wars, Britain collapsed in the winter of 1946–1947. In February 1947, Britain informed the U.S. government that it could no longer support Greece and Turkey. In other words, Britain could no longer contain Soviet efforts to realize long-term Russian ambitions.

Interestingly enough, Khrushchev, who eventually succeeded Stalin, later wrote in his memoirs that it had been Stalin who "frightened the Turks right into the open arms of the Americans. Because of Stalin's note to the Turkish government, the Americans were able to penetrate Turkey and set up bases right next to our borders." (Notably, Stalin's successors, within three months of his death in 1953, informed Turkey that there were no longer any territorial claims against Turkey and that after reconsidering the question of the Straits, Soviet security could in their view be assured by conditions acceptable to Turkey. Surely, this was also an admission that Stalin had harbored expansionist ambitions beyond any reasonable interpretation of Russian security interests as well as a statement of the withdrawal of Stalin's demands.[38])

Should the United States have accepted this Soviet intimidation of countries on its southern flank as a reflection of legitimate Russian security concerns and should the area have been considered as part of Russia's sphere of influence because of its location? And should the United States have ignored the desire of the nations in that area, so far away from America, to have the United States play a counterbalancing role? Their fear was Russian expansion, not American. They welcomed, indeed *wanted,* this extension of American power. For them, Russian expansion meant an end to their independence; America's involvement was a guarantee of it. That was the critical difference between Russian and American expansion, as were the initiating Russian role and the reactive American one.[39]

Britain's collapse confronted the United States with a new world. There were only two great powers left, the Soviet Union and the United States. America would now have to take the initiative, mobilize its own resources, and organize a collective effort to safeguard western Europe and prevent further Soviet expansion. The assumption underlying this shift was clear: The Soviet Union was an enemy. American policy makers assumed this posture reluctantly and only when left with no choice but to recognize the reality. At that point they realized that their hopes for postwar cooperation had turned out to be an illusion.[40] World War II started as an Anglo-French attempt to prevent Germany from dominating eastern Europe and destroying the European balance of power. Two years after the war, the domination of eastern Europe had been achieved by Russia. Ironically, if it were not for that Soviet presence, the United States would have withdrawn from Europe.*

---

*A former Director of the CIA and Secretary of Defense aptly said the following about this early postwar period:

> The Russians had committed a colossal blunder. . . . They had failed to understand — and exploit — the rhythms of the American democracy. . . . The Russians failed to grasp that the Americans simply did not think the same way. The Americans had not read Lenin or Clausewitz or Machiavelli. . . . In a profound sense it was Soviet misreading of the United States that induced America to accept its role in the central strategic relationship of the last 40 years." (James Schlesinger, "The Eagle and the Bear," *Foreign Affairs,* Summer 1985, p. 939.)

The Cold War: Inevitable or Accidental?

No power could have been less prepared for the rivalry with the Soviet Union than the United States. The test of any political culture, however meritorious its ideas might be intellectually and morally, is how appropriate it is in guiding policy makers in a conflict situation with an adversary. During World War II, the United States did not even expect the postwar conflict. It focused almost entirely on the task of militarily defeating Germany and Japan. Even if American leaders had been more adept at power politics, it is not entirely certain whether the postwar superpower rivalry would have been avoidable. But America might have been placed in a more favorable postwar situation and perhaps the conflict might have been less intense and of lesser scope.

The United States Failure to Bargain
The United States, for one thing, failed to maintain its military power as a bargaining tool with the Soviet Union. After Yalta, when the Soviets began to quickly consolidate their control in eastern Europe, Churchill urged that the U.S. Army stay in its foreward positions in Germany instead of withdrawing to lines previously agreed upon for the division of Germany. Churchill wanted to extend the American drive into Czechoslovakia and capture Prague and western Czechoslovakia so as to improve the western bargaining position on Austria and Czechoslovakia. He also urged that the U.S. Army in Europe remain strong until a settlement had finally been achieved. And when all these entreaties to Washington failed, he suggested that at least the U.S. Army drive to Berlin instead of swinging southward to round up the remnants of an already defeated German Army. The former capital of Germany was symbolically more important, and it was desirable therefore to capture it before the Russians did and to drive beyond in order to "join hands with the Russian armies as far to the east as possible."[41] Churchill's goal was to prevent the emergence of a powerful Russia in the center of Europe.

This suggestion too was turned down. The United States remained hypnotized by the purely military task of defeating what was left of the tattered German forces and completely disregarded the importance of using military power as a political weapon. In General Marshall's words, political goals such as Berlin were not worth the sacrifice of his soldiers' lives! Yet what are wars fought for but political goals? These classic words uttered as the war in Europe was ending showed the constancy of the U.S. style. Right after the Japanese attack on Pearl Harbor, at a cabinet meeting, Secretary of State Hull turned to Secretary of War Stimson and said, "It's your show now." Policy was to be subordinated to military strategy and the defeat of the enemy. The Secretary of State's job was presumably in suspense until the Secretary of War informed him that the victory had been achieved. Although Churchill was very realistic about the political situation developing in Europe, he had little power. Roosevelt until his death had the power but he was basically unrealistic. Only Stalin was both powerful and realistic, knowing what he wanted and how to get it.

Even more symptomatic of the U.S. style was the rapidity of America's postwar demobilization. An armed force of 12 million was quickly disbanded and the 1945 $81 billion military budget dropped down to $13 billion in two years. The nation had mobilized once it had been provoked, but now that the crusade was over the country could return to normalcy, focusing on domestic priorities and, at most, on hemispheric problems. Nationalist China, a member of the U.N.'s Security Council on which all the great powers were members, would police Asia; Britain and Russia would preserve the peace in Europe. By 1946 the United States had barely sufficient forces for the occupation of Germany and Japan. This state of affairs was hardly an incentive for Moscow to act with self-restraint. Rather, it was an inducement for Stalin to consolidate his gains and ignore American protests. Yet the irony was that at the end of the war the United States was at the height of its power and possessed enormous bargaining capability had it chosen to exercise it.

This demobilization, it must be added, included all the laboratories and facilities used in the research and production of the atomic bomb. The scientists went back to their universities. The stockpile of bombs grew very slowly. There were only two bombs in the stockpile by the end of 1945, nine by July 1947, and 50 a year later; none of them was assembled. By 1948, there were only about 30 bombers equipped to drop atomic bombs.[42] Given the relatively small stockpile, the large number of Russian targets, and the few bombers available for attacking the Soviet Union, the Joint Chiefs opposed any plans for war. Generals Eisenhower and Bradley, World War II heroes, and successive Army Chiefs of Staff afterward, also expressed moral indignation at the thought of carrying out an atomic attack. At no time immediately after the war did the United States try to use the bomb diplomatically and threaten Moscow privately or publicly with massive retaliation, as she was to do later or as the Soviets were to do with Britain and France when they invaded Egypt in 1956.

Yet it has been claimed that such "nuclear blackmail" is exactly what the United States did.[43] Critics have asserted that since Japan was on the verge of defeat, the two atomic bombs dropped on Japan were not militarily necessary. They were dropped only to demonstrate America's awesome new weapon to the Soviets and to intimidate Stalin. In reality, the bombs were necessary to bring about Japan's final surrender; and the attacks on Hiroshima and Nagasaki clearly did not frighten Stalin, if that was their intention. He continued to consolidate his grip on eastern Europe, and he was shortly to coerce Iran and Turkey. None of his actions would suggest fear of the American bomb. If anything, his behavior demonstrated "the impotence of omnipotence."[44] What exactly was it that American atomic blackmail was supposed to have prevented Stalin from doing? The fact remains that despite being the sole possessor of the most powerful weapon in history, the United

States abstained from using it politically, surely a unique instance of great power abstinence when a *Pax Americana* was in its grasp. Can anyone doubt that had Stalin been the sole possessor of this weapon he would have used it to achieve a more favorable postwar situation for the Soviet Union? As it was, the years when America had a monopoly on nuclear power were those during which the Soviets pushed the hardest.[45]

In fact, the United States did not really need the bomb politically because of the enormous productivity of American industry. American conventional power too was, to say the least, impressive. However, as in the past, only the perception of external provocation could stimulate America to mobilize itself and resort to force. Yet the only way the Soviet Union could have been restrained as World War II was ending was for the United States to have taken a hard-line and assertive attitude; and the sooner this would have been done after the invasion of France or, at the latest, after Yalta, the better. In retrospect, one has to wonder what would have happened had the United States asserted its powers more openly.

Stalin was a careful statesman. When he met firm opposition, he was willing to act with restraint. At one conference during the war, when Roosevelt was trying to convince him to show restraint in Poland, the Soviet leader asked, "How many divisions does the Pope have?" Later, he commented to another Communist leader on the importance of the Red Army in extending Soviet control beyond the Soviet Union's frontier. In short, Stalin understood the value of military power and would have respected it had the United States used it as an effective bargaining tool.

Stalin also knew something else: that the postwar Soviet Union, like tsarist Russia in 1815, was an exhausted country.[46] After four years of heavy fighting, after 20 million dead and much of European Russia laid waste, the Soviet dictator's bargaining strength was not as great as America's. Stalin needed to rebuild his nation's factories and collective farms; he therefore needed time. To be sure, he tried to see what he could pick off around the periphery of the area occupied by the Red Army, and in the process his satellization of eastern Europe shocked western sensitivities. But, as noted, in the countries closest to western power — Czechoslovakia and Hungary — the Soviets allowed free elections, and only slowly transformed eastern Europe into satellites. Stalin always kept a cautious eye on the United States and what it might *do* — as distinct from what it *said*. He could not afford a dangerous confrontation with America. Even though his weakened diplomatic leverage should have been obvious to any intelligent observer who had followed the bloodletting on the eastern front, it was apparently not seen by the American government. The Red Army's power and performance had blinded the west from noting Russia's political and economic vulnerabilities. Thus the United States was not even aware of its diplomatic strength. Symptomatic was the fact that America and Britain's leaders travelled eastward to all conferences with Stalin; Stalin never came westward beyond the Red Army's reach. Western leaders behaved as if they were suppliants, allowing the Soviet leader to control the agenda, never apparently realizing that they held the stronger hand.

The reluctance to use military power as a diplomatic tool was symptomatic of the American approach to international politics and suggests a fundamental difference between American and Soviet styles at the time: America hesitated to assert its power during the war in order to create a more favorable postwar situation. This attitude did not change until after the war when the Soviet Union tried to expand beyond the areas it had captured by the time the fighting stopped. Public opinion had been aroused against Germany; the aim of the war was its unconditional surrender. In addition, most Americans wanted to believe that there were no fundamental conflicts of interest between the United States and the Soviet Union, which, it was also widely believed, was largely abandoning communism and turning to democracy and capitalism. In the words of a March 1943 *Life* magazine issue: The Russians were "one hell of a people . . . [who], to a remarkable degree . . . look like Americans, dress like Americans and think like Americans."[47] This widely shared sentiment testifies to American wartime hopes as well as illusions, the rather facile transfer of American views about society and democracy to the world at large, the simultaneous ignorance of Russian history and Soviet ideology, and the expectation that since both powers had "used the same words and because they both desired the defeat of the Axis, [they] had identical expectations for the future."[48] Under these conditions, it would have been very difficult to initiate an anti-Soviet policy.

Failure of Western Leadership?

Still, the question that remains is: Should Roosevelt — and Churchill — not have tried to alert their publics anyway? The war had started over Poland's independence. Was Poland's future — whether it would govern itself and be a genuinely independent country — not exactly the kind of issue on which to mobilize opinion? Self-determination was the fundamental principle of western democracy, and American leaders had committed themselves to the defeat of Nazi Germany in order to realize this principle. Surely, an issue that involved not just the liberation from Nazi rule, but the substitution of Soviet domination for German domination, would have been comprehensible to most of the American public (and British public as well). After all, it had been the same U.S. and British governments that helped create their peoples' hopes and illusions in the first place. Could they not therefore have helped to dispel these hopes and illusions as well?

Perhaps, given its crusading style, America could not have bargained harder with Stalin until after the war. Perhaps the United States, in focusing its energies on the defeat of Germany and Japan, and believing simultaneously that anyone who fought with her against the common enemies had to be equally peace-loving, could not have avoided the rapid dismantling of its powerful military machine after its victories. It should be recognized that what prevented the United States from being more effective in the conduct of foreign policy during 1945–1946 was its past history of isolationism and its democratic nature. To put it another way, its political culture was unprepared for the world it became caught up in during World War II. Roosevelt was correct in believing that the American people wanted no post-war involvement in Europe and expected him to focus on winning the war. As a politician and commander-in-chief, the president was successful; but as a statesman, he failed because he possessed no real strategic sense of what the world would look like once Germany and its allies had been defeated.

Conflicts among states are inherent in the structure of the international system. Nations obviously have their own distinct "personalities" and do not act in the same way. To suggest, therefore, that the Soviet Union is merely a "mirror image" of the United States — that it is a state with normal security concerns which, if met by the western states, would lead it to behave peacefully, that its expansionist drives are essentially defensive, a reflection of its extreme concern for security, and that its often ruthless actions are usually reactions to western behavior the Soviets regard as hostile — is to misperceive Soviet conduct. Soviet behavior is *not* basically a mirror image of the United States; its policies are *not* merely reactions to American policies. Were that true, the western efforts to establish better postwar relations by satisfying her interests in eastern Europe and China would have been more successful. One thing about World War II is absolutely certain: *America's wartime leaders all believed that postwar cooperation with Russia was possible. Anti-Communism was not the cause of the Cold War.*

However, there was nothing accidental about the eruption of the Cold War. One cause was the international state system. Its bipolar character meant that the United States and the Soviet Union would regard each other as potential threats to their respective security. But Soviet policy made sure that the Cold War would be inevitable. If a state operates on the fundamental assumption that other states — even allies — are in fact enemies, they will become so. Stalin's determination to act unilaterally in eastern Europe, to ignore allied protests, to surround himself with subservient neighbors without ever indicating where his sphere of influence would stop (it even included control of all of Germany and a subservient western Europe) emptied the reservoir of goodwill that could have been the real basis for postwar Soviet security. Stalin's conception of security — whether defensively or offensively motivated, or inspired by traditional Russian security considerations, or spurred by Soviet revolutionary ideas — left little or no security for other states. This was obviously unacceptable to the European states, as well as to the United States.

America's wartime policy failed not because it tried to accommodate Soviet interests; the fact that it did try laid the basis for the domestic consensus to support the later containment policy. The real failure was that the United States did not oppose Stalin earlier, that it clung to its hopes for postwar cooperation despite growing signs to the contrary, and that it dissipated its strength immediately after the war. It should be remembered that Stalin was cautious and restrained when firmly opposed. Moreover, since Soviet security was an ever-expanding concept, it was America's responsibility to set the limits on Soviet aims.* America's failure to stop Stalin and foreclose his opportunities to extend Soviet power was thus an additional cause for the Cold War.[49]

Notes

1. Robert Gilpin, *War and Change in World Politics* (Cambridge: Cambridge University Press, 1981), pp. 199–200.

*Former Soviet Foreign Minister Litvinov, asked after the war if the west granted Moscow's demands, "Would that lead to goodwill and easing of the present tensions?" replied, "It would lead to the West's being faced after a more or less short time, with the next series of demands." Why? Because, the former Soviet Foreign Minister said, the "root cause" of east-west tension was "the ideological conception prevailing here [Moscow] that conflict between Communist and capitalist worlds is inevitable." (Interview with Richard C. Hottelot, *New York World Telegram*, January 28, 1952.)

2. Hans Morgenthau, *Politics among Nations*, 4th ed. (New York: Alfred A. Knopf, 1967), p. 504.

3. John Lewis Gaddis, "The Long Peace: Elements of Stability in the Postwar International System," *Inter-National Security*, Spring 1986, pp. 99–142.

4. Zbigniew Brzezinski, *Game Plan* (Boston: The Atlantic Monthly Press, 1986), p. 29.

5. For a more detailed analysis, see John Spanier, *Games Nations Play*, 6th ed. (Washington, D.C.: Congressional Quarterly, 1987), pp. 110–339. Also see Paul Seabury, *The Rise and Decline of the Cold War* (New York: Basic Books, 1967), pp. 10–13.

6. A. J. P. Taylor, *The Struggle for Mastery in Europe 1848–1918* (London, England: Oxford University Press, 1954), pp. XXIV–XXXII.

7. Ibid., p. xxxi. Also see Paul Kennedy, "The First World War and the International Power System," *International Security*, Summer 1984, p. 23.

8. Thomas W. Wolfe, *Soviet Power and Europe, 1945–1970* (Baltimore: The Johns Hopkins Press, 1970), pp. 10–11; Hannes Adomeit, *Soviet Risk-Taking and Crisis Behavior* (Boston: Allen & Unwin, 1982), p. 140. Khrushchev's figure was 2,800,000; even at that figure, the Soviet forces were far larger than western forces.

9. Louis Halle, *The Cold War as History* (New York: Harper & Row, 1967), p. 17.

10. Richard Pipes, *Survival Is Not Enough* (New York: Simon & Schuster, 1984), p. 38.

11. Ibid., p. 37 (italics added). Pipes tells the story that in 1890 the Russian General Staff did a history of Russian warfare and found that between 1700 and 1870 Russia had spent 106 years fighting 38 military campaigns, of which 36 had been "offensive" and only two "defensive." p. 39. Also see Robert V. Daniels, *Russia, the Roots of Confrontation* (Cambridge, Mass.: Harvard University Press, 1985), p. 361.

12. Zbigniew Brzezinski, "The Soviet Union: Her Aims, Problems and Challenges to the West," in International Institute for Strategic Studies, *The Conduct of East-West Relations in the 1980's*, 1984, Part I, p. 4.

13. Ibid.

14. Russell F. Weigley, *The American Way of War* (Bloomington,

52   *From Wartime Allies to Postwar Enemies*

Ind.: Indiana University Press, 1977), p. 347. Also see David
Eisenhower, *Eisenhower: At War* (New York: Random House,
1986) who emphasizes the dependence of the western front on
the eastern front and that Eisenhower's constant concern was to
prevent a split of the alliance with the Soviet Union.

15. *The New York Times,* October 5, 1985.

16. John L. Snell, *Illusion and Necessity* (Boston: Houghton Mifflin, 1963), p. 212.

17. Paul M. Kennedy, *The Rise and Fall of British Naval Mastery*
(Malabar, Fla.: Robert E. Krieger Publishing Company, 1982),
pp. 309–310.

18. John J. Mearsheimer, *Conventional Deterrence* (Ithaca, N.Y.:
Cornell University Press, 1983), pp. 91–92; Kennedy, op. cit.,
pp. 312–313.

19. As Richard Rosecrance ("International Theory Revisited," *International Organization,* Fall 1981, p. 108), has aptly commented, the building of the German navy before 1914 led to
Anglo-German tensions and eventually war. But the building of
the U.S. Navy led to the Washington Naval Agreement, not
rivalry.

20. Among others, see John Spanier, *American Foreign Policy Since
World War II,* 11th ed. (Washington, D.C.: Congressional Quarterly, 1988); Stanley Hoffmann, *Gulliver's Troubles* (New York:
McGraw-Hill, 1968), part II, pp. 87–213; Ken Booth, *Strategy
and Ethnocentrism* (London: Croom, Helm, 1973); and Colin S.
Gray, "National Style in Strategy," *International Security,* Fall
1981, pp. 21–48, and *Nuclear Strategy and National Style* (Lanham, Md.: Hamilton Press, 1986).

21. George Kennan, *Russia and the West under Lenin and Stalin*
(Boston: Little, Brown, 1961), p. 186.

22. Curtis Keebler, "The Roots of Soviet Foreign Policy," *International Affairs,* Autumn 1984, p. 563.

23. Nathan Leites, *The Operational Code of the Politburo* (New
York: McGraw-Hill, 1951); and Alexander L. George, "The 'Op-
erational Code': A Neglected Approach to the Study of Political
Leaders and Decision-Making," in Erik Hoffmann and Frederic
J. Fleron, eds., *The Conduct of Soviet Foreign Policy* (Chicago:
Aldine-Atherton, 1971), pp. 165–190.

24. George Kennan, *American Diplomacy 1900–1950* (Chicago: Chicago University Press, 1951), p. 118.

25. On the allied side, Herbert Feis, *Churchill, Roosevelt, Stalin* (Princeton, N.J.: Princeton University, 1957) is a standard source. Winston Churchill's six volumes, *The Second World War* (Boston: Houghton Mifflin, 1948–1953) are the superb memoirs of a participant. An older but excellent critique of the U.S. conduct in the war is Chester Wilmot, *The Struggle for Europe* (New York: Harper & Brothers, 1952).

26. See, for example, the intelligence forecast in Robert E. Sherwood, *Roosevelt and Hopkins* (New York: Bantam Books, 1950), vol. 2, pp. 363–364.

27. See, for example, the comments of Henry Hopkins, the president's closest adviser, after Yalta. Ibid., p. 516.

28. Quoted by Wilmot, op. cit., p. 659.

29. Gaddis Smith, *American Diplomacy During the Second World War* (New York: John Wiley, 1966), p. 9.

30. On Soviet wartime policy, William Taubman, *Stalin's American Policy* (New York: W. W. Norton, 1982), p. 39 and Voitech Mastny, *Russia's Road to the Cold War* (New York: Columbia University, 1979) are comprehensive and indispensable.

31. Ibid., p. 9.

32. Adam Ulam, *Expansion and Coexistence* (N.Y.: Frederick A. Praeger, 1968), pp. 399, 401.

33. Eduard Mark, "American Policy toward Eastern Europe and the Origins of the Cold War, 1941–1946: An Alternative Interpretation," *The Journal of American History*, September 1987, pp. 313–336.

34. See, for example, how power was seized by the Communist party in Hungary in Charles Gati, "The Democratic Interlude in Post-War Hungary," *Survey*, Summer 1984, pp. 99–134; also by Charles Gati, *Hungary and the Soviet Bloc* (Durham, N.C.: Duke University Press, 1986).

35. John Lewis Gaddis, *The United States and the Origins of the Cold War* (New York: Columbia University Press, 1972), pp. 133–173.

36. Ulam, op. cit., pp. 410–411.

37. For the Far Eastern Agreement at Yalta, see Warren I. Cohen, *America's Response to China* (New York: John Wiley, 1980), pp. 175–176.

38. Strobe Talbott, trans. and ed., *Khrushchev Remembers* (Boston: Houghton Mifflin, 1974), pp. 295–296.

39. Bruce R. Kuniholm, *The Origins of the Cold War in the Near East* (Princeton, N.J.: Princeton University Press, 1980); and David S. McLellan, "Who Fathered Containment?", *International Studies Quarterly,* June 1973, pp. 205–226.
40. Joseph M. Jones, *The Fifteen Weeks* (New York: The Viking Press, 1955).
41. Churchill, op. cit., vol. 5, *Triumph and Tragedy,* p. 512.
42. David Alan Rosenberg, "The Origins of Overkill: Nuclear Weapons and American Strategy, 1945–1960," *International Security,* Spring 1983, p. 14.
43. For example, Gar Alperovitz, *Atomic Diplomacy* (New York: Vintage Books, 1967).
44. Gaddis, op. cit., pp. 244–281.
45. Ulam, op. cit., p. 414.
46. Adam Ulam, *The Rivals* (New York: The Viking Press, 1971), pp. 3–11; and Mastny, op. cit., pp. 310–311.
47. *Life,* March 29, 1943. Also see, for example, General Eisenhower's similar comments in Dwight D. Eisenhower, *Crusade in Europe* (New York: Doubleday, 1952), pp. 457, 473–474.
48. Smith, op. cit., p. 178.
49. Mastny, op. cit., p. 309.

From Cold War I
to Cold War II

An Overview

The Cold War can be divided into two broad periods: Cold War
I from 1947 to 1962 — from the Truman Doctrine to the end of
the Cuban missile crisis — and Cold War II, which began with
the Soviet invasion of Afghanistan in December 1979.[1] In between was a period of détente, which can also be subdivided
into two periods: Détente I from 1963 to 1968 and Détente II
from 1969 to 1979. Cold War I was a period during which the
United States initially held an atomic monopoly and, after the
Soviet explosion of an atomic device in 1949, a vast strategic
superiority composed of intercontinental-range bombers (with
air refueling), later supplemented by intercontinental ballistic
missiles (ICBMs) and nuclear submarines with sea-launched
ballistic missiles (SLBMs).

During these years, the Soviet Union was also essentially a
Eurasian power, but after 1949 the Communist world spread
from East Germany to Communist China; only Yugoslavia had
successfully defected from the Soviet-controlled bloc in eastern Europe. Soviet attempts to expand its influence beyond
Eurasia were abortive; in the early 1960s, in both the Congo
and Cuba (during the missile crisis) the limits of the Soviet
Union to project its power were clearly revealed. The Soviet
Union attributed its humiliation in Cuba to its nuclear inferiority as well as its conventional naval inferiority. After the
missile crisis, whose outcome was the withdrawal of Soviet
missiles, Moscow embarked on a sustained military buildup of
both strategic and conventional forces, including a large surface fleet. This buildup required a period of relaxation. The
United States too required a respite, since it had become involved in Vietnam. This led to Détente I.

Detente II coincided with the emergence of American-Soviet strategic parity. America's nuclear superiority had ended.
It was also the decade during which the Soviet Union, like the
United States, became a global power. It acquired an air and
sealift capability that could extend beyond Eurasia. In the
wake of America's withdrawal from Vietnam in 1973, North
Vietnam's final victory in 1975, and the attendant reemergence
of an American mood of withdrawal from an activist foreign

policy, Soviet confidence grew in its ability to exploit the shift in the strategic balance and America's paralysis of will. A series of subsequent interventions in Africa, followed by the invasion of Afghanistan in 1979, helped destroy détente. Simultaneously, this period coincided with the breakup of the Sino-Soviet alliance and the Sino-American reconciliation.

A major symptom of the decline of détente toward the end of the 1970s was the collapse of the strategic arms limitation talks (SALT), which contributed to the worsening of the superpower relationship. Unlike Cold War I, then, Cold War II was waged between two superpowers who were of approximately equal strategic strength; whose alliances were losing the cohesion and unity that had once characterized them; who confronted a world in which many states — some allies or friends, others nonaligned third world states — played a more independent and assertive role; and who found themselves inexorably drawn to all regions of the world as their global interests and rivalry were projected into local quarrels and rivalries.[2]

More specifically, we will deal with the following phases:

Cold War I: Conflict, 1947–1952
              Conflict and Competition, 1953–1962
              Conflict, Competition, and Cooperation:
              Détente I, 1963–1968
              Détente II, 1969–1979
Cold War II: Confrontation, 1980–

Phase 1: Conflict, 1947–1952

This first period was basically one of Soviet expansion. Having already expanded into central Europe, Moscow consolidated its grip on eastern Europe and sought to exploit weaknesses to its south. By early 1947, both sides considered each other as enemies. Stalin had already announced in February 1946 that World War II had not been the result of an accident or mistakes; rather, it had been the product of world capitalism. And since this condition continued to prevail, the danger of war — this time with the United States — was still present. The message made explicit an assumption he had held throughout the war: that there was not much difference between Nazi Germany and democratic America; both were capitalist states and therefore enemies. President Truman's "declaration of (the cold) war" came in his March 1947 address to the Congress, requesting funds to support Greece and Turkey. The United States, he declared, could be secure only in a world in which freedom flourished. Thus the United States had to be "willing to help free peoples to maintain their institutions and their national integrity against aggressive movements that seek to impose upon them totalitarian regimes. This is no more than a frank recognition that totalitarian regimes imposed on free peoples, by direct or indirect aggression, undermine the foundations of international peace and hence the security of the United States."[3] In fact, this Truman Doctrine, as it was to become known, by posing the growing U.S.–Soviet conflict in traditional terms of democracy versus authoritarianism, supplied an ideological rationale whose purpose was to mobilize a public opinion that had sought to return to normalcy after the war for a struggle that had already been going for a year.

Rivalry Over Europe

The real focus of the major postwar conflict was western Europe. First of all, Europe was important because of its geographical situation as the western rimland of Eurasia. To contain the Soviet Union, the United States had to deny Moscow control of the Atlantic approaches to the western hemisphere. Second, the loss of Europe would result in a critical shift of power against the United States. There were five centers of military and industrial power in the world: the United States, England, Germany, Russia, and Japan. The Soviets controlled only one of these centers, and it was the aim of the United States to prevent any of the others from falling into hostile hands. Despite its postwar collapse, Europe's potential power remained great. Third, western Europe was vital because it was the home of democracy. Freedom in North America could not survive in isolation. As two world wars had amply demonstrated, American and western European security and democracy were inseparable.

The symptom of Europe's collapse was economic, although a more fundamental cause was psychological. Europe was emotionally exhausted after two world wars (1914–1918 and 1939–1945). Stalin's quest for Soviet security now extended beyond the control of eastern Europe; to secure the latter, he sought a pliant western Europe as well.[4] He had large armed forces deployed in central Europe, and he controlled large Communist parties in France and Italy. Russian prestige stood at an all-time high. These were formidable assets.

Symptomatic of Stalin's appetite was his rejection of a U.S. offer of a 25-year alliance to prevent German rearmament. Given only token American occupation troops in Germany, this would have left the Russian military forces supreme in Europe. The western European states, minus Germany, were no match for the Red Army.[5] If Stalin had merely Russian security in mind, how could he have refused such a proposal? But he did, presumably because "such an agreement would have given the United States a lasting foothold in Europe and a continuing voice in German affairs, whereas an American return to isolationism would have left Germany little choice but to accept the Soviet alternative for its future." Soviet policy favored German unity "on the grounds that political capture of a reunified Germany was possible."[6]

From Washington's perspective, the situation resembled that before World Wars I and II: a strong power seeking continental domination. The balance of power previously kept by Britain now had to be restored by injecting U.S. power into western Europe. Thus the Truman Doctrine for Greece and Turkey was quickly followed by a four-year multibillion plan of economic aid for Europe's recovery. Named after American Secretary of State George C. Marshall, it was called the Marshall Plan.

From Moscow's perspective, however, the economic recovery of western Europe would not only fill a power vacuum but also eliminate the opportunity for exploiting Europe's low morale and hunger. To counteract the Marshall Plan the Soviets tried to paralyze the governments of France and Italy by calling on the Communist-dominated trade unions to cripple their nations' economies. These efforts failed. The Soviets also saw the recovery of western Europe as a threat to their security, because this revival required the restoration of Germany which the western allies controlled under the postwar occupation. Instead of gaining control of all of Germany, therefore, the Soviet Union suddenly faced the prospect of two-thirds of Germany, the most populated and industrialized part before its destruction, being tied to the United States, a formidable combination. To prevent this from happening, the Soviets instituted the Berlin blockade in 1948, the year of the Marshall Plan.

Berlin, the former capital of Germany, had great symbolic importance and it had been divided among the victors plus France. Lying in the Soviet zone of occupation, West Berlin was highly vulnerable to Soviet pressure. The Soviets now cut off ground access to West Berlin. This was clearly a contest of wills. Moscow sought to push the western allies out of the city, demonstrating to West Germany's citizens which was the stronger power and, in effect, warning them not to align West Germany with the United States. If the Soviets succeeded in strangling West Berlin, their heightened prestige, together with the erosion of U.S. influence, could still help them gain control over West Germany, if not beyond. "By attempting to convert a local strategic advantage into a major American defeat, Stalin took a calculated military risk which drastically altered the whole East-West relationship."[7]

The western response was a massive airlift to supply West Berlin with all its needs. The Soviets gave in and reopened access to West Berlin by road and rail traffic in 1949. Stalin also failed to prevent the emergence of the new German state, the Federal Republic of Germany. However, the Soviet attempt to intimidate West Berlin and West Germany had made clear that all of western Europe would be subject to Soviet pressure and that western recovery could not really occur unless Europeans were sure of their security. After all, what motive was there for Europeans to work hard if they feared a Soviet takeover tomorrow? The Marshall Plan had already indicated Washington's awareness that U.S. security was linked to European security. The Berlin airlift reaffirmed that. But no formal American political commitment to European security had yet been made. Such a commitment was needed to signal friend and foe alike that America had finally left its isolationist shell. This happened in 1949 when the United States committed itself formally and publicly to Europe's defense. Thus the impact of the Berlin blockade on the U.S. assessment of the Soviet challenge was profound, and it precipitated the North Atlantic Treaty Organization (NATO).[8] Its principal members were Belgium, Britain, France, Iceland, Italy, the Netherlands, Norway, Portugal, and the United States. West Germany was not a member; it remained the former enemy, an occupied power. (Greece and Turkey became members in 1952 and Spain in 1982.)

The division of Europe was now clear. In one sense, it had been clear since the Soviet and American armies met at the Elbe River. It became even clearer with the consolidation of Soviet power throughout eastern Europe on the one hand and the Marshall Plan and the Berlin airlift on the other. NATO was the most unambiguous signal that could be given. There was no longer any doubt that western Europe's defense was America's first line of defense. Although no eastern equivalent of NATO existed yet, the presence of the Red Army, together with Moscow's clear-cut authority and dominance in eastern Europe left no doubt that the area was off limits to the west. The major exception was Yugoslavia whose leader, Tito, had mobilized national resistance to the German occupiers and then did the same thing when Stalin sought to control him. Yugoslavia was subsequently expelled from the Soviet bloc.

It is particularly interesting in retrospect that the Ber-

lin blockade and Stalin's excommunication of Tito's Yugoslavia from the international Communist movement came
simultaneously.

The Berlin and Belgrade ventures complemented each other by
being both aimed at reversing the American ascendancy in the
Cold War. In Berlin, the prize was to inflict on the adversary a
diplomatic defeat that would shatter the United States' credibility as the protector of western Europe; in Belgrade, Stalin's
own credibility as the undisputed master of eastern Europe was
at issue. Along with the anticipated success of the Berlin blockade, the expected subjugation of Yugoslavia would thus have
established in two bold strokes the preconditions of Moscow's
European supremacy that had eluded him after World War II.[9]

The failure of these "two bold strokes" was a setback for
Stalin who in 1948 had increased his control of eastern Europe,
launched the coup in Czechoslovakia, called on the Communist parties and Communist-dominated trade unions in
France and Italy to prevent their nations' economic recovery,
launched the Berlin blockade, and tried to destroy Tito.

NSC-68
In a revision of the containment policy, the Soviet Union was
identified as both a political and military adversary. In National Security Council (NSC) document 68, issued in April
1950 by the Truman administration, the Soviet Union was said
to be "unlike previous aspirants to hegemony, . . . animated
by a new fanatic faith, antithetical to our own, and seeks to
impose its absolute authority over the rest of the world." The
United States was regarded as the Soviet Union's principal enemy. It had to be "subverted or destroyed by one means or
another if the Kremlin is to achieve its fundamental design. . . . The assault on free institutions is world-wide now,
and in the context of the present polarization of power a defeat
of free institutions anywhere is a defeat everywhere."[10]
Nations have historically distinguished among their many

interests and objectives; some are vital, others less so. Like individuals, they have "champagne tastes and beer budgets" and therefore must establish priorities; they cannot afford everything. NSC 68, by boldly asserting that "a defeat . . . anywhere is a defeat everywhere" was suggesting that all American interests and commitments were equally important and must be defended. This deliberate overlooking of the distinction between primary and peripheral interests, motivated by a broad anticommunism, was a recipe for disaster. A great power, if it is prudent, concentrates its attention and resources for the conflict with its primary opponent. It does not involve itself in areas of secondary interest and spend enormous resources in struggles with less important adversaries, thus squandering the strength it needs to confront its principal enemy. Indeed, faced with two or more opponents, it should focus on the most powerful one and seek to isolate it by attracting the other(s) toward itself.

NSC 68 also called for a rapid military buildup. It foresaw the emergence of a nuclear stalemate, and once the U.S. deterrent would be neutralized by the Soviet bomb, it feared that the Soviet Union might risk a military attack. NSC 68 stated that this might occur by 1954. "It also puts a premium on piecemeal aggression against others, counting on our unwillingness to engage in atomic war unless we are directly attacked."[11] NSC 68 recommended a buildup of both nuclear and conventional forces. But President Truman paid little attention to the report. To implement it would cost too much, and therefore no massive increase in defense spending followed. If it had not been for the North Korean attack on South Korea in June 1950, the recommendations would have died. But Korea gave plausibility to NSC 68's forecast of aggression and militarized the containment policy. Thus, just as Soviet pressure right after the war had ended U.S. isolationism and led to NATO, so Berlin and especially Korea led to increases in the low postwar U.S. military budgets and a military buildup.

The United States sent General Eisenhower, who had been in charge of the allied armies in Europe during the war, back as supreme commander; it shipped four American divisions composed of approximately 60,000 troops to Europe, thereby visibly committing American manpower to underline the credibility of its NATO pledge to defend Europe; and it urged West Germany's rearmament as part of a general western rearmament. West Germany, the former enemy, joined NATO in 1955. East Germany, a Soviet satellite, became formally allied to the Soviet Union in 1955 when Moscow organized its NATO counterpart, the Warsaw Treaty Organization (WTO), or Warsaw pact. The division of Europe into two blocs had now been formalized.

War in Asia
Once the situation in Europe had sufficiently stabilized after the Marshall Plan, the Berlin airlift, and the organization of NATO, Soviet attention shifted to Asia. There, in contrast to the increasing western strength in Europe, the American position was being undermined. The Nationalist Chinese lost the civil war to the Communists in 1949. They lost mainly because the Nationalists represented the landowners while the Communists represented the vast majority of Chinese, the peasantry. The Nationalist government, inefficient, corrupt, and highly repressive, alienated the land-hungry peasants; the Communists, who had a better army and better political and military leadership, were the victors. The remnants of what was left of the Nationalists retreated to the island of Taiwan. The Chinese Communists had successfully aligned themselves with the forces of nationalism and reform.

The disintegration of Nationalist China translated into the rise of a major new Communist state. The Soviet Union signed an alliance in early 1950, which was a major setback for the United States. It also represented an opportunity for further exploitation. This opportunity was found in Korea, a peninsula to the south of China, jutting out to Japan. It was occupied by Japan during World War II, but after Japan's surrender the Soviets disarmed Japanese forces to the north of the 38th Parallel, the Americans doing so to the south. These respective zones grew into a Communist North Korea and a non-Communist South Korea. But in drawing up its defense perimeter in the Pacific after China's collapse, the United States omitted South Korea. The reason was that in a war with the Soviet Union, American sea and air power could neutralize the Korean peninsula. Therefore, it withdrew its forces and declared South Korea outside the defense perimeter.

The North Koreans, assuming that the United States had abandoned South Korea, thought they could pick it up "on the cheap" and unify the country. Stalin at least agreed, if he did not instigate the action, for North Korea could not have acted independently. In any event, the North Korean Army crossed the 38th Parallel and invaded South Korea in June 1950. The United States now changed its mind for reasons having little to do with the inherent importance of South Korea but for reasons having to do with the European and Asian balance of power, as well as the kind of world America was trying to create.[12] The United States had just organized NATO and pledged itself to the defense of its European allies. What would they think if the United States now abandoned South Korea? Admittedly, South Korea was not an ally, but it was America's protégé. The United States helped establish its government, provided it with aid, and trained its army. Thus a failure to defend South Korea would make its European allies wonder whether in like circumstances they too would be abandoned. If they believed this, NATO would disintegrate.

A second reason for America's defense of South Korea was that in the wake of Nationalist China's collapse, the United States had to do in Asia what it was also doing in Europe — look to a former enemy for an ally. Japan, with its sizable population and its large-scale industry, was an obvious choice if the United States were to create a position of strength in Asia as it had done in Europe. But Korea and Japanese security had historically been linked. At the turn of the century, when tsarist Russia made northern Manchuria a Russian sphere of influence and expanded its influence southward to Korea, the Japanese government offered to divide Korea at the 38th Parallel.

The Russians could have the northern half but not the southern half; this was essential to Japan's security. When the Russians attempted to spread their influence further south, Japan attacked Russia, defeating her in the war of 1904–1905. The Korean peninsula, lying between China and Russia to its north and Japan to its south, was thus a "dagger' that could be and had been pointed in either direction: by tsarist Russia against Japan, by an expansionist militaristic Japan in the 1930s against China, and by the Soviet Union against American-occupied Japan after World War II. A principal benefit for Moscow of a North Korean victory would therefore be to assure Japanese neutrality in the Cold War.

The result was that the United States fought its first "limited war" to confirm its alliance in Europe, attract Japan as an ally (which it did shortly afterward), and make clear that South Korea was in America's sphere of influence. It was to be a long three-year war in which the United States first hung on, then turned the tables on the North Koreans by defeating them, after which it invaded North Korea and marched to Korea's frontiers with China and the Soviet Union. The dagger, however, now having been turned around, brought Communist China into the war. The United States was the enemy. Not only was it a capitalist state but Washington continued to support the rump Nationalist regime on the island of Taiwan as the government of China; it refused to recognize the new Chinese government as the legitimate government, even though it controlled mainland China. Indeed, after the Korean War erupted, the U.S. Navy was sent to protect Taiwan (and was to remain there until the Nixon administration).

In addition, to China's south, in Indochina, the United States supported the French war against the Vietminh, or nationalistically motivated Vietnamese Communists. France, after Japan's defeat, tried to restore its colonial control over Indochina (Vietnam, Cambodia, and Laos). Refusing to grant Indochina national independence, France confronted national resistance organized by the Vietminh. Initially unsympathetic to France's efforts to restore colonial control, the United

States began to change its mind and gave France economic and military assistance in its fight. It needed French support for the containment policy in Europe, and after Communist China's rise to power and the eruption of the Korean War, American aid to the French grew even further. The United States was also about to ally itself to Japan, with whom China had just fought a long war. It was therefore no surprise that China intervened in Korea to drive the American and South Korean and other allied forces away from its frontier. In marching up to this frontier Washington badly miscalculated China's reaction and this blunder was to be very costly in lives, in prolonging the war, and in souring future U.S.–Chinese relations.

Allied forces soon recovered and by 1951 the war settled down in the area of the 38th Parallel. Subsequent armistice negotiations dragged on for two years until 1953 when the new Eisenhower administration threatened to use atomic weapons on China if a settlement were not reached soon. It was reached, and it reconfirmed that North Korea belonged to the Sino-Soviet sphere, while South Korea belonged to the American sphere. Neither side had allowed the other to conquer its half of the peninsula. Whether it was the atomic threat that ended the war is still not clear. What is clear is the influence of two other reasons: China's exhaustion and, probably most important, the death of Stalin. Since there is no legitimate process of succession in the Soviet Union, Stalin's death meant a period of jockeying among the principal Communist leaders. This required a time for calm and not foreign tensions, and it translated into a need to end what was the tensest situation between the superpowers, one that could escalate if the war were not brought to a conclusion.

The Effects on U.S. Foreign Policy
But two legacies from the Korean War were to haunt U.S. policy until the consensus on containment broke down during the later Vietnam war (1965–1973). The first was that Korea and more specifically China's intervention transformed containment from an anti-Soviet to an anti-Communist one. Despite

the missionary and universal language of the Truman Doctrine and NSC 68, containment had been practiced only to counter moves by the Soviet Union and its proxies like the North Koreans. It had been a limited and selective policy.[13] Now it had turned into a broader crusade against communism in general in which the distinction between vital and secondary interests sometimes became obscured. Previously, the Communist world was not seen as a monolith; take, for example, Yugoslavia's independence. But after the Korean War, all states except Yugoslavia were seen as either close allies or satellites of Moscow. Thus any expansionist moves by these countries had to be opposed because they would enhance the power and influence of the Soviet Union and the Sino-Soviet bloc, and a gain for the Communist world was seen as a loss for the "Free World." Bipolar politics thus became the politics of confrontation.[14]

This anticommunism as a policy was reinforced by U.S. domestic politics. The Republicans, after four losses in presidential elections, were looking for an issue. As the party of Herbert Hoover and the Great Depression, they could hardly run on their domestic record; they needed a foreign policy issue. The "fall" of China was a major setback for the United States. Since the Democrats were in power when it happened, they could be held responsible. While no policy could probably have changed the outcome of the Chinese civil war, the administration's fault was that it had justified U.S. policy with universal rhetoric; it had done so largely to mobilize public and congressional support for the containment policy. Now this came back to haunt the policy makers. If the central conflict of our time was between freedom and slavery, then it was difficult for the administration to explain why the United States did not do more to "save China." The Republicans charged the Democrats with betrayal, being "soft on Communism," and appeasement. These broad accusations against the Democrats, as well as against specific individuals, most of them reckless charges of loyalty and security risks, placed the administration on the defensive. Thus indiscriminate anticommunism at home affected foreign policy, and U.S. policy makers — especially Democrats — were prone to intervening in Asia for many years afterward.

The second legacy of Korea was a deep gulf between mainland China and the United States. For the Chinese Communists, it reaffirmed their view of capitalist America as their chief enemy. For the United States, which since the turn of the century had seen itself as China's protector and benefactor (although, in reality, it had been neither), China's turning Communist and then denouncing America as the "world bastion of reaction" and sending its forces into Korea against the American Army transformed what had previously been a "love affair" with China into genuine hatred. It became politically impossible to recognize The People's Republic, usually referred to as "Red China," in the 1950s and 1960s. Not until 1972 did the relationship between the two countries begin to thaw with the visit to the mainland by President Nixon, the first to call the regime by its proper name. But it was to be 1979 before the two nations exchanged formal recognition. For 30 years, the United States had continued to recognize the Nationalists on Taiwan as the legitimate government of China!

Phase 2: Conflict and Competition, 1953–1962

In 1953, Joseph Stalin died and a new administration came into office in the United States. It was also the year the Korean War ended. The new governments in both the United States and Soviet Union continued to wage their battles in the third world; the shift from Europe to Asia was expanded to the Middle East during these years. The American interest was in the areas around the peripheries of the Soviet Union and Communist China in order to encircle what in those days was generally referred to as the Sino-Soviet bloc. The Soviet Union's interest reflected both its military vulnerability and the dangers of a confrontation in Europe, as well as the opportunities for contracting western influence and expanding its own among the less developed countries (LDCs). The LDCs were highly nationalistic and Moscow sought to exploit this; U.S. blunders helped it do so. The fact that the Cold War was extended from Europe to the third world in the 1950s was symptomatic of a major change in the structure of international politics from the 1940s: The collapse of western colonialism which, starting after World War II, was accelerated in the 1950s with the birth of many new states, especially in Africa.

Encircling the Communist World
For the United States, the middle 1950s were years of great confidence. Even though the Soviet Union had exploded its first atomic device in 1949, the following years had not resulted in a closing of the atomic imbalance. Quite the contrary. During the 1950s, U.S. strategic superiority grew quickly. By the time the Eisenhower administration came into office in January 1953, the United States had hundreds of atomic bombs. It was also acquiring the first pure jet bomber, the B-47, with the capability to penetrate Soviet defenses, while the larger and first intercontinental bomber, the B-52, would soon go into production. The Soviets, with far fewer bombs, had only propeller-driven airplanes that could not easily penetrate American air space against the new generation of American jet fighters.

President Eisenhower sought to use this power to contain the Sino-Soviet bloc not only in Europe, as his predecessor had done, but in the third world as well. He did so by extending the lines of containment around the Sino Chinese-Soviet bloc. This was accomplished by two alliances, the Southeast Asia Treaty Organization (SEATO) and the Middle East Treaty Organization (METO), also known as the Baghdad pact. Eisenhower did not want to fight another Korea because he feared that a series of such conflicts would bankrupt the economy and result in the attrition of American manpower. A preferable strategy was to organize replicas of NATO to restrain the Soviet Union and Communist China, supplemented by a number of bilateral alliances, such as the defense pacts with Japan, signed during the Truman years, and the pacts with South Korea and Nationalist China, signed during the Eisenhower years. These alliances would encircle the Communist bloc and make clear to Moscow and Beijing that they were not to cross these lines. Backed up by the threat of massive retaliation against the two principal Communist states and their satellites, the Eisenhower administration felt certain that it could prevent further Communist expansion by means of limited wars at a reasonable cost. The money was to be spent on building up the Strategic Air Command so it could deliver that massive (nuclear) blow. There would be no need for maintaining expensive conventional forces, especially a large number of army divisions.

There were at least two problems with this approach. The first was that it was easy to threaten massive retaliation when the targeted nation could not respond, but it was quite another matter to make such a threat against an adversary whose capability to retaliate was growing. Even if such a threat sufficed to deter an all-out attack on the United States, it might not suffice to deter a Korean-type aggression. No nation would risk its survival to defend a limited, although important, stake. In 1950, the United States had not bombed Moscow but responded locally with conventional forces.

The second and more fundamental problem was that NATO could not be replicated outside of Europe. In Europe, the members of the alliance were united in sharing a common perception of the Soviet threat. In addition, the alliance gained strength from each state's sense of nationalism. That nationalism gave it a reason for defending itself against external danger and helped mobilize popular support for that task. The Eisenhower administration's global strategy, with the priority it gave to containing international communism, overlooked the quite different conditions outside of Europe. One was regional conflicts. SEATO included Pakistan who joined the alliance not because of a concern about Chinese expansion — much of the time the two countries shared friendly relations — but mainly to acquire U.S. weapons to use against India, its rival on the Indian subcontinent. This alienated India, a potentially very powerful state and one of the very few democracies among the LDCs. It also stimulated a local arms race in which India turned to the Soviet Union for weapons and political support. The Baghdad pact, on the other hand, included Iraq, as its name would suggest. But the administration wanted to attract Egypt, the strongest Arab state, for containment. However, the two Arab states were traditional rivals in the Middle East. Thus Egypt set out to destroy the alliance.

In its preoccupation with Soviet designs the Eisenhower administration also failed to take into account the strong sense of nationalism of the new nations. In Asia, the indigenous states were basically hostile to a western-organized alliance against communism. Their nationalism was instead directed against their former colonial masters, Britain and France, both members of SEATO, and against the United States, SEATO's organizer and the west's leading power. In fact, SEATO's only Asian members besides Pakistan were the Philippines, which joined because of its special relationship with America, and Thailand, the only state genuinely concerned about Communist China's expansion. Australia and New Zealand were not really Asian states.[15] In the eyes of Asians, the United States was repeatedly in the wrong: by refusing to recognize the new China, by continuing to recognize the discredited Nationalist regime, and by supporting the French in Indochina against those fighting for national independence. In the Middle East, Egypt's nationalism and its leading position in the area meant that it would have to place itself in the vanguard of all Arab states in opposing Israel — that was the one goal all Arabs could agree on. Given the strong American support for Israel, it seems utopian to have expected Egypt to align itself with the United States against the Soviet Union. And including Iraq in METO only served to strengthen Egypt's antiwestern stance.

Soviet Bloc Difficulties or Tensions
Quite apart from the weaknesses of the non-European replicas of NATOs and the difficulties of using them to contain communism, Soviet strategy shifted in the 1950s to exploit the ris-

ing tide of Third World nationalism. In the 1950s, over 40 new states were admitted to the United Nations, 30 of them from Africa. These ex-colonial states were too many to be ignored by Moscow. To do so might alienate them and drive them back into the imperialists' arms. The United States was already shifting its economic aid from Europe to the underdeveloped countries.

The emergence of Khrushchev in 1955, after a prolonged power struggle among Soviet leaders as well as the increasing Soviet contacts with key countries, including highly publicized visits by the new leaders to Third World states and highly visible economic aid projects, were key factors which inaugurated the first "mini-détente" of the postwar period.

Usually referred to as "the thaw" in the Cold War, this period witnessed the following events: Khrushchev's attempt at reconciliation with Yugoslavia; the withdrawal of Soviet and western troops and permanent neutralization of Austria (undoubtedly, among other reasons, to encourage West Germany to think of a similar solution and thereby undermine NATO); the first summit conference of Soviet, U.S., British, and French leaders, leading to euphoric western expectations about the "spirit of Geneva"; and Khrushchev's pronouncement that war was no longer "totally inevitable," a declaratory shift from Lenin that was obviously well received in the west. Whatever hopes all these and other moves aroused in the west for a better future relationship with the Soviet Union, they did not last long. Tensions soon rose again.

One reason was that the 1955 summit was barely over when Khrushchev, using Czechoslovakia as a proxy, signed an arms agreement with Egypt, which set the stage for the Suez War in 1956 (see Chapter 5). A second reason was that Stalin's death exposed several severe Soviet vulnerabilities. They stemmed mainly from Khrushchev's 1956 de-Stalinization campaign. Khrushchev portrayed the late dictator as far more terrifying than he had ever been portrayed by the most vehement anti-Communist propaganda: a mass murderer who had abused his power and systematically purged his colleagues. By attacking

Stalin as the symbol of Soviet injustice and tyranny, Khrushchev was suggesting that once these abuses had been removed,
communism would continue to be a sound and vital system.
Stalin's terror was a perversion of communism; communism
was not at fault. The Chinese, however, were upset by the de-
Stalinization campaign.[16] Khrushchev had raised the basic
question: Was Stalinism a product of Stalin's personality or
communism itself? The new Soviet leader blamed the former,
exonerated the latter. But leaders like the head of the Italian
Communist party were asserting that Stalinism was a reflection of the Soviet system. Had Khrushchev not placed the legitimacy of the Communist system in jeopardy by denouncing
the man who for three decades had been portrayed as the wise
and humane successor to Lenin and the benign leader of world
communism? Would these criticisms not lead to "polycen-
trism" or centrifugal pressures within the Communist world
and weaken the bloc's political and ideological unity? The
Chinese were very upset by Khrushchev's denunciation of Stalin as an absolute dictator (not unlike Mao in China).

The Chinese also questioned Khrushchev's emphasis on the
noninevitability of war and a nonviolent transition to socialism. This conflicted with the Chinese focus on a revolutionary
strategy — on the continuation of the class struggle and the
need for armed revolution — and apparent Chinese willingness
to risk nuclear war to promote Communist aims. The 1954–
1955 Taiwan Straits crises over the off-shore islands of Quemoy and Matsu had already demonstrated that the Soviets
were unwilling to confront the United States on an issue vital
to Communist China: the reunification with Taiwan. The same
was true in 1958. Indeed, the Soviets felt that the Chinese were
reckless and willing to precipitate an American-Soviet conflict
over Taiwan — hardly a key issue for Moscow. The Soviets
then changed their mind over helping China build its own
bomb. From Moscow's point of view, a nuclear-armed China
led by Mao Zedung, was too risky. During the Chinese clash
with India in a border dispute in 1959, the Soviets adopted a
neutral position instead of siding with the Chinese against a

"bourgeois" state. Soviet economic loans to China ended during this period, and Soviet technical experts helping China in its development were called home. In response, the Chinese abandoned the Soviet model of communism and in the subsequent Great Leap Forward in the 1960s set out their own radical program in which they claimed they had leapt ahead of the Soviets in the transition from socialism to communism. The Chinese denounced the Soviet leaders for being heretics and "modern revisionists"; the Soviets, in turn, denounced the Chinese for betraying Marxism-Leninism and becoming "Hitlerites." By 1960, with new border tensions between Russia and China, the Sino-Soviet alliance of 1950 was coming apart.

More significant, however, for the collapse of the "spirit of Geneva" was Stalin's legacy in eastern Europe. The national resentment and hatred for the Soviet Union confronted his successors with a serious dilemma.[17] If they preserved Stalin's tight controls, they would intensify existing dissatisfaction and opposition to Soviet-imposed industrialization and exploitation. An indication of what might then happen came soon after Stalin's death in the form of a 1953 uprising in East Berlin and East Germany, led by the alleged beneficiaries of proletarian rule, the working class, who were rebelling against the low wages, harsh discipline, and austerity of the "workers' state." The Red Army quelled the revolt. The alternative was to relax Soviet reins and hope to avoid such uprisings. But in relaxing its grip, Moscow in fact stimulated a demand for greater independence and the Soviet-controlled "thaw" became an uncontrollable flood in Poland and Hungary in 1956. In Poland, Soviet intervention was narrowly averted; in Hungary, because it threatened to defect from the Warsaw pact and because the Communist party had lost its monopoly of power, the Soviets did intervene militarily. The Soviet-Yugoslavia reconciliation foundered. In the countries he controlled, Khrushchev had demonstrated that he was determined to maintain bloc loyalty and that the Soviet Union would have the right to determine when and if to intervene. The Soviet military intervention in 1956 thus had a similar affect on Soviet relations

with the United States and its allies as the coup d'état in
Czechoslovakia had in 1948. It aroused western anger and
cleared away illusions.

The third reason for the revival of the Cold War was that a
shift in the military balance, acclaimed by Moscow, was seen
as a means of both ending the insecure situation in East Germany and destroying NATO politically. The insecurity of the
Soviet grip on eastern Europe was most evident in the late
1950s when thousands upon thousands of East Germans
"voted with their feet" by leaving for West Germany via West
Berlin. The stream of emigration was particularly devastating
because, among those fleeing, were the cream of the younger
generation, educated by the state, who were expected to serve
the state. The Soviet sense of vulnerability in its forward position facing NATO, already strong because most non-Communist states recognized the Federal Republic of Germany and
not what was often still called the Communist "zone of occupation," was thus heightened. To end this hemorrhage of
skilled and professional personnel, the Soviets decided to eliminate West Berlin and simultaneously compel western recognition of East Germany as a legitimate state.

Confrontations in Berlin and Cuba

In 1957, the Soviets saw a way of strangling West Berlin because that year they tested the world's first intercontinental
ballistic missile (ICBM).[18] Shortly afterward, the Soviet Union
made its first shot into space, another Soviet triumph, especially so since American technology had always been considered the most advanced while Soviet technology had long been
seen as backward. Now, the Soviets had achieved two spectacular technological achievements, and the implications of
these achievements for the balance of power were widely
noted, not least in Moscow. The Kremlin asserted that it was
no longer vulnerable to American bombers and that the distribution of power in the world was shifting in the Soviet Union's
favor. Khrushchev claimed that the Soviet Union was massproducing ICBMs and American intelligence began to talk of
a "missile gap," since the United States was behind in ICBM

development. Up to then strategically inferior, the Soviets, now acting on the belief that the changing correlation of forces should be reflected in territorial changes, demanded that West Berlin be turned into a "free city" and gave the western states six months to comply. If they refused to do so, the Soviets would turn access to the city over to East Germany; if the Allies tried to force their way through to Berlin, the Red Army would support the East Germans. In short, leave peacefully or face the possibility of war.

Thus, after shifting their attention and energy away from Europe in 1950 because the situation there had been stabilized and because challenging the United States would be too risky, the Soviets in 1958 once again focused their attention on Europe. If successful, the Soviets would not only stabilize the status quo in eastern Europe, especially East Germany, but destroy NATO. As in 1948, the credibility of the United States as western Europe's protector was at stake. At a time that Moscow was claiming a shift in the strategic balance, failure to uphold the western position in West Berlin would humiliate NATO, demonstrate American impotence, validate the Soviet claims, intimidate America's closest European allies, and drive them into neutralism. For NATO, the survival of the alliance became the issue.

Consequently the late 1950s and early 1960s were filled with a series of Berlin crises. The possibility of American and Soviet forces coming to blows was ever-present, especially in 1961 when Khrushchev first bullied President Kennedy at the Vienna summit meeting and then built the infamous Berlin Wall between the Soviet and western halves of the city. By 1961, however, the United States knew through reconnaissance satellites that the Soviet Union had been bluffing and that it had only a few ICBMs. The Soviets knew that the Americans had discovered this, and they also knew that there was now a real missile gap — in America's favor. The reason was that Soviet claims of mass production and repeated threats over Berlin had speeded up American missile production and deployment.

The Soviets now made a very dangerous move. They had a

lot of intermediate-range missiles and they shipped some of them to Cuba where Castro had only recently overthrown the pro-American Batista regime and in 1961 defeated an American-backed invasion of Cuba by Cuban refugees. The missiles were a "short-cut" to catch up with the United States. The Soviets shipped the missiles secretly, all the while assuring the new Kennedy administration that they were sending only defensive arms to Cuba. The president publicly warned them against sending offensive weapons, the category that they were shipping. The Soviet building of a missile base was discovered, however, before the missiles became operational. Clearly, this was an attempt to match the American ICBM buildup and reduce the missile gap. The missiles also posed a potential threat to American bomber and ICBM bases. If the United States did not object to the 70 odd Soviet missiles planned for Cuba, more might be added, increasing the threat to the American deterrent.

Furthermore, since 1957 Moscow had been claiming that it was becoming the world's leading power. Acquiescence in the Soviet missiles in Cuba, 90 miles off Miami and in the Caribbean where the United States under the Monroe Doctrine had historically claimed to be the dominant power, would be to underline the Russian claims and American impotence. Since the Soviets had also announced that they expected to resolve the Berlin problem by the end of the year, they could thus be expected to follow up the installation of missiles in Cuba with a renewed demand for a western exit from West Berlin. The fact was that American inaction would be perceived by most of the world, including the NATO allies and Moscow, as a confirmation of a changed distribution of power in the world. It was this that led President Kennedy to demand the withdrawal of the missiles.

The resulting confrontation was the most dangerous one of the entire postwar era. It ended when the Soviets finally withdrew the missiles after the United States had privately informed Moscow that it would attack those missiles if they were not removed. Khrushchev complied. The Soviet retreat, in

Moscow's eyes, reflected U.S. strategic superiority, not just local U.S. conventional military superiority.[19] This ended the missile crisis, as well as the pressure on the western powers to withdraw from Berlin. It also produced, on the one hand, the first lasting détente and, on the other hand, a Soviet determination never to be humiliated again by building up both its strategic and conventional forces.

Phase 3: Conflict, Competition, and Cooperation (I): The Kennedy-Johnson Years, 1963–1968

The years after the Cuban missile crisis were supreme years of American power. President Kennedy's 1961 inaugural address promised that "we shall pay any price, bear any burden, meet any hardship, support any friend, oppose any foe, to assure the survival and success of liberty." He had eloquently articulated U.S. globalism, and his triumph in 1962 had dramatically demonstrated the superiority of American power. The whole world had witnessed it. Ironically, this momentous success in facing Soviet power down led to the first step to détente because the Soviet Union needed time to recuperate and build up its military power so that no second Cuba would ever be imposed upon it. Thus the long-term effect of the victory in Cuba was in fact to undermine the strategic superiority which, together with local U.S. naval superiority, had made it possible. By the end of the decade, U.S. strategic supremacy had quietly disappeared and the Soviet Union was building a large navy as well.

During these years of enormous self-confidence, the United States also became deeply involved in Vietnam and squandered its power. Initially a relatively minor operation intended to help shore up a pro-American government in South Vietnam, it led to a large-scale expensive intervention when that government was about to collapse. The result was not only a defeat in Vietnam but, worse, a deeply divided society at home and the collapse of the postwar domestic consensus between the presidency, Congress, and public opinion on containment.

The years that Zbigniew Brzezinski has called the "cresting of American globalism"[20] were thus short and ended in disaster. By the end of the decade U.S. foreign policy found itself with neither its former strategic advantage nor public support at home for the conduct of what its critics were to disapprovingly call its "global policeman" role.

It seems paradoxical that Cuba led to Détente I. But both powers felt a need for some relaxation of tensions, because the "eyeball to eyeball" confrontation renewed their interest in arms control in order to avoid a nuclear war. Cuba raised the mutual awareness of their common interest in avoiding suicide and the need to cooperate in the arms area. The hot-line agreement, establishing direct crisis communication links between the White House and the Kremlin, and the limited nuclear test ban, were both signed in 1963; the multilateral non-proliferation agreement was signed in 1968. Simultaneously, the United States and Soviet Union proceeded with their own armaments program. Concerned by the Soviet bluff over Berlin after 1958 and what the Soviets might do as they acquired more missiles, the Kennedy administration set U.S. force levels at 1000 Minuteman ICBMs and 41 submarines with 656 missiles. While the U.S. secretary of defense announced confidently that the Soviets had lost the quantitative arms race and accepted their inferiority, the Soviets decided on a massive buildup.

The Need to Relax International Tensions

At the time of the Cuban missile crisis, the Soviets had 50 ICBMs; by 1964 it was 200. Between 1966 and 1969, they added roughly 300 ICBMs per year so that by 1969 their ICBM force surpassed that of the United States. Taking ICBMs and SLBMs into account, in January 1967 the United States was still far ahead: 1630 to the Soviets' 600. A year later, when the Strategic Arms Limitation Talks (SALT) were supposed to start, the ratio was 1710 to 1000. Thus the United States still held a strategic edge, especially in bombers and submarines. Yet each side now possessed the capability to destroy the other, regardless of who struck first. By November 1969, this U.S.–Soviet ratio had been reversed in the Soviet Union's favor: 1710 to 1900, and 1710 to 2350 by the time SALT I was signed in 1972.[21] In part, to keep up with the ever-increasing number of Soviet missiles, the United States began to place multiple warheads on its missiles (intercontinental bombers are not included in the above figures; these favored the United States by 3:1 by 1972, although the Soviets had far more extensive defenses against bombers). These armament efforts led President Johnson to propose that the two powers talk to each other about stabilizing the deterrent balance. The Soviets accepted, but the 1968 Soviet intervention in Czechoslovakia postponed the start of SALT.

In any event, in the years between the Cuban missile crisis and the beginning of the Nixon administration's in January 1969, the moment the Soviet Union overtook the United States in ICBMs, the Soviets wanted to reduce international tensions. They wanted to concentrate on their arms buildup; to avoid any more confrontations with the United States; to refrain from doing anything that might stimulate the United States to deploy more strategic weapons, as it had done after Khrushchev's pressure on Berlin; and not least, to gain time for the new post-Khrushchev leadership.

Cuba was among a number of things that led to Khrushchev's being accused of pursuing "hare-brained schemes." It also precipitated the coup against the Soviet leader in 1964. The new Brezhnev regime needed a détente to consolidate its hold on power. It was also faced with such other problems as the lagging Soviet economy; the increasingly wide rift with China; and the continuing instability in eastern Europe, where in 1968 the Czech attempt to develop a "communism with a human face" was militarily squashed by the Soviet Union. Indeed, at the time of the intervention Moscow announced the Brezhnev Doctrine, which made explicit what had already been implicit in Soviet policy in 1953 and 1956: that the Soviet Union had the unilateral right to intervene in the socialist com-

monwealth to prevent counterrevolutionary attempts to restore capitalism! Moscow also witnessed the fall of some of its
closest friends in the third world: Goulart in Brazil (1964), Ben
Bella in Algeria (1965), Nkruma in Ghana, and Sukarno in Indonesia (1966). It attributed their downfall to the United
States. The years of American strategic superiority were thus
seen as the years of counterrevolutionary efforts in eastern Europe and a new third world rollback policy seeking liquidation
of "progressive forces" and their replacement with "reactionary regimes."

The United States also had reasons for seeking some relaxation of tensions. One was the assassination of President Kennedy in November 1963 and his successor's primary interest in
domestic affairs. President Johnson's ambition was to outdo
his mentor Franklin Roosevelt by creating the Great Society.
Another was the American involvement in Vietnam,[22] the Soviet Union and China, like the United States, had accepted the
division of Vietnam after 1954. Only the North Vietnamese did
not. Its leader, Ho Chi Minh, considered himself and his Communist party as the rightful heirs to French colonial rule
throughout all of Indochina. This set the stage for the second
Indochina war. While Diem's arbitrary rule in South Vietnam
helped create fertile soil for an insurrection, the decision for
renewing the armed struggle in the south was made by Ho Chi
Minh. The National Liberation Front (NLF) and its military
arm, the Vietcong, were instruments of the North Vietnamese
to unify Vietnam under northern control.

President Eisenhower had talked of Vietnam as a "domino"; if it fell, it would be followed by the other countries of
southeast Asia. President Kennedy escalated his predecessor's
political commitment to Diem with over 16,000 military advisers, because he subscribed to the same belief. While no North
Vietnamese Army crossed the 17th Parallel, as the North Korean army had crossed the 38th parallel, North Vietnam was
just as surely in his perception trying to conquer South Vietnam. Guerrilla warfare was just another variant of the pattern

of Communist aggression which had to be contained. And behind Ho Chi Minh stood Moscow and Peking. Communism
was still perceived as a monolithic bloc. But even had the Sino-
Soviet split been recognized, China was seen as the more militant state; and Ho was seen as Mao's puppet.[23]

The Vietnam War
It was unfortunate that President Lyndon Johnson was in
power during 1964–1965.[24] Each predecessor had increased the
nation's commitment; each had done just enough to prevent
the loss of Vietnam. But by early 1965, a North Vietnamese
victory was only a matter of time. Johnson felt he had no
choice but to send U.S. combat forces. American prestige had
become increasingly committed in the escalating involvement
by earlier presidents. To withdraw now and lose Vietnam,
Cambodia, and Laos would not only make him the first president in U.S. history "to lose a war" but would profoundly affect the credibility of American power and commitments
elsewhere.

There was one other key factor: The Democrats had "lost"
China. Both Kennedy and Johnson did not want the Republicans to accuse them of having "lost Indochina." For Kennedy,
the military advisers he sent to Vietnam kept the situation from
deteriorating further for a while; Johnson confronted defeat
and therefore sent in the troops. In the context of U.S. domestic politics, accepting such a defeat was considered unacceptable. Johnson recalled that Truman was placed on the defensive by all the vicious accusations of appeasement and
betrayal; his domestic reform program had fallen victim to the
foreign policy charges. Johnson did not want to suffer the same
fate and jeopardize his future conduct of foreign and domestic
policies. Having won the presidency in his own right in 1964,
he did not want to endanger his presidency at the very start.
In Vietnam, the U.S. anti-Communist crusade was thus reinforced by domestic political considerations. A major intervention was considered less costly than disengaging from

Vietnam.[25] That was the price the nation paid for the vicious partisanship on the China issue.

Johnson tried to fight the war painlessly — without sacrificing his Great Society programs or raising taxes to pay for the war. As the war proceeded, despite continuous official optimism of "light at the end of the tunnel," opposition to the war grew. This was particularly so after late 1967 when taxes were raised, college students were no longer deferred from conscription, and reserve units were called up. This hurt the white middle class; a painless war now became painful. Antiwar demonstrations, protest meetings denouncing "Johnson's war," and draft resistance mounted. But it was the Tet offensive in February 1968 that broke the administration's back.

The Vietcong attacked every major city and town; in Saigon, South Vietnam's capital, they penetrated the U.S. embassy compound. If after three years of war and repeated forecasts of victory, the enemy was still strong enough to launch such a widespread offensive, the war's end was nowhere in sight. The fact that the Vietcong were decimated (after Tet, North Vietnamese forces bore the burden of the fighting) did not seem to matter. The television pictures of the fighting to clear Saigon and other cities and the reporters' discouraging news coverage made it appear that Tet had been a major defeat. Psychologically, it was. A war without a seeming end and the constant underestimation of the enemy's determination to win and capability to fight suggested a hopeless quagmire. A majority of Americans now felt that the United States should not have entered the war. Beset by doubts about the wisdom and the growing costs of the war — especially in lives — American public opinion turned negative. America's will to fight had evaporated, and while the Communists lost the battle they won a great political victory. The real domino had been American opinion. Johnson announced that he would not run for reelection; the North Vietnamese had in fact driven the president out of office.

The irony of the U.S. intervention in Vietnam, in retrospect, was that had American diplomatic representatives been in China in the early 1960s, Washington would have known that Ho Chi Minh was an ardent nationalist, that he was not a Chinese stooge, and that he would have opposed China's expansion into Vietnam. The chief reason for the U.S. intervention would thus have evaporated. But the American style in foreign policy, which transformed the initial anti-Soviet containment policy into a broad, indiscriminate anti-Communist policy, had forgotten after Tito that nationalism also infused Communist states. It was this kind of thinking that kept the United States from exploiting such nationalistic differences within the Communist world in order to isolate and weaken the Soviet Union. The powerful anti-Red Chinese feelings in America, which had made official recognition of the People's Republic impossible, reinforced this determination to oppose any Communist expansion. The United States paid a high price for its involvement in Vietnam in lives and in resources that could have been better spent on modernizing U.S. strategic and conventional forces, as well as on necessary domestic programs. Perhaps the biggest loss was the collapse of the 20-year public consensus on containment.

Extricating the United States from Vietnam thus became a top priority for the incoming Nixon administration. It was the major short-term reason for broadening détente with the Soviet Union *and* Communist China. If North Vietnam were politically isolated from its major allies, it might be more amenable to a negotiated settlement that would protect non-Communist South Vietnam. At the same time, how America left Vietnam became, in the Nixon administration's own eyes, critical. If Washington accepted a settlement that was tantamount to defeat — e.g., a coalition government controlled by the Communists — the United States would not be able to pursue its quest for détente. Why should an increasingly militarily strong Soviet Union settle for a mutually acceptable coexistence if it felt America was weak and could be pushed around? And why should the People's Republic of China move toward the United States if it could not count on American determination and strength to resist Soviet efforts to achieve Asian hegemony? Thus Vietnam and the fate of détente were seen as interlocked.

Détente II: The Nixon-Ford-Carter Years, 1969–1979

The word détente really came into vogue in the 1970s; it was rarely used to describe the years from 1963–1968. Both the United States and the Soviet Union had reasons for both broadening the relaxation of tensions and supplementing their relationship with cooperation on a number of key issues. Indeed, if Cold War may be defined as an adversary relationship, détente may be said to be an adversary partnership, a mixed relationship composed of elements of rivalry and cooperation. The highlights of this decade were the SALT arms control agreements. But between the first agreement in 1972 and the ratification effort of the second one in 1979 détente collapsed. Both powers were disillusioned by the end of the decade. The fact is that neither saw détente as an end of the Cold War; each continued to wage it in the different circumstances of the 1970s. Basically, détente was the continuation of the Cold War by other means.

The American Mood of Isolationism

By the time President Nixon assumed office, the United States needed to reassess the containment policy.[26] The issue was not whether to pursue containment — that was a given — but how to do so at a time of changed circumstances from the decades of the 1950s and 1960s. The key problem was that Vietnam had turned public opinion against a vigorous foreign policy. The mood of the country was isolationist. In the swing pattern so characteristic of American foreign policy, public opinion polls showed that Canada was the only country a majority of Americans were willing to defend. This mood of weariness with foreign intervention and wariness about new commitments was accompanied by a sense of guilt. America had abused its power in Vietnam. It was time to limit the U.S. role in the world to one more consistent with its "limited power." For many Americans, the problem was less the Soviet threat than America's "global policemanship." The consensus was that we should concentrate on problems at home in order to more fully realize the American Dream for all Americans, thereby purifying ourselves from the arrogance of power we had acquired internationally.

Above all, the powers of the presidency were to be cut back. Restraints were to be imposed because presidents had waged war without congressional declarations of war and subverting — or helping to subvert — regimes they considered inimical to American interests, such as the Allende government in Chile. It was to be 1973 before Congress would pass the War Powers Resolution to restrain the chief instrument of U.S. overt intervention and tighten control over the CIA, the chief instrument of covert intervention. In the meantime, however, it was not only clear that the popular and bipartisan agreement on containment was shattered, but there was no consensus on either what the U.S. role in the world should be (if any) or how the nation's foreign policy should be conducted. There was only one policy on which the country appeared to agree: "No More Vietnams."

This mood of isolationism was reinforced after 1973 by the shock of the quadrupling of oil prices during the Arab-Israeli war by the Organization of Petroleum Exporting Countries (OPEC). The shock effects of this rise of a barrel of oil (42 gallons) from $3 to $12 reverberated through all western economies: large-scale unemployment and economic recession on the one hand and galloping inflation on the other; stagnating economies and lowered expectations about future gains in the standard of living. The collapse of the pro-American Shah in Iran in 1979, resulting in a more than doubling of oil prices in just over a year, reinforced the American stagflation (simultaneous unemployment and inflation). Quite understandably,

Americans worried about keeping their jobs and paying their home fuel bills — indeed, all their bills. The Cold War was not the American people's primary worry.

While the economic pain exacerbated the preoccupation with domestic affairs, it was also a symptom of a declining economic capability. The immediate postwar supremacy of the U.S. economy reflected not only its extraordinary productivity but also the destruction and collapse of the economies of the European industrial nations as a result of six years of warfare. As these nations — and Japan as well — recovered and prospered, their share of world productivity rose relative to that of the United States. In fact, they became competitors in areas such as textiles, consumer electronics, and steel and automobile production, in which America had once reigned supreme. There were many reasons for the decline of the smoke-stack industries and sectors of consumer goods production. Among them were: the high price of American labor compared to foreign workers; the savings in transportation costs when manufacturing is nearer to the markets in which the products sell; and the fact that in western Europe, after the formation of the Common Market in 1958, the common tariff barrier raised prices of U.S. goods and made them uncompetitive — which was not true if U.S. companies built factories *in* Europe behind the tariff wall.

The faltering of the American economy as a result of underinvestment at home was already occurring when OPEC's action made all Americans aware of their vulnerability and, in an increasingly interdependent world economy, how sensitive the economy was to events overseas. The American economy that once had been virtually independent of imports and the need to export had in the past supported a rapidly increasing standard of living through high wages; a vast expansion, especially during the Johnson presidency, of the welfare state; and sizable military budgets and foreign aid programs. During the 1970s the economy, increasingly uncompetitive as it was becoming part of the world economy, no longer grew sufficiently to support all three of these programs.

Thus when the Nixon administration assumed office, both the national will to contain communism and the capability to do so were declining. Yet this period coincided with the growth of Soviet power and a more activist Soviet policy. The emergence of strategic parity meant that at best U.S. nuclear forces could neutralize Soviet strategic forces, but they would be less useful in restraining more limited Soviet challenges. The fact that the Soviets were also extensively modernizing their conventional forces was therefore very worrisome. Among the most important of their programs was the building of a major surface navy (they already had a great many submarines) and an airlift capability, which gave the Soviet Union the means for extending its power beyond Eurasia.

Russia, both tsarist and Soviet, had historically been a Eurasian power. Spanning Europe and Asia, tsarist Russia expanded into the areas surrounding her. The principal instrument of this expansion was the army. Likewise, Stalin's expansion coincided with the Red Army's advance. The United States, by contrast, had developed a sizable navy. American power in this century had to be projected across the Atlantic and Pacific oceans, and long-range air power gave added capability to America's stature as a global power. The Soviet Union, even though it faced an intercontinental enemy after 1945, did not initially develop a large-scale strategic capability. It continued to focus on the army and held America's European allies hostage, whereas the United States starting in the early 1950s developed a growing capability to hold Russia's population as hostage. By the 1970s this changed and the Soviet Union became transformed from a Eurasian, or continental, power into a global one.

The new Russian Navy was the symbol of the Soviet Union's global aspirations. Unlike America, the Soviets were not dependent on importing key raw materials or oil, so they really did not need a navy to control the world's seas. The buildup from an essentially coastal defense navy to one that could show its presence in all oceans is partly attributable to the wish to destroy American carrier battle groups and, even more, to destroy U.S. strategic and attack submarines. But, like Germany at the turn of the century, also a land power, the fact that the Soviet Union would build a large surface fleet, traditionally the possession of her principal rival, is psychologically revealing. For Germany, it meant a willingness to challenge England, which at the time was the world's premier naval power. The navy also became a symbol of Germany's determination to go beyond playing just a European role and to pursue a *Weltpolitik*. For the Soviet Union, a very status-conscious power that had finally achieved strategic parity with the United States, the navy represented similar ambitions.

Containment By Another Name

The central question for the United States was how to contain the Soviet Union at a time when its power was at a historical high while American unwillingness to contain it was at a post-war low and the capability to do so was also declining. The instrument of last resort, of course, remained the military. However, given the emerging nuclear parity, the risks and costs of resorting to it had risen from the days when the Soviet Union had been strategically inferior. And the American public seemed in no mood to resort to force anyway. Henry Kissinger — whose tenure ran through the Nixon and Ford years as national security adviser and then later as secretary of state (and for a while, he held both positions) — devised a political strategy involving three elements: (1) using American trade, technology, and credit to help the Soviet Union's increasingly stagnating economy; (2) linking all agreements (from Vietnam to trade and arms control, etc.) so that if the Soviets sought certain benefits from the United States in one area they would also have to accommodate American interests in another; and (3) exploiting the Sino-Soviet conflict and playing up to Communist China, which had become the Soviet Union's bitter enemy with claims on Soviet territory and as a competitor for the leadership of the Communist and third worlds. The United States and China were both determined to prevent what the Chinese called Soviet "hegemony." For American policy the reconciliation with China represented a critical shift: from a general anti-Communism back to the anti-Soviet opposition it had been before Korea and the Chinese intervention. Russia was the principal enemy. It had to be contained and if the United States could attract China and gain its help for that task, that was what had to be done. Balance-of-power logic had finally prevailed over the American penchant for crusading.

In short, U.S. policy sought to provide Moscow with the incentives for self-containment with a mixture of sticks and carrots: access to the American economy which could, however, be reduced or withdrawn if it "misbehaved"; signing agreements it wanted which likewise could be withheld in case of aggressive behavior; and, of course, compensating for U.S. weaknesses in will and capability by playing one large Communist state against another. Rather than use these means as sanctions, however, it was preferable to use the first two as incentives to give the Soviet leaders a vested interest in maintaining good relations with the United States; the advantages they would gain would give priority to cooperation over confrontation. Nevertheless, there could be no doubt that these means would give the United States some political leverage, which would be enhanced by America's growing ties to China, supplementing those which already linked the United States to NATO and Japan. Thus, despite a strategic parity that might perhaps be upset by the momentum of the Soviet arms buildup, the United States would be able to compensate for the American disinclination to use military power.

The Nixon-Kissinger strategy was clearly not based on any illusions that the Soviet Union had changed or, as was commonly heard in the United States at the time, that the "Cold War was over." Rather, détente was essentially a policy of containment for a period when Russia was a potentially greater threat than ever before, but the American will and capability to contain it were at a low ebb. Two key points in this must not be overlooked. First, there was to be no shrinking of U.S. commitments or a reduction in America's global role. The

United States would remain a global power with global interests. The containment of Soviet power and influence was only
to be carried out at a lower cost and in a less burdensome way.
Second, the American withdrawal from Vietnam after the Paris
agreements in January 1973 removed an albatross from the nation's neck and allowed the United States to give its attention
to other problems. It is notable that Henry Kissinger, President Nixon's national security adviser from 1969 and secretary
of state too (after the 1973 inauguration), could spend weeks
away from Washington, shuttling around the Middle East after
the 1973 Yom Kippur War and laying the foundations for peace
between Egypt and Israel (to be finally achieved by President
Carter in 1978). The nation no longer centered its energies on
Vietnam and tore itself apart at home.

Soviet Reasons for Improving Superpower Relations
Russia, for different reasons, was also searching for a détente.
The most important reason was undoubtedly economic. Soviet
agriculture had long been described as Russia's "Achilles
heel," but the short falls of grain were becoming more persistent at a time when the leadership had promised the Russian
people a more balanced diet, including meat. Industrially, too,
the Soviets had problems, on the one hand, simply producing
enough consumer goods of decent quality and, on the other
hand, keeping up with the new industrial revolution of computers and petrochemicals. The reasons were quite obvious:
ideological prescription, centralized planning and a rapid,
slow-moving bureaucracy with a vested interest in the status
quo. There were few incentives for workers to labor hard. Only
in the military-aerospace sector of the economy, separated
from the consumer economy, did the Soviets perform well. After 60 years of communism, the Soviet economy could not provide its citizens with a decent standard of living; what it could
produce well was enormous quantities of arms. Restructuring
the economy would run into bureaucratic resistance and would
also be risky for the party's monopoly of power. Importing
western techniques and goods was thus the best short cut for

remedying Soviet agricultural and nonmilitary industrial performance (and some industrial imports might even help in upgrading some arms, e.g., guidance systems for ICBMs). The Soviet Union was also very worried by China's increasing alignment with the West. The Chinese leadership was challenging the legitimacy of the Soviet government, denouncing it as heretical while claiming that it was the rightful heir of Marxism-Leninism. It also wished Moscow to admit that all the old treaties by which the tsars had seized Chinese territory were "unequal" and invalid. Border clashes had occurred in 1969 and afterward. Concerned by the Soviet Union's growing power and that Brezhnev might be tempted to apply his Doctrine to them, the Chinese had in characteristic balance-of-power fashion responded to the Nixon administration's quiet but clear signals for a desired improvement in Sino-American relations. The visit of Richard Nixon to China in early 1972 — significantly, before a scheduled summit with Soviet leaders — was a fundamental turning point. Moscow wanted to slow down this growing reconciliation and formation of an anti-Soviet U.S.-Chinese coalition.

A third reason why Moscow wanted a détente was its desire for a legitimation of the European status quo. The west had long recognized Soviet hegemony in eastern Europe and abstained from assisting efforts to change or end that hegemony. Yet the Soviet Union's insecurity remained. It was all too aware of its troubles in Czechoslovakia, tensions in Poland (where in 1970 the ship workers in Gdansk struck against meat price rises and shortages of food and consumer items and brought down the government!), and the broader Soviet unpopularity throughout eastern Europe. West Germany, whose democratically elected government claimed to represent all Germans, was seen by Moscow as revisionist. Moscow not only installed a Communist regime in Poland, it also shifted Poland westward, taking over the part of eastern Poland it had acquired from the Nazi-Soviet pact's division of that country; in compensation Poland was given part of eastern Germany. But West Germany did not formally accept this change of the

(East) German-Polish border. In 1969 West Germany's government initiated an *Ostpolitik,* signed a nonaggression pact with Moscow, recognized the new Polish-German frontier in a treaty with Poland, and exchanged official recognition with East Germany, the German Democratic Republic. The Soviets also negotiated with the western powers, guaranteeing their access to Berlin in 1971, and sought the western allies' de jure approval for these postwar changes (which they gave at Helsinki in 1975). This at last legitimated the territorial and political division of Europe and therefore served, in a sense, as a peace treaty ending World War II.

Finally, both superpowers had a continuing interest in arms control. Washington wanted to slow down the rapid Soviet strategic buildup which in 1969 overtook the United States in the numbers of land-based intercontinental ballistic missiles (ICBMs). Moreover, there seemed to be no end in sight to the Soviet production of ICBMs and sea-launched ballistic missiles (SLBMs). The United States was concerned with the deployment of an antiballistic missile (ABM) system by the Soviets around Moscow, perhaps the beginning of a nationwide deployment. In August 1968 the United States launched its first multiple independent reentry vehicles (MIRVs). MIRVs would allow the United States to inundate and overcome a Soviet strategic defense. By ensuring that the United States would still be able to destroy Soviet society, MIRVs were intended to preserve America's deterrent capacity. Still, these improvements on defensive and offensive technologies threatened to cause not only expensive arms races but also instabilities in the strategic balance.

Moscow's interest in arms control was political as well as military. Since the 1917 revolution, the Soviet Union had been weaker militarily than its enemies, first Germany, then the United States. Finally, seven years after its humiliating retreat during the Cuban missile crisis, Russia had caught up with America. The long postwar period of American strategic superiority was ended. The Soviets wanted a formal U.S. recognition of this new state of American-Soviet parity and wanted to be treated as an equal superpower. A strategic arms limitation agreement was, in its eyes, a critically important matter of prestige, not just a security matter.

Détente from 1972 to 1974 was symbolized by annual summit conferences, and by the first major SALT agreement which, in itself, was to become part of a continuing process of SALT negotiations. In fact, arms control became the centerpiece of détente. Agreements suggested that political relations between the two powers were improving, that the possibility of war had receded; lack of agreements suggested a deterioration of détente. Indeed, détente did not so much replace conflict with cooperation, confrontation with negotiation, as create a more mixed type of relationship combining conflict and cooperation. It represented the realization by the two powers that while their basic relationship remained an adversarial one, they also shared certain common interests, especially their survival.

Expectations and Disillusionment
The main reason for détente's downfall was the opposing interpretations the superpowers had of détente.[27] The U.S. government, and certainly American opinion, essentially perceived détente as mutual self-restraint (or, in reality, since the United States was in a mood of withdrawal from foreign affairs, *Soviet* restraint). Given the American disposition to think in terms of opposites — war or peace, force or diplomacy — détente was popularly understood as the opposite of Cold War: an end to their rivalry. The Soviet leadership did not, however, view détente as an ending of the ideological struggle or its support for national liberation struggles. Both sides welcomed a relaxation of tensions that would diminish the threat of nuclear war. But otherwise, they held quite different expectations.

American disillusionment started during the 1973 Middle East Yom Kippur War, the fourth Arab-Israeli war. At the 1972 summit conference the two powers agreed not to exploit tensions for unilateral advantage, to avoid confrontations, and to demonstrate mutual restraint.[28] Yet Moscow not only failed to alert Washington of the forthcoming Arab attack on Israel but, once hostilities had started, it encouraged other Arab states to join Egypt and Syria, sent in massive supplies of arms after initial Arab successes and, after the Arabs retaliated for the subsequent American arms shipments to Israel with an oil embargo, endorsed it.[29] They also threatened to intervene unilaterally with airborne troops if the United States did not join it to prevent Israeli forces from completely annihilating Egyptian forces. This attitude, considered alien to détente by Washington, was followed after 1975 by a series of Soviet-Cuban interventions: in Angola (with up to 20,000 Cuban troops); Ethiopia (16,000 Cuban troops); and a coup in Southern Yemen. The last two countries were situated, respectively, in the key Horn of Africa area opposite Saudi Arabia and on the Saudi peninsula, near vital western oil lines. Finally, when after the 1978 coup by Afghan Marxists the new government met nationwide resistance that threatened its survival, the Soviets intervened militarily in 1979. In U.S. eyes, détente began to look like a trick, intended to delude and relax the United States while the Soviet Union continued to build up its armaments and unilaterally gain geopolitical advantages at America's expense.

In Moscow, the picture of course looked quite different. From the beginning it said that détente did not mean the end of the international class struggle. Since when, in any event, should a great power refrain from seizing opportunities for gaining influence because the adversary power was in no mood "to play"? If the United States was in an isolationist mood, concerned mainly with not getting involved, was it not in fact presenting Moscow with every incentive to take advantage of existing opportunities since there would be no penalties to be paid for such efforts? The promise was one of all gains at no risks or costs. Moreover, had the United States not bombed the Soviet Union's Vietnamese ally while Moscow continued negotiations with Washington in the early years of détente? And had the United States — specifically Kissinger — after the Yom Kippur War not excluded Moscow from Middle East negotiations while unilaterally enhancing its influence throughout the area? Had President Carter not similarly pursued an Egyptian-Israeli peace agreement while reducing Soviet influence throughout the area? How did this approach differ from what the Americans were accusing the Soviets of doing in Africa? And what benefits had détente conferred upon the Soviet Union after 1972? Arms negotiations after SALT I had been unfruitful; the economic benefits that the Nixon administration had agreed to had not been delivered. (The U.S. Congress in the Jackson-Vanik amendment linked trade to Soviet emigration policies, especially of Soviet Jews. Moscow regarded this as intolerable interference in its domestic affairs and rejected the trade agreement.) During the early Carter years, the president attacked the Soviet Union on "human rights" ground. Later, despite the successful conclusion of SALT II after seven years of negotiations, Carter called for an increase in U.S. defense spending, a new MX (Missile Experimental) ICBM, and the installation in western Europe of 572 intermediate range missiles (to counter the deployment of Soviet SS-20s, each with three warheads). SALT II was withdrawn because of Senate opposition but, in Soviet eyes, Afghanistan merely served as the pretext for a "return of the Cold War" as the United States proceeded with its rearmament program, imposed high technology and grain boycotts on the Soviet Union after its invasion of Afghanistan and, in general, pursued a stronger anti-Soviet policy in an increasingly close association with China.[30]

Clearly, both sides found the results of détente disappointing. The collapse of arms control, which had become the symbol of détente, was an ominous warning of a renewed, more hostile relationship. For the Carter administration, which tended to reflect liberal America's sense of guilt for its past "abuses of power," especially in Vietnam, and had proclaimed "the end of the Cold War," détente was the prerequisite for concentrating on what it felt was the main problem: the division of the world into North-South (in Carter's words, "one-third rich and two-thirds hungry") and the building of a more

humane post-Vietnam and post–power politics "world order."
American public opinion was eager from the first to believe the
best, and each administration in turn, with an eye to the next
election, did little to discourage such high public expectations.
In fact, in public, even the Nixon administration sounded euphoric, talking of a "new era" of peace and a "structure of
peace." It was no wonder that such grandiose assessments led
public opinion to harbor high expectations and optimism about
the results of SALT and détente. But both were based, as it
was soon to be realized, on the same hopes and illusions as the
post–World War II expectations. The Soviets, it must be
added, were always straightforward about their definition of
détente. There was no attempt to deceive the United States;
the deception was self-induced.

The Soviet invasion of Afghanistan was the final blow to
détente, and particularly for President Carter who had so often
asserted that the United States had in the past frequently exaggerated the Soviet threat and had, therefore, overreacted.[31]
Soviet behavior in 1979 turned Carter into a "hard-liner." But
since a genuine hard-liner was already running for the presidency on the Republican party ticket, the nation turned to
Ronald Reagan. After Afghanistan, which had been preceded
by a revolution in Iran, the collapse of the strong American
position in that country, the seizure of the American embassy
and officials by the Iranians, and their being held for 444 days
during which the U.S. government floundered and appeared
helpless while the Iranians humiliated the United States, public opinion changed once again, swinging from its isolationist
mood to a more interventionist mood. It seemed to fall
somewhere between "no more Vietnams" (no more military
involvements) and "no more Irans" (no more national humiliations). Verbally, it resulted in tougher anti-Soviet rhetoric, a
strengthening of U.S. strategic deterrent forces, a declining interest in arms control, and a more activist foreign policy. Iran,
perhaps more than even Afghanistan, reawakened the nation's
consciousness that the United States was a great power; that
an attitude of "stop the world, I want to get off" only encour-

aged small as well as big hostile nations to take advantage of America; and that the end result of not exercising U.S. power (presumably, wisely) was the strengthening of the nation's enemies.

It is paradoxical but true that great powers often have to do what must be done regardless of their preferences, that it was Jimmy Carter who after the Soviet invasion of Afghanistan added a new area of the world to be defended by American military forces: the Persian Gulf and its oil sheikdoms (especially Saudi Arabia). The United States, and even more, western Europe and Japan, depended greatly on imported oil, much of it at the time from the prowestern Gulf states (plus Iran for Europe and Japan). The expansion of Soviet power toward the Gulf, even though the Soviet motivation may have been primarily defensive to shore up the pro-Soviet regime in Afghanistan, had to be a matter of great concern to America, whose industrial allies would be very vulnerable to Soviet pressure if Soviet power flowed into the Gulf (Iran being the most likely first target).

On the Russian side too, the hard line had also emerged before Reagan. Perhaps the Soviet Union was simply doing what came naturally: taking advantage of its opponent's desire for relaxation. The 1970s was not the first time that this happened. The first Cold War summit conference between Khrushchev and Eisenhower in 1955 was barely over before the Soviets made an arms deal with Egypt and the "spirit of Geneva" vanished. After its missile and space success in 1957, Moscow could not wait to cash in on its alleged missile superiority to drive the west out of West Berlin. Détente could not but end in disillusionment as the Soviets, together with the Cubans, expanded their influence in Angola, Ethiopia, and Yemen while Americans wanted "No More Vietnams." Afghanistan was merely the final blow in a series of moves that Moscow felt free to make because it felt it could do so with impunity. Neither the prospects of direly needed trade, technology, and credits, nor the prospects of a second SALT agreement provided the Soviets with incentives for self-restraint. The goodwill of countries the Soviet Union defined as hostile was hardly worth the sacrifice of possible strategic gains that would weaken its self-designated enemy.

The fact was that from the Soviet perspective détente did not change "objective conditions." The historically inevitable process of revolutionary change continued. Moscow could not stop this process, even if it wanted to accept the status quo. The regime's *raison d'être,* of course, was to help advance the historical process along, not to accept, let alone reinforce, the status quo. Thus the commitment to national liberation in the third world could not be disavowed. Indeed, détente was expected to improve conditions to wage the international class struggle. Clearly, the United States and Soviet Union held quite different interpretations of détente and, given their differing expectations, it is not surprising that each ended up being disillusioned and dissatisfied with détente's results. America expected Russia to contain herself; Russia, in turn, expected America to accept Soviet support for revolutionary changes in the third world as being compatible with détente. Détente, American-style and détente, Soviet-style, were incompatible.

Phase 4: Cold War II Confrontation, 1980–

As in 1917, 1940–1941, and 1945–1947, the pendulum-like swing of American public opinion following the events in Iran, Afghanistan and, not to be forgotten in that disastrous year of 1979, the Sandinistas' victory over Somoza in Nicaragua, led to a new postdétente containment policy starting with Carter, whose own opinions largely reflected that of the country, both before and after 1979; the new anti-Soviet policy was perhaps best symbolized by the U.S. boycott of the Olympic Games in Moscow. Since these games were the first to be held in the Soviet Union, Moscow, knowing they would get world-wide attention, tried to use the games to glorify both socialism and its superpower status. The refusal of the United States and some of its allies to participate robbed the games of some of its luster and propaganda value. (In 1984, the Soviets got their revenge and boycotted the Los Angeles Olympic Games, which turned out to be part of the reawakening of American pride in America and further stimulated this new mood.)

Nevertheless, it was the election of Ronald Reagan that best reflected the rejection of détente and the renewed emphasis of the American-Soviet rivalry. Reagan had long denounced détente; he had run against President Ford for the Republican nomination in the primaries in 1976, denouncing détente. There was no question of where Reagan stood on détente — he wanted no part of it. In one of his early pronouncements, he said the Soviet leaders would lie, cheat, and steal and do whatever was needed to expand their power; he declared shortly afterward that the Soviet Union was an "evil empire" and "the focus of evil in the modern world." Furthermore, he asserted, freedom was the wave of the future, not communism. Reagan thereby raised an issue of great sensitivity to Moscow: the legitimacy of the regimes in eastern Europe, including the Soviet Union.

The Revival of U.S.-Soviet Hostility

Since, unlike his predecessor, President Reagan saw the U.S.–Soviet conflict as central, all issues were judged in that light. Third world issues were not approached in terms of their own merits but were seen in an east-west context. It was in Central America where Reagan decided to make his mark almost immediately after the inauguration. It had been in the third world that the Soviet Union, together with its proxies, especially Cuba, had expanded its influence with impunity in the 1970s. The President was determined to stop it. Latin America had in the past been only intermittently involved in the Cold War. Largely ignored by both powers at first, it gained attention after Castro came to power in January 1959, as the result of indigenous causes. A halfhearted American-organized attempt to overthrow Castro in 1961 failed. In 1962, when the Soviets placed missiles in Cuba, the United States reacted vigorously; the missiles were withdrawn but Castro remained. Even before

Cuba, the United States had perceived a threat to its security when a Latin government looked (or was suspected of looking) to Moscow; after Cuba, it was even more sensitive to "another Cuba." Thus it intervened covertly in Guatemala (1954), overtly in the Dominican Republic (1965), and covertly in Chile (1970–1973). But it was not until after Somoza's fall in Nicaragua in 1979 that the United States was to worry seriously about "another Cuba" — and on the mainland too.

The Sandinistas, like Castro earlier, began to squeeze out their partners in the popular anti-Somoza revolution (the Catholic Church, business groups, trade unions, and political parties) as they moved toward authoritarian rule at home and turned toward Havana and Moscow in foreign policy. Claiming that Nicaragua was a base for the subversion of all its neighbors in Central America, such as El Salvador, the Reagan administration charged that the Soviet-Cuban-Nicaraguan activities in the area represented a security threat to the United States, as well as a test of American credibility: If the country could not take care of trouble in its own backyard, how could it do so elsewhere? Indeed, the United States had always assumed security in the western hemisphere and had, therefore, been able to project its power across the Atlantic or Pacific oceans without worrying about threats nearer home.[32] This "strategic rear," the administration argued, was now vulnerable and thus provided the Soviet Union and her allies with opportunities to weaken the United States in its own backyard. Indigenous revolutions, the administration claimed, were acceptable; revolutions tied to Havana and Moscow were not. Just to reinforce the message it was trying to send to Moscow, Havana, and Managua, it sent U.S. forces into the Caribbean island of Grenada to liberate it from its Marxist, pro-Cuban government.[33]

In Nicaragua, however, Reagan was unwilling to use the military because such an intervention would conjure up Vietnam and stir strong political opposition in Congress and the public. Instead, the administration organized the Nicaraguan "contras" to fight a guerrilla war against the Sandinistas. Despite calling them "freedom fighters," the president faced strong congressional criticism of this effort because they were led by officers of the overthrown dictator national guard, they were unsuccessful in the field, and, more fundamentally, the contras were unable to attract a popular following and exploit internal domestic dissatisfaction with the Sandinistas. The intense administration effort on behalf of the contras, it needs to be noted, was part of a larger U.S. effort to support anti-Marxist guerrillas in Afghanistan, Angola, and Cambodia. The aim of the Reagan Doctrine, as it came to be called, was to reverse the gains Moscow and its allies had made since the middle 1970s. The Soviet response was to step up their aid to their new-found friends while intensifying their own efforts in Afghanistan.

Indeed, the Reagan administration's policy in the third world was instinctively anti-Soviet. For instance, during the Iran-Iraq war, which had started in 1979, Iraq's ally, Kuwait, in 1986 asked for Soviet and U.S. protection of its oil-tankers against Iranian attacks. The Iranian attacks were in retaliation to Iraqi air attacks on tankers to and from Iran. The purpose was to reduce Iran's ability to earn the funds with which to continue the war which Iran might otherwise win because of its larger manpower reserves. But once Moscow agreed to help Kuwait, Washington offered to reflag Kuwaiti tankers as American ships and escort them with U.S. warships in order to minimize Soviet influence in the critical Persian Gulf. There was no threat to the oil flow from the Gulf nations to the rest of the world. Yet by its intervention, the United States risked a military clash with Iran.

Reagan's Rearmament and Anti-arms Control Policies
The administration also heavily emphasized an American arms buildup. Both expert and public opinion in the United States held that Soviet military growth had continued at a steady rate while the United States in the 1970s, hampered by the nation's antimilitary mood and lack of congressional funding, had not increased its arsenal of missiles beyond what it had in 1967

(although it had MIRVed just over half of its ICBM force and two-thirds of its SLBMs). The Soviet Union's biggest missiles, the SS-18s, and SS-19s, with ten and six warheads, respectively, had all been deployed since the 1972 SALT I agreement. American missiles were of the pre-SALT I (1960s) generation and American bombers, dating back to 1950, "were older than their pilots." Moreover, it was feared that the land-based missiles, the backbone of the U.S. deterrent, were becoming vulnerable to an attack by the Soviets' huge missiles with their large numbers of increasingly accurate warheads. Thus the president recommended a modernization program consisting of 100 large missiles with very accurate warheads, known as MX* (renamed by the president as Peace-keeper) and 100 B-1 bombers; he also continued the Trident submarine and missile programs (the Trident I and II missiles are both long-range; the latter, to be deployed after 1989, would also be very accurate).

But the administration had more in mind than modernization. It also emphasized the development of a nuclear warfighting doctrine and capability. When the United States had strategic superiority, it was easy to deter a Soviet attack. Now that the Soviet Union had achieved strategic parity plus a capability to attack U.S. missile silos in a first strike, deterrence might no longer be as certain as before. And if it failed, then would it not be preferable to limit the resulting nuclear conflict, attack military targets only, not cities, and try to end the war before it escalated? Yet mere talk of nuclear war fighting frightened many Americans because it suggested that the United States was moving away from the widely accepted proposition that nuclear war was suicidal and that the only function of nuclear weapons was as a deterrent. The president also proposed a major new direction for U.S. defense policy: a Strategic Defense Initiative (SDI) to banish "the specter of retaliation" by discovering the means for rendering missiles "impotent and obsolete." This major new American emphasis on defense against missiles meant that the arms race was increasingly

*Reagan only got 50 MXs.

being pushed into space. Quickly labelled Star Wars, this missile defense program — if the research were successful — could according to its proponents establish the superiority of the defense over the offense; or, according to its critics, it could give rise to an arms race in both defensive and offensive weapons.

This overall military buildup was accompanied by a hostile attitude toward strategic arms control, which the administration largely blamed for America's failure to keep up with the Soviets — indeed, for falling behind. In its vigorous opposition to arms control, it was the first administration since Truman not to engage the Soviets in serious negotiations. It opposed SALT II, negotiated by Presidents Nixon, Ford, and Carter, condemning it as "totally flawed." But because of public concern about the administration's negative attitude toward arms control, it said it would abide by SALT II. All other proposals were advanced basically to appease western public opinions. The Soviets denounced the Reagan administration for its buildup and Star Wars proposals, accusing the United States of seeking to regain its former strategic superiority, speeding up the arms race, and bringing the world nearer to the edge of war. But in 1986 Reagan declared that America would no longer abide by the terms of SALT II and the United States exceeded the SALT II ceilings on MIRVs. Moscow declared it would for the time being continue to abide by SALT II but then proceeded to deploy a new ICBM.

Ironically, President Reagan was driven toward arms control despite himself. This was in part because public opinion overwhelmingly favored arms control, in part because the president had badly hurt his own prestige, and arms control agreements were a principal means of restoring his historical reputation. In 1986, the news leaked that the United States had, despite its official policy of not dealing with terrorists and Reagan's frequent and strong condemnation of terrorism, done exactly that. It covertly sent arms shipments to Iran, which had direct links to the terrorist groups in Lebanon who in the early 1980s twice attacked the U.S. embassy and a marine compound, causing a large loss of lives. The terrorists subsequently kidnapped and held several Americans (as well as others, mainly westerners) as hostages. The arms-for-hostages deal, in which some were released, only to be replaced by newly seized hostages, was very unpopular with the American public. Iran, after all, had already once humiliated the United States during the closing days of the Carter presidency. Now it was happening to Reagan in his last two years in office. Moreover, the deal turned into a scandal when it was revealed that some of the money from the arms sold to Iran was diverted to the contras, despite a congressional cutoff in funds in 1984–1985. Both operations were carried out by the president's own national security staff in the White House. Although Reagan's memory of the arms deal was often hazy and he disclaimed any knowledge of the diversion of funds, the staff was clearly carrying out policies the president favored: freeing the hostages and keeping the contras alive until Congress would fund them once more. His competence, judgments, and credibility seriously questioned, his laid-back style of leadership on foreign policy — not knowing basic facts and unfamiliarity with issues — starkly revealed (even though it had been visible before), the president needed to rescue his tattered reputation. Arms control agreements were an obvious way of doing this. Thus, despite his earlier strong opposition, Reagan had the opportunity to go down in history as the nation's greatest arms control president. In 1986 the Soviets said they were interested in two agreements: the elimination of all intermediate-range nuclear missiles in Europe and a 50 percent reduction of offensive missiles in exchange for restricting research on Star Wars to the laboratory and a deferral of any SDI deployment for ten years. It was the European agreement that moved toward agreement in 1987; the strategic arms deal appeared unlikely because the president was wedded to SDI as his legacy and therefore was unwilling to compromise on any limits on SDI research.

One other factor might play a role in furthering arms agreements: the continuing economic problems facing the United

States. The United States could no longer afford both guns and butter in large amounts as in an earlier era. Because of the constraints of the economy, a choice had to be made. The Reagan administration chose guns, although it is fair to add, it would have cut welfare back anyway, given its antiwelfare attitude. (The Democrats, by and large, give priority to welfare.) Admittedly, the choice of butter or guns is one of degree, not one or the other. But whatever the final mix, a stagnating economy will reduce both; thus the administration placed great emphasis on stimulating an economic recovery by tax reductions. Cutting taxes, however, while greatly increasing the defense budget led to enormous budget deficits and an appreciation of the value of the U.S. dollar. This, in turn, priced American products out of international markets and led to a flood of cheaper imports into the United States. Partly because of this growing trade deficit, the economy became increasingly uncompetitive in world markets, not only in older traditional industries but also increasingly in high technology areas and agricultural exports. In the 1980s, the United States became the world's largest debtor nation. Its economy remained sluggish. The issue of how many guns versus how much butter, therefore, became a critical political issue; so was the issue of whether the country could afford all of its foreign policy commitments.

The Soviet "Time of Troubles"
For Moscow, the early 1980s were disappointing years. First, it had hoped that the election of a conservative Republican president would mean the restoration of a Nixon-style détente. Moscow had found the latter more "businesslike" than liberal Democratic administrations. The Republicans tended to talk tough but were quite willing to meet at summits and negotiate; Democrats, more predisposed to liberal (anti-Communist) values, were frequently militantly anti-Soviet and prone to interventionism in the pre-Vietnam era. Carter, however, frustrated the Soviets with his inconsistencies: wanting to improve American-Soviet relations on the one hand, attacking them on hu-

man rights violations on the other; giving SALT II priority and not linking it to Soviet behavior, then suggesting that the U.S. Senate would make such a link if the Soviets did not mend their ways; telling Moscow that it had a choice between cooperation or conflict; not reacting to Soviet moves in Africa but then sharply reacting to the invasion of Afghanistan; and swaying between the often conflicting advice of his secretary of state (Vance) and his national security adviser (Brzezinski). Thus another hard-line anti-Soviet Republican in the White House who would be consistent in his behavior and with whom the Soviets thought they would be able to deal was a relief. But this relief did not last long. It soon became apparent that Reagan was a different kind of Republican and that he was more eager to confront the Soviets than to negotiate with them.

Second, while Reagan, the oldest American postwar president, sounded the anti-Soviet call to arms, the Soviet leadership suffered a geriatric problem. Leonid Brezhnev, who had hung on to power despite several years of serious illness, died in 1982. He was replaced by the former head of the secret police, Yuri Andropov, who died in 1984. He was succeeded by the third leader in two years, Konstantin Chernenko. It wasn't until he also died, in 1985, that a member of the younger generation, Mikhail Gorbachev, finally became leader of the Soviet Union. Since Brezhnev during the last years of his life was not fully in charge, the Soviet Union had for at least five years not had the kind of leadership it needed to make major decisions departing from old policies in both the economic realm as well as foreign policy.

Third, the Soviets were concerned by the scheduled U.S. weapons deployments for the late 1980s and 1990s: the MX missile; the B-1 bomber (reportedly to be followed by a new Stealth bomber, which would be able to evade radar detection); the Trident II SLBM; and subsonic but highly accurate cruise missiles that could be launched from the air, ground, or sea. These weapons would degrade the value of Soviet ICBMs, the heart of their deterrent forces, and render Soviet anti-bomber defenses largely obsolete. The Soviets therefore had to again be concerned with a shift in the strategic balance. Soviet fear about America's growing first-strike capability was heightened by the Star Wars proposal. They did not see it as a defensive system. Rather, since they believed that no complete antimissile defense was possible, they viewed this program as offensive and aggressive. United States missiles would attack Soviet missiles; those left after an American strike would then be prevented from retaliating by the American missile defenses. Star Wars thus strengthened the incentive to launch a disarming strike on the Soviet Union.

While many American critics thought that the development of space-based defense was technically not possible, the Soviet feared that it might be. They also feared that, given the U.S. lead in high technology, they might not be able to match the American effort. Thus, after walking out of arms control talks in 1983, they returned to them even though none of their earlier conditions for resuming such talks were met. Clearly, if Moscow wanted to avoid SDI deployment, one way of doing so would be to offer a radical reduction of the Soviet Union's first-strike missiles in exchange for a U.S. postponement of Star Wars deployment long enough for Soviet technology to catch up. While the powers talked about such a deal at the 1986 Iceland summit meeting, the president was unwilling to limit research to the laboratory because he believed that that would kill SDI. The "grand compromise" thus remained out of reach for the time being.

Fourth, even in western Europe, where the Soviets had expected some successes because of European-American differences with NATO, the results turned out to be disappointing. The United States and its European allies had for some years increasingly seen relations with the Soviet Union in quite different ways. The United States was disillusioned with détente and saw only the vast Soviet rearmament drive and expansionist activities in the third world. The Europeans, by contrast, had benefited from détente: They enjoyed profitable trade relations with the Eastern bloc, an absence of Cold War crises in Europe, and an exchange of recognition by East and West

Germany, normalizing to some degree the relationship among the two Germanies. While the United States wanted less détente, its allies wanted more détente. As a result, the west European governments began to distance, or "uncouple," themselves from the United States on foreign policy while at the same time continuing to rely on America for their defense. This increasing split within the western alliance on fundamental policy toward the Soviet Union was further widened by growing public opposition in Europe to U.S. defense policy, especially with regard to the deployment in western Europe of U.S. missiles to counter the Soviet deployment of SS-20 intermediate range missiles (each armed with three accurate warheads) aimed at western Europe. Vast crowds protested the plan in the streets. Fear of nuclear war, mixed with pacifism, neutralism, and anti-Americanism, were all represented in these repeated demonstrations. The Social Democrats in West Germany and the Labour party in England, two major parties, now in opposition, came out against the U.S. deployment. Indeed, the Labour party came out for Britain's unilateral nuclear disarmament and the elimination of U.S. nuclear bases in Britain. Nevertheless, the British, West German and Italian governments favored the U.S. deployment of Pershing II cruise missiles and, despite the street demonstrations, they remained steadfast.

The Soviets adamantly opposed American missiles. They insisted on their own deployment while refusing to accept any American missiles because the SS-20s, they argued, merely represented a modernization of an older generation of intermediate range missiles. To prevent the U.S. deployment, they sought to exploit the widespread European fears. When this failed, they walked out of all arms control negotiations in the hope that European opinion, even more frightened at the collapse of all arms control negotiations, would intensify European pressure on Washington to comply with the new Soviet demand to dismantle the U.S. missiles before they would resume arms control talks. Star Wars, however, changed their mind and brought Moscow back to the negotiating table where the steadfastness of European governments and the determination of the United States to counter the SS-20 deployment, paid off when Moscow accepted an earlier U.S. proposal for no deployment of intermediate-range missiles by either side and added all of its short range missiles to the deal.

Fifth, the future prospects of the Soviet Union were troublesome. Apart from its enormous military power, it was beset by economic problems: (1) Its rate of growth had declined each decade (from 7 to 8 percent annually in the 1950s to a projected 2 percent in the late 1980s). (2) It could not feed its people a balanced diet and had difficulty in keeping up with high technology (which, when possible, it tried to steal or buy furtively from western countries). (3) There was a decline in the growth of its labor force and the productivity of Soviet workers. (4) There was the prospect that the Great Russians — who had first always ruled Russia — were about to become a minority among the multitude of non-Russian ethnic groups. (5) The Soviet ideology was losing its appeal at home, and, more broadly, the Soviet model of development in the third world was becoming less attractive. In the Communist world, its neighbors in eastern Europe, especially Poland, remained restive and potential sources of trouble; hatred for the Soviet Union was deep and widespread, and China remained alienated. As one wit is reported to have said: The Soviet Union was the only Communist country in the world surrounded by Communist enemies. Indeed, in a real sense, Soviet foreign policy had grossly failed because its main result had been to drive western Europe, Japan and China together and encircle itself. The consequence of this was not likely to diminish the Soviet paranoia about its security.

The Soviet Union as a One-Dimensional Power

In the early 1980s the Soviet Union was thus very much a one-dimensional power, unable to offer friends and allies either an example of a successful economy or much economic assistance; nor could it present to the world a society culturally and politically appealing. Nevertheless, the Soviet Union remains a formidable adversary because of its huge military machine and its persistent determination to expand its influence. In the third world, it is not the Soviet domestic system but Soviet power, the abundance of weapons it can give to antiwestern states and self-styled revolutionary groups, the Soviet military advisers and Cuban proxy forces it can send to help them achieve and/or stabilize power, and the Soviet authoritarian methods of central political control and police surveillance that appeals to some leaders in the less developed countries. In the western world, the fear of Soviet military power and intimidation remained. France's Socialist President told the West German Parliament in the midst of the SS-20 crisis in the early 1980s, he saw Soviet missiles in the east and pacifists and neutralists in the west. He added that this was not a balance that could ensure a peaceful and free Europe. The fact is that if it were not for her military power — which has been achieved with only half the gross national product of the U.S. — the Soviet Union would not be seen as a superpower, and clearly, Moscow spends so much on its military forces because it expects its investment to pay off politically.

But the Soviet economy can no longer afford the large-scale investment in the military. Like the United States, Russia must pay more attention to its basic economy. Among other things, the Soviet leadership must concentrate on fundamental reforms in its economy. This, in turn, requires slowing down the arms competition with the United States. The result has been a string of Soviet arms control proposals and a stated desire for improved Soviet-American relations. Without a reversal of its economic problems, the Soviet Union's status as a member of an exclusive club of two will be threatened, as well as its ability to maintain a strong and technologically-up-to-date military. Mr. Gorbachev's future as the Soviet Union's leader may well depend on his turning the economy around and reaching arms control agreements with the United States.

The Legacy of the Past

Each decade has left its imprint on the Cold War. The legacy of the 1940s is the superpower rivalry, a rivalry that is still with us today. Its beginning fulfilled the prophecy of Sainte-Beuve who, in 1847, had said "Europe has had its day. . . . The future of the world lies between these two great nations [Russia and America]. One day they will collide, and then we will see struggles the like of which no one has dreamed of."[34]

It is ironic that it was the issue of eastern Europe that constituted the first blow to the wartime alliance. The satellization of the area, carried out in the name of Soviet security, has left the Soviet Union insecure. Not only were the United States and Britain alienated but most of the peoples of the affected countries have never willingly accepted Soviet control. Three times Moscow has had to intervene militarily and once the Polish Army had to do it instead. Each intervention has raised Cold War bitterness. In 1956 it helped undermine the thaw after Stalin's death while in 1968 it delayed the start of the SALT talks. By the time they were resumed, the United States had started the multiplication of warheads on missiles, a development whose overall effect on the nuclear balance was negative (see Chapters 3 and 4). Thus events in eastern Europe that helped precipitate the Cold War have continued intermittently to profoundly affect its course. One reason for the large Soviet army in the area is less to face NATO than to assure the loyalty of its Communist regimes. The instability in this area remains potentially dangerous. It is perhaps useful to recall that it was in eastern Europe that both world wars started: World War I after the assassination of the Austrian Archduke in 1914, World War II a year after the Munich appeasement in 1938. And it was the Soviet coup in Czechoslovakia in 1948 that signaled the full onset of the Cold War in Europe.

The resulting U.S. containment policy evolved during the 1940s and 1950s. During the late 1940s when the United States defined the limits beyond which Soviet expansion would not be tolerated — a task it had refused to do during the late stages of World War II — U.S. policy had restricted itself to countering its principal adversary. But after 1950 containment lost its sense of proportion with the demise of Nationalist China, the signing of the Sino-Soviet alliance, the Korean War, and Communist China's intervention. Anti-Sovietism became anti-Communism. Before these events, the United States was quite willing to assist Communist Yugoslavia after its break with Stalin and anticipate exploiting the likelihood of Sino-Soviet differences. Subsequently, the Sino-Soviet bloc was seen as a monolith; all Communist states were believed to be puppets of either Moscow or Beijing. China's differences were seen as only tactical differences over how to wage the Cold War against the capitalist west, a task on which they were united with Moscow. Vietnam was one result of this faulty perception and its impacts were disastrous: Besides losing the war, the United States squandered resources against a secondary adversary in an area of secondary interest. Even worse, it divided the United States domestically and destroyed the consensus that had been the basis for an activist U.S. postwar foreign policy. The failure to exploit the Sino-Soviet conflict because of this crusading habit was a strategic error of the first order; the Vietnam war was one cost of this mistaken policy.

The legacy of the first two decades was therefore that of a bipolar world. The United States and Russia viewed the Cold War in zero-sum terms: "What you gain I lose; I must therefore try to prevent any losses." In a two-power system, such a perception was hardly surprising. The balance was constantly seen as being at stake. A setback anywhere — be it a "loss" of Hungary or South Korea — might lead to further setbacks elsewhere; a tolerable and acceptable shift in the balance might thus lead to a series of defeats, producing a major and unacceptable change in the distribution of power. This perception has continued as the world moved beyond bipolarity after the middle-1950s, as the cohesion of both NATO and WTO began to loosen, and as the new third world nations began to play a more prominent role on the world stage. The superpower rivalry now extended to southeast Asia and the Middle East; after 1979, it extended to the Persian Gulf, Central America, and the Caribbean. Regional issues were rarely seen on their own merit but rather on how they related to the superpower competition.

The arms control talks during the 1960s and 1970s also demonstrated that the U.S.–Soviet relationship was a mixed one consisting of conflict and common interests, rivalry and cooperation. Arms control agreements were a form of antisuicide pact. The very destructiveness of nuclear weapons and the necessity to avoid war compelled the adversaries to work together. Historically, great powers have always been concerned with their national security; indeed, if one power were militarily stronger than the other, so much the better. In a dangerous world, it was better to be safe than sorry. This approach to national security obviously still influences the superpowers. But nuclear weapons were in a special category. A nuclear war would destroy both the United States and the Soviet Union. Thus they also shared common security concerns. Neither could think in purely national security terms any more; each one's security depended on the other. Arms control talks therefore became politically popular and a barometer of the state of American-Soviet relations. Agreements were a sign of détente; inability to arrive at agreements was a symptom of tensions. The Reagan administration, opposed to détente, thought it a virtue to be against arms control during the first years. Only later, partly because of public expectations, partly to salvage its tattered reputation, did the administration show an interest in arriving at agreements with Moscow. Arms control thus qualified the zero-sum attitude.

Despite arms control cooperation and the détente of the early-middle 1970s, there have been further dramatic changes since the 1970s and these are still very visible in the 1980s: the Soviet Union's achievement of strategic parity, its attainment of a conventional capability to project power beyond Eurasia, and the finding of proxy regimes whose interests coincide with those of Moscow. In America, the changes include the return to an anti-

Soviet approach to foreign policy, the willingness to align itself with anti-Soviet Communist regimes, especially with a Communist China, the continued public reluctance to use force in more than a quick, relatively painless manner against ministates, and the continuation of both the arms competition as well as the arms control efforts to assure both national security and ensure that nuclear war shall not occur. How nuclear weapons keep the "war" cold is discussed in the next two chapters.

Notes

1. For broad overviews and analyses, see John Spanier, *American Foreign Policy Since World War II,* 11th ed. (Washington, D.C.: Congressional Quarterly, 1988) and Joseph L. Nogee and Robert H. Donaldson, *Soviet Foreign Policy Since World War II,* 2d ed. (New York: Pergamon Press, 1984), as well as Alvin Z. Rubinstein, *Soviet Foreign Policy Since World War II,* 2d ed. (Boston: Little, Brown, 1985) and Adam Ulam, *Expansion and Coexistence,* 2d ed. (New York: Praeger Publishers, 1974).
2. While the timing of the different phases of the Cold War is somewhat different, the use of "C" words to describe the different periods was first suggested by Charles and Toby Gati, *The Debate Over Detente* (New York: The Foreign Policy Association Headline series 234, February, 1977).
3. Spanier, op. cit., p. 30.
4. Vojtech Mastny, "Stalin and Militarization of the Cold War," *International Security,* Winter 1984–1985, pp. 110–112.
5. Edward Mark, "American Policy toward Eastern Europe and the Origins of the Cold War, 1941–1946: An Alternative Interpretation," *The Journal of American History* (September 1981), pp. 313–336.
6. Thomas W. Wolfe, *Soviet Power and Europe, 1945–1970* (Baltimore: The Johns Hopkins Press, 1970), p. 15.
7. Mastny, op. cit., p. 120.
8. Ibid., p. 121.
9. Ibid.
10. Samuel F. Wells, Jr., "Sounding the Tocsin: NSC 68 and the Soviet Threat," *International Security,* Fall 1979, p. 131.
11. Ibid., p. 133.

12. John Spanier, *The Truman-MacArthur Controversy and the Korean War*, rev. ed. (New York: W. W. Norton, 1965).

13. John Lewis Gaddis, "Was the Truman Doctrine a Real Turning Point?", *Foreign Affairs*, January 1974, pp. 386–402.

14. John Spanier, *Games Nations Play*, 6th ed. (Washington, D.C.: Congressional Quarterly, 1987), pp. 142–143.

15. Louis J. Halle, *The Cold War as History* (New York: Harper & Row, 1967), p. 304.

16. On the beginnings of the Sino-Soviet conflict, see Donald Z. Zagoria, *The Sino-Soviet Conflict 1956–1961* (Princeton, N.J.: Princeton University Press, 1962) and David Floyd, *Mao Against Khrushchev* (New York: Frederick A. Praeger, 1963).

17. Zbigniew Brzezinski, *The Soviet Bloc* (Cambridge, Mass.: Harvard University Press, 1960).

18. Hans Speier, *Divided Berlin* (New York: Frederick A. Praeger, 1961); Arnold Horelick and Myron Rush, *Strategic Power and Soviet Foreign Policy* (Chicago: The University of Chicago Press, 1966); Robert M. Slusser, *The Berlin Crisis of 1961* (Baltimore: The Johns Hopkins Press, 1973); and Alexander L. George, "The Cuban Missile Crisis, 1962," in George, David K. Hall and William E. Simons, eds., *The Limits of Coercive Diplomacy* (Boston: Little, Brown, 1971), pp. 86–143.

19. See, for example, the "Essay," written by, among others, Dean Rusk, Robert McNamara, Theodore Sorenson, and McGeorge Bundy, entitled "The Lesson of the Cuban Missile Crisis," *Time*, September 27, 1982, p. 85.

20. Zbigniew Brzezinski, "How the Cold War Was Played," *Foreign Affairs*, October 1972, p. 193.

21. Wolfe, op. cit., pp. 432–437; David Holloway, *The Soviet Union and the Arms Race*, 2d ed. (New Haven, Conn.: Yale University Press, 1984), p. 43; and Raymond L. Garthoff, "SALT I: An Evaluation," *World Politics*, October 1978, p. 8.

22. George C. Herring, *America's Longest War* (New York: John Wiley & Sons, 1979); David Halberstram, *The Best and the Brightest* (New York: Random House, 1969); Guenter Lewy, *America in Vietnam* (New York: Oxford University Press, 1978); and Townsend Hoopes, *The Limits of Intervention* (New York: David McKay Company, 1969).

23. Norman Podhoretz, *Why We Were in Vietnam* (New York: Simon & Schuster, 1982), p. 49.

24. Larry Berman, *Planning a Tragedy* (New York: W. W. Norton,

1984); and Herbert Y. Schandler, *Lyndon Johnson and Vietnam* (Princeton, N.J.: Princeton University Press, 1977).

25. Leslie Gelb and Richard K. Betts, *The Irony of Vietnam* (Washington, D.C.: The Brookings Institution, 1979), p. 68.

26. The best books on this decade are by participants: Richard Nixon, *The Memoirs of Richard Nixon* (New York: Grosset & Dunlap, 1978); Henry Kissinger, *The White House Years* and *The Years of Upheaval* (Boston: Little, Brown, 1979 and 1982, respectively); and Zbigniew Brzezinski, *Power and Principle* (New York: Farrar, Straus, & Giroux, 1983). For an analysis of America-Soviet relations from Nixon to Reagan, see Raymond L. Garthoff, *Détente and Confrontation* (Washington, D.C.: The Brookings Institution, 1985). While often very critical of U.S. policy, this lengthy book is excellent in explaining Soviet perceptions and interests.

27. Other reasons often cited by conservative critics are that détente was based on the illusion that the Soviet Union had become a status quo power and that Moscow had taken advantage of America's relaxation of its vigilance. Defenders of détente like Henry Kissinger blame the failure on the emasculation of President Nixon's authority as a result of Vietnam, the Watergate scandal which forced Nixon to resign the presidency, Congress' general attack on the "imperial presidency," and specific interventions such as depriving the president of his economic tools or preventing U.S. reactions to Soviet-Cuban moves. See, for example, Soviet expert, Dimitri Simes, "The Death of Detente?", *International Security,* Summer 1980, who says that before the Jackson-Vanik amendment and the collapse of presidential authority, Moscow was cautious (p. 13).

28. Garthoff, op. cit., pp. 290–298.

29. It was probably too much to expect the Soviets to betray Egyptian and Syrian confidences. They had invested too much for too long in both countries to sacrifice this influence in order to warn Washington of the pending attack. They may have believed that specific moves like the evacuation of Soviet civilians from Egypt would be picked up by U.S. intelligence and provide the necessary warning of war.

30. For Soviet reasons for invading Afghanistan, see Garthoff, op. cit., p. 887ff. and Thomas T. Hammond, *Red Flag over Afghanistan* (Boulder, Col.: Westview Press, 1984).

31. The Carter and Reagan policies toward the Soviet Union, after 1979, are discussed in Garthoff, op. cit., p. 966ff. and Alexander Haig Jr., *Caveat* (New York: Macmillan, 1984).
32. *The Report of the President's National Bipartisan Commission on Central America* (known also as the Kissinger Report) (New York: Macmillan, 1984).
33. The president then proceeded to undermine this point by intervening ineffectively in Beirut, Lebanon, by becoming involved on one side of a civil war between the prowestern and pro-Israeli Lebanese Christians and the Moslems, who looked to "pro-Soviet" Syria for political and military support. The small U.S. marine contingent was thus placed in an untenable situation. After a suicide mission on the marines, which could not have been carried out without Syrian knowledge, if not assistance, left 241 dead, the pressure to withdraw the marines became overwhelming. In turn, this left Syria which already had troops in Lebanon and had influence with the various Moslem factions in that country, the dominant power. Small Syria had humiliated and humbled the mighty United States. This squandering of American prestige and power and the resulting undermining of western influence in Lebanon, countered the so-called "lesson of Grenada."
34. Quoted by André Fontaine, *History of the Cold War* (New York: Vintage Books, 1970), vol. I, p. 11.

Nuclear Arms, Deterrence, and Keeping the War "Cold"

Why It Remained "Cold"

Before nuclear weapons, states considered war as a legitimate and rational instrument of policy. War was legitimate because in an anarchical state system each state defined its national interests and had the right to use force to protect itself. It was also rational because it was cost-effective. When a nation went to war, it was presumably because vital interests were at stake. It could calculate that the costs in terms of loss of life or territory or finance might be high. But such costs, however painful, were deemed acceptable. Gains would exceed losses.

War in the twentieth century has thrown both war's legitimacy and rationality into doubt, because the cost of war has risen astronomically. The first world war (1914–1918) consumed an entire generation of young men, especially in France and Britain, countries whose populations were much smaller than their enemy's, Germany. Their appeasement policy toward Germany in the 1930s reflected deeply felt national antiwar moods. By comparison, during the second world war (1939–1945) the loss of life among the armies on the western front was considerably less; only on the eastern front did the four years of heavy fighting between the Russian and German armies resemble the carnage of World War I. Overall casualties, however, military plus civilian, were considerably greater.

The war ended with the two atom bombs dropped on Hiroshima and Nagasaki to compel the surrender of Japan. These bombs symbolized the increasing destructiveness of war in this century. Now that one airplane and one bomb could instantly destroy so much of a city's population and housing, the essence of war had changed.[1] The survival of society now became questionable; the cost of war would exceed any conceivable gains. As the megatons (millions of tons of explosives) of hydrogen bombs replaced the kilotons (thousands of tons) of atomic bombs, this conclusion seemed even more obvious. Not fighting, but deterring war, was now seen as the only conceivable purpose of such "absolute" weapons. So it was "absolutely" imperative to avoid a nuclear war.

Throughout past history, nations never had the ultimate power to destroy themselves. Hence states could make war, knowing that their survival was guaranteed, no matter how terrible the slaughter may be. Since Hiroshima, some states have had too much power. The result, as President Eisenhower said in 1955 at the Geneva summit conference, is that "there is no alternative to peace." In the nuclear age the superpowers have no choice but to engage each other in the manner of porcupines making love — very carefully. President Eisenhower put it simply: "You can't have this kind of war. There just aren't enough bulldozers to scrape the bodies off the street."[2]

This suggests that if in the past national leaders had been able to gaze into a crystal ball and see the future before they went to war, they would not have fired any shots. If the leaders of Russia, Germany, and Austria-Hungary in 1914 had been able to see that they would not be around four years later, or Hitler that his thousand-year Reich, only six years old in 1939 when he invaded Poland, would be lying in rubble in 1945, none of them would have resorted to war. The point about nuclear war is that one does not need a crystal ball. There is no question of the outcome. The possibility of nuclear war forces government leaders to concentrate on avoiding suicide and devising the safest possible strategy of deterrence, thus ensuring that the Cold War will stay cold.

The American View of Deterrence

In 1946, Bernard Brodie, who would become a famous writer on strategy, said

> The first and most vital step in any American security program for the age of atomic bombs is to take measures to guarantee to ourselves in case of attack the possibility of retaliation in kind. The writer in making this statement is not for the moment concerned about who will *win* the next war in which atomic bombs have been used. Thus far the chief purpose of our military establishment has been to win wars. From now on its chief purpose must to be avert them. It can have almost no other useful military purpose.[3]

These comments on the significance of what had happened in Hiroshima are almost commonplace today, but they were novel at the time. The U.S. strategy of deterrence evolved gradually. During the period of the U.S. monopoly on the atom bomb, the stockpile was tiny: two bombs at the end of 1945, nine by July 1946, 13 a year later, and 50 by July 1948. None was assembled. The bomber force that could deliver these bombs was also small: only about 30 B-29s.[4] By 1950, the Strategic Air Command (SAC) had just over 300 aircraft capable of carrying the bomb. In 1951, SAC's capability improved with the delivery of the first B-47 jet bomber; of medium-range, it was based overseas around the Soviet Union. The Soviets exploded their first bomb in 1949, but U.S. strategic superiority grew during the 1950s. By 1959, SAC reached its peak strength with 1,366 B-47s, stationed within two to three flying hours distance from their targets, and 488 intercontinental range B-52s (which came into service after 1955), plus 1,000 tanker aircraft to refuel the bombers and 174 reconnaissance aircraft. At the same time, the atomic stockpile doubled to 2,000 between 1953 and 1955. Above all, after 1954 SAC's destructive capacity was enormously increased by the hydrogen bomb.

SAC planners in 1955 expected the destruction of at least three-quarters of the population of Russia's 118 cities, approximately 77 million people, 60 million fatally[5]; by the time the Kennedy administration came into office, they expected to destroy 90 percent of all cities and towns in the Soviet Union, 2500 targets with the deaths of 350 million Russians and Eastern Europeans in a few hours (Chinese casualties were also included since all of Moscow's allies were targeted; radiation would also spread to neutral states like Finland, killing many more). By contrast, American intelligence believed that the Soviet Union had only a few atom bombs in the early 1950s and a small force of propeller-driven bombers based in the Soviet Union; these bombers, after a long flight, would have had difficulty penetrating U.S. air defenses with their jet interceptors.

The Eisenhower "New Look," with its emphasis on strategic air power, had three aims, two of which it had inherited from the Truman administration: deterring an attack on the United States and preventing an invasion of western Europe. The new aim was to threaten Moscow with massive retaliation in order to prevent it from instigating or allowing its client states to launch more limited challenges like Korea. While it was always questionable whether the administration would in fact precipitate a war with the Soviet Union over another Korea in Asia or elsewhere, the Soviet leaders remained cautious. They were careful by nature, unwilling to risk exposing their country, "the bastion of the world revolution," to complete destruction. This remained true even as the Soviet capability for striking the United States grew with jet bombers and hydrogen bombs after the middle 1950s. While SAC in a single blow expected to leave the Soviet Union a "smoking, radiating ruin at the end of two hours,"[6] the United States too would suffer great destruction — as Eisenhower recognized early — if some of the Soviet bombers got to their targets. Nevertheless, the U.S. capability still sufficed to deter both a nuclear Soviet strike against America as well as an invasion of western Europe. The danger of an escalation to nuclear war was simply too great for Moscow to risk unleashing the Soviet Army.

But while America's continuing strategic superiority could neutralize both the Soviet Union's increasing strategic forces and its large conventional forces facing NATO, the threat to attack Moscow in response to some limited challenge outside of Europe was even less believable than it had been at the time of Korea when the Soviets could not have retaliated against the United States. It simply was not credible that the United States would precipitate an all-out war to defend an important, but nevertheless limited, interest. This line of thinking grew even further after the Soviets tested the world's first intercontinental ballistic missile (ICBM) in 1957. America's bombers were concentrated on 58 bases; Russian ICBMs, with their speed, might in a surprise attack be able to destroy most of them. The assumption was that Moscow would, as it said it was doing, build enough of these ICBMs to launch a "disarming" strike. The incoming Kennedy administration therefore focused its attention on coping with these two problems. Suicide or surrender — holocaust or humiliation — were not realistic policy alternatives. Future Koreas would have to be met locally by conventional forces and the United States would have to build up such "limited war forces." It would also have to modernize U.S. strategic forces, replacing most of the increasingly vulnerable bombers with missiles, to ensure the future of deterrence. This strategy was named "flexible response."

The Irrationality of Nuclear War

Many of the students of the new field of national security — almost all civilians — who in the 1950s had spent their time thinking and writing about deterrence, arms control, and limited war now became officials in the executive branch. They established the strategic force levels that the United States was to possess for over two decades: 1,000 land-based Minutemen ICBMs (plus 54 older ICBMs) — the Air Force had requested 2,400 — and 41 nuclear-powered submarines (with 16 missiles per submarine), or 656 sea-based missiles. It downgraded bombers, retiring all B-47s but keeping 600 B-52s in service. They also set out in detail the rationale for America's deterrent policy.

While this explanation hardly had unanimous support among those who participated in the debates over national security policies, there was widespread agreement on the central ideas of deterrence and arms control. These ideas, first elaborated in the 1950s, were refined in the 1960s during the Kennedy-Johnson administrations and remained the consensus until the 1970s.[7] While the challenge to them was to be a formidable one, the original ideas remain influential even today.

The elaboration of these concepts has consistently started from the premise that nuclear war would be a catastrophe and must therefore be avoided. Nuclear weapons were so destructive that there would be no winners or losers. Everyone would lose. The function of nuclear weapons was to deter an all-out war. From this proposition, so evident to all persons of common sense and rationality, was deduced a whole series of other propositions. These propositions were so logical that it was believed that they were the consequence of nuclear technology rather than American ways of thinking; the Soviets, if they put their minds to it, would arrive at the same conclusions. In short, with regard to nuclear weapons, there was no American or Soviet way of thinking; logical and deductive reasoning would arrive at universal conclusions regardless of nationality.

The key to successful deterrence was holding the adversary's society hostage. It was the threat to annihilate his urban-industrial complex that would give the potential attacker the incentive for self-restraint. This type of attack against cities was called a "countervalue" attack because presumably the enemy would place high value on the survival of urban areas, which are the centers of industry and population.* The term that came into vogue in the 1960s to describe the damage to be inflicted was "unacceptable damage." During the 1960s, the Kennedy administration set this level at killing 25 percent of the Soviet population and 50 percent of Soviet industry.[8] President Kennedy talked of 100 million Russians, 100 million Europeans, and 100 million Americans dying in a large-scale nuclear war. Secretary of Defense Harold Brown, during the Carter administration in the late 1970s, said that destroying the Soviet Union's 200 largest cities with 34 percent of the population and 62 percent of the industry constituted "unacceptable damage."[9] Whatever the number killed, the point remains that a society without most of its cities, industries, skilled personnel, medical facilities, transportation systems, and food (much of it contaminated with radiation and, in any event, unable to be shipped for distribution to the urban areas of the country) would be one in which "the living would envy the dead," as Premier Khrushchev was reported to have said. When both sides possessed this capability for inflicting assured destruc-

---

*The other form of attack against the enemy's deterrent forces was called "counterforce." The Kennedy administration subscribed to it briefly but soon abandoned it. However, in the 1970s counterforce came into vogue again. See below.

tion, it was referred to as mutual assured destruction, better known as MAD.

In 1983–1984, the perception that nuclear war was suicidal was reinforced by the thesis that nuclear war would create a "nuclear winter."[10] A major nuclear attack on cities would produce so much smoke and soot that sunlight would be blocked for weeks, if not months, plunging a darkened world into subfreezing temperatures, leading to the extinction of species of plants, animals, and microorganisms not only in the northern hemisphere but globally. Agriculture would be destroyed if the war occurred just before or during the growing season and surface water would be frozen to a depth of several feet. Life for the survivors would be tenuous at best because of the drastic climatic change. When combined with the direct effects of a nuclear explosion on the inhabitants of targeted cities, there might eventually be no survivors in the northern hemisphere's mid-latitude belt encompassing the United States, Canada, Europe, Russia, China, and Japan. Human beings, animals, and plants in the southern hemisphere would also suffer enormously because the smoke would spread rapidly. An ironic finding was that since this winter would spread to the whole world, the power that struck first, even if it were successful and could prevent any retaliation, would "win" — but only for a week or two!

While this scenario was to be sharply questioned,[11] the fundamental question did not change: How could one make sure that deterrence would not fail? What were the minimum requirements to make deterrence credible to the opponent? Essentially these were twofold. The first was to have forces whose size left the opponent with *no* doubt that the threat of destruction was a very real one. The deterrent forces had always to be at wartime strength and ready to strike 24 hours a day, 365 days a year. The second requirement was the permanent superiority of the offensive over the defensive. There was one danger: If the rapid technological changes that characterized the postwar period allowed the defense to catch up with the offense, thereby weakening the deterrer's ability to inflict assured destruction, the enemy might be tempted to launch an attack. Thus technology would have to ensure that the means of delivering the nuclear arsenal would stay far ahead of any countermeasures.

If these requirements were met, would an enemy risk launching an attack, knowing that if it did it would be signing its death warrant? While rationally it should be dissuaded, the fact was that historically states have been repeatedly caught by surprise. In 1941, Stalin did not believe that the Germans were about to attack; less than six months later the United States was caught napping at Pearl Harbor.[12] What made the danger of a first strike in the postwar years a possibility was the increasing speed of modern delivery systems. The pure jet bomber flying at 600 mph had the capacity to launch a surprise attack if the enemy's bombers were not on alert. The surviving planes would then no longer be able to retaliate fully, and their numbers could be whittled down even more by jet interceptors and other means of defense alerted for the bombers' arrival. The resulting level of damage might then be acceptable because the benefit would be enormous: the opponent's elimination.

The vulnerability of bombers, then, rendered the deterrent balance unstable because it gave each side the incentive to strike the initial blow. Nuclear war might therefore occur despite the awful destructiveness of modern weapons. Clearly, merely possessing the bomb was not enough to prevent war. That could only be achieved by eliminating the vulnerability of the deterrent forces. It was this concern that gave birth to the topic of "arms control."

The Rationale for Arms Control

Strategic arms control has focused mainly on the issue of the delivery systems.[13] Its aim has been to find an alternative to certain solutions for resolving the likelihood of nuclear war erupting, such as transforming the structure of the sovereign state system and eliminating all nuclear arms. Arms control accepted the world as it was. Nation-states would not disappear because of the threat of nuclear extinction: international conflict and rivalry would continue. Nuclear weapons, furthermore, could not be disinvented; the knowledge of how to build the bomb was here to stay. Thus the problem was how to learn to live with the bomb and specifically to prevent nuclear war by dealing with the most likely cause of such a war. If neither the cause of conflict nor nuclear arms could be eliminated, the best hope for secular salvation lay in their "control." In this sense, arms control was seen not as an alternative but a supplement to more traditional defense policy since both aimed at achieving the same goal: to protect the nation by deterring nuclear war. Arms control's emphasis was not so much in reducing the nation's *capability* to fight — it was compatible with military reductions or, if necessary, increases — as it was in removing the *incentive* to launch a first strike.

There were two forms of such a strike. One was a "bolt out of the blue" or preventive attack unprovoked by the opponent. The other, the more likely one, was a preemptive attack provoked by the fear that the opponent might attack. The greatest danger of the latter is in a crisis period when the superpowers are locked in confrontation. Neither side may want to strike first, but neither is sure that the other will not do so. Each may therefore fear not attacking and feel that it has no choice in the matter. "Crisis instability" is thus a major danger. The assumption underlying the possibility of either preventive or preemptive attack is the same: namely, that the forces that are supposed to deter the opponent are vulnerable to attack themselves and thus they provide the enemy with a strong incentive to strike.

But the motivations for these two types of attack are different. Preventive war is offensively oriented. The attack occurs even if at the moment relations between the two states are relaxed. The assumption is that war will happen in the long run; therefore, eliminate the enemy when possible. And what better time to do it than when relations are reasonable and the enemy does not expect an attack? Preemptive war is, by contrast, defensively motivated. The desire is to avoid war altogether, but because of the mutual fear that the opponent may strike, one side launches the attack to get in the first blow. The only defense is the offense. The possibility of suffering 20 to 30 million casualties might restrain an attacker from launching a preventive attack when the alternative is not to attack at all and suffer no losses. But in a crisis, when the fear of being struck is greatest, each may feel compelled to preempt regardless of the casualties it might have to accept.

Arms control thus focused on the delivery systems because it was these systems that rendered the deterrent balance unstable. In seeking a solution to the first-strike problem, arms control was based on two assumptions: first, that both the United States and the Soviet Union shared a common interest in avoiding a nuclear war and second, although the basic cause for their conflict was political, the delivery systems constituted an independent cause for risking a nuclear war. The two superpowers would thus benefit from cooperating in this area. But how could the deterrent balance be made safe, or "stable"? That was the critical question. In the nuclear era a balance of power, or mutual deterrence, was not a guarantee that war could be prevented; it now had to be a *stable* balance. This could be attained in the following ways.

Stabilizing MAD

First, and foremost, the deterrent forces had to be made invulnerable. Arms control thinking drew a careful distinction between the totality of nuclear forces and second-strike forces.[14] It was the latter — those that would be left after absorbing an opponent's first strike — that were the critical component. The more invulnerable the second or retaliatory strike forces were, the stabler the balance. In the bomber era (when arms control thinking began) it was the bomber that was increasingly believed to be the principal cause of instability because they were kept on relatively few airfields and thus vulnerable, or "soft," targets — a strong temptation for either side to make a sneak attack. The three-pronged forces that were later developed were believed to be more invulnerable and therefore creating a more stable balance. This triad consisted of: (1) ICBMs, which were protected in underground silos and so well dispersed that even a direct hit on a silo would destroy only one missile; also, ICBMs could be fired instantly because of their solid fuel; (2) SLBMs, which could be both concealed under water and be made mobile so that enemy submarines could never be sure of their exact location (SLBMs could remain "on station" under water for months at a time); and (3) bombers, a percentage of which would always be on alert, ready for a quick takeoff (the number could be increased during a crisis). But the main burden of deterrence was to fall on land- and sea-based missiles, not the bombers, which were drastically cut back in numbers.

From this perspective, then, arms control thinking (aided by the usual interservice rivalry) resulted in an *increase* in arms. A triad of deterrent forces would greatly complicate an aggressor's plans for a first strike; even if he succeeded in eliminating one leg or two legs of the triad, one or two would survive to retaliate fully and devastatingly. A triad would also enormously complicate the aggressor's ability to defend himself from assured destruction. In these circumstances, when most of the attacked party's second-strike forces would survive, what rationale for a first strike could there possibly be? A surprise attack could not sufficiently disarm the enemy to ensure one's survival and recovery.

Invulnerable second-strike forces possessed by both powers thus stabilize the mutual deterrent balance. Disarmament advocates often assert that arms and peace are incompatible and that the more arms deployed, the greater the threat to peace. Arms control proponents, by contrast, suggest that it is not the numbers of arms that are the key to the preservation of peace but the maintenance of stability.[15] Although fewer arms may contribute to that aim, an increase could also achieve that end. The critical criterion is that the weapons deployed be the "right" kind, that is, they contribute to the stability of the balance; the "wrong" kind will destabilize the balance and this is to be avoided. Bombers, for instance, were bad when they constituted the backbone of deterrence. The 1960s generation of missiles, however, were good. They were sufficiently inaccurate to hit silos so that each side's deterrent forces were safe from the other's first strike, but they were sufficiently accurate to hit large urban-industrial centers.

A second ingredient of arms control thinking was that cities and their inhabitants were to be left deliberately unguarded. Traditionally in war, nations try to protect their populations from attack. To attempt to do so in the nuclear age, however, would convey to the adversary that you are trying to seriously reduce his ability to destroy you; in turn, this might suggest to him that you may be thinking of launching a first or disarming strike against him. If your population is protected, and his retaliatory forces are largely destroyed in a first strike, the remaining crippled forces may no longer have the capacity to impose unacceptable damage upon you. In these circumstances, the side with the unprotected population would feel compelled to preempt. It is the mutual ability to destroy each other, often referred to as "mutual assured destruction," or MAD, that is at the heart of deterrence. Arms control thinking, then, rejects the charge that MAD is an irrational strategy. It is completely rational — indeed imperative — for both sides to leave their populations — the hostages — undefended. There can be no destabilizing of civil defense or antibomber and antimissile defenses to protect the population.

The key point is that while each nation's population is left undefended, it is in fact safe as long as its strategic forces remain invulnerable. Not people, but military hardware, needs to be protected. This, in turn, requires that the deterrer take not only the necessary measures to ensure his forces' invulnerability but also that the adversary not make his weapons accurate enough to overcome that invulnerability. Attacking cities does not require very accurate weapons because urban areas are large targets. Attacking missiles in silos or nuclear submarines in port, both small targets, require accurate warheads. Such counterforce weapons are to be foresworn because they would be destabilizing and again instill the fear of a first strike and create a mutual hair-trigger situation. To sum up: stable mutual deterrence requires invulnerable second-strike forces and vulnerable cities.

The third component of U.S. arms control thinking focused on the meaning of the term "balance." According to this mode of analysis, balance does not mean an approximately equal number of bombers and missiles. What is needed is a second-strike capability to destroy the other's society. When one has that, one has "sufficiency"; when both sides have the capability to retaliate, regardless of who strikes first, parity has been achieved.[16] The number of weapons and the mix between bombers, ICBMs, and SLBMs is a matter for each side to decide for itself and is likely to vary with its calculations of what it will take to accomplish this purpose. One factor influencing both sides is a general conservatism and tendency to be cautious. Large numbers of weapons are a reminder to the opponent that a sufficiently large retaliatory force is likely to survive a preemptive blow. There is reason to be cautious: A small force would presumably be easier to destroy in a first strike and would therefore be less of a deterrent to the opponent. Indeed a small force might tempt a strike. If both sides reduced their current huge arsenals to small forces (without an extensive inspection system in place), there would be an incentive to cheat and each side would keep a large enough missile capability to launch a successful disarming strike.

What about an upper limit? The term "overkill" would suggest that the real problem is that the United States and the Soviet Union have too many nuclear arms. What, it is asked, is the point of killing every Soviet man, woman, and child more than once? There are only a finite number of cities on both sides to target. The difficulty is deciding how much is enough. No one really knows. For the United States, is it the force structure it has built? After all, no war has started. Or could deterrence be implemented by half that force or a dyad instead of a triad? The answer cannot be known for certain unless war erupts. Then perhaps it can be said that the numbers and the mix of weapons did not suffice to deter aggression.

There are additional unknowns that make force level calculations difficult. Will all deterrent forces be operational at the time of an enemy attack? Not all nuclear submarines are on station or bombers on alert. How many of them may therefore be destroyed in the attack? How many of the surviving land-based missiles will be able to take off? How many will malfunction during flight? And how many missiles will miss their targets? Each power is likely to calculate the forces it needs for a second-strike somewhat differently, given its estimates of how invulnerable it thinks it is, how reliable it believes its deterrent forces to be, and how large its target list is.

These characteristics of American arms control thinking about deterrent strategy were logically deduced from the nature of nuclear weapons and the fundamental belief that their principal function was to deter a war, not fight one. The irrationality of nuclear war, the emphasis on deterrence, second strike, countervalue targeting, invulnerable offensive forces, and abstinence from population/industry defenses were all thought to be so obvious that American arms control proponents felt it was imperative for them to communicate these premises to the Soviet leadership. In the final analysis, stable mutual deterrence would be brought about best if the two superpowers cooperated, and this cooperation demanded a convergence of ideas. If the Soviets still held traditional military notions that regarded war as an instrument for realizing national objectives, population defense, and so on, they had to be disabused of them because such notions were anachronisms left over from an age when war was not suicidal. It was America's task to educate the Soviet Union on the realities of the nuclear era. The proponents of arms control not only believed that other cultures would come to accept American strategic ideas but they were optimistic that Soviet thinking and behavior could be changed. Educating the Russian leaders therefore was the fourth point of American arms control thinking.

This goal could be achieved in two ways. Speeches by

American leaders and congressional testimony would convey the ideas. Unilateral actions, such as shifting deterrence from primarily bombers to missiles, would be consistent with such ideas and convey to the Soviets that the United States was pursuing policies like these both to enhance its own security *and* Soviet security. But it was imperative that the Soviets follow our lead and pattern their forces and strategy on the American model. The other means of communicating American ideas on nuclear strategy was by means of bilaterally negotiated arms control agreements. In the wake of the 1962 Cuban missile crisis, such negotiations began and resulted in a number of agreements, ranging from a White House–Kremlin hotline to nuclear nonproliferation. Not until 1972, however, did the two superpowers conclude an agreement dealing with their strategic forces.

SALT I

The first Strategic Arms Limitation Talks (SALT) appeared to embody the American ideas of stable mutual deterrence: vulnerable cities and invulnerable second-strike forces.[17] SALT I encompassed two agreements. The first agreed to limit antiballistic missiles (ABM) to 200 for each side. The Soviets had deployed about 60 ABMs around Moscow, and it was possible that they might deploy them nationally to protect their cities. They believed that a weapon whose only purpose was to protect people's lives was a good weapon. In SALT I, however, they agreed to a low limit on ABMs so that the ABMs each side was allowed to deploy could not protect their populations. The United States, which had decided to go ahead and build its own ABM arsenal to match the Soviets, abandoned the ABM altogether after a further agreement in 1974, which reduced ABMs from 200 to 100. What this suggested was that both powers had surrendered the idea of defending their populations; the Soviets — and this was the critical point — apparently had accepted the American concept of mutual assured destruction.

In the second agreement the two powers agreed to freeze

their offensive missile forces for a period of five years. At the end of this time the expectation was that a longer-term set of lower and mutually agreed-upon ceilings on various types of strategic weapons would have been negotiated. The purpose was to reduce the Soviet first-strike threat to the United States. The freeze was an interim measure to give the United States and the Soviet Union time to negotiate. In the meantime American forces were frozen at 1,710 (1,054 ICBMs and 656 SLBMs) while the total Soviet number was frozen at 2,358 (1,618 ICBMs and 740 SLBMs), almost 40 percent higher than the American level. But these figures did not include either bombers, in which the United States held a 3 to 1 lead (about 450 to 150), or multiple warheads, which the United States had already begun to install on its missiles. These multiple independent reentry vehicles, or MIRVs, were originally intended to overcome a Soviet ABM system by saturating it. Enough warheads would then still be able to penetrate and inflict assured destruction, no matter how thick the ABM defenses were. When after Vietnam the Congress, reflecting the nation's antimilitary and isolationist mood, was in no mood to appropriate the funds for more missiles, the Nixon administration decided that by multiplying the warheads on missiles the United States could continue to match the Soviet missiles building program. (Not much thought was given to what would happen to the strategic balance when the Soviets, who had much bigger missiles, would MIRV as well, as they were permitted to do under SALT I.)

In any event, if bombers and MIRVs were added to the SALT numbers on offensive missiles, an approximate parity would be established. What was really believed to be important by arms control advocates at the time was the apparent convergence of American and Soviet strategic doctrines. The benefits were obvious: an end to the arms race (since when each power had enough forces to inflict assured destruction on the other neither would need more) and the eternal nature of deterrence (since neither would ever dare to attack the other).

There are a few more points about American thinking on

deterrence and arms control. First, it was consistent with the U.S. approach to foreign policy.[18] It was formulated by civilian "defense intellectuals," not — as one might have expected — by military officers.[19] From its premise that a nuclear attack on America could be avoided as long as the United States preserved its capacity to inflict unacceptable damage on the Soviet Union, other propositions followed: nuclear superiority was meaningless in an assured destruction environment; Soviet parity was acceptable since mutual deterrence would be most stable when each side had invulnerable second-strike forces; population protection was discouraged because defenses were a greater threat to peace than offensive weapons; and offensive weapons were to be used not to destroy the enemy's arms in order to reduce his ability to destroy the United States but to retaliate against the civilians living in cities. Weapons targeted against people reduced the risks of war while arms targeted against other arms raised the likelihood of war. All these axioms were contrary to traditional military logic: that military superiority is desirable; that the nation's population is to be defended; and that the aim of military strategy is to destroy the adversary's capability and impose one's will upon him. MAD seemed to be aptly named: Whoever had heard of a strategy whose philosophy was "killing people is good and destroying weapons is bad"?

Second, arms control logic fit the American way of thinking about peace and war: no war or total war. Peace was the normal state of existence. But once the United States had been attacked or provoked, it launched a punitive crusade against the aggressor to teach him a painful lesson for violating America's peace. The crusade was also an instrument of reform. By demanding the aggressor's unconditional surrender, eliminating his warlike regime, and democratizing his nation to make it peaceful, the United States was in fact seeking to eliminate power politics itself. The American way of war was one of total war, "a war to end all wars." Nuclear weapons and deterrent strategy were consistent with this American way of perceiving the world. The new weapons should suffice to deter an attack, since no nation would deliberately court suicide. Thus "a war to end all wars" would no longer have to be fought. MAD, a war-avoidance — not war-fighting — strategy was the best means to realize this long-sought goal in the nuclear age.

Third, arms control was characteristically American because of its central technological and apolitical orientation. The cause of strategic instability and a possible war was technological. So was the solution. It was simply a question of what kinds of weapon systems were deployed. The superpowers could create a stable deterrent structure that would promise an end to the arms race and provide eternal peace despite their political differences. Indeed, the whole structure of deterrence and stable mutual deterrence elaborated in the 1950s and 1960s by the defense intellectuals was thought to be logically deducible from the basic technical facts of a nuclear explosion. MAD was a politically neutral strategy; no other reasonable conclusions could be drawn. Fighting and winning wars was no longer a rational proposition; deterrence was the only feasible course; stabilizing mutual deterrence was therefore in the interests of both powers. Their cooperation was fundamental to achieving such an antinuclear suicide stance.

There was a kind of intellectual arrogance and naive optimism about this formulation: arrogance that the American way of thinking about nuclear strategy was the correct way and that U.S. strategic ideas were both timeless and universal; and optimism because once this way had been explained to the Soviet Union, its leaders would recognize their own strategic illiteracy and the benefits of "Americanizing" their strategy. This optimism in our own enlightenment and belief that it was this nation's task to educate Moscow was, however, to run into historic Russian ways of thinking.

The Nuclear Age and Soviet Strategy

Until Stalin's death in 1953, Soviet strategy canonized the Russian leader's conclusions about World War II, namely, that the Soviet Union had won because of certain permanently operating factors such as larger armies, superior morale and social systems, and greater war production; these were decisive in deciding the outcome of the war. Surprise attack was not decisive. Hitler's surprise attack on Russia in 1941, initially very successful, had been halted and defeated. Presumably, Stalin's lessons from that war applied to a surprise attack with atomic weapons. Of course, Stalin could hardly admit that an atomic first strike could be decisive. He had to play down the American advantage of an atomic monopoly while simultaneously urging his scientists to develop a Soviet atomic bomb. Thus the Soviet experience, as seen by Stalin, and shrewd diplomacy reinforced each another. The months following Hitler's invasion had been devastating, "more comparable to the loss from a nuclear assault than anything else experienced by a great power in modern times."[20] In 1941 the Soviets lost control of 40 percent of their population, 40 percent of their grain production, about 60 percent of their coal, iron, steel, and aluminum production, and almost 95 percent of certain critical military industries such as ballbearings. Militarily, they lost 4 million soldiers in dead, wounded, and prisoners and over two-thirds of their tanks and aircraft.[21] Yet the Soviet Union survived and triumphed in the end. Thus the question arises: Did Stalin's minimizing of the importance of a new weapon he did not have reflect his actual reading of World War II or was it simply a diplomatic tactic? He was certainly anxious to produce a Soviet bomb.

In any event, after Stalin's death, Soviet military doctrine was reexamined and adjusted to the new atomic era. The result was quite different than in the United States. The reason was that the Soviets distinguish between the political and military aspects of military doctrine.[22] The former focuses on the actual decision to *initiate* war; the latter, on *preparing* operational plans for the hostilities. This distinction between preventing war and waging it reflects a basic division of labor between the Communist party and the military. The issue of deterrence is a political matter to be decided by the Soviet Union's leaders. Consistently since Khrushchev succeeded Stalin (after an initial brief succession by Malenkov), Soviet leaders have stated their commitment to preventing a war rather than starting one. Khrushchev's view from 1956 on was that regardless of how a war would start, it would escalate to a nuclear one. However, he emphasized that war between capitalism and communism was no longer "fatally inevitable" as Lenin had once predicted. Subsequently, he reduced Soviet conventional forces and in 1959 gave priority to the newly created Strategic Rocket Forces.

The Focus on Preemption and Counterforce
Soviet military officers, by contrast, concentrated on war fighting if deterrence should fail because "the imperialists unleash it." In a complete reversal of Stalin's deemphasis on surprise attack, Russian officers upgraded its role.[23] The initial phase of an atomic war was critical. If the advantage of a surprise attack was so beneficial, the enemy would recognize that as well and therefore the Soviet Union had to seize the initiative and strike preemptively if war was about to erupt. Unlike Stalin, who had considered surprise as conferring only a transitory advantage and whose experience had been that of a war of attrition, the Soviet military after his death came to grips with strategy against an overseas (rather than continental) opponent who held a nuclear superiority. American military and civilian officials had already recognized the importance of a surprise attack. Pearl Harbor, six months after Hitler had taken Stalin by surprise, left a deep scar and the atomic bomb served to underline the importance of surprise attack in the nuclear era.

Soviet officers also downgraded the role of attacking the enemy's population and industrial centers. Whereas America's strategy was a retaliatory strike to destroy Russian society, the Soviet Union clung to a more traditional military strategy. In part, this reflected its reading of World War II in which the decisive factors, as in most wars, had been the destruction of the enemy's military capability. It was the defeat of the German Army and four years of hard fighting by the Red Army that had, in Soviet eyes, been chiefly responsible for the allied victory, not the American bombing of German cities and factories engaged in military production. The key strategic objective in war remained the defeat of the enemy's military forces. In part, the traditional approach also reflected the emphasis on the importance of preemption. To strike at cities would not prevent retaliation. But to strike at the opponent's strategic forces might degrade them and limit the damage from a subsequent retaliatory blow.

During the 1940s and 1950s, however, the Soviets did not have the capability to launch a preemptive strike at U.S. bomber bases. Soviet deterrence remained dependent mainly on its large army facing NATO. This army, supplemented by a large medium-range bomber force, held western Europe hostage while SAC held Russia's population hostage. Even several years after the shock of the first Soviet ICBM test in 1957, and at the time of the Cuban missile crisis in 1962, Russia had only 50 rather large missiles. Also, they were liquid-fueled and not protected in silos and therefore very vulnerable to an American first strike. The United States had over 200 missiles, protected by silos. By October 1966, about the time the American land-based deployment ended, the Soviets had only 340 ICBMs and 30 SLBMs. Thus, despite their preemption and counterforce planning, they had to be very careful about challenging the United States. They could not afford to risk escalating a crisis. As in Cuba, they had to desist and withdraw their missiles once Washington reacted to the attempt to change the status quo in the Caribbean. American nuclear strength set limits to Soviet "adventures."

But by the time the Nixon administration came into power in 1969, Soviet strategy did matter. First, because the Soviets under Brezhnev, recognizing the impact of U.S. nuclear superiority during the Cuban missile crisis, rapidly built up their ICBM force. From 340 in late 1966, the figure rose to 720 in 1967, 900 in 1968, and 1,060 in 1969. The smaller liquid-fueled SS-11, comparable in capability to the U.S. solid-fueled Minuteman, reached 850 in numbers by 1971, to which 180 were added later for a total of 1,030. In addition, there was the very large, or "heavy," SS-9 missile with its 20-25 megaton warhead. Clearly, the Soviet purpose was to attain parity with the United States, strengthen the Soviet Union, and not repeat the humiliation it had suffered in the Cuban missile crisis.[24]

Second, and more important, the reason Soviet strategy did matter in the 1970s was that contrary to MAD doctrine and American hopes for a convergence of goals, the Soviet military emphasized nuclear war fighting and winning.[25] The replacement of the 308 SS-9s with the huge SS-18 capable of carrying over 30 warheads each (but limited by SALT II to 10) and 360 SS-19s with six warheads each greatly concerned U.S. strategists, who saw them as "silo-busting" missiles or, in the language of the experts, they had a "hard target kill capability."

Each Soviet missile force, the 308 SS-18s *or* the 360 SS-19s,* was increasingly believed by the United States to be capable of destroying 80 to 95 percent of the Minuteman force by itself. The Soviets had three-quarters of their warheads on their ICBMs. The United States had three-quarters on SLBMs, but these were not counterforce weapons. Each SS-18, carrying eight to ten warheads, could attack four to five American ICBMs (the assumption being that with two accurate warheads the attacking side could be sure of destroying the opponent's hardened silo); an SS-19 with six warheads could "take out" three U.S. Minuteman missiles. One study concluded that "This meant that the Americans had more silos to shoot at with fewer ICBMs, and the Soviets had fewer silos to shoot at with more ICBMs. By 1982, the Soviet could, in principle, allocate about six warheads for each U.S. missile silo."[26] Another study noted:

> The United States currently [1985] has approximately 1,500 warheads deployed on [550] Minuteman IIIs; the U.S.S.R. has over 4,000 warheads deployed on SS-18s and SS-19s.

---

*In 1985 the CIA in a revised estimate said the SS-19 was not as accurate as believed earlier and that therefore the SS-19 was no longer considered a major threat to U.S. missile silos. The Pentagon has not publicly accepted this reevaluation.

The more than 1,000 U.S. ICBM silos could be targeted on a
2:1 basis and still leave the Soviets with more than 2,000 SS-18
and SS-19 warheads in reserve. In contrast, the more than 1,500
warheads on the Minuteman III could destroy only half of the
nearly 1,400 Soviet ICBM silos. Hence, the Soviet Union has
the potential to destroy the entire U.S. ICBM force with its
ICBM force; the United States does not.[27]

In fact, the command, control, communications, and intelligence (C³I) system* is even more vulnerable than ICBMs.
The physical destruction of satellites, or radars, or transmis-
sion towers for submarines and launch control centers for
ICBMs, or worse, Washington and the entire political leadership (referred to as "decapitation") raise the question of
whether anything more than a crippled retaliatory strike is
even likely in a situation in which C³I may not survive for more
than a few hours, if that, let alone several days or weeks.[28]

Soviet doctrine, with its emphasis on seizing the initiative
at the outset of a war, plus the Soviets' growing counterforce
capability, was thus a very worrisome matter to the United
States. Soviet ICBMs were clearly intended to limit the damage to the Soviet Union from American retaliation by destroying as much of the U.S. strategic forces and C³I as possible
before it could retaliate. One point needs reemphasis in this
context: Soviet strategic planning has shown no eagerness for
nuclear war. Quite the contrary. But it has assumed that deterrence was not foolproof, that it could fail, that contingency
planning had to cover that possibility, and that the best way to
deter war was to be ready to fight one. A strategy of retaliation
might not be enough; it might fail to deter at precisely the moment it was most needed — in a crisis.[29] The only way to deter
war was to have a "prewar fighting posture" and ability to

*The C³I is composed of satellite sensors, ground relay stations, early warn-
ing radar stations, plus a vast array of computers and other communication
links that would first note an attack, assess its size, warn the president,
secretary of defense, and chairman of the Joint Chiefs of Staff (collectively
referred to as the National Command Authority), transmit the orders to
retaliate and, if the conflict continues, control its conduct.

confront the potential aggressor with "annihilation" and "defeat."[30]

Moreover, Soviet doctrine combined a counterforce strategy and preemption with strategic defense. This included active defense, such as ground-to-air missiles against bombers, as well as passive defense, that is, civil defense. Shelters have reportedly been built to protect many of the party, military, and secret police leaders. The ABM deployment, of course, was limited by SALT I. The United States abandoned the ABM altogether after 1974 and optimistically assumed that the Soviet agreement to limit the ABM meant their acceptance of the stabilizing MAD strategy. But it is now widely believed that the Soviets wanted to eliminate the American ABM because they perceived it as a threat to their preemptive strike capability against the United States. Currently, however, the greater concern is that the Soviets might in the next decade deploy a network of phased-array radar that could be used in the battle management for a more extensive ABM system.[31] Thus after a massive first strike against U.S. ICBMs, the defense might be able to further reduce the destruction of a crippled U.S. retaliation strike.

This divergence of doctrine provided American conservative critics of SALT with sufficient ammunition to oppose the 1979 SALT II treaty. The goals of SALT II, shared by Presidents Nixon, Ford, and Carter, were, first, to provide for equal numbers of all strategic delivery systems (including bombers) and, second, to lower Soviet first-strike capability (although the United States had already made it clear that SALT III would try to lower the SALT II ceilings substantially). The equal ceilings for both powers were 2,400 strategic nuclear delivery systems, of which 1,320 could be MIRVed (and of these, 1,200 could be MIRVed ICBMs and SLBMs, the rest would be bombers carrying cruise missiles). This ceiling, which was to be lowered to 2,250 in 1981, affected only the Soviets since the United States would have had to build up to reach this level of missiles; of the 1,320 MIRVed launchers, no more than 820 could be ICBMs. The Soviets retained the 308 heavy missiles permitted them under SALT I. Despite the existence of majority support in the U.S. Senate for approval of the SALT II treaty, enough senators, mainly conservative, opposed the treaty because, they charged, the 820 MIRVed ICBMs would give the Soviet Union strategic superiority and a first-strike capability.[32]

The rationale for the SALT process had been to enhance the stability of mutual deterrence by limiting the threats to the survivability and effectiveness of strategic forces. In SALT I, this meant limiting the SS-9, but under SALT II, the Soviets would, according to the conservatives, retain such a large first-strike capability that the agreement represented a failure of the United States to accomplish its principal goal. Even some liberals opposed the treaty because its high ceilings were said to stretch the meaning of the word "limitation" too far. SALT, it was said, had merely legitimated all the offensive systems both sides possessed or were planning on deploying; the only deployment that had been limited was the ABM. (This was not a minor achievement, considering that its deployment would have given a major impetus to the offensive arms race. As it was, it was a key reason for the American MIRVing which, when it was not abandoned after the ABM limitation, led to the increasing vulnerability of the U.S. ICBM force.) More important in accounting for SALT II's defeat were two factors: (1) Soviet foreign policy behavior and its clear violation, as seen in the United States, of the spirit of détente and (2) the continuing rapid Soviet military growth not only in strategic weapons but in conventional arms. This massive military expansion across the board after the Soviets had achieved parity suggested that this expansion was to serve needs beyond simply defense. The building of a large surface navy appeared especially symbolic of a desire to extend Soviet influence beyond Eurasia.

Soviet Rhetoric versus Military Doctrine

In these circumstances, the gap between the Soviet political leaders' repetitive assertions that Soviet policy was defensive and the military's emphasis on victory in nuclear war was perceived in the United States to be "at best ambiguous, at worst threatening."[33] Yet Soviet political leaders' conclusions about nuclear war reflected those of their American counterparts. During the 1970s and early 1980s Khrushchev's successor, Leonid Brezhnev, frequently proclaimed statements such as "it is dangerous madness to try to defeat each other in an arms race, to count on victory in nuclear war." The initiation of a nuclear war could only be the act of one "who has decided to commit suicide," since retaliation was unavoidable. Brezhnev also denied that the Soviet Union was seeking military superiority with the aim of launching a first strike; he condemned such charges as "absurd and utterly unfounded." While he committed himself to preventing the reemergence of U.S. superiority, he and his successors all stressed that nuclear war represented a "danger to all mankind." Yuri Andropov, Brezhnev's immediate successor after Brezhnev died in 1982, said that nuclear war would be "fatal for mankind"; Konstantin Chernenko, who succeeded Andropov after he died a year and a half after succeeding Brezhnev, had already earlier proclaimed that nuclear weapons posed "a threat to the whole of civilization, even to life in our world." It was "criminal," he said, "to look upon nuclear war as a rational, almost legitimate continuation of policy."[34]

The Soviet political leadership thus appeared to accept the notions of deterrence and mutual vulnerability — notions at odds with the frequent references to victory in nuclear war put forth by Russian military officers. (Such military comments were heard less frequently after 1972.) In part, the new Soviet emphasis on the irrationality of nuclear war was to tone down the military views which, when quoted in the West, were a political liability. Thus the Soviets began to talk of nuclear war in terms acceptable in the West: deterrence, stability, and parity.[35] The other reason was that while the political leaders focussed on deterrence, the political dimension of Soviet military doctrine, the military's responsibility was confined to the operational or military-technical realm — preparing the armed forces for nuclear war and the plans for conducting it should deterrence fail because the "imperialists" had launched an attack. This meant that whereas in the United States, deterrence and war fighting were juxtaposed as mutually exclusive, in the Soviet Union the two were considered complementary. The Soviet force structure and strategy are designed to convince a would-be aggressor that a victory over the Soviet Union in a nuclear war is not possible. The Russian military has therefore "thought about the unthinkable" because of its traditional belief that a "nuclear war can be prevented only if the Soviet Union is prepared to wage one." There is no Soviet equivalent to the American theory of deterrence.[36] Nevertheless, the political and military aspects of Soviet military doctrine were not in fact that different from the American approach. The latter was characterized by a disjunction between the civilian strategists' declaratory doctrine, which emphasized deterrence and arms control to stabilize the deterrent equation, and SAC's operational planning, which always included strikes against military targets and, if necessary, a preemptive strike.

Notes

1. Bernard Brodie, *Strategy in the Missile Age* (Princeton, N.J.: Princeton University Press, 1959).

2. The Harvard Nuclear Study Group, *Living with Nuclear Weapons* (New York: Bantam Books, 1983), pp. 43–44; Gregg Herken, *Counsels of War* (New York: Alfred A. Knopf, 1985), p. 116.

3. Bernard Brodie, *The Absolute Weapon* (New York: Harcourt, Brace, 1946), p. 76. (Italics in original.)

4. David Alan Rosenberg, "The Origins of Overkill: Nuclear Weapons and American Strategy, 1945–1960," *International Security,* Spring 1983, pp. 14–15.

5. Norman Palmer, *Strategic Weapons,* rev. ed. (New York: Crane Russak, 1982), pp. 9–25; Herken, op. cit., p. 83.

6. David Alan Rosenberg, "'A Smoking Radiating Ruin at the End of Two Hours': Documents on American Plans for Nuclear War with the Soviet Union, 1954–55," *International Security,* Winter 1981/1982, p. 11. For U.S. assessments of its own vulnerability

during the 1950s and early 1960s, see Betts, Richard K., "A Nuclear Golden Age? The Balance Before Parity," *International Security*, Winter 1986–87, pp. 3–32.

7. In lieu of many, Michael Mandelbaum, *The Nuclear Question* (Cambridge, England: Cambridge University Press, 1979), Jerome H. Kahan, *Security in the Nuclear Age* (Washington, D.C.: The Brookings Institution, 1975), especially Part Two, and Lawrence Freedman, *The Evolution of Nuclear Strategy* (New York: St. Martin's Press, 1983).

8. Alain C. Enthoven and K. Wayne Smith, *How Much Is Enough?* (New York: Harper Colophon, 1972), pp. 175, 207.

9. Harold H. Brown, *Annual Report, Department of Defense, Fiscal Year 1979* (Washington, D.C.: U.S. Department of Defense, 1978), p. 55.

10. Carl Sagan, "Nuclear War and Climatic Catastrophe: Some Policy Implications," *Foreign Affairs*, Winter 1983/1984, pp. 257–292.

11. The nuclear winter thesis has been questioned scientifically by Stanley L. Thompson and Stephen H. Schneider, "Nuclear Winter Reappraised," *Foreign Affairs*, Summer 1986, pp. 981–1005; and strategically by Albert Wohlstetter, "Between an Unfree World and None," *Foreign Affairs*, Summer 1985, pp. 962–994.

12. Richard K. Betts, *Surprise Attack* (Washington, D.C.: The Brookings Institution, 1982), pp. 34–50.

13. Thomas C. Schelling and Morton H. Halperin, *Strategy and Arms Control* (New York: Twentieth Century Fund, 1961) remains the classic statement of what came to be the prevailing U.S. view on arms control; also Hedley Bull, *The Control of the Arms Race*, 2d ed. (New York: Frederick A. Praeger, 1965). For the spectrum of views on nuclear arms, U.S. defense policy, and relations with the Soviet Union, see Robert A. Levine, *The Arms Debate* (Cambridge, Mass.: Harvard University Press, 1963).

14. Albert Wohlstetter, "The Delicate Balance of Terror," *Foreign Affairs*, January 1959, pp. 211–234.

15. Michael Howard, *The Causes of War*, 2d ed. (Cambridge, Mass.: Harvard University Press, 1984), pp. 265–284.

16. David Holloway, *The Soviet Union and the Arms Race*, 2d ed. (New Haven: Yale University Press, 1984), p. 149.

17. John Newhouse, *Cold Dawn* (New York: Holt, Rinehart & Win-

ston, 1973); Thomas W. Wolfe, *The SALT Experience* (Cambridge, Mass.: Ballinger Publishing Company, 1979); and Garthoff, op. cit., pp. 127–198.

18. Colin S. Gray, "National Style in Strategy: The American Example," *International Security,* Fall 1981, pp. 21–48.
19. For a critique, see Fred Kaplan, *The Wizards of Armageddon* (New York: Simon & Schuster, 1983).
20. Raymond L. Garthoff, *Soviet Strategy in the Nuclear Age* (New York: Frederick A. Praeger, 1958), p. 90.
21. Ibid.
22. Douglas M. Hart, "The Nuclear Freeze and Soviet Perspectives on Nuclear War," in William J. Taylor, ed., *The Nuclear Freeze Debate* (Boulder, Colo.: Westview Press, 1983), pp. 172–173; Holloway, op. cit., pp. 29–35.
23. Herbert S. Dinerstein, *War and the Soviet Union* (New York: Frederick A. Praeger, 1959).
24. William G. Hyland, "The USSR and Nuclear War" in Barry Blechman, ed., *Rethinking the U.S. Strategic Posture* (Cambridge, Mass.: Ballinger, 1982), p. 52.
25. Richard Pipes, "Why the Soviet Union Thinks It Could Fight and Win a Nuclear War," *Commentary,* July 1977, pp. 21–34; and W. T. Lee, *Understanding the Soviet Military Threat: How CIA Estimates Went Astray* (New York: National Strategy Information Center, 1977).
26. Richard Smoke, *National Security and the Nuclear Dilemma,* 2d ed. (New York: Random House, 1987), p. 201. For the CIA's revised estimate of the SS-19s' accuracy, see *The New York Times,* July 19, 1985.
27. Robbin F. Laird and Dale R. Herspring, *The Soviet Union and Strategic Arms* (Boulder, Colo.: Westview Press, 1984), pp. 53–54.
28. Paul Bracken, *The Command and Control of Nuclear Forces* (New Haven, Conn.: Yale University Press, 1983) and Bruce G. Blair, *Strategic Command and Control* (Washington, D.C.: The Brookings Institution, 1985). Also see Richard Ned Lebow, *Nuclear Crisis Management* (Ithaca, N.Y.: Cornell University Press, 1987).
29. Benjamin Lambeth, "Uncertainties for the Soviet War Planner," *International Security,* Winter 1982/1983, p. 141.
30. L. Gouré, F. D. Kohler, and M. L. Harvey, *The Role of Nuclear*

Forces in Current Soviet Strategy (Miami, Fla.: Center for Advanced Studies, 1974), p. 5. Also see Derek Leebaert, ed., *Soviet Military Thinking* (Boston: Allen & Unwin, 1981), p. 86; and Joseph D. Douglas Jr. and Amoretta M. Hoeber, *Soviet Strategy for Nuclear War* (Stanford, Calif.: Hoover Institution Press, 1979).

31. Zbigniew Brzezinski, *Game Plan* (Boston: The Atlantic Monthly Press, 1986), pp. 108–109.

32. On the SALT II negotiations, see Strobe Talbott, *Endgame* (New York: Harper Colophon Books, 1980). For SALT II and the Senate, see Stephen T. Flanagan, "The Domestic Politics of SALT II: Implications for the Foreign Policy Process," in John Spanier and Joseph Nogee, eds., *Congress, the Presidency and Foreign Policy* (New York: Pergamon Press, 1981), pp. 44–76.

33. Holloway, op. cit., p. 54.

34. Quotes from Dan L. and V. Rebecca Strode, "Diplomacy and Defense in Soviet National Security Policy," *International Security,* Fall 1983, p. 91; Raymond L. Garthoff, *Detente and Confrontation* (Washington, D.C.: The Brookings Institution, 1985), pp. 771–785 and "Mutual Deterrence and Strategic Arms Limitation in Soviet Policy," *International Security,* Summer 1978, pp. 112–147.

35. Benjamin S. Lambeth, "Has Soviet Nuclear Strategy Changed?" in Roman Kolkowicz, ed., *The Logic of Nuclear Terror* (Boston: Allen & Unwin, 1987), pp. 211–230.

36. Holloway, op. cit., p. 33. Also see Dimitri K. Simes, "Deterrence and Coercion in Soviet Policy," *International Security,* Winter 1980/1981, pp. 80–93.

Nuclear Strategy in the Era of Parity

Why the Cold War Remained "Cold"

United States's operational planning for the implementation of deterrence showed a remarkable similarity to Soviet military planning. Early Strategic Air Command targeting favored hitting 100 urban centers "selected with the primary objective of the annihilation of population, with industrial targets incidental."[1] The Joint Chiefs of Staff's targeting plan, however, gave priority to destroying the Soviet capability to deliver atomic bombs to the United States, then to retarding the Soviet advance into western Europe, and only lastly, Soviet industry. Historically, military planning has always focussed on destroying the enemy's capability to wage war.* But General Curtis LeMay, SAC's commander, protesting the operational demands of the missions, was committed to one single knockout blow attacking all targets simultaneously. The forces at his command were growing, the Soviet air force was comparatively small, and after 1954 the hydrogen bomb made the idea of a single strike even more enticing. Consistent with this aim, LeMay reportedly sought the development of a single bomb powerful enough to destroy the entire Soviet Union. Preventive war was ruled out from the beginning by President Truman but SAC did not rule out the possibility of a preemptive strike.

The atomic age posed an obvious dilemma: If the United States wanted to avoid a Soviet first strike, could it avoid considering preempting? In the bomber era, American intelligence calculated that it would have several days, if not weeks, of warning because of the time it would take the Soviets to prepare for a strike against the United States. Just what would constitute an unambiguous warmomg of Soviet readiness to attack was never clarified. However, after the Soviets exploded their first thermonuclear device in 1955 President Eisenhower, very much aware of the nuclear dilemma, had seri-

*One might add that it has also been part of the Western tradition not to target noncombatants. Although this tradition has been increasingly violated, especially in this century, targeting civilians still causes bouts of conscience, if not charges of crimes against humanity. See George Quester's excellent chapter, "Cultural Barriers to an Acceptance of Deterrence" in Roman Kolkowicz, ed., *The Logic of Nuclear Terror* (Boston: Allen & Unwin, 1987), pp. 82–108.

ous misgivings about a preemptive counterforce strike. Soviet hydrogen bombs could inflict enormous damage on the United States even if only a few bombers survived an American first strike. After 1957 the appearance of Soviet ballistic missiles with their ability to strike in minutes made a U.S. preemptive attack even less likely. Now the fear was of a *Soviet* first strike; their ICBMs would make it difficult just to get U.S. bombers into the air, let alone fly to the Soviet Union to locate and destroy the missiles before they were fired. (The U.S. Navy now recommended that since a U.S. disarming strike was impossible and U.S. land-based bombers were increasingly vulnerable, thus inviting attack, the country needed a secure second-strike force — which just happened to be the Navy's new nuclear submarines.[2]) For all of the counterforce targeting before 1960, the fact was that mutual deterrence was in place because the bombs were so utterly destructive that attacks would cause enormous population and urban damage.

A strategy of avoiding cities and limiting nuclear war to military targets was, nevertheless, seriously considered once more by the incoming Kennedy administration. The United States, declared its Secretary of Defense,

> has come to the conclusion that to the extent possible, basic military strategy in a possible general war should be approached in much the same way that more conventional military operations have been regarded in the past. That is to say, principal military objectives . . . should be the destruction of the enemy's military forces, not his civilian population . . . giving the possible opponent the strongest possible imaginable incentive to refrain from striking our own cities.[3]

But the administration soon dropped the idea of a counterforce attack. It concluded that the weapons then available were not accurate enough and McNamara did not like the first-strike implications of a counterforce strategy. Further, in his opinion, the generals would use it to ask for ever-more weapons to hit a growing list of targets. By contrast, cities were easy to hit, and, given their finite number, this required only a limited force and a limited investment of money. Mutual assured destruction (MAD) became official U.S. strategy.

Deterrence Credibility and a U.S. War-Fighting Strategy

The emergence of strategic parity plus the capability to multiply warheads and enhance their accuracy led to a reexamination of the MAD strategy, since accurate MIRVs permitted both sides to think again about counterforce or disarming strikes against each other. While each had missiles with single warheads, a first strike made little sense because missiles were initially inaccurate; even later, after the accuracy of their guidance systems had improved, neither superpower had deployed the 2:1 numerical superiority required. The SALT I 1,054 (United States) to 1,398 (Russia) ratio did not endanger American ICBMs, the most accurate leg of the triad. A Soviet disarming strike would leave enough American ICBMs to destroy the Soviet Union in a second strike. But the multiplication and increasing accuracy of warheads once more allowed both powers to think of using nuclear weapons to strike a quick and overwhelming counterforce blow.

One of the ironies of American strategic thinking is that having sought to "Americanize" Soviet strategy, it ended by patterning itself after Soviet strategy in its concern with war fighting.[4] This occurred gradually during the 1970s and early 1980s, for two reasons. First was the emergence of U.S.–Soviet strategic parity. Deterrence had become symmetrical. The United States could threaten the Soviet Union with annihilation, but the Russians could now also annihilate America. The threat of massive retaliation, which was at the heart of the deterrent strategy, was therefore losing its credibility. Thus the central question about nuclear deterrence was raised again: If deterrence should ever fail, how should the United States respond? As early as 1971, President Nixon said:

> I must not be — and my successors must not be — limited to the indiscriminate mass destruction of enemy civilians as the sole possible response to challenges. This is especially so when

that response involves the likelihood of triggering nuclear attacks on our own population.[5]

The end result, or so it was implied, might well be self-deterrence unless the United States had the capability to fight a "limited nuclear war."

The second reason for the U.S. shift to nuclear war fighting was the option of more discriminating targeting due to the increasing accuracy of land-based missile warheads. With accurate guidance systems, it was possible to zero in on missile silos located some distance from large concentrations of population.* Counterforce targeting, by deliberately avoiding cities, therefore seemed to hold out the possibility that nuclear war no longer had to mean a nation's self-destruction. A counterforce exchange, one which would presumably not escalate into an all-out war, might kill more people than in past wars (American estimates range from 2 to 20 million in both countries depending on the type of attack launched),[6] but these totals fell far short of annihilation.

There were two situations that administrations from President Nixon on worried about. One was that strategic parity might tempt the Soviets to launch a first strike in a crisis. More specifically, the concern was that the Soviets, possessing hard target-killing ICBMs, might launch them against American ICBMs and airfields. The other was that deterrence might eventually fail as a result of irrational behavior, escalation, or miscalculation. Would the Soviets not be deterred, as in the past, by the threat of massive nuclear retaliation from American submarines? The answer was no because SLBMs were inaccurate and useful only against large targets such as cities. If the United States did retaliate against Russian cities, the Soviet Union could use its remaining ICBMs and SLBMs to strike once more — this time against American cities. This was the nightmare vision to which President Nixon had alluded: the threat of a Soviet *third* strike might deter an American *second*

---

*In the United States, nuclear forces were generally some distance from urban areas; this is less true in the Soviet Union.

strike. As long as U.S. cities remained hostages to a Soviet attack, a president might not retaliate. In fact, the Soviets would not even have to launch their missiles in an initial strike. In a situation where they had accurate warheads and the United States had mainly anti-city ones, just the Soviet threat of a strike might compel Washington to comply with Moscow's demands. The future was one of Soviet nuclear blackmail — "Cubas-in-reverse."

It was in this context that American administrations for over a decade favored the development of the MX (Missile Experimental), renamed Peacekeeper by President Reagan. Its advantages were claimed to be twofold: It was mobile so it would not be, as the Minuteman, vulnerable to Soviet attack and with 10 accurate warheads, it could pose the kind of counterforce threat the Soviet SS-18s and 19s posed to the U.S. ICBMs. Its purpose was to deter a limited Soviet strike on U.S. ICBMs and, if that were not feasible, to deter a nuclear escalation and, hopefully, terminate hostilities before the war got out of control. In the era of parity, the United States needed a whole range of options to different kinds of Soviet challenges. A capability to destroy Soviet cities was no longer sufficient to deter limited strikes. After the initial counterforce exchanges, the remaining capability to obliterate each other's cities would give each side the incentive to end the war quickly before it escalated. A counterforce capability was therefore needed to *supplement* the nation's countervalue capability. The ability to fight a limited nuclear war would once more restore the credibility of U.S. deterrence. War fighting was no longer seen as an alternative to deterrence. As Secretary of Defense Caspar Weinberger said in 1986,

> Our "warfighting" capability to defeat an attack and restore the peace is therefore not something separate from our strategy of deterrence. In fact, it forms the foundation of effective deterrence.[7]

The MAD Advocates' Response
MAD advocates rejected this conclusion for a number of rea-

sons.[8] First, if administrations really believed that nuclear war could be fought and society would survive, they might be more likely to risk war. And while 5 to 25 million dead was preferable to 100 million or more, the lower figures "can only be considered 'limited' by comparison with those that might result from a direct nuclear attack on urban-industrial areas"; moreover, such figures also probably underestimated the actual number of people who would die in the long run.[9] In any event, the threat of mutual assured destruction remained the most effective deterrent to war.

Second, once both sides had first-strike weapons, they could not in a crisis afford to sit back and retaliate only if struck. Each would feel compelled to preempt lest it be caught napping. Indeed, the Reagan decision to place MX in silos intensified this compulsion "to use them or lose them."* The very fact that the Soviets might not believe that the MX was to be used in a second-strike might force them to launch a disarming strike. And the United States, knowing that, might feel that it had better beat the Soviets to the draw. Thus the crisis instability of the bomber era was revived in the age of accurate MIRVs, and the momentum set in motion by a limited nuclear exchange would *inevitably* escalate into a full-scale nuclear war.

Even worse, C³I was so vulnerable to attack that the means of controlling the strategic forces would not survive more than a short time after a Soviet strike. Instead of a conflict in which nuclear weapons are used selectively against nonurban military targets, in relatively small numbers and over a period of weeks or longer, the United States must recognize that "the limited nuclear war-fighting option is a chimera, and that policies which depend upon the ability to maintain escalation control of a nuclear exchange are ultimately incredible."[10] Indeed, communication networks are so vulnerable that it has been asserted that U.S. strategy, like Soviet strategy, has no choice

---

*Congress for this reason limited the administration's request for 100 MXs to 50; in order to receive 50 more, the administration in late 1986 proposed placing MX on railroad cars in order to make an attack upon them harder in a crisis.

but to preempt.[11] Finally, keeping a conflict limited required Soviet cooperation, but Moscow officially rejected the idea of limited nuclear options (LNO). All in all, the critics charged, LNO weakened deterrence and might well bring on an all-out nuclear war.[12]

Are the Soviets Risk-Takers or Minimizers?

A lot of polemics were exchanged between those who continued to believe in the old deterrent strategy and the advocates of limited nuclear war. The latter characterized the former as irrational because they believed that the MAD strategy was still credible in the age of parity, while proponents of MAD dismissed those who articulated a counterforce strategy as virtual warmongers.[13] Ironically, neither side paid much attention to actual Soviet behavior, something obviously quite relevant for an evaluation of these competing versions of deterrence. The fact was that Soviet foreign policy behavior reflected little of the daring that was attributed to it by those who claimed that in a situation of strategic parity the Soviet leadership might risk a limited strike in the belief that there would be no U.S. retribution. Theoretically, that was a genuine option. In reality, Soviet policy has on the whole been cautious and not prone to taking large risks.[14] Ominous rhetoric and constant opportunism aside, the Soviet political leaders have used force only where they have judged their stakes to be vital — so critical to their security that they saw no practical alternative to intervention — where the likelihood of U.S. intervention was minimal, and where the prospects of quick success at relatively moderate costs were high. Such a *risk-minimizing* strategy has been pursued only in eastern Europe, on its southern border in Afghanistan and, briefly in local clashes, along the Sino-Soviet border in 1969; and only in Afghanistan did the Soviets miscalculate. Even in Hungary (1956) and Czechoslovakia (1968), where the intervention was perceived as a necessity if these states were not to defect from the Warsaw pact, the Soviet leaders hesitated. Despite their overwhelming military power and the unlikely possibility of American intervention in the Soviet sphere of influence, they deliberated at length, changing their minds several times as they calculated the risks and costs, as well as gains and losses.[15]

The Soviets did not intervene in Yugoslavia in 1948 after Stalin "ex-communicated" Tito, or later in Romania when it showed increasing independence on foreign policy issues, or in Albania when it moved closer to China, or in Poland in 1980–1981 where the regime's authority was being undermined. All these states are close to the Soviet Union, if they do not border it.

Soviet behavior then, as noted earlier, reflects an awareness that a nuclear war will be catastrophic. Quite apart from their memories of Russia's bare survival in World War II and the tremendous cost in lives paid for the victory over Germany, Russian military experience is such that there seems to be a greater awareness of the "frictions of war," that war plans look fine on paper but are subject to Murphy's Law ("If things can go wrong, they will") within hours of the breakout of war. In Soviet operational discussions there are so many repeated warnings of a "misplaced belief in the prospect of an easy victory"[16] that it is dubious that Moscow really "thinks it could fight and win a nuclear war." Operational planning may give the impression of utter certainty, and phrases like "fighting and winning a nuclear war" seem to suggest that it can actually be done. But wise officers and political leaders know that carrying out war plans entails unexpected problems.[17] It is one thing to calculate on a computer that U.S. ICBMs are highly vulnerable, but operationally it is quite another matter to achieve an 80 to 95 percent kill rate.

If — and that is an enormous if — anything goes wrong with a comprehensive preemptive strike, the penalty is devastating: possible extinction. After all, neither superpower has ever launched hundreds of missiles at about the same time to hit targets thousands of miles away in silos. Therefore, neither can have any experience upon which to base any confidence about a successful disarming strike. Before the Soviets can feel confident about carrying out a successful first strike, they must be able to plan and execute a virtually perfect plan. Yet there are simply too many unknowns: the reliability of ICBMs and warheads; their accuracy on a north-south course which involves flying over the North Pole (both powers have tested them only on an east-west course); and the ability to coordinate such a large-scale attack so that each warhead hits its target after flying over thousands of miles at the exact second it is supposed to do so. The Soviets must also believe that the American missiles will still be in their silos when the Soviet warheads arrive. However, there is the possibility that the United States will launch-under-attack and that the silos will be empty. Indeed, given the fact that C³I is even more vulnerable than the ICBMs, U.S. strategists will have every incentive to launch. Furthermore, the Soviets must believe that an American president would rather surrender than order a retaliatory strike with SLBMs and any ICBMs as well as bombers that escaped destruction. After all, the president may be extremely angry, act before he knows the attack was a limited one, believe that the war is bound to escalate anyway, or think a major retaliation will limit another Soviet strike. In these circumstances, would the Soviet leaders really risk a first strike in what former Secretary of Defense Harold Brown has called "a cosmic roll of the dice"? The fact is that the vulnerability of U.S. land-based missiles is more theoretical than real.

Americans alarmed about Russian strategy have often cited the Soviet Union's losses of over 20,000,000 people in World War II as evidence that Soviet society was able to survive despite an over 12 percent loss of population. They have argued that a comparable loss would be approximately 30 million and that if Soviet strategy disarmed the United States in a first strike it could hold retaliatory losses below that figure because of Soviet civil defense measures.[18] These arguments seem specious. Stalin did everything he could do to appease Hitler to avoid an attack; he did not attack Germany. Furthermore, Soviet losses were spread over a four-year period, and the tremendous devastation is still memorialized everywhere and constantly with enormous statues and eternal flames. It is inculcated into every new Russian generation, including visits by school children to memorials and young honor guards at these memorials. Thus it is more likely that the memories of World War II will reinforce Soviet reluctance to risk all-out nuclear war with a strike against ICBMs. Indeed, if war is a continuation of policy by other means, what political aim is worth the risk of obliteration? Nuclear war is the negation of policy.

This is especially so if one critical factor normally neglected in American military analyses of Soviet strategy is taken into account: the multinational composition of the Soviet Union. The fact that the Great Russian and ethnic Slavs are becoming a minority is often noted in terms of its political consequences but not its impact on Soviet calculations of whether to risk a nuclear strike against the United States. An American attack on the Soviet Union, even a counterforce one, would result in a disproportionate number of Great Russians dead relative to their percentage of the total population (because half of the ICBM fields are in western Russia, some near large population centers). This would threaten the Great Russians' control of the Communist party plus the governmental and military-security police bureaucracies. As the Congress' Office of Technology Assessment has perceptively noted, the survival of the Soviet state would be at stake:

> The attack could cause "derussification." The U.S.S.R. is a nation of nationalities, of which the Great Russians — who dominate politics, industry, and much else — comprise about 48.5 percent of the population. Most Great Russians live in cities, so an attack would reduce their numbers and influence. Derussification could weaken Great Russians' control of the U.S.S.R. with unforeseeable consequences.[19]

Thus Soviet foreign policy remains anxious to avoid nuclear war and opportunistic and incremental in its search for expanding its influence.

Nor is it surprising, moreover, that Soviet military writings since 1977 have stressed that under the nuclear umbrella, a long conventionally fought war might be feasible again. Given the Soviet and Warsaw pact edge in manpower and great superiority in the numbers of tanks, armored vehicles, self-propelled artillery, and the like, the possibility of a Soviet *Blitzkrieg* (a war conducted with lightninglike speed) against NATO — and if that did not work, an attrition strategy — meant that a conventional war might once more become a "continuation of policy by other means."[20] Whereas earlier the Soviets had stated that a conflict that started conventionally would quickly escalate to nuclear war, now the Soviets talked of "general conventional war," which might encompass Europe, the Middle and Far East, involve as many countries as World War II, and last "over many years." In 1981, the Soviet military carried out the first all-conventional exercise since 1960. Soviet nuclear forces were now relegated to a primary retaliatory role; that is, their main purpose was to inhibit American/NATO escalation.[21] This posed a major problem for the deterrence the United States had extended to its European allies in 1949.

NATO versus the Warsaw Pact

It may be that the trend toward more warheads and greater accuracy in guidance systems allowed the United States to design a more traditional strategy; it may also be that in an age of strategic parity it made sense to have more options that just suicide-or-surrender in case of a limited strike on the U.S. ICBMs, as unlikely as that possibility really was. But if there has been one overwhelming reason for a U.S. counterforce strategy, it has been the defense of western Europe. The Soviet leaders would still have to fear that an American president in response to any strike against U.S. territory might respond with an attack, even on Soviet cities. Whether he would risk the destruction of the United States in response to an attack on America's European allies was less certain. This is the reason why the deterrence that the United States extended to its European allies against a Soviet attack has been declining in credibility since the late 1950s. But not until the 1970s did it become a critical issue.

Extending U.S. Deterrence

How has the United States in the past four decades attempted to deter a Soviet attempt to invade western Europe? First, it signed the NATO treaty in 1949, thereby clarifying to Moscow that Washington regarded western Europe as vital to its security interests. Second, it sent four American divisions to Europe in 1951 to reinforce the U.S. NATO commitment. If the Red Army were to invade western Europe, American soldiers would be killed; this, in turn, would trigger the SAC. Thus, just in case Moscow did not believe that the United States really would risk war to defend western Europe, Washington removed the doubt.

As Europe recovered economically, it began to mobilize its armed forces. But NATO never matched the Red Army's strength. At first, that was because Europe was economically shattered; later, the European nations concentrated on their individual economic growth, the building of what were to become extensive welfare states and the Common Market. By the late 1960s Europe's economy was competing strongly with that of its protector. More important, western Europe did not see the necessity of or want to mobilize expensive larger forces, especially armies. There was no need to do so because America's nuclear superiority at that time meant that the Soviets could not afford to risk an invasion. America's nuclear weapons were a cheap substitute for European (and U.S.) manpower. Thus Europe got its defense on the cheap. To make up for the imbalance of ground forces, the United States armed its troops with tactical or battlefield nuclear weapons. So why worry? But the time for worry did come. The Soviet ICBM test and first Sputnik launching in 1957 suggested that the time was nearing when the Soviet Union would acquire sizable intercontinental-range forces to hit the United States and make massive retaliation mutual. While America had its atomic monopoly and later its strategic superiority, defending Europe was considerably less costly than a Russian attack would have been for the Soviet Union. But now, defending its European friends might cost America its national existence.[22]

Deterrence was therefore losing some of its credibility; at the very least, a degree of uncertainty hung over the American commitment. As one means of preventing such an erosion, the United States has repeatedly articulated a counterforce strategy since the early 1960s. Inasmuch as a counterforce exchange would allegedly avoid risking its survival, the U.S. commitment to defend its allies was supposed to remain credible in Moscow's eyes. While the Kennedy administration soon abandoned counterforce for mutual assured destruction, counterforce came back in the 1970s during the Nixon and Carter administrations as technology made it a feasible strategy.

As noted earlier, the United States had already proposed a more flexible strategy for the defense of western Europe in the 1960s. The Europeans should raise larger conventional forces; only if such a conventional defense failed would the alliance first use tactical nuclear arms. This was not only to contain the Red Army and its allies but also to warn Moscow that if it did not desist, the United States would use its strategic nuclear forces to destroy the Soviet Union, if there were no other choice.

However, this stance only added to the Europeans' reluctance to raise larger conventional forces. From the American perspective, the idea was to avoid an all-out nuclear war if deterrence failed and then limit the subsequent fighting to a conventional conflict confined to Europe. But from the European perspective, defense held no interest after two destructive and exhausting wars in this century. War avoidance was Europe's goal. The Soviets would be deterred only by the fear of American nuclear retaliation against their homeland. If NATO's smaller armies could not stem the advance of the Warsaw pact forces, then NATO would have to quickly resort to its tactical nuclear arms as an equalizer. Once used, these tactical weapons — now also available to the Red Army — would inevitably lead to an all-out nuclear war. The desire to avoid this was presumably what deterred the Soviets from attacking. Thus,

> a permanent inferiority in conventional forces, originally seen as dangerous, came to be viewed as strategically useful to the extent that any large-scale Soviet invasion would inevitably lead to U.S. nuclear weapons being used, simply because European conventional forces were not meant to fight a prolonged "large-scale war."[23]

Deterrence would therefore remain effective in a situation of NATO's conventional inferiority. On the other hand, the Europeans feared that a conventional defense would suggest that the American pledge to respond to a Soviet invasion with a nuclear strike against the Soviet Union was no longer credible. And if the Soviets really thought that Europe's defense was becoming uncoupled from the American deterrent, they might be tempted to risk an invasion.

Soviet Military and Political Aims

While NATO's problem from the beginning was essentially the conventional superiority of the Red Army and eastern European divisions, the Soviet problems were quite different. Unlike the western Europeans who had asked the United States for assistance to balance Soviet power, the countries of eastern Europe had no choice. Soviet domination was imposed upon them. One reason for the large size of the Warsaw pact forces was to preserve this Soviet order in eastern Europe. Soviet divisions were used repeatedly to quell revolts (East Germany in 1953, Hungary in 1956, and Czechoslovakia in 1968) or threaten intervention (Poland in 1956 and Poland 1980–1981 before the *Polish* army in fact took over power). Soviet force calculations must also be influenced by the possibility of uprisings and resistance in eastern Europe in case of a war with NATO. The numerical superiority of the Warsaw pact forces, in any event, does not look quite as formidable when it is recalled that slightly more than half the alliance's divisions are non-Soviet. How reliable most of these eastern European divisions would be in a war with NATO remains a question mark.

The Warsaw pact's large forces, however, were obviously an effective instrument not only to deter a NATO attack (it is hard to believe that the Soviets, looking at NATO forces, took that possibility seriously) but, more important, to threaten an invasion of western Europe. Russia has historically been a Eurasian power with the army as the senior service. After 1945, she simply did not have the means to come to grips with an enemy protected by several thousand miles of water. Even when she gained such a capability, the first generation of Soviet intercontinental bombers was not very good and not many were built. While the Soviet ability to hit the United States and hold America's population hostage was minimal for the first decade of the Cold War, the Soviet army was a most persuasive means of holding America's allies hostage. But the army plus a very large force of medium-range bombers, supplemented by intermediate range missiles after 1959, had at least four other objectives after holding western Europe hostage became less important after Soviet strategic forces had been built up.[24]

The first was to target America's strategic forces, most of which during the 1950s were deployed overseas around the Eurasian continent, including western Europe. Second, after the United States in the 1960s came to rely principally on intercontinental-range forces based in the United States, the Soviets remained concerned about America's forward based systems (FBS) in Europe. While the role of these weapons in the defense of western Europe was defined by Washington as tactical, the Soviets defined them as strategic. Anything that could hit the Soviet Union was considered to be strategic (Soviet weapons that could hit targets in western Europe from Russia were tactical, however, by Soviet definition since they could not reach the United States!). That this forward based system had only a limited capacity relative to the U.S.-based strategic forces' enormous power to destroy the Soviet Union was beside the point.

The third reason for maintaining sizable Soviet regional strategic forces against Europe (more recently called "Euro-strategic") was that the British and French developed their own national nuclear forces. Initially composed of bombers, later mainly SLBMs, these forces were tiny compared with the strategic forces the superpowers developed. But as MIRVing began, the growth of these European deterrents, especially the French one, made them more formidable. Moscow also had to be concerned about a growing Chinese nuclear capability and threat in Asia.

A fourth reason for Russia's regional strategic forces was political: to pressure or intimidate western Europe into a more accommodating mood, if not into neutralism, and drive the United States out of Europe. As early as the 1948 Berlin blockade, the Soviets had sought to use their conventional military superiority in Europe to strangle the western powers in their half of the city. From 1958 to 1962, the Soviet numerical advantage on the ground plus medium-range bombers was supplemented by Khrushchev's claim that the Soviet Union was mass-producing ICBMs. This turned out to be an enormous bluff but that was not known until a series of potentially very dangerous confrontations had occurred in Berlin from 1958 to 1962 when, with the end of the Cuban missile crisis, the Berlin crisis faded away. After 1964, of course, the Soviets launched their drive to catch up and overtake the United States in ICBMs and SLBMs.

It was in this situation of conventional superiority and strategic parity that in 1976–1977 Moscow deployed an intermediate-range missile, the SS-20. That deployment demonstrated how much the political situation in Europe had changed as a result of parity. The Soviet rationale for deploying the SS-20 was the need to modernize Soviet intermediate-range missiles aimed at western Europe. The older missiles, large, liquid-fueled, slow to fire, and vulnerable to a U.S. strike, were to be replaced by mobile, solid-fuel missiles, each armed with three warheads. As a better missile with more accurate warheads and less vulnerable to an American preemption, its deployment for an older, less stable system seemed justified. Regardless of whether modernization was in fact the only reason for the replacement of the older missiles, as the Soviets claimed, the Europeans, especially the West Germans, tended to attribute the SS-20 deployment to more ominous motives.

Moscow's Missiles as Political Weapons

In the old asymmetric deterrent balance in which the United States held the Soviet population hostage and the Russians held the Europeans hostage, American strategic power had neutralized not only the growing Soviet intercontinental capabilities but also stalemated the Warsaw pact armies. But symmetrical deterrence changed all this and the credibility of America's NATO commitment, initially raised by the Soviet ICBM tests in 1957, was now raised in a starker and more agonizing fashion. First, the superpowers' deterrent forces neutralized each other. Second, Soviet conventional forces, having been upgraded, especially in quality, retained their superior offensive capabilities. Third, the emerging imbalance in intermediate nuclear forces (INF) meant that NATO, outmatched in the size and capabilities of its conventional forces, would be discouraged from escalating hostilities by resorting to tactical nuclear arms. Why would NATO resort to them when the inevitable Soviet nuclear response would inflict greater destruction on Europe than a conventional war? A credible deterrent could not be based on an incredible action. Suicide, Henry Kissinger had once said, is not a believable policy. Thus the prospect of a failure to deter a Soviet attack on western Europe appeared to rise.

The Europeans, therefore, asked the United States to deploy a counterbalancing intermediate-range missile in western Europe.[25] In response, the United States offered 108 Pershing II missiles, each equipped with one accurate warhead, and 464 subsonic ground-launched cruise missiles (GLCMs). The critical element was that both missiles had the range to hit the western part of the Soviet Union. The Pershing could do so in just a few minutes. No American nuclear-armed missiles deployed in Europe after 1963 had that capability. Why was this so important when U.S. strategic forces already targeted the Soviet Union? The answer was that a new means had to be found to couple Europe's defense to the U.S. strategic forces in order to reassure the Europeans. Initially, this linkage had been the U.S. ground forces. But now Europeans were quite unsure that even if American soldiers were killed, the United States would unleash its strategic forces while America itself remained immune to attack. The Pershings and GLCMs were to restore faith in this coupling: Once American missiles hit the Soviet Union, even if these missiles came from western Europe rather than the United States, the Soviets would hardly limit their retaliation to western Europe; they would hit back at the United States itself. This would, of course, unleash a U.S. retaliatory strike. The Soviets would thus continue to have to choose between triggering World War III and not attacking Europe.

What the Europeans themselves would contribute to the deterrent capability of the alliance, however, was an issue the Europeans preferred not to face. Western Europe had, in a sense, come to "the end of the road." As the Kennedy administration had foreseen, the answer to this nuclear stalemate was sizable conventional forces to hold the Red Army without risking nuclear escalation. But "the end result of 20 years of Soviet military buildup and 20 years of voluntary European blindness," said one astute French observer, "is that Europe finds itself in 1982 back to square one, that is, with its only serious option being a buildup of its conventional forces to a sufficient level so as to prevent Moscow from being tempted to call the nuclear bluff."[26]

But the Europeans, whose combined population, technology and wealth far exceeded that of the Soviet Union, remained unwilling to raise those armies. Europe had become used to leaving its defense largely in American hands, as symbolized by the series of American generals who commanded NATO's forces.[27] In the process, many Europeans no longer felt responsible for their own defense (the French, having withdrawn from NATO's command, were the exception); indeed, after a generation of peace, many took that peace for granted. Presumably, it was not linked to the military balance.[28] Rather than make an effort to raise larger conventional forces, European governments fell back on their only alternative: nonmilitary policies toward the Soviet Union. They tried to preserve their own détente, despite Afghanistan, the squashing of Solidarity in Poland, the continued Soviet military growth, and the SS-20 deployment facing NATO.

Simultaneously, as the time for the U.S. deployment of Pershings and GLCMs approached, as noted earlier, huge crowds throughout most of western Europe (except France) took to the streets to protest the American missiles.[29] What occurred was a "battle of the streets" in which massive demonstrations in the streets and around U.S. bases tried to reverse NATO's 1979 decision for a U.S. counterdeployment, a decision endorsed by the British, West German, and Italian governments. In the first two countries that decision had been endorsed by their respective electorates in the reelections of the British Conservative party and West German Christian Democrats. (Both governments, however, also favored Europe's separate détente.)

The result was a contest of political will. Moscow was determined to prevent any U.S. counterdeployment. It claimed that with French and British strategic forces and American FBS, a balance already existed in Europe, that the U.S. Pershings and GLCMs would upset that balance, and that what Washington was really doing was an end-run around the recently agreed-to SALT II ceilings on strategic systems. Yet Moscow deployed well over 400 SS-20s with over 1300 warheads (about 500 targeted against Asia) to zero for the United States.

The western European governments, as well as the United States, continued to view the Soviet deployment as an offensive political maneuver. The deployment of the SS-20s was seen as an attempt to drive a wedge between the United States and the Europeans and intimidate the latter.[30] The Soviet deployment, which came as détente with the United States was collapsing, was consistent with past Soviet aims in the repeated Berlin crises: to weaken American influence by driving the United States out of western Europe and to frighten the west Europeans into a more accommodating attitude toward Soviet interests. In that sense, the SS-20s represented a resurrection of the earlier Berlin confrontations because "the Soviet Union sought to change radically the European balance and the European perception of the balance."[31]

Soviet political strategy was not to make any concessions to avoid a U.S. deployment; it would simply support the European "peace movement" and exploit Europe's fears, pacifism, and growing neutralism in order to compel its governments to exercise unilateral arms control. By being deliberately diplomatically inflexible, it sought to increase the pressure on Washington for concessions. The Reagan administration, however, stood firm. It really could not forgo the deployment. To have reversed itself under Soviet pressure and the street protests would have left Moscow triumphant, NATO humiliated, and the U.S. will to defend NATO commitment widely questioned. Moscow would then be in an excellent position for future "nuclear blackmail" of western Europe. When the first Pershings were deployed in 1983, the Soviets walked out of all arms control negotiations, vowing not to return until the U.S. missiles were withdrawn. The Soviets sought to raise the pressure on Washington and the European governments even higher by intensifying the fears of the peace movement. Simultaneously, Moscow promised to match the U.S. deployment, especially with a "palisade" of missiles along East Germany's border with West Germany, the principal target of Moscow's antimissile campaign. If it could separate West Germany from NATO, the western alliance would collapse.

While the Soviets did return to the negotiating table in 1985 because of President Reagan's proposal for a strategic defense in space (see the next section), the SS-20 episode raised a serious question about the viability and cohesion of NATO and the shortcomings of extended deterrence in an era of strategic parity. The Soviets might not have prevented the U.S. counterdeployment but, whether or not they had originally intended only to modernize their Eurostrategic weapons, the SS-20 episode turned out to be an important political tool. It gave impetus to European neutralism and pacifism and directed these attitudes in an anti-American direction. It also fueled the peace movement's desire to separate Europe from the western alliance. And in Britain and West Germany, it helped destroy the postwar NATO consensus as the British Labour party and West German Social Democratic party turned against the U.S. deployment and became increasingly critical of their nations' memberships in NATO. So did other socialist parties in Europe (except for the French, which was in favor of the deployment).

The Double Zero Solution
Nevertheless, having lost the initial battle, Moscow reversed itself and accepted the zero-zero IRBM deployment for both powers it had rejected when President Reagan first proposed it, largely as a propaganda move to place the Soviets on the defensive, to placate the antimissile European crowds, and to enable the United States to go ahead with its missile deployment. Now, Washington was trapped by its own proposal; it could hardly reject it, even though it would, according to the original rationale for the deployment, "uncouple" Europe's defense from the U.S. deterrent. It did initially qualify its acceptance, arguing that 0-0 would give the Soviet Union the advantage in short-range missiles since the United States had not deployed any. But Gorbachev replied that if these were the stumbling block to NATO's acceptance, he would eliminate these missiles as well. Thus 0-0 turned into 00-00.

The result was that this made Europe's defense more dependent than ever on the U.S. strategic deterrent. Yet at the 1986 Iceland summit meeting with Soviet leader Gorbachev President Reagan had paradoxically committed the United States to the abolition of the nation's ballistic missiles, if not all strategic weapons, within a 10-year period to match a similar Soviet offer. If this were to be realized, Europe's security would of course have to depend on conventional deterrence. Only large-scale mobilization in Europe and the United States could build up the sizable forces necessary to confront Moscow with a long, costly war if it were to attack NATO, a war that it might not in fact win. But the whole postwar history has demonstrated that while Europe has the material resources, it lacks the will to mobilize them. And to believe that in the midst of the euphoria of the largest and most important disarmament effort in history, the European governments (as well as that of the United States) could pose the Soviet Union as a great threat requiring an immediate large-scale conventional mobilization staggers the imagination; the United States does not even have a draft.

A European defense without nuclear weapons is, in any case, inconceivable. Even larger conventional forces can never by themselves be as effective a deterrent as one backed by nuclear weapons, because it is the possibility of escalation and the horror of nuclear war that remains the ultimate deterrent. The use of nuclear arms in Europe's defense may not be as credible today as it once was, but the remote chance that they might be should suffice to deter a Soviet attack. In any event, there is no alternative at present. It was for this reason that the President, after his return from Iceland, backpedalled on the elimination of all U.S. ICBMs as alliance pressure on him to keep the U.S. deterrent intact grew.

But this just squares the circle. If the defense of Europe remains dependent in the final analysis upon the U.S. nuclear deterrent, the question remains the same: how credible does the threat of retaliation remain in response to an invasion; or, if the initial response is a conventional one, how believable will it be to Moscow that if the conventional defense fails, the United States will escalate to strategic missiles? In short, can the alliance continue to depend for deterrence on MAD or did it not make sense to shift to a counterforce strategy for more reliable deterrence? Should war occur because the Soviets may doubt that the United States would use nuclear weapons to defend its allies, was it not rational that the United States should think of how to limit damage to itself?

The Revival of Strategic Defense

The Reagan administration came into power skeptical of arms control, if not all negotiations with the Soviet Union.[32] The President was the first post-war president who said that the United States was number two and that the Soviets had gained superiority in the strategic balance; and he attributed this to a large extent to past arms control negotiations. Because the United States was behind and arms control was partly responsible for this, the emphasis of the administration's effort was on unilateral rearmament rather than bilateral arms talks. The modernization program of the strategic forces thus preoccupied the Reagan administration in its initial years while a continuous battle raged within the administration over whether to engage in any arms negotiations at all; and if it did, on what terms. One key problem was what the United States would bargain with since the only immediate new missile that might worry the Soviets was the MX. But because the MX was a counterforce weapon which the Reagan administration planned to place in what it had loudly trumpeted were vulnerable Minuteman silos — thus enhancing the Soviet's incentive to preempt and destroy them before they destroyed Soviet ICBMs in a first strike — it worried Congress too. The result was that Congress limited the number of MXs to be deployed to 50. However, even if the administration could have satisfied Congress with a more mobile and less vulnerable mode of deployment, the 100 MXs Reagan had asked for were hardly much of a bargaining chip to get Moscow to radically reduce its 1398 ICBMs.

SDI and Domestic Politics

Thus two sets of circumstances came together in March 1983, leading to President Reagan's proposal for a Strategic Defense Initiative (SDI) to make missiles "impotent and obsolete."[33] One was that since the Soviets were not about to drastically cut back on their ICBMs, the best U.S. strategy was to outflank Soviet offensive forces and neutralize Moscow's heavy investment in the post-1964 strategic buildup. The second factor, and perhaps even more important, was the growth of an antinuclear movement. The collapse of détente, the harsh words exchanged by Moscow and Washington during the early Reagan years, the extensive American rearmament program and, most important of all, the talk of nuclear war fighting and "prevailing" in such a conflict, plus the MX missile program, raised widespread public concerns about a new "arms race" and the possibility of war.[34] Would deterrence last? Rather than strengthen deterrence, would the acquisition of first-strike weapons by each power not weaken deterrence as in a crisis each would feel compelled to preempt? Was it really sensible under the best of circumstances to expect deterrence to hold, never to fail? By the mid-term 1982 election the nuclear freeze movement to first freeze the testing, production, and deployment of all nuclear weapons, to be followed by their reduction and, if possible, their elimination, had a widespread popular following and all Democratic presidential candidates except one were soon to endorse it. In addition, the Catholic bishops, then the Methodist bishops, condemned all uses of nuclear weapons, even for retaliation; nuclear arms were condemned as immoral.

In this political atmosphere, when nuclear offensive modernization looked unlikely and the antinuclear movement's argument that nuclear weapons were not only unhealthy for the body but for the soul might cast doubt on the future legitimacy of nuclear deterrence, the Reagan vision of an antimissile defense to protect populations was a timely and astute political stroke. The president virtually stole the antinuclear movement's clothes. Nuclear deterrence with its ever-present threat of mankind's extinction was to be replaced by a new and more hopeful world of SDI. The dark and menacing time of MAD would be followed by a bright and, finally, safer future. He rejected looking "down to an endless future with both of us sitting here with these horrible missiles aimed at each other. And the only thing preventing a holocaust is just so long as no one pulls the trigger."[35] Rejecting the fundamental assumption of deterrence — that prospects of such a holocaust would prevent war — the president proposed building what critics called a nonnuclear "astrodome" over the United States in order to protect its people and ensure the survival of American society. Why not seek to escape the nuclear nightmare based on MAD, Reagan asked, with MAS (Mutual Assured Security)? SDI, the President said, "isn't about war, it's about peace. It isn't about retaliation, it's about prevention. It isn't about fear, it's about hope."[36] Was this not more moral than killing millions of people in vengeance? Was MAS not consistent with the bishops' moral rejection of nuclear deterrence? And would SDI not create a far safer world than the MAD strategy all of his predecessors had endorsed, a strategy that relied on mutual deterrence and arms control agreements to help stabilize the deterrent balance?

The ABM Precedent

The Reagan SDI proposal with its mix of real and utopian motives was not the first time that the idea of a defensive shield had been suggested. In the 1960s, the Soviets deployed an antiballistic missile (ABM) system around Moscow; perhaps this system would become part of a wider national system. The Soviet ABM, however primitive, caused great concern and anxiety in the United States because a later, technologically more effective ABM might at some future point rob the United States of its capability to retaliate massively against the Soviet Union and thus weaken deterrence. The less damage the United States could cause in a retaliatory or second strike, the less inhibiting the U.S. deterrent would be on Soviet behavior. The fear was that a Soviet ABM buildup might be the prelude to a Soviet first strike. No ABM system could protect most of Russia's population against a full-scale U.S. launch. But if the Soviets hit first with a disarming strike and crippled much of the American retaliatory capability, and then an alerted defense could shoot down a sizable percentage of what was left of the U.S. second-strike force, the Soviet Union might suffer only "acceptable" damage and losses. Their survival and recovery assured, the combination of large numbers of relatively accurate warheads plus an ABM defense might indeed be an enticement to launch a first strike.

The initial American response had been that rather than build an American ABM, it was simpler and cheaper to overcome the Soviet ABM by saturating Soviet defenses. The way to do this was by multiplying warheads. Thus the defensive and offensive arms races were linked, even though the Soviets had at one time denied this linkage and claimed that defensive weapons were good weapons since they saved peoples' lives. But in terms of American arms control thinking, population defense was bad, and stimulating an offensive buildup was also bad. Later, the United States also decided to develop an ABM, which was to become a bargaining chip during SALT I. The Soviets (had to worry about whether U.S. ABMs would weaken a Soviet preemptive strike, should it ever be necessary to launch one.

During the SALT I negotiations the Soviets therefore pushed hard for some sort of ABM limitation. The United States was willing but only if it were linked to limits on Soviet offensive forces, especially the ever-growing ICBM force. The American position was — and this needs to be emphasized — that there was a strict relationship between U.S. strategic defenses and Soviet offensive capability. Before agreeing to limits on ABMs, the United States needed to know what the ceilings on Soviet ICBMs would be (and more broadly, ICBMs and SLBMs, but it was the potential counterforce capability of the ICBMs that was the main concern). The SALT I deal was a limit of 200 ABMs (which in 1974 was lowered even further to 100) for each side while simultaneously freezing the offensive forces of both sides and leaving the ceilings to be imposed on different weapons systems to the SALT II negotiations. Since for all practical purposes ABM defenses had been abandoned and the Americans thought the Soviets had accepted MAD, the debate over ballistic missile defense ceased.

Benefits and Liabilities

The president's SDI proposal was to revive the debate and many of the arguments. Reagan's proposal was, of course, far more ambitious. If the research could be realized, the aim was a defensive system that could intercept and destroy enemy missiles in flight before they hit the United States. This defense was to occur in three phases. The first was the boost phase during which the ICBMs would rise out of their silos; this phase would last no longer than five minutes. Yet this initial phase was the critical period, for in phase two, the midcourse, the warheads would separate from the missiles and the number of targets to be destroyed would vastly multiply. Obviously, the success rate of destroying this larger number of targets would be far more difficult — and impossible if in the first phase a majority of missiles had not been destroyed. The third phase was the terminal one: destroying the incoming warheads that had survived.

If the research were successful and an astrodome defense feasible, there would be no point in having missiles. Indeed, the president — like the Catholic and Methodist bishops — has said the elimination of all missiles was his ultimate goal. A second intermediate-range objective was also cited, especially after critics pointed out that no leakproof defense was possible, that even a 95 percent successful defense would allow enough warheads to get through and destroy America's cities and millions of people. This second purpose was to defend ICBMs with terminal defense, the technology for which already exists. While the administration claimed that there was no contradiction between these two purposes — missile defense was all that was currently possible — in fact population and ICBM defense were opposing objectives. The first seeks to do away with missiles and move beyond deterrence; the second, to keep the missiles and defend them, thereby strengthening deterrence. Despite the incompatibility of the two objectives, the administration claimed that SDI would make the world a safer place. An attacker could not know in advance how well or badly SDI would perform so that he could not know how many people it would save or how many missiles it could protect. In short, SDI raised the uncertainties about a successful first strike and this would therefore stabilize deterrence. The administration could have quoted a Soviet source from the mid-1960s: "The creation of an effective anti-missile defense system by a country which is a potential target for aggression merely serves to increase the deterrent effect [of its retaliatory force] and so helps avert aggression."[37]

The critics of SDI, however, were legion. The president's plan quickly became dubbed as Star Wars. It was so enormous and complex that one of the obvious criticisms was that it would be technologically impossible: that it would be enormously expensive (official and unofficial estimates ranged from $500 billion to $1 trillion); that it could never be fully tested until the moment of attack, when it would have to work perfectly the first time it was used, an unlikely prospect for such a terribly complex system; that it could be overcome if saturated with incoming warheads (as the United States had planned to do in the 1960s by MIRVing its missiles to overcome Soviet ABMs); that it would lead to an offensive arms race since the Soviets would build more missiles and/or multiply warheads; and that it would also result in a defensive arms race because the Soviets, like the United States earlier, would match the American effort, which would undermine the 1972 ABM treaty.[38] The resulting competition between defensive and offensive technologies — e.g., maneuverable warheads, or MARVs, to penetrate a defensive shield — would cause an unstable balance, which would leave both sides less secure (as well as less wealthy since the cost of the offensive arms to overcome SDI would have to be added to SDI's development costs). And since SDI could not protect the nation against low-flying bombers and cruise missiles, defenses against these weapons would also have to be developed at further costs.

Some critics charged that SDI was a characteristically American proposal — a technological way of recovering the sense of almost absolute security it had during its century of isolationism from international politics. But there was no "technical fix" to what was essentially a political and diplomatic problem — how to coexist with the Soviet Union in a nuclear world. This would require a more serious arms control effort than the administration was making to avoid a new arms race in space and stabilize the one here on earth.

Soviet Perceptions and Fears

One result of SDI was to reverse the U.S. and Soviet positions in the early 1970s. In the ABM debate, the Russians argued that defending people was good; this time it was the Americans. Then the United States expressed its fear that the Soviet ABM would induce a Soviet first strike and it developed MIRVs to overcome a potential nationwide Soviet ABM defense; SDI led the Soviets to express their concern about an American first strike and to say that one of their countermeasures would be to build up their missile/warhead force. This time the Soviets, not the Americans, argued that strategic defenses were destabilizing. As Brezhnev's successor, Yuri Andropov, said a few days after President Reagan's SDI proposal:

> . . . the strategic offensive forces of the United States will continue to be developed and upgraded at full tilt and along quite a definite line at that, namely that of acquiring a first nuclear strike capability. Under these conditions the intention to secure itself the possibility of destroying with the help of the ABM defenses the corresponding strategic systems of the other side, that is of rendering it unable of dealing a retaliatory strike, is a bid to disarm the Soviet Union in the face of the U.S. nuclear threat.[39]

In short, the Soviets viewed SDI not in isolation, but in the context of the changing U.S. military doctrine of fighting a limited nuclear war and the attendant U.S. offensive build-up with its focus on 100 B-1 bombers (being deployed presently, to be followed perhaps in the 1990s by a Stealth bomber virtually invisible to current radar detection), counterforce ICBMs (50 MXs scheduled to be operational by 1989), and SLBMs (Trident II, scheduled for deployment starting in 1989 in up to 20 Trident submarines). These forces would be targeted against the Soviet ICBM force, which carried most of the Soviet Union's warheads. (For the United States it is the submarines that carry most American warheads. With Trident II missiles, 13–15 of the Trident submarines, each with 24 tubes and each missile carrying 8 warheads, could alone destroy more than 90 percent of the Soviet Union's 1398 ICBMs.) Thus the Soviet leaders, like American leaders, had to be increasingly concerned about the vulnerability of their ICBMs, the backbone of Soviet strategic forces since they have few bombers and keep only about ten percent of their nuclear submarines at sea. After a U.S. first strike, the crippled surviving Soviet ICBMs might, no longer be able to inflict "unacceptable damage" on a United States defended by SDI. Indeed, by the time the Reagan modernization program is completed in the 1990s, the United States will have about 75 percent of the nuclear strength needed to destroy Soviet leaders in their shelters in addition to Russia's nuclear forces, conventional forces, and war industry.[40] In these circumstances, uncertain in a crisis whether they could retaliate, the Soviets might feel compelled to use their ICBMs or lose them.

Thus there were in fact three SDIs: SDI I incorporated the president's vision of a space-based population defense; SDI II consisted of the more limited and feasible ground-based missile defense; and SDI III was the Soviet perception of SDI as part of an American offensive strategy, even though it might be disguised as a defensive system. Such a perception was consistent with earlier U.S. concerns about Soviet ABM deployment, the changes in U.S. strategic doctrine and targeting, and the acquisition of more accurate warheads. And these U.S. changes in doctrine and weapons were, of course, also consistent with similar Soviet changes since both nations had become increasingly concerned with limiting damage to themselves — just in case deterrence failed.

The switch of positions between the United States and the Soviet Union from the ABM to SDI negotiations was ironic but not the only irony. Another was that while American scientists doubted that SDI could be achieved the Soviets, with their respect for U.S. technology, feared it could be. A third irony was that SDI might reinforce targeting cities because, if only a limited number of missiles could get through to strike at military targets, the attacking side would have no choice but to strike at cities in order to maintain its assured destruction capability as much as possible. Thus strategic defenses would not, as the president asserted, take the world away from MAD but assure its continuation. A fourth and even greater irony was that if both powers could perfect defenses against nuclear weapons and thereby nullify the fundamental cause for the post-1945 peace, conventional war would be more likely. The United States, which had for four decades relied on nuclear arms rather than large and more expensive conventional forces to preserve the peace, would then have to again build up such forces once SDI was in place.

A final irony was that America's European allies were skeptical about what SDI would do for them.[41] Not only did they think the shorter flight time for a missile from Russia to western Europe than to the United States meant that SDI could not defend them, but if the Soviets deployed their own version of SDI the British and French feared that their nuclear forces, developed at such great expense and effort, would be rendered useless. But the biggest question for the Europeans was: If SDI were successful and could protect America, would this not lead to a resurgence of U.S. isolationism? And if it did, would the United States abandon them? Or would SDI, precisely because it could now safeguard the United States, make the United States more willing to defend western Europe since the cost for doing so was no longer self-immolation? For America's NATO allies these were life-and-death questions.

Stalemate in Arms Control

The result of the U.S. and Soviet positions on SDI was a stalemate in the arms control negotiations. The United States wanted a radical reduction of the Soviet ICBM threat. This time it was the Soviets who argued that they could not reduce their ICBM force because they did not know how many they would need to penetrate American defenses if the SDI research and deployment were successful. (The research was, of course, impossible to stop on both sides.)

Thus the prospects for an arms control agreement initially looked bleak. President Reagan was firmly convinced not only that SDI was the answer to the Soviet first-strike capability against the U.S.'s retaliatory land-based missiles but that SDI was the key to a world free from nuclear weapons. He believed that the United States, like the Soviet Union, should therefore proceed with the research, and if this proved fruitful, the two powers should negotiate mutual defensive deployments. (Indeed, if Soviet research were inadequate, America should share its knowledge with the Soviets so that both sides could phase in their strategic defenses while reducing their offensive forces. Otherwise, the Soviets might believe that the United States was getting ready for a first strike and decide to preempt while the American SDI was being phased in. But it would take a lot of faith and trust by the Soviets to believe that having attained a quantum leap forward in science, the United States — the capitalist enemy — would share this most advanced military technology.)

As noted earlier, the Soviets feared that SDI might work. They undoubtedly also feared its *offensive* capabilities. In any event, they had to be genuinely concerned about a new and very expensive arms race that they could not afford and feared they might lose. It was perhaps for these reasons that the Soviets kept up an insistent anti-SDI barrage in every international forum. Probably what they feared most, however, was that SDI would focus the U.S.–Soviet competition in

> an area where the United States seemed to have a clear technological edge (an advantage all the more impressive in light of long-standing Soviet research efforts in the field). As one analyst has put it, "For the Soviet Union, the U.S. SDI program is quickly becoming symbolic of a more fundamental challenge between states — or perhaps, between social systems — calling

into contention the political, economic and industrial, scientific and technological, and military potentials of the superpowers."[42]

Thus the president's renamed SALT talks — START (Strategic Arms Reduction Talks) — got stalled. Clearly, the United States held a more potent bargaining chip than MX if it wanted to use it. The Soviets were not seemingly against strategic defense as such. Their objection to SDI was that it was part of an offensive strategic buildup and first-strike strategy. They offered deep cuts in their strategic forces, deeper cuts than those they rejected out of hand when presented by President Carter in 1977. Such deep cuts in Soviet ICBMs with their first-strike potential had been a Reagan goal from the beginning. SDI was proposed precisely because of the numbers and accuracy of Soviet warheads. Moreover, it was essentially a long-term research program to discover the feasibility of exotic SDI laser and particle beam technologies. The president could therefore potentially meet the Soviet desire to reaffirm the ABM treaty prohibitions on space-based ballistic missile defenses while continuing intensive research since the results would probably not be known until 2010 or 2020.[43]

The outlines of a far-reaching arms deal or "grand compromise" thus became visible: deep Soviet cuts in ICBMs for the postponement of any American SDI deployment while research in the laboratories went on. But at the 1986 Iceland summit meeting when the Soviets offered to eliminate all medium-range missiles in Europe and a 50 percent cut of strategic forces, the president rejected the proposal. He did so because the Soviets wanted a *strict* interpretation of the 1972 ABM treaty, confining ABM research to the laboratory, while he wanted the Soviets to accept a *broader* interpretation that would permit some research, development, and testing outside of the laboratory, with deployment possible at the end of a 10-year period. The president charged that in sticking to the strict interpretation the Russians were trying to "kill" SDI, a charge not all the scientists working on SDI accepted; the president obviously wanted no practical restraints on the program.

But even if it did restrain the SDI research program, was the Soviet offer not worth it? SDI had originally been proposed to reduce the Soviet first-strike threat and close what the president had called "the window of vulnerability." In that sense, it was a bargaining chip, something to trade for a radical cut in Soviet ICBM forces. But when the Soviets appeared willing to make major concessions, SDI was seemingly no longer up for barter. SDI had taken on a life of its own as if it were already a reality. The reason for proposing SDI was all but forgotten when the Soviets offered the administration a cut of their own ICBMs sufficiently large to greatly reduce, if not eliminate, their first-strike potential.

Indeed, if one took at face value the 1986 Iceland summit talk of eliminating all ballistic missiles, if not in fact all nuclear strategic weapons, there would be no Soviet missile threat.* Possibly, the United States might retain a bomber/cruise missile capability if only missiles were eliminated; but SDI had never been intended to protect the nation against bombers or cruise missiles. Yet despite the fact that there would be no missiles to defend against and that SDI would not be able to cope with air-breathing systems, the president clung to SDI. In a missile-free environment, the rationale for SDI shifted to "insurance" — insurance against Soviet cheating, accidents or attacks by third countries, although it remained unclear to which countries this referred (Britain, France, China and India, or whom?) In any event, such an SDI IV could be provided by a smaller, ground-based system using current or soon-to-be-available technologies.[44]

Indeed, the basic question remains whether nuclear deterrence is not only a cheaper but a safer way of avoiding nuclear war if the incentives for each side to preempt are removed.

*After Iceland, there was considerable confusion on this point with Gorbachev insisting the two men had agreed on the 10 year elimination of all strategic arms and the president saying that while he had agreed with this ultimate goal he had assented only to the abolition of all strategic missiles, not bombers and cruise missiles. In a later communique issued after Prime Minister Thatcher's post-Iceland visit to President Reagan, even the abolition of all ballistic missiles in ten years was dropped; it now became only a long-term goal.

Thus we return to the central issue of stability. There are many ways to achieve that: relying more on nuclear submarines; relying less on MIRVed missiles with accurate warheads; replacing them with a single war-headed mobile ICBM; even a ground-based defense of siloed ICBMs; and, not least, arms control arrangements reducing the opponent's hard-target "kill" capability. The main point is to preserve the survivability of U.S. retaliatory forces. If these can survive any preemptive attack, the nuclear balance will remain stable.

It was precisely because the triad of bombers, ICBMs and SLBMs would complicate a Soviet attack, as well as Soviet defenses against a U.S. retaliatory strike, that it was developed. Even if one leg of the triad became vulnerable, the two other legs would each still have sufficient assured destruction capability to deter an attack. Of the three, the SLBMs were the most invulnerable. It is one thing to seek a major reduction in these forces or, as Reagan sought to do, to abolish entire categories of nuclear weapons; it is quite another to eliminate those forces that make it impossible for the enemy to gain an advantage from a first strike and contribute the most to stabilizing the balance. The point is not merely to reduce numbers but to reduce the possibilities of an eruption of nuclear war. It therefore boggles the mind that a U.S. president could in 36 hours over a weekend, apparently without much preparation or examination by either the State or Defense Departments, quixotically offer the abolition of all missiles, if not all strategic weapons, which have provided the United States and western Europe security for four decades. It suggests that neither the president nor his advisers apparently understood either this point or the simple fact that without the nuclear deterrent the Soviet Union would achieve conventional superiority against NATO.

Gorbachev and the Propaganda War

In the meantime, Gorbachev sought to exploit the president's attachment to SDI to gain a propaganda advantage. The new Soviet leader had since shortly after he gained power sought to exploit western Europe's antinuclear and propeace mood to see if appealing arms control plans might divide Europe from the United States. The goal was old, but instead of trying to intimidate the Europeans, Gorbachev tried seduction. He first suspended all nuclear testing in 1985; this moratorium was to place the United States on the defensive and make President Reagan appear to be the obstacle to a relaxation of international tensions. The president had repeatedly said he would not stop testing since it was necessary to test older warheads in the deterrent arsenal to make sure they worked; presumably he also wanted a free hand to test the Star Wars components. Thus the two leaders played a game: Gorbachev would extend the moratorium on testing and call for the end to all testing, and each time Reagan would turn him down. In January 1986, Gorbachev also proposed the phased elimination of all the world's nuclear arms by the year 2000, a blatant propaganda move. In Iceland he upped the ante by proposing the elimination of all Soviet and U.S. intermediate-range nuclear missiles in Europe plus an initial 50 percent cut in offensive strategic missiles by 1991 with a total elimination of all strategic forces by 1996. The "joker" was that he tied all these concessions to the strict adherence of the ABM treaty for a 10-year period.[45] In earlier negotiations, the Soviets had separated the European missiles from strategic missiles and SDI; only the latter two were linked.

The president had all along insisted that he would not make concessions on SDI; administration officials had also consistently expressed their displeasure with the ABM treaty as an obstacle to SDI research and testing. Gorbachev may well have gambled that he was safe in making his concessions, appearing flexible, and assuming the mantle of peacemaker; for if Reagan were consistent, he would not budge but reject all of Gorbachev's "concessions." Reagan would therefore be seen in many countries as the major obstacle to a safer world. In Europe especially, this might strengthen anti-American opinion and divide the Western alliance, even though the European governments supported the United States. That is why in early

1987, Gorbachev again unlinked INF. His record was one of proposing one arms control plan after another, of making the Soviet Union appear as a reasonable power while NATO — especially the United States — constantly reacted, often less than enthusiastically. He could not really lose: A European missile agreement would be a significant achievement, especially in slowing down the arms competition and improving U.S.–Soviet relations; a failure would pin the responsibility on the alliance. The key problem was the European governments' fear of denuclearization and being left to face Soviet conventional superiority. The Soviet proposal thus created intra-allied conflicts and U.S. pressure on allied governments. Washington knew that NATO could not turn down its own offer. But for its European members, their lack of conventional strength continued to haunt them and leave them with the fear of being abandoned by the United States. In any event, Gorbachev was the beneficiary: in 1987 he was rated by Western public opinion as being far more strongly for peace than President Reagan; even the 0-0 proposal was thought to be Gorbachev's!

In the meantime, while the superpowers could not resolve their differences over SDI, SDI did produce some beneficial results: It blocked the elimination of nuclear missiles, saved the nuclear deterrent, and rescued the president from the consequences of his own weekend folly in Iceland. In any case, by 1987 SDI was stalled. On the one hand, the Reagan administration kept on pushing for a broad interpretation of the ABM treaty. On the other hand, the Democratically controlled Congress, already skeptical over the purposes, feasibility, and cost of SDI, and angered over the SALT II violations by the United States, insisted on the traditional, or narrow, interpretation of the ABM treaty. In the Senate, there was considerable support for the view that the Nixon administration had presented it with the restrictive view and that is what had been ratified. Confronted with opposition in Congress, which faced continuing budget deficits, the administration's cutting of social services, and presidential opposition to tax increases, and which was already skeptical of SDI and critical of the administration's renunciation of SALT II, the administration proposed an early deployment of ground and space-based homing rockets that kill their targets by smashing them. Sensing that SDI was in trouble and that its time in office was running out, the administration clearly wanted to ensure a commitment from which a future president and especially Congress would not be able to retreat. Reportedly, it also shifted funds away from the exotic technologies that gave SDI the name of Star Wars to the rockets, sensors, and battle-management systems for deployment by the middle 1990s. But Congressional opposition was strong. And in 1987 when a distinguished group of physicists, among them some of the world's leading experts in laser and particle beams, stated that it would be 10 or more years before it would be known if these were feasible technologies, this opposition was strengthened. It is therefore perhaps surprising that President Reagan, to restore his historic reputation after the Iran-Contra scandal, did not use SDI as a bargaining chip to arrange not one but the two largest arms reduction agreements any U.S. president had ever achieved. Of course, a 00-00 European agreement is in itself a significant agreement, abolishing about 1,400 Soviet warheads, most of which were aimed at western Europe. The president continued to cling to his vision of Star Wars for his long-run historical reputation. Unless Reagan changes his mind, his successor will decide whether to accept the "grand compromise."

The Restraining Impact of Nuclear Weapons

The principal impact of nuclear weapons for the last 40 years has been to discipline the exercise of power. Not only has it prevented a total war between the United States and the Soviet Union despite the scope and intensity of their rivalry, but it has led them to manage their crises very carefully whenever they erupted. These crises have occurred repeatedly at points where the American and Soviet (Sino-Soviet for a while) spheres touched. When one power tried to change the status quo, the other resisted, determined to preserve it, as in Berlin in 1948–1949, and again repeatedly from 1958–1961, or in Quemoy-Matsu in the Taiwan Straits in 1954–1955 and 1958, or in Cuba in 1962. If the possibility of the use of violence lies behind much of international politics, this possibility rises close to the surface in the crises between the two superpowers. Crises, in this sense, stand at the crossover point from peace to war, even if their occurrence suggests that the balance is being kept.[46] Crises are thus very dangerous; yet none has erupted into a general war, as would in all likelihood have happened in a prenuclear period when the penalty for going to war did not involve the price of extinction. Since 1945, in both deterrence and crises, the United States and the Soviet Union have resorted only to the threat of force. Both are trying to avoid a nuclear catastrophe.

When force itself is used, as in Korea and Vietnam, it is used only in limited wars.[47] Again, as in crises, there is a perceived threat to the equilibrium. While in crises the threat of using force is employed to shift the status quo, limited wars result from the actual crossing of the frontier between the superpower spheres and the perceived requirement to restore the status quo. Unlike World Wars I and II where the political goal was the enemy's unconditional surrender — that is, the elimination of the regimes that started the wars — the aim of U.S. intervention in Korea and Vietnam was to deny the North Koreans and North Vietnamese the conquest of the southern halves of these countries, which Washington defined as being in the U.S. sphere. (Just as in reverse, when U.S. forces crossed into North Korea and approached Communist China's frontier after defeating North Korea's army, China intervened to restore the status quo at the 38th Parallel, which divided the two Koreas.) Total victory over the enemy was not the goal, if only because as Korea had shown, it led to escalation of the fighting, a prolongation of the war, higher casualties and, above all, the intervention of one of the two major Communist powers. These were the major reasons that in Vietnam the army was confined to operations in South Vietnam.[48]

Even more significant was that on the Communist side, the Soviets tended increasingly to resort to wars by proxy since the mid-1970s in such places as Angola and Ethiopia. Soviet forces were never involved and therefore the Soviet Union did not present the United States with a direct challenge. Cuban troops with Soviet arms and East bloc personnel were used instead. While Fidel Castro was undoubtedly also pursuing his own revolutionary goals, his interests in these instances coincided with those of Moscow, which daily invested several million dollars in Cuba to keep the economy going (for a total of between $4 to $5 billion/year by the early 1980s). Only in Afghanistan, on its border, an area not likely to involve U.S. troops, did the Soviets intervene with their own forces. Similarly, the United States aided indigenous groups seeking the overthrow of Marxist governments in Nicaragua, Angola, and Afghanistan. In addition, both powers have frequently resorted to "showing the flag," that is, using "force without war."[49]

The chief role of nuclear weapons in peacetime, then, is their nonuse. If war should erupt and nuclear weapons are used, they will have failed to perform their principal function. Their basic test is not whether the enemy can be defeated, but whether they can prevent nuclear war. The fear on both sides that, even with more accurate MIRVs, first strikes will not be successful in disarming the opponent and that limited nuclear wars may not be controllable means that the two superpowers will continue to face the real possibility of committing mutual suicide. The basic deterrent balance therefore remains fundamentally stable. Both powers can continue to see their common fate in the crystal ball.

This restraining effect deserves special emphasis because of the increasing number of criticisms of deterrence.[50] These criticisms of deterrence are not really new, at least the threats to the physical survival of the nation, if not the world. The atom bomb, long before the hydrogen bomb, had made policy makers and the public aware that people were living in a new era of unprecedented destructiveness. Who has tried to deny that nuclear weapons were dangerous to one's health? Has that not been the reason for the emphasis on deterrence and arms control?

What these attacks on deterrence do is deliberately ignore its track record: Since 1945 it has preserved the peace between the United States and the Soviet Union. None of the many crises have erupted into war. The Soviets have used force only against their allies in eastern Europe and Afghanistan, all neighboring states. Europe, the area of most vital interest to both superpowers, has enjoyed its longest period of uninterrupted peace in a century. Large United States and Soviet forces, representing the two most powerful nations in history, locked in an ideological antagonism and a global struggle as profound as any in history, have despite repeated crises and periods of tension kept their powder dry.

The conclusion might be summed up as follows: *If nuclear weapons were eliminated, relieving fears of a nuclear holocaust, one of the ironic results might well be to make wars between the major powers more likely because such hostilities would be considerably less damaging.* There is clearly a trade-off between the destructiveness of war and the incidence of war. If the abolition of all nuclear weapons were possible, as the two powers talked about in Iceland, it would present a cruel dilemma: On the one hand, it would remove the fear of national, if not global, suicide; on the other hand, it would make it more probable that war would again become a national instrument of policy in which the gains would exceed losses. Nuclear weapons have, after all, eliminated not only nuclear wars but *all wars* between the major powers for 40 years. This is not likely to remain true if SDI is deployed. For if it works, as the president hopes, it will make missiles "impotent and obsolete," even if they have not been eliminated by 1996, the date the superpowers talked of at the Iceland summit in 1986. The irony will be that if the goal of abolishing nuclear weapons were to be achieved, the United States and its allies would have to mobilize very large and expensive conventional forces; nuclear arms have for over 40 years served as a cheap substitute for manpower. Thus SDI, in ridding the world of nuclear missiles, may make the world go back to fighting more bloody conventional wars.

The fact is that the United States and western Europe cannot eliminate nuclear deterrence.[51] Not only NATO but U.S. security depend on it. U.S. offensive nuclear forces remain the *only* deterrent. President Reagan's SDI may shoot down most of the enemy missiles, but some may get through the defense shield. Furthermore, SDI cannot guard the nation from bombers, cruise missiles, or depressed trajectory submarine-launched missiles, let alone a merchant ship or just a suitcase filled with nuclear explosives. In fact, SDI cannot be a technological solution to the nuclear arms problem any more than nuclear disarmament. The best guarantee against attack remains the threat of punishment — nuclear punishment. If it is true that a deterrent capability must be retained, the key question remains what size and kind of nuclear forces should be deployed to minimize their vulnerability to a first strike, and what kind of arms control arrangements are necessary to maintain a stable deterrent balance — in order to keep the Cold War cold.

Notes

1. Rosenberg, "The Origins of Overkill: Nuclear Weapons and American Strategy, 1945–1960," *International Security,* Spring 1983, p. 15. For the history of the nuclear age from the perspective of the civilian strategists, see Stegg Hecken, *Counsels of War* (New York: Alfred A. Knopf, 1985).
2. Ibid., pp. 56–57.
3. Commencement Address, University of Michigan, June 16, 1962.
4. Donald W. Hanson, "Is Soviet Strategic Doctrine Superior?" *International Security,* Winter 1982/1983, pp. 61–83.
5. Quoted by Lynn Etheridge Davis, "Limited Nuclear Options: Deterrence and the New American Doctrine," *Adelphi Papers*

(London, England: International Institute for Strategic Studies, 1975/1976), p. 3.

6. Among others, see Office for Technology Assessment, *The Effects of Nuclear War* (Washington, D.C.: U.S. Government Printing Office, 1979), p. 4.

7. Caspar W. Weinberger, "U.S. Defense Strategy," *Foreign Affairs,* Spring 1986, pp. 678–679.

8. Michael Mandelbaum, *The Nuclear Question* (Cambridge, England: Cambridge University Press, 1979). Pp. 110–112 sums up the critics arguments as well as anyone.

9. Desmond Ball, "Can Nuclear War Be Controlled?" *Adelphi Papers* (London, England: International Institute for Strategic Studies, 1981), pp. 28–29. Also see Desmond Ball and Jeffrey Richelson, eds., *Strategic Nuclear Targeting* (Ithaca, N.Y.: Cornell University Press, 1986).

10. Desmond Ball, "U.S. Strategic Forces: How Should They Be Used?" *International Security,* Winter 1982/1983, p. 60. The above issue of Ball's *Adelphi Papers* is, as the title suggests, devoted to this issue.

11. Daniel Ford in *The Button* (New York: Simon & Schuster, 1985) argues that this is precisely what the U.S. Air Force plans to do.

12. For a persuasive statement of the opposite view, including the point that the Soviet political leaders will have every incentive to act with restraint and use nuclear weapons selectively and in limited numbers, see Albert Wohlstetter, "Between an Unfree World and None," *Foreign Affairs,* Summer 1985, pp. 962–964.

13. Spurgeon M. Keeny, Jr. and Wolfgang K. H. Panofsky, "MAD vs. NUTS: The Mutual Hostage Relationship of the Superpowers," *Foreign Affairs,* Winter 1981/1982, pp. 287–304.

14. Jan F. Triska and David D. Finley, *Soviet Foreign Policy* (New York: Macmillan, 1968), pp. 310–349; Michael P. Gehlen, *The Politics of Coexistence* (Bloomington, Ind.: Indiana University Press, 1967); and Hannes Adomeit, *Soviet Risk-Taking and Crisis Behavior* (Boston: Allen & Unwin, 1984).

15. For example, see Jiri Valenta, *Soviet-Intervention in Czechoslovakia* (Baltimore, Md.: The Johns Hopkins Press, 1966); also Garthoff, *Détente and Confrontation,* pp. 915–937.

16. Lambeth, "Uncertainties for the Soviet War Planner," *International Security,* Winter 1982/83, p. 157.

17. Lambeth's comment on this is worth reproducing. "In practical terms, all doctrine does for Soviet planners, aside from pre-

scribing broad guidelines for force procurement, is to indicate
the most sensible modes of combat in the best of all worlds.
Because of its irresolution about the precise contours a war
might assume and its appreciation that things could go badly despite the best efforts of the leadership to control events, doctrine
scarcely offers a hard prediction of how the Soviets would actually respond, or much comfort in the way of 'instant courage'
for the Soviet strategic decisions-makers." Ibid., p. 142.

18. Indeed, Richard Pipes, *Survival Is Not Enough* (New York: Simon & Schuster, 1984), p. 34, has argued that if one adds up the
lives lost in *both* world wars, those killed in the civil war after
the Bolshevik revolution, a later famine, and the various purges
— about 60 million dead — the conclusion has to be that the
Soviet Union may calculate "unacceptable losses" completely
differently than the United States.

Albert Wohlstetter in "Bishops, Statesmen, and Other Strategists on the Bombing of Innocents," *Commentary,* June 1983,
p. 27, has made the same point: Soviet dead as a result of Stalin's
collectivization of the peasantry, famine, purges, and those
killed by the secret police during World War II

> do not suggest that Soviet leaders value the life of Russian cit-
> izens above political and military power. If the West responded
> to Soviet military attack by destroying military targets, it would
> be something on which Soviet leaders continue to lavish a huge
> part of their painfully scarce resources . . . the prospects of
> such a Western response would be the best deterrent to their
> initiating war.

19. Office of Technology Assessment, op. cit., p. 102. Also see Gary
Guertner, "Strategic Vulnerability of a Multi-National State:
Deterring the Soviet Union," *Political Science Quarterly,* Summer 1981, pp. 209–223, and George H. Quester, *The Future
of Nuclear Deterrence* (Lexington, Mass.: Lexington Books,
1987), pp. 173–182.

20. John J. Mearsheimer, *Conventional Deterrence* (Ithaca, N.Y.:
Cornell University Press, 1983), pp. 165–202; and P. H. Vigor,
Soviet Blitzkrieg Theory (New York: St. Martin's Press, 1983).

21. James M. McConnell, "Shifts in Soviet Views on the Proper Focus of Military Development," *World Politics,* April 1985, pp.
330–339; Christopher Donnelly, "The Development of the So-

viet Concept of Echeloning," *NATO Review*, December 1984, pp. 14–16; and Michael McGuire, *Military Objectives in Soviet Foreign Policy* (Washington, D.C.: The Brookings Institution, 1987).

22. Books that dealt with this central question at the time were Robert E. Osgood, *NATO* (Chicago: The University of Chicago Press, 1962); Henry A. Kissinger, *The Troubled Partnership* (New York: Anchor Books, 1966); and Raymond Aron, *The Great Debate* (New York: Anchor Books, 1965). For a recent history of the alliance with the focus on the politics of NATO, see Gregory F. Treverton, *Making the Alliance Work* (Ithaca, N.Y.: Cornell University Press, 1986).

23. Pierre Lellouche, "Does NATO Have a Future?" *The Washington Quarterly*, Summer 1982, p. 47. For a critical assessment of the U.S. decision, see Leon N. Sigal, *Nuclear Forces in Europe* (Washington, D.C.: The Brookings Institution, 1984).

    Quite apart from this military logic, the European deemphasis of large armies and reliance on the U.S. deterrent meant a cheaper defense. This money could instead be invested in Europe's welfare system.

24. Garthoff, *Détente and Confrontation,* (Washington, D.C.: The Brookings Institution, 1985), pp. 849–886 and "The Soviet SS-20 Decisions," *Survival,* May/June 1983, pp. 110–119. Garthoff, however, specifically denies that the SS-20 deployment was to be used for purposes of politically intimidating the western powers.

25. Andrew J. Pierre, ed., *Nuclear Weapons in Europe* (New York: Council on Foreign Relations, 1984); and David N. Schwartz, *NATO's Nuclear Dilemma* (Washington, D.C.: The Brookings Institution, 1983).

26. Lellouche, op. cit., p. 48.

27. Lellouche, op. cit.; Jeffrey Record, "Should America Pay for Europe's Security?", *The Washington Quarterly*, Winter 1982, pp. 19–23; and Hedley Bull, "European Self-Reliance and the Reform of NATO," *Foreign Affairs*, Spring 1983, pp. 874–892.

28. Michael Howard, "Reassurance and Deterrence," *Foreign Affairs*, Winter 1982/1983, pp. 316–319.

29. Why there were no popular protests in France is explored by Theodore Draper, "The Phantom Alliance," pp. 1–27 in Robert W. Tucker and Linda Wrigley, eds., *The Atlantic Alliance and*

Its Critics (New York: Praeger, 1983). Also Howard, op. cit., pp. 321–324 and Ball, op. cit.

30. William G. Hyland, "The Struggle for Europe: An American View," in Pierre, op. cit., pp. 29–36.

31. Ibid., p. 31.

32. Strobe Talbot, *The Russians and Reagan* (New York: Vintage Books, 1984) and *Deadly Gambits* (New York: Knopf, 1984).

33. See the series on Weapons in Space in *The New York Times* from March 3 to 8, 1985. For background to SDI, see Paul B. Stares, *The Militarization of Space* (Ithaca, N.Y.: Cornell University Press, 1986). For a strongly argued pro-SDI position, see Keith B. Payne, *Strategic Defense* (Lanham, Md.: Hamilton Press, 1986) and Zbigniew Brzezinski, ed., *Promise or Peril* (Washington, D.C.: Ethics and Public Policy Center, 1986).

34. Robert W. Tucker, "The Nuclear Debate," *Foreign Affairs,* Fall, 1984, pp. 1–32.

35. *The New York Times,* March 30, 1983.

36. *The New York Times,* March 30, 1983.

37. Quoted by David B. Rivkin Jr., "What Does Moscow Think?" *Foreign Policy,* Summer 1985, pp. 88–89.

38. Union of Concerned Scientists, *Why Space Weapons Can't Protect Us* (New York: Vintage Specials, 1984) focuses largely on the technical side of SDI; McGeorge Bundy, George F. Kennan, Robert S. McNamara, and Gerard Smith, "The President's Choice: Star Wars or Arms Control," *Foreign Affairs,* Winter 1984/1985, pp. 264–278; Robert McNamara, *Blundering into Disaster* (New York: Pantheon, 1986); and Sidney D. Drell, Philip J. Farley, and David Holloway, *The Reagan Strategic Defense Initiative* (Cambridge, Mass.: Ballinger, 1985).

39. Bundy et al., op. cit., pp. 270–271. There was some evidence that the Soviets would focus their response to SDI by trying to knock it out rather than overcome it with offensive weapons. *The New York Times,* December 18, 19, 1986.

40. *The New York Times,* October 24, 1986.

41. Ibid., May 13, 1985.

42. Jeremy Azrael and Stephen Sestanovich, "Superpower Balancing Act," *Foreign Affairs* (America and the World 1985), pp. 481–482.

43. See, for example, the pessimistic estimate of the American Physical Society, the U.S.' largest professional association of

physicists, which reported that so many breakthroughs would be required to develop laser and particle beam weapons that it would be a decade or more before it would be known whether they were feasible. *The New York Times,* April 23, 1987.

44. For perceptive and critical comments on the Iceland summit, see Charles Klauthammer, "Reykjavik and the End of Days," Leon Wieseltier, "The Ungrand Compromise," and Albert Gore Jr., "Stability for Two," *New Republic,* November 17, 1986, pp. 19–31.

45. John Spanier and Joseph L. Nogee, *The Politics of Disarmament* (New York: Praeger, 1962).

46. Glenn Snyder, "Crisis Bargaining," in Charles F. Hermann, ed., *International Crises* (New York: The Free Press, 1972), pp. 217–218; and Alexander L. George, et al., *Managing U.S.-Soviet Rivalry* (Boulder, Colo.: Westview Press, 1983), pp. 365–398.

47. On deterrence of crises and limited wars, see Alexander L. George and Richard Smoke, *Deterrence in American Foreign Policy* (New York: Columbia University Press, 1974).

48. It may well be that these "lessons in Korea" were irrelevant in Vietnam. For the few years after 1966 China's attention was mainly focused domestically, occupied with the Cultural Revolution to restore China's "revolutionary" spirit by reversing the increasing bureaucratization of party and government through purges.

     Thus the memories of Korea, it has been charged, paralyzed U.S. strategy, preventing the application of sufficient pressure to compel North Vietnam to desist from the war in the south. Col. Harry G. Summers, *On Strategy* (New York: Dell Publishing Co., 1984).

49. Barry M. Blechman and Stephen S. Kaplan, *Force Without War* and Stephen S. Kaplan *Diplomacy of Power* (Washington, D.C.: The Brookings Institution, 1978 and 1981, respectively).

50. See especially the National Conference of Catholic Bishops, *The Challenge of Peace: God's Promise and Our Response* (Washington, D.C.: United States Catholic Conference, 1983); and the best seller by Jonathan Schell, *The Fate of the Earth* (New York: Avon Books, 1982), part I, p. 3ff.

51. George H. Quester, *The Future of Nuclear Deterrence* (Lexington, Mass.: Lexington Books, 1986).

China and the Global Balance of Power

The Impact of a New Actor

As the Cold War emerged from the ashes of World War II the structure of the international system became increasingly bipolar. Almost no one had foreseen such a concentration of power by the United States and the U.S.S.R. Certainly it was understood that Germany and Japan would be demilitarized and reduced for a time as political actors. But the assumption was widespread that among the victors, Britain and France would regain their status as great powers and that China would be a major factor in keeping the peace in the Far East. Formal recognition of these great powers was given in the United Nations Charter which made the United States, the Soviet Union, France, Great Britain, and China permanent members of the United Nations Security Council (and thus endowed with the power of the veto). As events developed, neither Great Britain nor France retained the great power status they had acquired before the war; indeed, few people understood in 1945 just how badly British and French power had been sapped by the war.

China, however was a different case. It emerged from the war a weak power. Although a large Asian state, on the winning side of the war and a permanent member of the United Nations Security Council, China's real status in the international hierarchy was low. The reasons for China's weaknesses were several. For one, the Japanese had devastated much of the country during the war. China survived not because of its resistance to the Japanese, but because Japan was conquered by the United States. Even more debilitating was the civil war that divided the country. At the end of that war the Communists under Mao Zedong's leadership had won control over large segments of the nation, particularly in northwest and north central China. By 1945 approximately one-quarter of the population and 15 percent (exclusive of Manchuria) of the territory were under Communist control. The Nationalists under Chiang Kai-shek were the recognized government of China, but that regime was authoritarian, corrupt, incompetent, and unable to unite the country.

However, while Britain and France declined in comparison to their prewar status as great powers, China eventually enhanced its position. China always had the potential to become a great power. It comprised a large population with a long history of cultural achievement. Although lacking the skills of a modern industrial society, the Chinese people were talented enough to acquire them, and the country was rich in natural resources. The fundamental reason for China's weakness was its inability to create a political system that could unite the country and harness the economic skills of its people. The first step toward overcoming this weakness was the unification of the country (except for Taiwan) under the Communists in 1949. More than a generation later the post-Mao leadership would introduce the economic reforms that would unleash the productivity of the Chinese people.

During the course of the Cold War China has become a great power, though not a superpower. As such it has played a dynamic role in the global balance of power. The dynamism of China's policy was rooted in its capacity to shift its alignment between the superpowers, which it has done twice. The major hallmarks of those shifts were the Sino-Soviet alliance, the Sino-Soviet rift, and the Sino-American rapprochement. We can divide China's relations with the superpowers into five general periods as follows:

1. 1945–1949 Nationalist government in power on mainland
2. 1949–1959 Sino-Soviet alliance
3. 1959–1969 Sino-Soviet rift
4. 1972–1979 Soviet-American rapprochement
5. 1980–present shift toward equidistance

As we will observe in examining each of these periods, the relations between the Soviet Union, the United States, and China were always complex and often contradictory.

The Period of Nationalist Dominance

There were some interesting similarities between U.S. and Soviet policies toward China after the war. One was the assumption in both Moscow and Washington that Chiang Kai-shek would survive the Communist challenge. Both governments recognized that Mao Zedong controlled a large segment of the Chinese people, but neither believed that he was capable of overthrowing the Nationalist government. Moscow apparently even agreed with the United States that China should have a coalition government. The American effort through General George Marshall to induce Chiang to admit the Communists into the government is well known.[1] According to Milovan Djilas, Stalin also "invited the Chinese comrades to reach an agreement as to how a modus vivendi with Chiang Kai-shek might be found."[2] Stalin acknowledged that Mao ignored his advice, and even admitted that Mao was correct in doing so.

Stalin, who carried cynical expediency in modern diplomacy to unparalleled heights, managed to maintain good relations with both sides in the Chinese civil war. On August 14, 1945, China and the Soviet Union signed a treaty of friendship and alliance whereby Moscow recognized the regime of Chiang Kai-shek as the legitimate government of China and promised to provide it with military and other material resources. Of course, there was a price. Chiang was operating from a position of extreme weakness and had to concede to the U.S.S.R. several of its longstanding objectives in China. Among these were Chinese recognition of the independence of the Mongolian People's Republic (Moscow's first true satellite); Soviet participation in the operation of the Chinese Eastern Railway; joint Sino-Soviet use of the naval base at Port Arthur; and internationalization of Dairen.[3] Basically, Stalin sought to recover the sphere of influence in China that tsarist Russia lost in the Russo-Japanese War of 1904–1905.

But there is no doubt that Stalin favored the Communist cause of Mao Zedong. Perhaps if he could have foreseen what a rival China would become, he might have had second thoughts. However, it is more likely that he thought of a Communist China as a potentially subordinate ally, perhaps not as obedient as the satellites of eastern Europe but certainly willing to cooperate against the imperialist foe. In the "two-camp" theory which he resurrected after the war Stalin viewed Mao as a fighter in the "antiimperialist and democratic" (i.e., Soviet) camp. Also, Stalin could not have forgotten the treachery of Chiang in 1927 when the Nationalist leader betrayed the Kremlin's confidence and virtually wiped out the military arm of the Chinese Communist party.

Following the Japanese surrender in 1945 the Soviet forces in control of large areas of northern China gave considerable assistance to the Chinese Communists, who occupied major portions of Manchuria. The Soviet military forces obstructed Chiang's attempt to take over Manchuria, and they gave large quantities of captured Japanese weapons to Mao's troops. This is not to suggest that Mao's ultimate victory was made in Moscow. Far from it. The Chinese civil war ended with the victory of the Communists because of internal conditions — basically the inability of the Nationalists to win the hearts and minds of the Chinese peasants, workers, and the emerging middle class.

Soviet policy in this period was less revolutionary than nationalist. Stalin was less concerned with promoting Chinese communism than in creating the conditions for a weak China that would be dependent on Soviet goodwill. One graphic example of Soviet self-interest in China was the removal of virtually all industrial plant, rolling stock, and usable equipment from Manchuria before the province was turned over to the Communists. This rapacity was also carried out in the German zone of Germany and parts of eastern Europe. However, in the case of Europe it could be rationalized that the U.S.S.R. dealt with an enemy that had inflicted terrible damage on the Soviet economy. No such case could be made for the Soviet stripping of Manchuria.

If Moscow's policies had a subversive impact on the Nationalist government, those of the United States cannot be said to have been strongly supportive. Some U.S. assistance was provided but nothing on the scale offered to Europe under the Marshall Plan. There was pressure from the U.S. Congress to increase financial and military assistance to China, but the Truman administration was discouraged by previous efforts to unify China with a coalition government of Communists and Nationalists. There was a growing pessimism that the Nationalists were losing control of China and a hope that should the Communists win, the United States could do business with them.[4] It should be noted that before his appointment as secretary of state George Marshall had spent a year in China trying to arrange a truce and some sort of coalition government. He held the Nationalists as responsible as the Communists for the failure of his endeavors. In July 1947 President Truman sent General Albert C. Wedemeyer to China for a fresh appraisal of the situation. Wedemeyer bluntly told Chiang Kai-shek that drastic economic and political reforms were necessary. Even so, on his return to the United States he urged President Truman to intervene actively in the Chinese civil war without waiting for the Nationalist government to make the desired reforms. Counseled by George Marshall and Dean Acheson, Truman rejected Wedemeyer's proposals. By this time the United States and the Soviet Union were in open conflict in Europe and Truman sought, if possible, to avoid an extension of that conflict to the mainland of Asia.[5] No one can say with certainty what the outcome of a large-scale program of military and economic aid to Nationalist China would have produced; but it seems clear that, as in eastern Europe, a sizable U.S. involvement to prevent a Communist takeover was more than the U.S. government or the American people were prepared to make. In the fall of 1949 Maoist troops forced Chiang Kai-shek to evacuate his forces to the island of Formosa, and on October 1 Mao Zedong proclaimed the People's Republic of China.

The Sino-Soviet Alliance

The victory of the Communists in China was welcomed in Moscow even though Stalin must have realized that under the new regime he could not retain all the concessions that he had extracted from Chiang Kai-shek. Nevertheless, a Communist China opened up horizons for the Kremlin that Lenin may have dreamed of but which Stalin hardly considered realizable at the time. Stalin, however, was enough of a realist to appreciate how much a Sino-Soviet alliance could cause a shift in the global balance of power. The "antiimperialist and democratic camp" that Andrei Zhdanov had described at the founding of the Cominform now composed one-third of the world.

The new relationship between the Soviet Union and China required a replacement of the 1945 Sino-Soviet treaty. To accomplish this Mao Zedong went to Moscow in December 1949 where he remained for almost 10 weeks. He and the Soviet leaders bargained long and hard. The results were three treaties that represented concessions on both sides. Moscow agreed to return the Chinese Changchun Railway and the naval base at Port Arthur. The commercial port of Dairen was recognized as belonging to China. Stalin promised to give China a $300 million credit, an amount so small that it displeased rather than assuaged Mao. Finally, they concluded a 30-year treaty of alliance directed at Japan or any other state that should ally with Japan, i.e., the United States.

The Sino-Soviet alliance was not the only factor shifting the balance of power toward the Soviet bloc. On September 23, 1949, President Truman announced that the Soviet Union had successfully detonated an atomic device. Only four years after America built an atomic bomb the U.S.S.R. had duplicated that feat. Although the Communist victory and the atomic explosion did not add immediately to Soviet military power, they did presage a trend that was favorable to the Soviet bloc. At the beginning of 1950 Stalin was probably at the peak of his power in the international arena. Unquestionably this altered configuration of global power contributed to the outbreak of war in Korea in June 1950 even though Stalin himself probably did not order the invasion. The Korean forces were Soviet-supplied and could not have attacked unless Stalin approved.[6]

The Impact of the Korean War
The Korean war was to have a profound impact on Sino-Soviet and Sino-American relations. Basically it sealed the Sino-

Soviet alliance. For more than a decade the United States was a common enemy to both Communist states. American opinion toward China hardened as a result of that war. There is good reason to believe that Sino-American relations may have been reasonably normal, if not actually good, had the Korean war not intruded. Shortly after the Communist victory in China the Truman administration released a White Paper on U.S.–China policy. It was critical of the way Chiang used U.S. military and economic aid. Moreover, as a gesture of friendship as well as a recognition of realities, it even suggested that the People's Republic be recognized as the legal government of China. Truman also announced that U.S. forces would not be used in the defense of Formosa and that military aid to the Nationalists would cease.[7] Traditionally, the Americans and the Chinese had been friends. To the extent that the United States involved itself in Chinese affairs it had supported the territorial integrity and political independence of China. The so-called open door policy was aimed at preventing other great powers from establishing protected markets in China.

Korea changed all that. Within four months after the war began U.S. forces had reached the Yalu River, the boundary between North Korea and China. Disregarding Chinese warnings that they would intervene, General Douglas MacArthur pushed to the north. In late November 1950 massive Chinese forces attacked U.S. forces (technically U.N. forces since the Security Council had authorized the use of a U.N. flag and command), and for the first time the United States and China were engaged in a de facto war against each other. One consequence was a massive shift of opinion in both countries against the other. Americans viewed China as much of an enemy as North Korea. It was almost a generation before American public opinion changed enough to allow a new policy toward China. Another consequence was the de facto alliance that developed between the United States and the Nationalist government on Formosa. On June 27 President Truman ordered the Seventh Fleet to patrol the Formosa Straits, thus dooming any possible Communist seizure of the island of Formosa. From the Chinese perspective the United States had become a party to their civil war. Finally, the Korean war made Beijing more dependent on Moscow than ever before. As it turned out the limited Soviet assistance to its Chinese comrades contributed to the evolving disenchantment between the two allies; yet Chinese dependence on Soviet support through the 1950s limited Mao's options considerably.

The Sino-Soviet alliance endured for about a decade although it did not formally terminate until 1980 when China chose not to renew the treaty of friendship and alliance. In general the 1950s was a period of cooperation between the two governments. In vital ways both countries were vulnerable, so each had something to gain by sticking together and much to lose by disbanding the partnership. By Soviet standards Moscow gave China considerable financial and economic assistance. From 1950–1955 Soviet loans to China totaled $1,325 million. Moscow boasted that "China's achievements in various fields of building a new life were based on the Soviet people's comprehensive experience and tremendous material aid."[8] According to Russian sources, new agreements for Soviet aid to China were signed in every year from 1953 through 1957. These agreements provided for building power stations; constructing or modernizing hundreds of industrial projects; transferring shares of joint stock companies in oil and metalworks; giving blueprints, equipment, and scientific and technical data; supplying machine tools, cranes, compressors, pumps, diesel engines, generators, vehicles, and farm machines; carrying out joint exploration and research of China's natural resources; and transferring Soviet-built hospitals to Chinese cities.[9] Unquestionably, some generosity was shown by the U.S.S.R. but nothing like the extravagant claims made by Moscow. The vast bulk of Soviet assistance had to be paid for in Chinese goods delivered to the Soviet Union or in hard currency.[10] Of particular importance was the agreement of April 27, 1955, under which the Soviet Union helped China to build her first experimental atomic pile and cyclotron. At the time Moscow was probably unaware of China's intention to use such aid to produce nuclear weapons.[11]

During the 1950s Moscow and Beijing had different domestic and foreign policy agendas. Political leadership was in transition inside the Kremlin, culminating ultimately in the ascendancy of Nikita Khrushchev. At the Twentieth Party Congress he began his campaign against the "cult of the individual" to rid Soviet society of some of its harshest Stalinist features. China was in the throes of even greater revolutionary change including the building of a leadership cult around Mao. During 1954–1955 the Chinese Communist party engaged in a bitter intraparty struggle to purge its ranks of political heretics. Mao emerged from this struggle more fully in control, and in 1958 he introduced the national campaign for domestic transformation, which became known as the "Great Leap Forward." Neither country fully understood or approved of what was going on in the other, but each recognized the value of the alliance and avoided doing anything that would disrupt it. There was no doubt in either Moscow or Beijing that Washington was the main threat and the major enemy.

In their respective foreign policies the U.S.S.R. and China supported each other. Moscow fully endorsed China's leading role at the Afro-Asian meeting in Bandung, Indonesia, in April 1955 at which the nonaligned movement was created. The Chinese defense minister attended the organization of the Warsaw pact in May 1955 and offered to provide Chinese forces in the event of a war in Europe. Of particular value to Moscow was China's endorsement of the Soviet suppression of Hungary's effort in 1956 to liberate itself from the Soviet bloc. Twice during the decade (September 1954 and August–October 1958) China bombarded the Nationalist-held offshore islands of Quemoy and Matsu in what appeared at the time to be preparatory steps to invading them. The more serious of the two offshore crises was the 1958 attack. Politically (though not militarily) Moscow supported the Chinese actions. In the face of American support for Nationalist China under a U.S. administration whose secretary of state defended brinkmanship as a foreign policy tactic, Nikita Khrushchev warned President Eisenhower on September 7 that Moscow would interpret "an attack on the People's Republic of China" as "an attack on the

Soviet Union."[12] On the propaganda front Moscow's unity with Beijing on the Quemoy and Matsu issue was solid. In the realm of action, however, caution prevailed on all sides. Neither Moscow nor Washington wanted to get into a fight over the offshore islands, and Beijing, then just beginning its Great Leap Forward, was in no position to engage the United States single-handedly.

China's revolutionary policies — both domestic and foreign — put a severe strain on the alliance in the 1950s. Barely six months after the crisis over Quemoy and Matsu China was involved in a conflict with India, which proved to be very embarrassing to the Soviet Union. The Sino-Indian conflict had its origins in the sympathy that India gave to the Tibetan nationalists who rebelled early in 1959 to challenge Chinese domination of the Himalayan kingdom. The Dalai Lama, Tibetan government leaders, and thousands of refugees fled to India, thus producing a wave of anti-Chinese feelings in India and anti-Indian sentiments in China. Possibly in order to punish India for its support for the Tibetan nationalists, but also as a show of its growing importance in Asian politics, the Chinese created a series of border incidents along the Sino-Indian frontier including the seizure of a frontier post in Indian territory. Moscow was caught in a bind because of its close ties to India. Khrushchev went to great pains to avoid offending either side, but the impartiality of the Soviet attitude was itself offensive to the Chinese. This incident was the first time since the Sino-Soviet alliance that Moscow had not given unqualified support to its ally on an important issue in international affairs.[13] This was an outward sign that the alliance was under serious strain.

The Sino-Soviet Rift

By the 1960s the Sino-Soviet alliance was not just under strain; it was dead. Actually, there was evidence of a growing rift throughout the whole decade. At first the signs were verbal and polemical; by the end of the decade the two Communist giants were engaged in a mini-war. Before we examine the manifestations of this rift we should ask the question: Why did the Sino-Soviet alliance collapse? On the surface there was a strong case for the durability of the coalition: The U.S.S.R. and China shared a common Marxist-Leninist ideology; they were both authoritarian regimes controlled by a Communist party; both governments were expansionist and opposed to the status quo; and perhaps most important, both were vulnerable to the power of the western alliance led by the United States. Although all of the above reasons in support of the alliance are subject to serious qualification, there is an element of truth in each of them.

On the question of ideology it can be argued that the differences were more significant than the similarities. Certainly the Soviet interpretation of Marxism-Leninism, emphasizing the importance of the industrial proletariat in the revolution, was quite different from the Maoist emphasis on the role of the peasant. As to the nature of their regimes, both were one-party dictatorships, but even that label concealed important differences such as the more developed bureaucratic structure in Russia than in China and the increased power of the military in Chinese politics. As to expansionism, there were also important differences. China was a country territorily divided by the revolution, while the Soviet Union had not only achieved territorial unity and integrity but had enormously expanded its sphere of control in eastern Europe. Regarding the vulnerability of both nations to American power, there is less question. That argument alone should have buttressed the coalition. In classical balance-of-power theory weaker states tend to unite when confronted with a stronger state. There is no doubt that U.S. strategic power exceeded that of both its adversaries combined.

So we return to the question: Why did the Sino-Soviet alliance break up? The essential explanation can be reduced to two words: nuclear weapons. In the decade of the 1950s the Soviet Union and the United States both built a nuclear inventory and delivery systems for atomic weapons. Eisenhower's "New Look" strategy stressed the role of nuclear weapons to

counter Soviet expansionism. Following the Soviet success
with Sputnik in 1957 the United States accelerated its production of Titan, Minuteman, and Polaris missiles.[14] By the end of
the decade the United States was strategically superior to the
Soviet Union although Moscow clearly had a deterrent capability. Peace was kept, in the words of Albert Wohlstetter, by
"the delicate balance of terror."[15] Khrushchev realized the
folly of a nuclear war and increasingly came to see the importance of building a stable relationship with the United States.
China was not the reckless power depicted in America and
later by Soviet propaganda, willing to risk a nuclear war to
destroy imperialism, but it was prepared to take more risks
than its ally. Beijing's revolutionary propulsion to expand conflicted with Moscow's caution. Thus the Sino-Soviet alliance
failed to achieve China's foreign policy objectives, notably
with regard to Formosa and India. For the Kremlin the alliance
became a nuisance because of the continuing threat of a confrontation with the United States, a confrontation Khrushchev
wanted to avoid, if at all possible.

Moscow's Nuclear Nightmare

Another danger that Moscow came to appreciate in the 1950s
was the spread of nuclear weapons. Soviet support for a nuclear test ban, which was strongly opposed by its ally, was
designed in large part to halt nuclear proliferation. When Nikita Khrushchev wrote to Chou En-lai in April 1958 explaining
the Soviet decision to suspend nuclear testing, he argued that
"if the tests are not terminated now, other countries may develop nuclear weapons. . . ."[16] One can only speculate on
Chinese sensitivity to this argument as they contemplated
being included among the "other countries." Undoubtedly
Khrushchev was shocked that year when the People's Republic announced its intention to become a nuclear power. Certainly the Kremlin had to be somewhat apprehensive about
Mao Zedong's depreciation of the dangers of a nuclear war
during the offshore islands crisis that year. As Benjamin Lambeth noted, "The Soviets were rudely awakened to the oner-

ous possibility that in some future crisis, in which China possessed its own atomic bombs, the way out might not be so easy, and Moscow might then be dragged into a catalytic nuclear confrontation with the United States because of some irresponsibility on the part of its allies in Beijing."[17] These Soviet fears led to the suspension of all atomic materials to China between the summer of 1958 and 1959. In June 1959 the Soviet government unilaterally abrogated the 1957 agreement that provided for atomic aid to China.

We know that nuclear weapons and China became almost obsessive concerns of Nikita Khrushchev. As the Sino-Soviet rift unfolded Soviet sources quoted Mao Zedong as having almost a bloodthirsty view of nuclear war. According to *Pravda*, for example, Mao told Jawaharlal Nehru "that if half of mankind were destroyed in a nuclear war, the other half would survive, and, moreover, imperialism would be fully liquidated and socialism would triumph throughout the world, and in half-a-century or a full century the population would again grow, perhaps by over half."[18] By the summer of 1962 the Soviet government had become committed to stopping China from acquiring nuclear weapons. But how to achieve this? Even among friends it is difficult for one nation to influence the nuclear policy of another, and by the early 1960s Moscow and Beijing were not exactly friends. Adam Ulam speculates that Khrushchev's scheme to put nuclear-armed missiles in Cuba in 1962 was part of a grand plan to stop nuclear proliferation in both West Germany and China. Part of China's incentive would be the American abandonment of Formosa.[19] There is no confirmation of this hypothesis, but it is not beyond the realm of political possibility. Of course, if that was what Khrushchev had in mind, he failed completely. And worse, from the Soviet perspective, China moved steadily toward the acquisition of nuclear weapons.

Even if the argument that the nuclear issue doomed the Sino-Soviet alliance is valid, it does not explain the Sino-Soviet rift. It is one thing for two parties to cease to be allies; it is quite another for them to become enemies. But that in fact is what happened during the 1960s. The causes of the Sino-Soviet conflict are multiple and complex. Some of the roots go deep into history. For 200 years during the thirteenth and fourteenth centuries Russia was conquered and dominated by the Mongol Tatars, the ancestors of today's Chinese. Quite likely this historical memory still colors the Russian perception of its oriental neighbor. Recent western scholarship suggests that the Mongol yoke may not have been as brutal as once believed, but the fact is that in Soviet history the Mongols are treated as cruel overlords. More recent history witnessed a reversal of political fortunes when the tsars in the nineteenth century forced the Manchu emperor to cede territories to Russia under the so-called unequal treaties. These territories involved large parts of Soviet Siberia north of the Amur and east of the Ussuri rivers and the island of Sakhalin. For a time China was demanding the renegotiation of these unequal treaties, a demand Moscow had steadfastly resisted.

The antagonism between China and Russia developed under the leaderships of Khrushchev and Mao, a point that has led some observers to focus on the personalities of the two leaders as a factor in the rift. Indeed there could hardly be a greater contrast between the intellectual Chinese who prided himself on his poetry as well as philosophy and the earthy, garrulous Russian. There was little affection between them. Khrushchev in his memoirs accuses Mao of playing politics "with Asiatic cunning, following his own rules of cajolery, treachery, savage vengeance, and deceit."[20] But at most we can credit the leaders' styles and personalities with exacerbating rather than causing the enmity. For one thing, there was conflict over more vital issues than the rhetoric that passed between them. For another, the political demise of Khrushchev in 1964 and the death of Mao in 1976 did not restore amity between China and the Soviet Union. It is believed that one of the reasons for Khrushchev's removal in October 1964 was the Politburo's desire to normalize relations with China. If that was so, then the effort was in vain. Beijing only accused Moscow of practicing "Khrushchevism" without Khrushchev.

Ideological Differences

Another factor in the antagonism was Sino-Soviet differences in ideology. Though both regimes claimed to be adherents of the same Marxist-Leninist doctrines, the fact is that in domestic and foreign policy they applied those doctrines in very different ways. A bitter debate erupted when the Chinese announced their plan to establish a communes program in the summer and fall of 1958 in connection with their Great Leap Forward. Under this plan the commune would become the basic social unit of China's Communist society. Agricultural cooperatives were to be combined with small-scale industry, thus replacing large industrial complexes (some built with Soviet aid) with hundreds of thousands of small and medium plants. These communes, China claimed, would "accelerate socialist construction, complete the building of socialism ahead of time and carry out the gradual transition to Communism."[21] Beijing implied that this was a short cut that would bring China to communism before its Soviet ally, which had a 32-year head start.

Moscow was outraged at the arrogance of Beijing's claims. Not only were the Chinese rejecting the Soviet model of economic development, they were heading down a disastrous path that would waste huge amounts of resources including aid given by the Soviet Union. Furthermore, they clearly saw the Chinese communes as an ideological challenge. There is no doubt whom the Soviets had in mind when *Pravda* in June 1960 asserted that

> The claims of the contemporary "Left-wingers" in the international Communist movement that when you have power in your hands, Communism can be introduced immediately, bypassing definite historical stages of development, are wrong. Such claims contradict Leninism.[22]

But was this fundamentally an ideological issue? The problem with debates that are ideological in form is that it is sometimes difficult to distinguish form from substance. We often confuse ideological posturing with theory. Ideological arguments can easily be rationalizations for political objectives. In those instances it is important to understand the real political objective behind the doctrinal debate. Essentially the debate over the communes and the road to communism was a contest for power because Mao had in effect claimed to have solved the problem of building communism in underdeveloped (or developing) countries. As Donald Zagoria notes, "For the Russians to concede this would be tantamount to conceding to Peking the leadership of the revolution in Asia, Africa, and Latin America."[23]

Just as China and the Soviet Union differed over the issue of building communism at home, so did they clash on the question of the global strategy to follow in the fight against imperialism. Strategy for Communists is an essential element of doctrine and as such is viewed as scientific in nature. A central question for Communist theoreticians is the nature of the epoch and what constitutes the balance of forces (in the Soviet terminology, the "correlation of forces") between socialism and capitalism. The power relationship between Communists and their enemies determines the overall strategy to be pursued. An assessment that minimizes the strength of the enemy is a "leftist deviation" that results in policies of adventurism and risk. A "rightist deviation" is one that overestimates imperialism's strength and leads to inaction or unnecessary compromise.

From Moscow's point of view Mao became a left deviationist; i.e., he was guilty of urging a premature forward strategy and recklessly risking a nuclear confrontation. Mao saw Khrushchev as a right deviationist because of the Soviet leader's determination to avoid a military confrontation with the United States. Apparently the two sides' perceptions of the correlations of forces differed because of differences over the significance of the Soviet accomplishments with ballistic missiles in 1957. On August 26 Tass announced the successful Soviet test of an ICBM, something the United States had not yet achieved. This was followed up with an announcement on October 4 of Moscow's successful launch of an earth satellite (the Sputnik), again a first. The Chinese concluded from these events that the Soviet Union had surpassed the United States in overall military capability, a view expressed in the slogan ". . . it is not the west wind which is prevailing over the east wind, but the east wind prevailing over the west wind."[24]

While Khrushchev was espousing "peaceful coexistence" in order to avoid a nuclear confrontation with the United States, Mao was willing to challenge the "paper tiger" of imperialism with his own brand of brinkmanship. Mao resented the Soviet failure to back him up with military support in his struggle for the offshore islands and with India. Added to this was Chinese resentment over Khrushchev's diplomacy, which appeared overly and increasingly accommodating to the west, sometimes even at the expense of Chinese prestige. Such, for example, was their perception of the Soviet handling of the crisis in the Middle East in the summer of 1958. The crisis involved western intervention in Lebanon and Jordan. To support prowestern governments American marines were sent to Lebanon and British paratroopers to Jordan. Khrushchev's response was to propose a heads-of-government conference comprised of Russia, the United States, Britain, France, and India! Adding insult to injury the Soviet leader even agreed to President Eisenhower's proposal that a conference take place within the framework of the United Nations Security Council (which at that time would have brought the Nationalist Chinese into the picture). Apparently under pressure from Beijing Khrushchev backed away from the idea of meeting within the framework of the Security Council. But shortly thereafter he made his first visit to the United States, an adventure that produced the disquieting — to the Chinese — "spirit of Camp David."

Khrushchev's effort to achieve a détente with the United States intensified in the last years of his rule, much to the displeasure of the Chinese. The Cuban missile crisis in the fall of 1962 marked a turning point in U.S.–Soviet relations. China strongly disapproved of the compromise that ended that crisis because it resulted in the dismantling of the Soviet bases on the island. As a demonstration of its feeling the Chinese government sent Cuba a telegram pledging to remain "reliable comrades-in-arms" and to stick by the Cuban people "through thick and thin." As Khrushchev moved closer to accommodation with the United States Chinese resentment grew even more. It boiled over when the U.S.S.R. joined Britain and the United States in signing a partial nuclear test ban treaty in 1963. Beijing denounced the treaty as a "dirty fraud." The Kremlin was accused of having "willingly allowed U.S. imperialism to get military superiority"; of having "betrayed the peoples of the Socialist camp" including the Russians and the Chinese.[25] Behind all these ideological and polemical fireworks was a profound sense of betrayal by what Beijing felt was Khrushchev's willingness to court the imperialist United States and the neutralist countries.

Conflicts of Interest
A major contribution to the growing Sino-Soviet enmity were the conflicts of interest between the two nations. Three in particular aggravated relations: (1) the competition for leadership of the Socialist camp, (2) the termination of Soviet economic aid to China, and (3) territorial claims made by China. The Soviet Union has always viewed itself as the leader of the Socialist camp. So did the Chinese Communists while Stalin was alive. Mao deferred to Stalin, but he was unwilling to do the same for his successors because he believed that his prestige was higher. Nevertheless, for a time Mao made no effort to challenge the primacy of the U.S.S.R. even during the Malenkov and early Khrushchev years. Chinese loyalty was strongly affirmed at the gathering of Communist parties in Moscow in November 1957 to mark the fortieth anniversary of the Bolshevik revolution. Mao explicitly acknowledged Soviet hegemony: "Every organization must have a head and the C.P.S.U. is best fitted to be the head of the international Communist movement."[26] After 1958, however, the Chinese position changed, in part as a result of disillusionment with

Khrushchev's policies and in part out of ambition to assume what Beijing believed to be its rightful place in the Socialist camp. At first the rivalry was covert. It burst into the open on the occasion of the ninetieth anniversary of Lenin's birth in April 1960 with the publication of a bitter critique of Moscow's leadership. The polemic was entitled "Long Live Leninism." In it the Chinese claimed that they, not the Russians, were the true standard bearers of Lenin's revolutionary tradition. That was the beginning of years of public polemics, which grew increasingly bitter through the 1960s. At the Twenty-second Party Congress Khrushchev publicly attacked the Chinese through their ally, Albania. Shortly before he was toppled in a coup Khrushchev organized a world conference of Communist parties for the probable purpose of expelling China from the Socialist camp. Only his overthrow in 1964 prevented an all-out Soviet effort to formally expel China.

Mention has been made of Moscow's repudiation in 1959 of its nuclear aid agreement with China. This was followed by Moscow's withdrawal of all its technical aid to China in the summer of 1960. According to Chinese accounts 1,390 Soviet experts were withdrawn, 343 contracts for technical aid were canceled, and 257 scientific and technical projects were terminated. The consequences were very damaging to the Chinese economy. These unilateral actions caused as much resentment in China as anything yet done by the Russians.

Potentially the most disrupting issue between both countries involved territorial and border claims, although the problem did not arise until after the recall of Soviet technicians from China. Chinese and Soviet sources claim that border incidents began in July 1960. The first public indication to the non-Communist world that China sought a revision of the Sino-Soviet frontier was made in March 1963 when the *People's Daily* mentioned nine treaties that former Chinese governments had been forced to sign including the treaties of Aigun and Beijing in the nineteenth century. These claims were made at about the same time that numerous incidents occurred along the border between Xinjiang and Soviet central Asia. In boundary negotiations begun in 1964 the Chinese laid claim to over 580,000 square miles of Soviet territory. *Pravda,* in an editorial shortly before Khrushchev was overthrown, declared that "We are faced with an openly expansionist programme with far-reaching pretensions." It warned that "any attempt to re-carve the map of the world" could lead to "the most dangerous consequences."[27]

As the Great Proletarian Revolution unfolded during 1966–1968 relations reached a nadir. Border incidents occurred frequently. The polemics on both sides became bitter. Moscow charged the Chinese with persecuting Kazaks, Uighers, and other nationalities in Xinjiag. Beijing replied with accusations of Soviet subversion. As the border tensions increased in the late 1960s Soviet troops were sent from eastern Europe to the Sino-Soviet border to bolster security. The number of Soviet divisions in the Far East was increased from 15 in 1967 to 21 in 1969, an increase that greatly disturbed the Chinese.

The culmination of these tensions was a pitched battle on March 2, 14, and 15, 1969, between Soviet and Chinese frontier guards. The fighting took place on a small uninhabited island in the Ussuri River known to the Russians as Damansky Island and to the Chinese as Chenpao Island. A Chinese attack was repulsed by the Soviets with a considerable loss of life on both sides. For a brief period Soviet troops penetrated deep into Chinese territory. Although both sides had acted provocatively in the crisis, and in spite of virulent and bellicose propaganda sallies in the press, neither side wanted the issue to be pressed to the point of war. But they came close. Diplomatic steps were taken to limit the damage, but the Damansky incident clearly revealed the existence of deep-seated animosities on both sides.

Leonid Brezhnev himself was faced with the same basic dilemma that had confronted his predecessor, and his response was basically the same: containment of the People's Republic. A conference of world Communist parties was convened in Moscow in June 1969 in part to isolate China. Brezhnev introduced a plan for an Asian collective security system not unlike the idea John Foster Dulles had promoted in the 1950s as a means of containing China. The idea was not endorsed by the conference. The failure of the conference's final document to mention China by name revealed the strong resistance within the Communist parties against formalizing a split in the world movement.

The Sino-American Rapprochement

China was profoundly isolated and potentially very vulnerable. On August 28, 1969, *Pravda* even warned the Chinese of the dangers of nuclear weapons if war ever broke out.[28] By the early 1970s the Chinese had virtually no allies politically or otherwise. In fact, as a consequence of the Great Proletarian Revolution Chinese relations with the rest of the world were more limited than at any time since the revolution. The logic of balance-of-power politics virtually compelled China (and the U.S.S.R.) to move toward an accommodation with the United States. And that is precisely what did happen. International politics acquired a triangular structure that profoundly affected the foreign policies of all three nations.

Triangular Politics

Triangular politics is not the same thing as tripolarity. China was nowhere near the equal of the two superpowers militarily and economically notwithstanding its large territory and huge population. But China was in a critical position to shift the balance between the United States and the Soviet Union. That leverage, however, depended on its willingness to maintain a flexible foreign policy. Until the Sino-Soviet rift China had not pursued a flexible foreign policy. In general, it maintained a high degree of rigidity as an ally of the Soviet Union and the sworn enemy of American imperialism. For Moscow the Sino-Soviet alliance was critical because throughout the period of the alliance the U.S.S.R. was considerably weaker than the United States. It needed the combination with Chinese power to come even close to rivaling America. So it was a case of two weaker states uniting to combat the power of an adversary stronger than both. It is no accident that China's move to "the other side" came about at the same time that the Soviet Union was reaching true military parity with the United States.

An important ingredient of triangular politics is the extent to which each of the parties fears collusion between the other two. During the 1950s and 1960s the United States more or less assumed it was dealing with a monolithic Communist bloc adversary. That fear (unfounded as of the 1960s) was a potent factor propelling the United States into the Vietnamese civil war. Little did the Kennedy or Johnson administrations realize how much their support for South Vietnam was producing the united Communist front they so feared.

Other collusive possibilities always existed. Theoretically the United States and the Soviet Union could enter a partnership directed against China; and China and the United States could align themselves against the U.S.S.R. The rift between Moscow and Beijing made these hypothetical arrangements real possibilities. It is clear that as relations between the Communist governments soured the Soviet Union came to fear the Chinese — not China alone, perhaps, but China in alliance with America or Japan or both. That fear was a major motivation for the Soviet Union's move toward détente with the United States in the 1970s.[29] Brezhnev and his colleagues wanted to use the United States as a means of pressure against China and at the same time to prevent China from being used by the United States as pressure against Moscow.

Another possibility in the triangular relationship was collusion between the United States and the Soviet Union against China. And it should be stressed that — unlikely as it was — the Chinese genuinely feared that Moscow and Washington would gang up against them. From the moment the Nixon administration started wooing the Chinese it affirmed its determination not to join with the Soviet Union to seek some form of global hegemony. Of the three possible alignments considered here the U.S.–Soviet was always the least likely because Washington never doubted for a moment that the main threat to its security lay in Moscow and nowhere else. Triangular politics developed essentially at the point when China came to that same conclusion. From then on China's foreign policy moved away from ideology toward geopolitics.

There remains finally a consideration of the factors that drove the United States into partnership with China. It certainly required a radical change in U.S.–Chinese relations to make triangular politics a reality. American motivation can be summed up simply: the Vietnam war. The Nixon administration came to power determined to disengage the United States from Vietnam. It hoped to do so by negotiation, since outright military victory seemed impossible. Domestic politics had made the achievement of U.S. goals by military means unattainable. Added to that was Hanoi's diplomatic intransigence. Nixon and his foreign affairs adviser, Henry Kissinger, saw in the Sino-Soviet rift an opportunity to bring pressure on Hanoi. If America could restructure its relations with both the Soviet Union and China, then it might be possible for one or both to help the United States disengage from Vietnam on terms acceptable to Washington. Henry Kissinger saw, as he records in his memoirs, "the possibilities of triangular diplomacy to help settle the war."[30]

Détente between the United States and China required a major change of perception of the other in both capitals. For 20 years U.S. policy makers and the public alike viewed China as a fanatic, aggressive — and at times irrational — power. Vietnam's expansionism was seen as a manifestation of Chinese aggression. Also, there were serious unresolved differences between the two nations, especially the issue of Taiwan. The United States was committed to the defense of Taiwan from Chinese attack, while Beijing was determined to ultimately bring Taiwan under the sovereignty of the People's Republic. Lesser problems involved American claims to compensation for nationalized property and Chinese efforts to recover its assets in the United States. For almost 15 years these and a few other issues had been the subject of sterile discussions between diplomats in the Polish capital of Warsaw.

Rapprochement

The rapprochement between China and the United States had its beginnings precisely on January 20, 1970. On that date the first official meeting between representatives of the Nixon administration and the People's Republic of China took place in Warsaw at the Chinese Embassy. This was the 135th meeting of a series that had taken place on and off for over 15 years. At that session Ambassador (to Poland) Walter Stoessel proposed sending a U.S. representative to Beijing for direct discussions. The response, to the delight of the White House, was positive. Henry Kissinger believed that the Chinese were interested in improving relations with the United States because they "wanted strategic reassurance, some easing of the nightmare of hostile encirclement," which the new administration was prepared to provide. "What the Chinese really wanted to discuss was the global balance of power," Kissinger said.[31] He was quite right.

China's concerns were not about the balance of power in the abstract. There were real fears of a Soviet strike, possibly with nuclear weapons. In the summer of 1969 a Soviet official asked a member of the State Department how the United States would react to a preemptive Soviet strike against Chinese nuclear facilities. The position of President Nixon was that the United States could not allow China to be "smashed."[32] While these exchanges were taking place the New China News Agency publicly accused the U.S.S.R. of preparing for war.

Thus both countries were ready for détente, but the process had to be carefully nurtured. Between the time when the Chinese government signaled its readiness to receive a U.S. emissary and Kissinger's secret visit to Beijing in July 1971 the United States communicated its desire to improve relations with China in a variety of ways. Nixon publicly referred to the country by its official name, the People's Republic of China; restrictions on travel and trade in nonstrategic goods were eased; regular patrolling of the Taiwan Straits by the Seventh Fleet ended. In various indirect ways China reciprocated. For example, the Chinese reaction to the U.S. expansion of the Vietnam war into Cambodia drew a relatively mild response. Also, the Chinese invitation to an American table tennis team to come to China was a clear sign of its intentions.

The principal purpose of Kissinger's secret negotiations with Chou En-lai in Beijing was to arrange for a presidential visit to China. On July 15, 1971, Richard Nixon delivered before a television audience the shocking announcement that he had accepted an invitation to visit China before May of 1972. For the first time the international community was made aware of the reality of triangular politics. No country was more affected by the new distribution of global power than the Soviet Union. Moscow understood well the implications of the new international reality and moved quickly to limit its negative consequences. The Kremlin sought an improvement in its relations with Washington. For Moscow a summit meeting with the American president became a necessity. Anatoly Dobrynin, the Soviet ambassador to Washington, even tried (unsuccessfully) to encourage a presidential visit to Moscow before Beijing.

Richard Nixon's historic visit to Beijing in February 1972 achieved the understanding that its architects had wanted. Henry Kissinger summarized that achievement as follows:

> There were no reciprocal commitments, not even an attempt to define coordinated action. A strange sort of partnership developed, all the more effectual for never being formalized. . . . Two great nations sought cooperation not through formal compacts but by harmonizing their respective understanding of international issues and their interests in relation to them. Cooperation thus became a psychological, not merely a legal, necessity. . . . The focus of the discussion . . . was on the requirements of the balance of power, the international order, and long-term trends of world politics. Both sides understood that if they agreed on these elements, a strategy of parallel action would follow naturally; if not, tactical decisions taken individually would prove ephemeral and fruitless.[33]

At the conclusion of the visit a statement, known as the Shanghai Communiqué, summarized both sides' positions. Taiwan was acknowledged as the crucial issue obstructing normalization of relations. Beijing maintained its claim that Taiwan was a province of China. The United States was unwilling to abandon its commitment to the Nationalist government, but it agreed that there was "but one China and that Taiwan is a part of China" (a point neither Chinese government disputed). It committed itself to a progressive reduction of U.S. forces and military installations on the island as tension in the area diminished with the ultimate goal being a total U.S. withdrawal. Essentially both sides had agreed not to let the Taiwan issue impede their cooperation on more fundamental questions. They both declared their opposition to the hegemony of any power (i.e., the Soviet Union) in Asia. As Kissinger put it succinctly, "We agreed on the necessity to curb Moscow's geopolitical ambitions."[34]

Normalization of Sino-Soviet relations proceeded steadily through the 1970s, unimpeded by major changes of leadership in both countries. Richard Nixon was forced to resign in 1974 because of the Watergate scandal. Gerald Ford, who followed Nixon and who himself visited China in 1975, was succeeded in the White House by Jimmy Carter, a Democrat. In China the leadership changes were more profound. Mao's death in 1976 led to a succession struggle ultimately won by Deng Xiaoping. Deng purged Mao's radical colleagues, the "Gang of Four," and undertook a major reform of the economy, abandoning many of the harshest features of Mao's collectivist policies. And even though Carter and Deng represented new leaderships (and new domestic policies), they maintained the policy of rapprochement of their predecessors. On January 1, 1979, the People's Republic of China and the United States exchanged diplomatic recognition and ambassadors. This was followed by an official visit by Deng to Washington.

Benefits Realized
Did the United States and China obtain the benefits expected from their tacit alliance? It is difficult to identify specific con-

sequences of broad shifts in political alignment. The results are often subtle and of a long-term character. Still some benefits were discernible. For America the principal gain was the deepening of Soviet Russia's commitment to détente and the initiation of important arms control agreements. While détente did not survive the decade, collaboration with the Chinese did give the United States more flexibility in its diplomacy than it would have otherwise had.

Détente with China did not secure U.S. objectives in Vietnam — principally the preservation of an independent government in the south — but that goal was unattainable with or without a Chinese alliance. However, it is probable that the change in China's U.S. policy limited the long-term damages of the collapse of South Vietnam. The great fear in Washington was that a Communist-dominated Vietnam would lead to a Communist-dominated southeast Asia, the so-called domino theory. As it turned out the only dominos to fall after the collapse of Saigon were Laos and Cambodia. Almost certainly the Vietnamese have been constrained by the pressure from China acting in concert with the United States.

For the Chinese the benefits were less apparent but no less real. The danger of a Soviet military challenge to China eased. Moscow continued to pose a threat with its sizable modern forces along the 4,500-mile northern border of China. And even after the failure of Leonid Brezhnev's efforts to build a system of collective security to contain China, the Kremlin strengthened its influence in countries that bordered China. It signed a 25-year treaty of friendship with Vietnam in November 1978 and invaded and took control of the government of Afghanistan in December 1979. Yet Moscow was cautious about engaging in threatening gestures toward its former ally. When China invaded Vietnam in December 1978 (in the aftermath of Vietnam's invasion of Cambodia and the expulsion of some 200,000 ethnic Chinese from Vietnam), the Soviet Union limited its response to warnings, although under the terms of its treaty of alliance it was committed to "taking appropriate effective measures" in the event "one of the parties becomes the object of an attack." The Soviet Union wanted no war with China. More than that, Beijing's alliance with Washington pushed Moscow toward an improvement in Sino-Soviet relations just as it had led to the U.S.–Soviet détente. China, the Soviet Union, and the United States are such major actors in the international system that none would choose to be at the mercy of a coalition of the other two.

Another significant benefit to China was the opening of its economy to western technology. The overriding goal of the post-Mao leadership was the modernization of the country. The normalization of relations permitted an expansion in trade between China and the United States. American companies were permitted to open permanent offices in Beijing and enter into joint ventures with Chinese corporations. On March 2, 1979, an agreement was signed on the settlement of outstanding claims. This paved the way for a trade agreement in July under which the United States granted China most-favored-nation status. The Carter administration agreed to sell military equipment for defense purposes. Between 1978 and 1981 the total value of trade between the United States and China increased from $1.1 billion to $5.5 billion.[35] Because of the Sino-American rapprochement China is in a position to obtain U.S. technology to modernize its economy in a way that is not yet open to the Soviet Union.

The Move Toward Equidistance

Triangular politics are inevitably dynamic. The Sino-American coalition formed in the 1970s could no more be permanent than the Sino-Soviet alliance of the 1950s. Both coalitions were based on a combination of ideological, geopolitical, and national interests that were bound to change over time. The most basic of all these considerations was the geopolitical one, i.e., the calculation of which power configuration offered the greatest security. The security or geopolitical factor was closely linked to the question of whom each state considered to be the greatest threat to its security. As we have seen, in the 1950s

China and the Soviet Union both viewed the United States as the greatest threat to their security. In the 1960s there was a dramatic shift in threat perception. Russia replaced America as China's greatest threat and China ceased to be viewed as a major threat to the United States. Thus neither China nor the United States came to fear each other, although both felt threatened by the U.S.S.R. This combination of perceptions gave Moscow the least room for maneuver and China the most. As China has become more active in international politics her foreign policy has been flexible and subtle.

The fundamental global conflict of the second half of the twentieth century remains the Cold War between the United States and the Soviet Union. China, while the weakest of the three, is in a position to play the role of balancer. It can do so, however, only to the extent that ideological or national interests do not bind her to one side or prevent her from aligning with one side. In the decade of the 1980s Beijing took advantage of its pivotal position by moving toward a more equidistant position between Moscow and Washington.

The movement was neither steady nor consistent. After Mao's death Sino-Soviet and Sino-American relations fluctuated widely. At times China's Soviet policy seemed to be on the mend as relations with the United States deteriorated, only to be followed by shifts in the opposite direction. These fluctuations were the result of a number of factors, which had the cumulative effect of weakening the Sino-American rapprochement. Although the fundamental conditions that led to that rapprochement remain in place, several developments have made it in China's interest to move closer to the center. By the early 1980s there were clear signs of a limited détente between China and the U.S.S.R.

China Moves Closer to Moscow

The reasons for China's shift are varied. Mao's death in September 1976 opened the way for an improvement in Sino-Soviet ties because his anti-Sovietism had become so strong as to preclude any kind of normal relations with the Kremlin. After his death Moscow signaled its desire for an improvement in relations. Although China's response was negative, the persistence of Soviet diplomacy (with an occasional reversal) in trying to come to terms with its former ally contributed substantially to wearing down Beijing's anti-Sovietism. Leonid Brezhnev sent a message congratulating Hua Guofeng on his new post as Party Chairman (it was rejected). The Soviet leader used the Twenty-sixth Party Congress in 1981 to propose measures to build confidence between the two countries. Again, China was negative. Shortly before he died Brezhnev delivered an important speech in Tashkent again proposing better relations with China. In the fall of 1979 the Chinese did agree to participate in negotiations to discuss their differences, and these negotiations have continued intermittently to the present time. Andropov continued Brezhnev's efforts at reconciliation, but his administration was too brief to consummate a détente with China. Chernenko was preoccupied with other issues. Mikhail Gorbachev, who took power in March 1985, put Sino-Soviet détente back on the agenda.

So far China has taken a generally hard line in negotiations with the Soviet Union. Beijing has demanded Soviet concessions on the three obstacles that stand as a barrier to normal relations: (1) a unilateral reduction of the Soviet armed forces in the area bordering on China, (2) a disassociation of Soviet support for the Vietnamese, and (3) a withdrawal of Soviet troops from Afghanistan. While anxious to improve relations Moscow has to date been unwilling to concede on any of these three points. That stubbornness, or rigidity, however, has not kept the Chinese from continuing the effort.

Both governments have abandoned the polemics of earlier years. As a result of the internal changes introduced since Mao's death, the Soviet Union is able to view China as more ideologically acceptable than in the past. The leaderships on both sides are now willing to concede that the other constitutes a "Socialist state." For Communist parties, which claim to be guided by doctrine, such matters are important.

A factor of some importance for China has been the fear of

losing its independence if it should align itself too closely to what is still viewed as an imperialistic nation. The Chinese still want to play a leadership role among the developing countries but they found that their alignment with the United States seriously undermined their credibility in the third world. That and the greater resources that Moscow was willing to invest in the third world induced the Chinese to reduce their active involvement in some regions such as Africa.

Of greater importance has been a change in the geopolitical confrontation between the two Communist nations. Neither is quite as fearful of the other as before. China no longer presses her demand for territorial revision or undoing the annexations of the unequal treaties, although that remains a potentially disturbing problem. On the other side China has come to view the Soviet military buildup in Asia as less of a menace than it once seemed. During his visit to the United States in 1984 Premier Zhao Ziyang observed that the increase in Soviet military forces in East Asia was primarily directed against the United States, not China. Gerald Segal suggests that Beijing's change of view of the Soviet menace may be the result of the quagmire in Afghanistan and the high cost of support for Vietnam.[36] One tangible sign of the improvement in military relations has been the sharp decline in border incidents since 1976.

Finally, the Reagan administration, which came to power in 1981, helped push China toward the center. The issue, of course, was Taiwan. Before he came to office Ronald Reagan was very critical of the U.S. abandonment of its military support for Taiwan, again raising the Chinese fear of a "two Chinas" policy. In his March 1982 speech at Tashkent Leonid Brezhnev compared Soviet support for one China to U.S. support for Taiwan and two Chinas. It was a point that carried great weight with Beijing.

The United States is not unaware of the importance of its ties with China. Taiwan is a particularly difficult issue for conservatives who have long been among the strongest supporters of Nationalist China. For many of them it is an issue of principle, which they are not willing to sacrifice for the cause of realpolitik. A strong supporter of China in the Reagan administration was Secretary of State Alexander Haig (who once referred to China as "NATO's sixteenth member"). In a visit to the People's Republic in 1981 he announced a new U.S. policy approving the sale of nonlethal arms to China. That same year it was announced that China was permitting the C.I.A. to monitor Soviet missile tests from a station in Xinjiang. Reagan has attempted to retain some of the momentum of previous administrations as evidenced by his visit to China in April 1984. The highlight of the visit was the initialing of an accord on peaceful nuclear cooperation. A clear indication of the new balance in China's superpower relations was the censorship of the anti-Soviet remarks made by Reagan during his visit.

Even if a détente with the Soviet Union develops, China will not break her ties with the United States. Aside from the political leverage, there is the importance of trade with the west for modernization. In recent years Sino-Soviet trade has increased, but it remains very marginal for both economies, less than 3 percent of their total trade as of 1985.[37] Only western technology can overcome the backwardness of the Chinese economy. In order to help finance her modernization China (unlike the U.S.S.R.) has joined the International Monetary Fund and the World Bank. The Soviets were successful in 1984 and 1985 in negotiating several important economic agreements that will expand Sino-Soviet trade into the 1990s, but their efforts to bind the Chinese politically have failed. Early in 1986 the Chinese foreign office announced that Beijing had "categorically rejected" a proposal for a mutual nonaggression pact that Moscow had been pushing for a number of years.[38] China's point was reaffirmed by her refusal to send a delegation to the Twenty-seventh Congress of the Soviet Communist party which met in the spring of 1986. In the early stages of the Sino-Soviet normalization Donald Zagoria predicted that "The détente will not constitute a far-reaching strategic change in the international balance of power, as did the U.S.–PRC rapprochement in the 1970's."[39] It has not nor does it seem likely to do so.

We conclude this look at triangular global politics by returning to the central theme of this book. The basic conflict in world politics today is between the United States and the Soviet Union. In this conflict China is an ally of neither side. The conflicts that do exist between China and the two superpowers are serious but not likely to lead to war. Chinese relations with the United States and the Soviet Union will fluctuate as its leaders determine how best to maximize China's interests and also according to their perception of which of the superpowers most threatens their country. These interests and perceptions inevitably change over time.

While China may be neutral in the U.S.–Soviet quest for global hegemony, she is not indifferent to the prospects of war between these powers. Simply put: China does not want the Soviet-American conflict to take the form of a military confrontation. Should developments move in that direction China can be expected to take whatever action possible to prevent a violent U.S.–U.S.S.R. confrontation. Exactly what such action — political or military — would be is difficult to foresee in advance of events. Although one cannot predict the future shifts in China's foreign policy, one can say with certainty that China will play an important role in world politics and thus be an important factor in the outcome of the Cold War.

Japan

A final point concerns the role of Japan in the Cold War. The question could be asked: Why has Japan not played a more dynamic role in the struggle for power between the superpowers? Economically Japan far surpasses China. Indeed with the world's third largest economy Japan in an economic sense is itself a superpower. But its role in international politics has never been commensurate with its economic strength. There are two fundamental reasons why this has been so. First, Japan's military power never grew in proportion to its economic power. External pressure as well as internal political forces have kept Japan from becoming a nuclear power. In the 1970s Japan ratified the nonproliferation treaty, thus formally eschewing a nuclear role for itself. More than that Japan has refused to spend more than 1 percent of its gross national product for arms. Only in 1987 has it gone slightly above the 1 percent self-imposed limit. The other factor has been Japan's alliance with the United States which of necessity required Japan to align its military-security policies with those of America. Since the U.S.–Japanese bilateral security pact came into force on April 28, 1952, Japan has relied on the United States to protect it from outside attack. To this day Japanese security is guaranteed by the American nuclear umbrella.

Relations between the Soviet Union and Japan have fluctuated in the postwar period, but full normalization has been frustrated by Moscow's refusal to return four islands in the southern Kuriles (the "Northern Territories") taken from Japan at the end of World War II.[40] Japan has made their return a condition for a peace treaty between two countries and substantial Japanese investment in the Soviet Far East. Notwithstanding Mikhail Gorbachev's expressed desire for an improvement in Soviet-Japanese relations he has refused to dismantle Soviet military formations on the islands, let alone return them to Japan. Thus, in the Cold War Japan's fundamental interests link it solidly to the western bloc.

Notes

1. This effort is described in Herbert Feis, *The China Tangle* (Princeton, N.J.: Princeton University Press, 1972).
2. Milovan Djilas, *Conversations with Stalin* (New York: Harcourt, Brace and World, 1962), p. 182.
3. Alvin Z. Rubinstein, *Soviet Foreign Policy since World War II, Global and Imperial,* 2d ed. (Boston: Little, Brown, 1985), p. 68.
4. Herbert Feis, *From Trust to Terror, the Onset of the Cold War, 1945–1950* (New York: W. W. Norton, 1970), p. 204.
5. Ibid., pp. 255–259.
6. See Allen S. Whiting, *China Crosses the Yalu, the Decision to Enter the Korean War* (Stanford, Calif.: Stanford University Press, 1960), chap. 3; Marshall D. Shulman, *Stalin's Foreign*

Policy Reappraised (Cambridge, Mass.: Harvard University Press, 1963), chaps. VI and VII. For a dissenting view see Robert R. Simmons, *The Strained Alliance: Peking, P'yongyang, Moscow and the Politics of the Korean Civil War* (New York: The Free Press, 1975).

7. John Spanier, *American Foreign Policy since World War II*, 10th ed. (New York: Holt, Rinehart & Winston, 1985), p. 60.

8. O. B. Borisov and B. T. Koloskov, *Sino-Soviet Relations* (Moscow: Progress Publishers, 1975), p. 58.

9. Ibid., pp. 61–64, 85–87.

10. J. M. Mackintosh, *Strategy and Tactics of Soviet Foreign Policy* (London: Oxford University Press, 1962), pp. 146ff.

11. See Joseph L. Nogee, "Soviet Nuclear Proliferation Policies: Dilemmas and Contradictions," *Orbis*, vol. 24, no. 4, Winter 1981, p. 754.

12. Robert C. North, *Moscow and Chinese Communists* (Stanford, Calif.: Stanford University Press, 1965), p. 281.

13. Mackintosh, op. cit., p. 256.

14. Jerome H. Kahan, *Security in the Nuclear Age, Developing U.S. Strategic Arms Policy* (Washington: Brookings Institution, 1975), pp. 68–73.

15. See Albert Wohlstetter, "The Delicate Balance of Terror," *Foreign Affairs*, vol. 37, no. 2, January 1969.

16. Quoted in Christer Jonsson, *Soviet Bargaining Behavior: The Nuclear Test Ban Case* (New York: Columbia University Press), p. 89.

17. Roman Kolkowicz et al., *The Soviet Union and Arms Control: A Superpower Dilemma* (Baltimore: Johns Hopkins, 1970), p. 89.

18. Borisov and Koloskov, op. cit., p. 84.

19. The United States presumably would agree to this as part of a deal involving Soviet withdrawal of its missiles in Cuba. See Adam Ulam, *Expansion and Coexistence, Soviet Foreign Policy 1917–1973*, 2d ed. (New York: Frederick A. Praeger, 1974), p. 669.

20. Nikita Khrushchev, *Khrushchev Remembers* (Boston: Little, Brown, 1970), p. 461.

21. Quoted in Donald S. Zagoria, *The Sino-Soviet Conflict, 1956–1961* (Princeton, N.J.: Princeton University Press, 1962), p. 97.

22. Quoted in Ibid., p. 77.

23. Ibid.
24. Ibid., p. 160. This section draws upon chap. 5 of Zagoria's book.
25. Quoted in Peter Jones and Sian Kevill, *China and the Soviet Union, 1949–1984* (New York: Facts on File Publication, 1985), p. 46.
26. Quoted in Mackintosh, op. cit., p. 247.
27. Quoted in Jones and Kevill, op. cit., p. 91.
28. Rubinstein, op. cit., p. 145. The *Pravda* article only hinted at the possibility of nuclear war; it was not made explicit.
29. Joseph L. Nogee and Robert H. Donaldson, *Soviet Foreign Policy since World War II*, 2d ed. (New York: Pergamon Press, 1984), pp. 248–269.
30. Henry Kissinger, *White House Years* (Boston: Little, Brown 1979), p. 695.
31. Ibid., pp. 685 and 690.
32. Ibid., p. 183.
33. Ibid., p. 1074.
34. Ibid., p. 764. For the Shanghai Communiqué see pp. 1074–1087.
35. Jones and Kevill, op. cit., pp. 121–123.
36. Gerald Segal, "Sino-Soviet Relations after Mao," *Adelphi Paper No. 202* (London: International Institute for Strategic Studies, 1985).
37. Ibid., p. 25.
38. Bohdan Nahaylo, "Sino-Soviet Relations Still Bittersweet," Radio Liberty Research Bulletin, April 9, 1986, p. 2.
39. Donald Zagoria, "The Moscow-Beijing Détente," *Foreign Affairs,* vol. 61, no. 4, Spring 1983, p. 868.
40. For an analysis of the Northern Islands issue see Lawrence M. Njoroge, "The Japan-Soviet Union Territorial Dispute," *Asian Survey,* no. 5, 1985.

The Origins of Rivalry in the Third World

How and Where It Was
Played

The Cold War began in Europe in the 1940s and became global in the 1950s. Today the principal arena of east-west competition is in the third world. Nothing reveals more clearly the general character of the struggle between the Soviet Union and the United States than the fact that its locus has continually shifted over the past four decades. Traditional conflicts of national interest have usually been geographically based and fixed. States fight over boundaries, principalities, provinces, spheres of influence, ports, islands, or resource-rich chunks of real estate. The objectives of most conflicts of interest may be economic or political, but traditionally they focused on control over specific territory. It is a measure of the profound and enduring character of the Soviet-American conflict that it transcends control or influence over any single region or territory. Speaking at the United Nations on its fortieth anniversary President Ronald Reagan singled out five countries where the United States opposed the presence of Soviet forces (or forces allied to the Soviet Union): Afghanistan, Nicaragua, Angola, Ethiopia, and Cambodia. A decade earlier Soviet-American conflict centered in other regions: Vietnam and the Middle East. In the 1960s superpower conflict took place in the Belgium Congo (now Zaire) and Cuba. And in the decade before that Korea and southeast Asia were major east-west battlegrounds. Notwithstanding the huge concentration of military forces in Europe — or perhaps because of them — that continent is not likely to reemerge as the battleground between east and west. For the foreseeable future the Soviet-American struggle will be fought primarily in the third world.

Stalin and the Third World

During Stalin's administration Soviet involvement in the third world — then referred to as the underdeveloped nations — was limited. There were several reasons why. Perhaps foremost was Stalin's geostrategic preoccupation with Europe. Ever since the Bolshevik revolution the greatest threats to Soviet power had come from Europe, and Stalin had little doubt that such would be the case in the future. Soviet foreign policy in the interwar period had focused primarily on relations with European powers, so almost as a matter of habit Stalin viewed Europe as the decisive theater of international politics. A political realist, Stalin always thought in terms of power, and the basis of military power was industrial power. Though Europe was devastated by the war, it was only a matter of time before Europe would rebuild its industry and again become militarily powerful. To Stalin the major threat was still Germany in alliance with Britain, France, and the United States. He could not imagine the underdeveloped nations of the world as industrial or military powers.

Furthermore, Stalin had little understanding of the revolutionary potential of the third world. One might have expected better from a disciple of Lenin inasmuch as Lenin had outlined a global revolutionary role for the colonized populations of the world. But Stalin had a deep distrust of the newly independent nations; he considered them mere pawns of their former colonial masters.[1] He distrusted the bourgeois leaders of these states as well as the bourgeois leaders of national liberation movements then still struggling for independence. Nationalist leaders like Ghandi, Nehru, and Sukarno were in his view merely "imperialist lackeys." Stalin may have been reacting to the unpleasant and unsuccessful experience he had in dealing with bourgeois-nationalist leaders in the interwar period, like Chiang Kai-shek. Certainly his profound suspicion of those whom he could not control would not incline him to treat the emerging third world leaders as allies.

Finally, his interpretation of Marxist-Leninist doctrine downgraded the importance of bourgeois-nationalist leaders and regimes. Stalin's last formal analysis of the international situation was presented at the Nineteenth Party Congress in 1952 under the heading "Economic Problems of Socialism in the U.S.S.R." Its title notwithstanding, the document was an analysis of the strategic position of the Soviet Union in the global balance of power. What is particularly notable was the low priority it gave to the third world. Stalin did acknowledge the growth of the national liberation struggle, but fundamentally he saw international politics divided along the lines of the two-camp doctrine, i.e., between the progressive camp led by the Soviet Union and the aggressive, undemocratic camp led by the United States.[2] Though Stalin acknowledged that the collapse of the colonial system weakened the imperialist camp, he offered no guidance for a Soviet strategy in the third world. He failed to recognize the potential of the national bourgeoisie as an ally of the Soviet Union. Instead, he urged support for full Communist revolutions in newly independent states, relying on the dogmatic view that "the solution of colonial slavery is impossible without a proletarian revolution."[3]

Thus, in contrast to the aggressive and at times risky (e.g., the Berlin blockade) policy pursued in Europe, the Soviet Union in the waning years of Stalin's administration pursued a limited and cautious policy in the third world. The Soviets made very little use of military forces either directly or indirectly. They involved themselves in local conflicts only with regimes that were contiguous to the U.S.S.R. And when they did initiate a probe, they kept the doors open for a retreat.

Stalin's caution did not mean that the Soviet Union was indifferent to opportunities in the third world. The collapse of western colonialism left a power vacuum in many parts of Asia, Africa, and the Middle East, and Stalin sought to exploit such situations, though not always with success. As noted before, one of the earliest was in 1945 in Iran where the Soviet Union refused to withdraw its troops. Indeed Moscow used military forces to help create separatist republics along the Soviet-Iranian border. But because of political pressure from the United States and the U.N. Security Council and concessions made by the Iranian government (later repudiated) Moscow did withdraw its forces in the spring of 1946. Very soon thereafter the Soviet-sponsored republics collapsed. At about the same time the Soviets sought to penetrate Turkey. They demanded the cessation of the Turkish provinces of Kars and Ardahan as well as joint Soviet-Turkish control of the straits at the Bosphorus. Turkey resisted, and the signing of a U.S.–

Turkish military pact forced Moscow to back down on its demands. Another third world probe frustrated by the west was
V. M. Molotov's request that the Soviet Union be given a trusteeship over Libya and later that a joint great power trusteeship
be extended over the former Italian possession in Africa.

An exception to Stalin's practice of not transferring arms
abroad except to Communist clients was the military aid given
(through Czechoslovakia) to Zionist forces fighting for a Jewish state. Thousands of small arms, ammunition, and even a
few Messerschmitt planes were provided to the Haganah organization. Moscow's objective was to weaken the British position in the Middle East; at that time support for Israeli
nationalism seemed to be a better strategy than support for
Arab nationalism.

Confrontation in Korea

Soviet involvement in the North Korean attack on South Korea was in marked contrast to Stalin's cautious and limited activity in the third world. It could be argued that the war in
Korea from 1950 to 1953 was a conflict between the two Koreas, China, and the United States inasmuch as the Soviet
Union was not directly engaged and there is no firm evidence
that Stalin initiated the Korean war. Nikita Khrushchev claims
that Kim Il-sung initiated the plan, but Stalin was involved in
the planning of the war, provided the weapons necessary to
fight it, defended North Korea's action publicly, and initiated
the negotiations that led to the truce agreement in 1953. The
Korean war was probably another Soviet probe but one on a
grand scale. Undoubtedly, the Soviet Union, assuming that the
United States would not respond, wanted to show Japan how
unreliable an ally the United States would be.[4] Moscow was
well aware that the United States was about to turn Japan into
an ally and nothing would have frustrated the American design
more than a Communist takeover of the Korean peninsula. If
Khrushchev's testimony is correct — and there is no reason to
doubt it — Stalin was fearful about the American reaction: "I
remember Stalin had his doubts. He was worried that the

Americans would jump in, but we were inclined to think that if the war were fought swiftly — and Kim Il-sung was sure that it could be won swiftly — then intervention by the USA could be avoided."[5]

Why indeed did the United States "jump in"? As already seen, President Truman's immediate response to the North Korean attack can be explained in terms of the administration's general attitude toward U.S. security in a bipolar world and more specifically in terms of the impact of doing nothing on the NATO alliance.[6] The American world view of the international situation had coincidentally been spelled out just before the Korean war by National Security Council (NSC) document 68. NSC-68 was a comprehensive examination of U.S. global interests, threats to those interests, and feasible responses. It stressed the necessity of maintaining the existing balance of power and the importance of a perimeter defense in stopping Soviet expansionism. Ranking in importance with preventing an accretion of Soviet power was the need to maintain the credibility of the United States as willing and able to defend its interests when they were challenged. The Communist invasion of South Korea was thus perceived as being exactly the kind of a threat the United States could not afford to let go unchallenged. As President Truman explained it to a national radio and television audience in September: "If aggression were allowed to succeed in Korea, it would be an open invitation to new acts of aggression elsewhere. . . . We cannot hope to maintain our freedom if freedom elsewhere is wiped out."[7]

Militarily the Korean war ended inconclusively. Kim Il-sung failed to unite the Korean peninsula under Communist rule, but then the goal of uniting the country under a democratic regime as endorsed by the United Nations on October 7, 1950, was not achieved either. The final frontier between the two regimes as agreed in the 1953 truce was very close to the original dividing line of the 38th Parallel. Politically, however, Moscow was the major loser. The Korean war stimulated a series of developments — U.S. rearmament, western unification, German rearmament — all of which were to strengthen the western side of the global balance of power at the expense of the Soviet bloc, and this shift, which Moscow and Pyongyang had inadvertently started, continued throughout the life of the Stalin administration.[8]

The real change in Soviet policy toward the third world was made by Nikita Khrushchev. In expanding Soviet horizons Khrushchev resurrected an orientation developed by Lenin in the early years of Soviet power. Lenin clearly envisaged the possibilities of destroying western capitalist power by uniting Soviet power with the forces of the third world. In his day, of course, the term third world did not not exist. He used the expressions "the East," "colonies," and "backward peoples" to refer to what we know today as the third world. The statement that "the road to Paris runs through Peking" or the "road to London is through New Delhi" is probably apocryphal although there is no doubt of Lenin's belief that decolonization would undermine western "imperialism." He advised the second Comintern Congress in 1920 that "a policy must be pursued that will achieve the closest alliance, with Soviet Russia, of all the national and colonial liberation movements."[9] In a general sense Lenin transformed the Marxist idea of revolution from social change within societies to national changes in the international system. There continues to be remnants of domestic revolutionary change in the meaning of Communist ideology, but the dynamics of Soviet doctrine and practice are in the changes in political relations between states. In other words, the Leninist component of Marxism-Leninism has supplanted the Marxist element, at least so far as Soviet politics is concerned.

Emergence of the Third World

Nikita Khrushchev and Dwight Eisenhower came to power at a time when the international system was undergoing rapid change. The decade of the 1950s witnessed the emergence of an international order different from that which existed before the second world war. In retrospect we can see that the transformation of the international system that took place in the post–World War II period had its origins in the aftermath of World War I. Possibly, that change might have occurred without the enormous upheavals of these two world wars, but they undoubtedly accelerated the change.

Foremost among the features of the new international order was the decline of Europe's domination of world politics. That domination originated with the European exploration and colonialization in the fifteenth century and culminated with the great empires of the twentieth century, which controlled much of Africa, Asia, and the Middle East. World War I destroyed the intra-European empires of Austria-Hungary, Turkey, and Russia. World War II paved the way for the collapse of Europe's overseas empires, notably the British, French, Dutch, Belgian, and Portuguese. Between the end of the second world war and the decade of the 1950s some 800,000,000 people, whose new governments constituted almost half of the United Nations membership, had gained independence.

Thus in the 1950s the third world emerged as a new force in international politics, not by any means a cohesive, unified actor comparable to the eastern or western blocs, but nevertheless a group sharing a common political heritage and a strong commitment to anticolonialism. In April 1955 representatives of 29 Asian and African third world states convened in Bandung, Indonesia, to formally declare the existence of a new political order in world affairs. The western world was put on notice that "colonialism in all its manifestations is an evil which should speedily be brought to an end."[10] Understanding full well the antiwestern potentialities of this anticolonial theme Moscow welcomed the Bandung convocation and its declaration. Khrushchev gave formal endorsement to the Leninist idea of a grand coalition of Communist and third world states at the Twentieth Party Congress in February 1956 when in delivering the report of the Central Committee he declared that:

The forces of peace have been considerably augmented by the emergence in the world arena of a group of peace-loving European and Asian states which have proclaimed nonparticipation in blocs as a principle of their foreign policy. . . . As a result, a vast "peace zone," including both socialist and nonsocialist peace-loving states in Europe and Asia, has emerged in the world arena. This zone embraces tremendous expanses of the globe, inhabited by nearly 1,500,000,000 people — that is, the majority of the population of our planet.[11]

The United States, with its own revolutionary tradition, was not unsympathetic to the aspirations of the former colonial populations for independence and freedom, but in some instances it suffered from its close identification with so many of the European states that had formerly been the colonial masters of the newly independent states. Indeed with the formation of the North Atlantic Treaty Organization (NATO) in 1949, the United States became an ally with several of the colonial powers. U.S.–third world relations were thus at times complicated by Washington's need to consider the interests of allied and friendly western powers. This was particularly true with Israel, even though Israel was not a colonial power.

Notwithstanding the differences in ideology, interests, and historical relations between the superpowers and the underdeveloped countries, the imperatives of the international system imposed on Moscow and Washington a parallel mode of behavior vis à vis the third world. The bipolar international system induced both great powers to garner as much support as possible in the third world. Both sides felt that a shift by any segment of the third world in favor of the other would mean a potentially damaging loss of power in the global balance. This reaction was understandable inasmuch as each side viewed the other as the principal — if not sole — threat to its security. In the language of game theory a "zero-sum" mentality prevailed whereby Moscow and Washington saw the addition of any of the newly independent states to the camp of the other as a loss for itself. If not quite the same as the domino theory, it was psychologically similar.

What about the pawns in this game, the newly independent states? Why should they have permitted themselves to become participants in the Soviet-American war? It should be noted that some third world countries did in fact pursue a policy of neutrality. Some states, for example Burma and Afghanistan, genuinely sought to avoid alignment with either the Soviet Union or the United States. But these were more the exception than the rule. Most of the newly independent states gravitated toward one side or the other even if only temporarily. Did they have a choice? The answer is yes and no.

An important factor limiting the options of these countries was their poverty and lack of development. Most of the former colonial territories had very small per capita incomes, often not exceeding $100, when they acquired independence. They were overpopulated, with large numbers of their population illiterate, undernourished, and in ill health. The economies of most of these countries depended on the export of mineral or agricultural commodities. Few had an industrial base of any size. They were thus economically vulnerable and desperately in need of outside assistance. Most would have preferred economic aid without strings, but many were prepared to accept the strings in order to get the aid.

Not all third world alignments, however, sprang from economic necessity. Some regimes were captured by elites committed to radical ideologies that predisposed them toward one side or the other, often toward Moscow. Mention has been made above to the anticolonial mentality that predisposed many third world elites against the west in general. But perhaps of greater significance was the fact that many of the new states were involved in regional cold wars of their own. India and Pakistan and Israel and its Arab neighbors were classic examples of antagonistic nations from the moment of their creation. In some instances third world countries were involved in imperialist ventures, like Indonesia with its conflicts with Malaysia over West Irian. Some conflicts involved struggles for regional supremacy, such as those between Egypt, Iraq, and Syria. Others were the result of historic enmity, economic gain, boundary controversies, tribal animosities, or efforts to

bring about ethnic unification. In all, the reasons for intra–
third world conflict were numerous and varied. In several
cases the parties to these conflicts found it in their interest to
enlist the support of one or another of the superpowers. They
were thus hardly pawns in the hands of the more powerful actors. Indeed it seems evident that the mainspring of third world
behavior vis à vis the superpowers was not fundamentally different from that of the latter toward the former, namely, to
pursue the national interest by whatever alignment could best
promote that interest. In other words, for small and large states
alike, the rule of the balance of power applied.

Among the techniques of balance-of-power politics have
been alliances (formal and informal), assistance (military and
economic), and diplomacy (multilateral and bilateral). The rivalry between the Soviet Union and the United States in the
third world involved the utilization of all of these techniques.
Sometimes the principal beneficiaries were the superpowers
and sometimes the smaller states.

The strategy developed by the United States to stem
the advance of communism became known as containment.
George Kennan established the political rationale for that
strategy in his famous article written for *Foreign Affairs* in
1947. He wrote: ". . . Soviet pressure against the free institutions of the western world is something that can be contained
by the adroit and vigilant application of counter-force at a series of constantly shifting geographical and political points,
corresponding to the shifts and manoeuvres of Soviet policy. . . ."[12] NSC-68 was essentially an elaboration and to some
extent a redefinition of the containment strategy. The geographical focus of containment during the Truman administration was Europe. The Truman Doctrine, the Marshall Plan,
and NATO were basically designed to prevent the expansion
of Soviet power into the heart of western civilization. Even
American resistance to communism in Korea was related to
deterrence in Europe. During the period when Eisenhower and
Dulles guided U.S. foreign policy containment expanded into
the third world. One of the principal techniques of that strategy

was the formation of military-political alliances with countries
along the periphery of the Eurasian land mass. Secretary of
State Dulles in some of his rhetoric may have condemned the
policy of containment as "negative" and "futile" but the several alliances negotiated by him were essentially applications
of that strategy. Two regions in particular were the focus of
U.S.–Soviet third world rivalry in the decade of the 1950s:
southeast Asia and the Middle East.

The Crisis Shift to Indochina

After the Korean truce in mid-1953 the crisis in Asia shifted to
Indochina where the faltering French effort to establish control
over its Indochinese colony threatened to lead to the extension
of Communist domination of the entire Indochinese peninsula.
The United States had come to the conclusion that the security
of southwest Asia required the containment of communism in
that region of the world. It should be noted that the Soviet
Union here was not the cause of the threat; in fact, Khrushchev had carefully avoided committing either Soviet forces or
prestige to the Vietminh insurgency. The threat to Asia's balance of power appeared to come from China, which in the mid-
1950s was still an ally in good standing with the Soviet Union.
In the spring and early summer of 1954 a conference was convened in Geneva to negotiate an end to the fighting between
the French and Vietnamese Communists. Before the Geneva
conference a preparatory strategy meeting was held in Moscow between Khrushchev, Chinese Foreign Minister Chou En-
lai, and Ho Chi Minh, Vietnam's Communist leader. The Soviet and Chinese estimate of the prospects for the Vietnamese
was very bleak until the surprising defeat of the French at
Dienbienphu on May 7, which occurred while the Geneva conference was in session. "I'll confess," said Khrushchev in his
memoirs, "that when we were informed of this news from Geneva, we gasped with surprise and pleasure. We hadn't expected anything like this."[13]

   Dienbienphu marked the end of French colonial rule in Indochina. As a result of the weakened western position Vietnam

was divided along the 17th Parallel with a Communist government in the north and a non-Communist government in the south. The instrument devised by the Eisenhower administration to contain communism (emanating, it was believed, from China) was the Southeast Asian Defense Treaty (SEATO) formed in September 1954.[14] The failure of SEATO to prevent North Vietnam from extending its rule throughout Indochina will be examined below.

Rivalry in the Middle East

In the mid-1950s the United States extended its line of containment around the Sino-Soviet periphery with the creation of the Baghdad pact. This pact united a "northern tier" of Middle Eastern states — Turkey, Iraq, Iran, and Pakistan — with Britain in the Middle East Treaty Organization (METO). The pact was later renamed the Central Treaty Organization (CENTO). It was to be a barrier against Soviet expansion southward. Although technically not a member of METO or CENTO, the United States was associated with the pact through bilateral agreements with each of the three Moslem members. Eventually the United States joined the economic, military, and countersubversion committees of the pact.

CENTO proved to be worse than unproductive; it was counterproductive. Moscow, of course, condemned it, but so did many Arab nationalists who saw it as a vestige of western colonialism. One Arab leader in particular who opposed the Baghdad pact was Gamal Abdel Nasser who emerged in the 1950s as Egypt's new leader and spokesman for Pan-Arab nationalism. Egypt and Iraq were traditional rivals for leadership in the Arab world, so it is not surprising that as Iraq aligned itself with the west Nasser looked increasingly to the Soviet Union for leverage against his Arab rivals. Nasser's antiwestern sentiments were only strengthened by the growing Israeli ties with the west, so in his mind opposition to Zionism and western colonialism coalesced into a general strategy of building a counteralliance to the Baghdad pact and subverting pro-western Arab governments.

Khrushchev saw an opportunity, and he seized it. He shifted Soviet policy solidly behind the cause of Arab nationalism, utilizing Egypt as the principal Soviet vehicle for influence in the Middle East. Moscow moved increasingly to an anti-Israeli, pro-Arab posture. To a much greater degree than his predecessor Khrushchev saw the importance of the Middle East: economically (because of the oil resources), and geostrategically (because of the Suez Canal), and most important, politically (because of the potential for leverage with the newly independent developing states). If western influence could be destroyed in that region where it had been dominant for centuries, then it would be weakened everywhere throughout the third world.

In 1955 the Soviets created a diplomatic sensation when they delivered a large quantity of Soviet arms to Egypt. This was the first time that weapons in such quantity had been given by the Soviet Union to any country outside of Moscow's direct control. It made Nasser an immediate hero of Arab nationalism. The consequences of the arms deal were to unfold for years to come. In July 1956, partially as a reaction to the growing Egyptian-Soviet ties, the United States revoked its offer to finance the construction of the Aswan Dam. The Aswan Dam was intended to be the centerpiece for raising Egypt's standard of living. It was designed to harness the Nile River, to prevent annual flooding of the Nile Valley, to irrigate new farmland, and to provide electricity for industrial development. Outraged, Nasser struck back with the most powerful weapon available to him: seizure of the Suez Canal, whose revenues, he claimed, would be used to finance construction of the Aswan Dam. Again, an opportunity was opened to Moscow and Khrushchev seized it. He endorsed Nasser's canal seizure and subsequently agreed to subsidize the construction of the high dam.

Egypt was not the only recipient of Soviet arms and aid. In 1956 Syria fell under the control of the antiwestern Ba'ath party (Arab socialist renaissance) and it too received Soviet weapons. In 1957 Syria's President Shukri Al-Quwatli visited the U.S.S.R. and received generous credits. In 1958 the west suffered a major setback when the prowestern monarchy in Iraq was overthrown by a faction of the Ba'ath party headed by Abdul Karim Qasim. Iraq not only withdrew from the Baghdad pact but the Qasim government turned to an obliging Soviet Union for military aid, credits, and technical assistance. Also in 1958 came the temporary unification of Syria and Egypt into the short-lived United Arab Republic.

As Arab-Israeli relations deteriorated the Arabs came more and more to depend on the Soviet Union for aid — both material and political. A case in point was the war that followed the Suez crisis in the fall of 1956. A coordinated Israeli, British, and French attack was mounted against Egypt in October. Nasser could not have stopped the coalition arrayed against him and would have suffered a major defeat had not the United States decided to oppose the invasion and pressure the three powers to withdraw. Eisenhower saw the invasion as wrong and believed that by opposing it he could restore American friendship and influence in the Middle East. He therefore supported calls in the United Nations for the removal of troops from Egyptian territory and, more significantly, threatened to deny Britain vital oil supplies if it did not withdraw from Egyptian territory. It did, and France and Israel had no choice but to follow suit. Ironically, it was not the United States but the Soviet Union that benefited from the end of hostilities in the Sinai. Moscow had taken a strong position against the western invaders, even going so far as to threaten Britain and France with nuclear weapons. The threat was clearly a bluff and had little to do with the withdrawal of forces, but it had a lot to do with gaining kudos among Arabs already hostile to the west. The net political consequence of the 1956 Suez war was a further erosion of American influence in the Middle East and a corresponding rise in Soviet penetration.

In January 1957, in an attempt to bolster the position of the United States, President Eisenhower announced that he would

give military aid to any Middle East country threatened by
aggression from "a country controlled by international communism." Endorsed by the U.S. Congress as a joint resolution
this commitment became known as the "Eisenhower Doctrine." Although the language of the Eisenhower Doctrine
could mean much or little depending on how it was interpreted,
the purpose was very clear: to protect those governments in
the Middle East from internal subversion or invasion by any
government closely associated with the U.S.S.R. The government most closely associated with the Soviet Union at the time
was Egypt.

Within a short time the United States had an opportunity to
apply the Eisenhower Doctrine. In the spring of 1957 an internal crisis developed in prowestern Jordan as a result of disorders led by pro-Nasser and pro-Communist forces. King
Hussein charged that international communism was attempting to overthrow him. Immediately the United States responded with economic and military aid. The crisis was
overcome. The following year Jordan again faced internal disorders triggered by pro-Egyptian and pro-Soviet domestic elements and so did Lebanon. This time the United States
(shaken by the overthrow of the prowestern Iraqi government
in the summer) along with Britain responded with military
force. The British sent paratroopers into Jordan and the United
States sent a contingent of 14,000 men into Lebanon. Moscow
threatened intervention of its own but in the end did not follow
through. The decisive American and British action did stabilize and strengthen the governments of Jordan and Lebanon —
but the victory was only temporary. By the end of the decade
Soviet influence in the Middle East had become entrenched,
even if it was not dominant. Khrushchev had made the Middle
East a major battlefield for the struggle over the third world,
and it has remained so to this day.

Khrushchev's moves into the third world were multifaceted,
involving more than military aid, using or threatening military
force, or supporting subversion. He also initiated the Soviet
Union's program of economic assistance. Beginning with Af-

ghanistan in 1954 and India in 1955 Moscow soon expanded its economic and trade agreements to include a number of countries concentrated in the Middle East and South Asia. India and Egypt were the two largest recipients, which indicated the importance attached to each of these states in their respective regions.

The economic programs designed by Moscow and Washington reflected different ideological and economic perspectives though in both instances the overriding objective was to win the hearts and minds of third world elites. The United States gave priority to economic projects in the private sector and sought to finance activities that could be productive in economic terms as well as political. The Soviets placed much greater emphasis on the state sector by encouraging the expansion of public ownership of industry. Believing that the growth of heavy industry would wean the developing countries from the world capitalist economy Moscow pushed large heavy-industry projects such as steel mills and machine-building plants. Big projects like the Aswan Dam in Egypt and the Bhilai and Bokaro steel mills in India became giant show pieces to demonstrate Moscow's commitment to third world development.

Although American aid was larger than Soviet aid, it was dispersed over more countries and included many smaller projects, often involving projects to increase food production. As a result, its political impact was diluted. By comparison Soviet programs were highly selective and concentrated in countries where Moscow believed it had the best opportunities to achieve a quick political payoff. In the 1950s more than 90 percent of Soviet-bloc aid went to only six countries: Egypt, India, Indonesia, Iraq, Afghanistan, and Syria.[15] Also, the terms of economic aid were often more appealing to the Soviet recipients than those of the United States. Soviet aid often was given in the form of long-term credits repayable at low interest rates. Unlike U.S. loans, which were repayable in hard currency, Soviet loans could be repaid either in local currency or in commodities exported by the recipient. Thus to a greater degree than the United States Soviet aid was closely linked to its foreign trade.

Competition in Africa

During the 1960s Africa joined the Middle East and southeast Asia as a major arena of east-west confrontation. In the decade from the mid-1950s through the mid-1960s a large part of Africa became liberated from colonial rule. The collapse of western colonialism had a destabilizing effect on both domestic and international politics on much of the continent. Many of the newly liberated states were very poor, lacked political unity, and were unable to provide the basic services of government. The old idea reflected in the original United Nations trusteeship system that territories had to be prepared and ready for independence was categorically rejected by the United Nations in 1960 when it adopted a declaration on colonialism calling for "immediate" action to end all colonial rule "without any conditions or reservations." It is no defense of colonialism to observe that for parts of Africa the implementation of this policy brought chaos, at least temporarily. Several countries experienced civil disorders either as a result of the lack of strong central power to maintain authority or as a result of civil war. In the latter case internal forces struggling for supremacy or secession often looked to outside forces for assistance. Sometimes the former colonial ruler returned to help strengthen the government of the newly independent regime or to support one of the contending factions in a civil conflict.

Nowhere were the problems described above illustrated more sharply than in the case of the Belgian Congo, which was unexpectedly given its independence in the summer of 1960 and became the Republic of the Congo (now Zaire). Almost immediately the new republic disintegrated into chaos. Belgium had done nothing to prepare the country for independence. Public services collapsed; the army mutinied against its officers (most of whom were white); Europeans were attacked and property seized; and perhaps most serious of all, the first of several secessionist movements were started by Moise Tshombe in the province of Katanga. Complicating the political disorders was a bitter rivalry between the two principal leaders of the central government: President Joseph Kasavubu who was prowestern and Prime Minister Patrice Lumumba who was pro-Soviet. The United Nations was asked to intervene to restore order and spur the removal of Belgian troops who had returned to the Congo in order to protect European lives and property and to help Tshombe's secessionist movement. Belgium's intervention in the civil war of its former colony had little to do with the Cold War per se. The Belgian government was anxious to protect Belgian-owned mining interests, which were extracting the huge mineral resources, particularly copper and cobalt, in Katanga. Secretary-General Dag Hammarskjöld was authorized by the U.N. Security Council to use international forces to aid the central government, but he was prohibited from interfering in the country's civil war, a mandate that proved impossible to execute.

Patrice Lumumba initiated the steps that brought the Congo crisis into the folds of the Cold War. Angered that Hammarskjöld would not use U.N. troops to suppress Belgian-supported forces, he invited the Soviet Union to send in forces to do the job. Moscow was only too willing to oblige, though its capabilities in the 1960s were limited. President Kasavubu thereupon proceeded to dismiss Lumumba and together with his successor, Col. Sese Seko Mobuto, forced the removal of those Soviet-bloc personnel who had come to aid Lumumba. Unexpected events brought continued changes in the fortunes of the many parties enmeshed in the Congolese quagmire. Among these were the murder of Lumumba by his political enemies and the death under mysterious circumstance of Secretary-General Hammarskjöld in an airplane crash. In 1962 the United Nations reversed its original stand and ordered Hammarskjöld's successor, U Thant, to use military force to defeat Tshombe's secessionist army. By 1964 the turmoil in the Congo had largely subsided.

The net result of the many conflicts intersecting in that hapless country was the restoration of a unified central government under a moderately prowestern leader. But many governments were bitterly disappointed by the outcome and blamed the United Nations. Opinion in western Europe objected to the role of the U.N. in frustrating the birth of what would have been a staunchly prowestern regime in Katanga. Even more bitter were the Soviets who believed (erroneously) that Hammarskjöld and U.N. forces had played a part in the death of their hero, Lumumba. They were not at all happy to see Col. Mobuto emerge as the ruler of the new country. Soviet disillusionment with the United Nations led Nikita Khrushchev to press for his ill-fated plan to replace the office of Secretary-General with a three-member troika, a collective office representing the Communist bloc, the west, and the neutrals.

The Congo crisis also led to the financial crisis that has plagued the U.N. to this day. Moscow intensified its opposition to a strong United Nations, rejecting the use of peacekeeping forces by that organization unless they were authorized by and under the control of the Security Council where the Soviet Union had a veto. The Congolese peacekeeping operation showed Moscow the dangers of permitting the General Assembly (where there is no veto) to create a peacekeeping force that might act contrary to its interests. Since ONUC (the acronym for the name of the Congolese forces in French) operated under a General Assembly mandate, the Soviet Union (and several other nations, including France) refused to pay for its share of the costs, thus precipitating a financial crisis. The long-term consequences of the Soviet position was to stifle the development of a strong peacekeeping function for the United Nations.

Moreover, the Soviet bloc was not the only group of U.N. members unhappy with the outcome of events in the Congo. Supporting Moscow were a group of militant African states whose antiwestern leaders sought to build a coalition of Socialist states on the continent. Nasser of Egypt was, of course, the most prominent spokesman, but in addition there were Kwame Nkruma of Ghana, Muhammed Ben Bella of Algeria, Sekou Toure of Guinea, and Mobido Keita of Mali. These and other antiwestern African leaders were viewed by Khrushchev as the hope for the future of Soviet interests in Africa. They supported Moscow on a wide range of foreign policy issues such as decolonization, reorganization of the United Nations, nuclear disarmament, and the role of national liberation movements in the third world. In return for their support Khrushchev was generous in his economic aid to these countries. The Patrice Lumumba Friendship University in Moscow was established to educate and indoctrinate students from third world countries who were expected to return to their countries and assume positions of leadership.

Khrushchev's great expectations for many of Africa's radical leaders proved to be unwarranted. Some of them (Nkruma, Ben Bella, and Keita) were overthrown in domestic coups. (Sukarno in Indonesia was another major Soviet hope that was dashed by a military coup.) Others (Toure and Anwar Sadat, Nasser's successor) changed their country's foreign policies. Indeed these leaders illustrated the unpredictability of radical-nationalist politicians in Africa and elsewhere. One of the many, though perhaps lesser, reasons for the coup that over-threw Khrushchev himself in October 1964 was dissatisfaction with the high cost and relative unprofitability of the Soviet commitment to third world leaders. The Brezhnev-Kosygin leadership that replaced Khrushchev pursued a more cautious and pragmatic policy in the third world. Economic aid continued though with fewer new credits. Commercial considerations became more prominent in Soviet economic activity in the newer countries than had been the case with Khrushchev.

New leaders came to power in both Washington and Moscow in the first half of the 1960s. For both, third world issues took a back seat to more pressing problems. Leonid Brezhnev and Alexei Kosygin were faced with the particularly pressing need for economic reform (a problem they transmitted to their successors). The Cold War at this time focused on the competition in the field of nuclear arms, which is discussed elsewhere. John Kennedy and Nikita Khrushchev, shortly before his removal, with their nuclear test ban treaty and the hot line agreements, took the first steps toward a cautious détente but not before the Cold War came perilously close to erupting into a hot war because of the stationing of intermediate-range missiles armed with nuclear warheads in Cuba.

The Cuban missile crisis in 1962 basically involved nuclear strategic — not third world — competition, even though the locale was in a third world country. Fidel Castro's seizure of power in 1959 turned out to be a major blow to the United States and a corresponding gain for the U.S.S.R. although at the time the significance of the Cuban revolution was not fully appreciated in either Moscow or Washington. Castro's movement toward communism was neither engineered in the Kremlin nor was it the by-product of mistakes made in Washington. Given the political circumstances of the time, one can almost conclude that it was inevitable that Cuba would drift into the Soviet orbit, but Castro's movement was an authentic domestic revolution, not one made in Moscow. Whatever his Marxist inclinations Castro came to power with an anti-Yankee ideology along with a memory of U.S. support for his bitter enemy Batista. That alone was bound to bring him into conflict with the United States, and given the bipolar character of international politics, an anti-United States posture created a powerful gravitational pull toward the Soviet Union.

The Middle East and Southeast Asia

U.S.–Soviet third world rivalry in the 1960s centered in two regions: the Middle East and southeast Asia. The war that erupted in June 1967 between Israel and Egypt, with Jordan and Syria also getting involved, created a major crisis in U.S.–Soviet relations and provided the Johnson and Brezhnev-Kosygin administrations with an unwanted opportunity to test their skills in crisis management. As was so often the case in the Middle East, events there were beyond the control of the two superpowers both of whom were compelled to react to protect their clients and who were thus pushed into a confrontation that each would have preferred to avoid. It is unlikely that any of the parties to the Six Day War desired to go to war, although Gamal Abdel Nasser's reckless brinkmanship and his inflammatory rhetoric gave the impression that Egypt was in fact preparing for a showdown with Israel.

The June War

Nasser's actions in the months before the outbreak of the 1967 war were motivated by the need to establish his leadership in the struggle against Israel and the competing claims of rivals in the Arab world. Arab terrorist attacks against Israel, particularly from Syrian territory, followed by Israeli reprisals produced a tense situation in the spring of 1967. Threats made by Israeli leaders to take drastic action against Syria led to rumors in April that Tel Aviv was massing troops along the Syrian border for an attack on Damascus. The rumors were unfounded, as revealed by U.N. observers who confirmed the absence of troop concentrations. Israel even invited Soviet Ambassador Chuvakhin to see for himself, but he refused. We cannot be certain to what degree the Soviet leadership actually believed an Israeli invasion was imminent, but Moscow did advise the Egyptian and Syrian governments that Israel was planning to attack Syria. Nasser, who in late 1966 under Soviet persuasion had signed a defensive pact with Syria, was under strong pressure to act. On May 16 he declared a state of emergency for his armed forces and ordered the United Nations Emergency Force, which had stood as a barrier between Egypt and Israel since 1956, to withdraw from the Sinai. On May 22 Nasser set up a blockade of Israel by closing the Straits of Tiran. He proceeded to move the mass of his army into position for an invasion of Israel and told the Egyptian National Assembly on May 29: "We are now ready to confront Israel."[16] As it turned out, he was far from ready; the Israelis struck first in a preemptive attack and in six days completely destroyed the Egyptian, Syrian, and Jordanian armies. At the end of the war Israel was in control of the entire Sinai Peninsula, all of Jerusalem, the West Bank of Jordan, and the Golan Heights of Syria. The consequences of that war have yet to be resolved.

Although Moscow had played a provocative role in the period leading up to the war, there is little doubt that the Soviet Union did not wish to see an outbreak of fighting. At the height of the crisis in late May the Soviet ambassador to Cairo urged Nasser not to be the first to open fire (as did the U.S. ambassador). Soviet sources claim that they were not informed in advance of Nasser's intention to impose a blockade on Israel, an act of war under international law, and had they known of it, they would have objected.[17] In all probability Moscow, in its attempt to protect Syria, had miscalculated how far Egypt and Israel would go to secure their interests.

In the final analysis the Soviet Union wanted what all great powers seek but rarely attain, namely, the fruits of victory without having to fight for them. Nasser in the weeks before war broke out was "on a roll," winning what appeared to be victory after victory. His stature in the Arab world skyrocketed and his successes created a widespread feeling of euphoria in Cairo. Had he been able to sustain this psychological advantage he would have inflicted upon Israel a major political defeat without ever having to face the test of arms in the battlefield. And Cairo's victory would have been Moscow's as well. The Soviet Union would have taken a giant step toward supplanting western influence in a critical region. Once the war began Moscow had no choice but to offer its "resolute support" for the Arab cause. The problem for Moscow was to keep a defeat from becoming a disaster.

Lyndon Johnson was faced with some of the same dilemmas as his Soviet counterpart. He too wanted to avoid another Middle East war; he wanted to protect Israel from an Arab assault; but he was no more in control of Israeli actions than Moscow was of Egyptian behavior. Washington understood full well that Israel would go to war if necessary to break an Egyptian blockade of any of its ports. The United States attempted unsuccessfully to mobilize joint action by other maritime powers against the blockade. It could, of course, have acted unilaterally in Israel's defense, but that was risky. Already bogged down in a war in Vietnam, Washington was extremely worried about getting enmeshed in a Middle East war.

Another danger for Moscow and Washington was a direct confrontation with the possibility of nuclear consequences. As a show of support for Nasser Moscow sent a large naval force into the Mediterranean, which raised the specter of a potential clash between U.S. and Soviet navies in the eastern Mediterranean. Moscow's awareness of the danger of the situation is revealed by a remark made to the Prime Minister of Algeria, Houari Boumedienne, who went to Moscow on June 12 to urge the Soviet government to put the Arab cause above Soviet-American relations. Allegedly Boumedienne asked, "Where is the line at which peaceful coexistence ends?" To which Brezhnev retorted, "What's your opinion of nuclear war?"[18]

That question expressed a fundamental contradiction between both the superpowers and their regional clients, namely, that as global powers the United States and the Soviet Union had interests that in some instances conflicted with those of their third world allies. Thus, while the Soviet Union gave diplomatic support to Nasser during and after the June war, the Kremlin was careful to avoid provocative action toward the United States. Immediately after the outbreak of fighting the Kremlin took the precaution of activating the hot line to Washington for the first time. Lyndon Johnson used the teletype communication to refute the charge made publicly by Nasser that U.S. aircraft had participated along with Israeli planes in attacking Egyptian targets. Moscow obviously did not take the charge (which was false) seriously, as evidenced by the lack of press commentary on it.

In defeat Nasser was bitter and not all of his antagonism was directed against the Zionist and imperialist enemy. On June 9 he engaged in the ploy of resigning as president, intimating in his radio broadcast that the Soviet Union bore some responsibility for the debacle. Some Arab governments, particularly Algeria, Iraq, and Libya, were quite open in their criticism of the Soviet Union, arguing that Moscow failed to support the Arabs to the same extent that Washington backed Israel. Both to counter Arab ire and to strengthen the Arab position the Soviet Union undertook a campaign of political and material aid to Egypt. On June 10 Moscow severed diplomatic relations with Israel. Two days later a massive Soviet airlift of military equipment was sent to Egypt. By the end of June the U.S.S.R. had sent some 200 MIG aircraft and toward the end of the year approximately 80 percent of the aircraft, tanks, and artillery lost to the Israelis had been replaced.

On the diplomatic front Brezhnev sent Soviet President Nikolay Podgorny to Cairo as a show of solidarity with its ally. Also in June Prime Minister Kosygin met with President Johnson in the unlikely diplomatic setting of Glassboro College in New Jersey to press the Arab cause. Kosygin's participation in the U.N. debate on the Middle East in the General Assembly emergency special session was an indication of the importance Moscow attached to restoring some of the diplomatic leverage lost by the Arab defeat. After a fruitless debate in which the Assembly failed to muster a two-thirds vote the issue was referred back to the Security Council. Several months of intensive negotiations produced a compromise resolution, the famous U.N. Resolution 242 of November 22, 1967. Its essential elements called for the "withdrawal of Israeli armed forces from territories occupied in the recent conflict" and the termination of the state of belligerency. Because the resolution failed to call for Israeli withdrawal from *all* the conquered territories, it was acceptable to Israel and the United States. The wording on this resolution was, as is so often the case with U.N. resolutions and other diplomatic communiqués, a papering over of an issue whose solution was simply not possible at the time.

Did the Soviet Union really want a solution to the Arab-Israeli conflict? One can easily conclude that it did if the solution fully met the Arab terms, since that would have clearly redounded to Moscow's benefit. But such a solution could not be attained. Realistically, a solution to the deep differences in the Middle East would have required a compromise, and one in which the Arabs would have had to make substantial concessions because Israel had won on the battlefield. A test of Moscow's seriousness was the degree to which it was prepared to put pressure on a client very much dependent on the Soviet Union. The evidence, according to Alvin Rubinstein, is that "In the hierarchy of Soviet regional and global objectives, a political settlement in the Middle East ranked very low."[19] Soviet interests at the time were better served in building a united Arab front that could be molded into an anti-American coalition. Therefore, even though there were some risks in rebuilding the Arab military arsenal — a danger of unleashing yet another Mideast war — the Soviet Union felt that they were worth taking. And indeed when the Egyptian military had been substantially rebuilt in the summer of 1969 Nasser initiated his war of attrition against Israel. This was another phase in the continuing turmoil in that volatile region whose violence even now shows no signs of abating.

By the end of the 1960s the structure of international politics was undergoing a very fundamental change. The simple bipolarity of the postwar years was largely gone. The world had not become multipolar in the eighteenth- and nineteenth-century sense and the Soviet Union and the United States continued to be militarily supreme, but a combination of factors tended to erode the domination of world affairs by the two nuclear giants. For one, the growth in numbers and sophistication of nuclear weapons created a condition of mutual deterrence that limited superpower freedom of action. Moscow was rapidly approaching nuclear parity with Washington and the United States no longer enjoyed the option of using nuclear weapons for political leverage as it had in the past. Nuclear weapons did not confer on their possessors a political power commensurate with their military capability.

We have already referred to the growth of the third world as a consequence of the termination of the colonial empires. The international system became more complex as new nations emerged and older nations became more powerful. In the latter category was the evolution of the defeated Axis powers — Germany and Japan — into industrial giants. Also, China, after the economic chaos of the Great Leap Forward of the 1950s and the Cultural Revolution of the 1960s, began to put its house in order and gave signs of pursuing an independent foreign policy.

One manifestation of the erosion of superpower hegemony was the difficulty the United States and the Soviet Union had in controlling their respective alliances. For the United States the major challenge came from France and the Gaullist foreign policy of its leaders. In the early 1960s Charles DeGaulle developed France's independent nuclear *force de frappe* and in 1966–1967 extricated France from NATO's military organization altogether. Moscow's problems with alliance cohesion were even more severe. The Soviet invasion of Czechoslovakia in 1968 to crush a reform movement left the Warsaw pact in a state of disarray. Only East Germany and Poland actively supported Moscow's military intervention. Even more damaging was the Sino-Soviet split which culminated in March 1969 in open, though limited, warfare over a boundary dispute. Although the Sino-Soviet alliance was not to be formally terminated until over a decade later, for all practical purposes it had become defunct.

Indochina

No upheaval illustrated more clearly the limits of superpower control over third world conflicts than the war in Vietnam. In some ways it was like the Korean war. It was both a civil and an international war: a conflict between indigenous forces in Vietnam and between the two leading Communist powers (the U.S.S.R. and China) and the United States. The Geneva accords in May 1954 partitioned Vietnam along the 17th Parallel with a Communist government in the north headed by Ho Chi Minh and a non-Communist government in the south headed by Ngo Dinh Diem. While technically the 17th Parallel was not considered to be an international boundary, politically it did in fact become one. One of the provisions of the Geneva accords was for general elections throughout Vietnam to be held in July 1956, though there is reason to doubt that either side believed they would ever take place. Hans J. Morgenthau observed in 1956 that:

> The provision for free elections which would solve ultimately the problem of Vietnam was a device to hide the incompatibility of the Communist and Western positions, neither of which can admit the domination of all of Vietnam by the other side. It was a device to disguise the fact that the line of military demarcation was bound to be a line of political division as well. In one word, what happened in Germany and Korea in the years immediately following 1945 has happened in Vietnam in the years following 1954.[20]

Knowing full well that the elections in the north would be rigged (free elections in Communist societies are virtually non-existent), Diem refused to be a party to the plan. Arguably, the rulers in Hanoi did not consider North and South Vietnam to be separate states but many others including Moscow and Washington did. In 1957 the Soviet Union sought the admission of North and South Vietnam into the United Nations. Although the General Assembly failed to register the two-thirds vote necessary to do so, a solid majority of the U.N. membership supported the proposal.

   Washington considered the 17th Parallel the boundary between the Communist and non-Communist world every bit as much as the 38th Parallel in Korea and the Elbe River in Germany. To bolster anti-Communist forces in Asia the United States and its European allies, France and Great Britain, joined with Australia, New Zealand, Pakistan, the Philippines, and Thailand to form the Southeast Asia Treaty Organization (SEATO) in 1954. Although none of the Indochinese states were members of the organization, SEATO unilaterally extended its protection to Laos, Cambodia, and South Vietnam (Cambodia rejected the unilateral SEATO protection almost at the outset). SEATO was the Asian equivalent of NATO in a generalized policy of containment, but in reality there were many differences between NATO and SEATO, the most fundamental being the different security concerns of the members of SEATO as compared with NATO. The link between the American defense of South Vietnam and its postwar policy of containment was described by Eugene Rostow, a member of the State Department during the Kennedy-Johnson administration:

> In Indochina the North Vietnamese government has broken the first and most basic rule of Peaceful Coexistence: That the frontiers of the two systems not be altered unilaterally, or by military action. To cite a clear parallel, it has been deemed self-evident in Washington and in Moscow that it would be unthinkably dangerous for either East Germany or West Germany to attack the other, either openly or through infiltration. Yet what North Vietnam . . . is attempting in Indochina — to conquer a country the United States has agreed to protect — is the precise analogue of such a hypothetical German conflict, or of the Korean war of 1950-53, or of the Soviet Union's early postwar probes against Greece, Turkey and Iran.[21]

Washington assumed that North Vietnam, China, and the Soviet Union were acting in concert.

But were they? Were the Communist powers acting in collusion? The reality of Sino-Soviet-Vietnamese relations was always more complicated than the image of a monolithic Communist movement held by the Kennedy-Johnson administration. While the three Communist powers shared a common ideology and a strong opposition to the presence of American power in the Pacific, they each had different interests and differing estimates of the risks that could be taken. In the late 1950s Hanoi gradually increased its efforts to overthrow the Diem government with active support for the Viet Cong insurgency in the South. Moscow increasingly found itself caught in a bind. In principle it supported the North Vietnamese–Viet Cong war as a legitimate "war of national liberation." It further felt compelled to give political and moral support to Vietnamese unification so as not to lose influence to the Chinese. On the other hand, Khrushchev apparently was concerned that the Chinese would push the Vietnamese too far, that Chinese-Vietnamese militancy might bring the United States more directly into the conflict. Thus, while Khrushchev was in power Soviet objectives in Vietnam were ambivalent and at times contradictory. Khrushchev is believed to have pressed Hanoi to take a course of moderation, which apparently did not sit well with the North Vietnamese. Clearly, while Khrushchev was in power the Soviet Union was very careful to avoid involvement with the war in Vietnam. Economic aid was provided but very little military assistance.

Soviet moderation was also evident in its policies toward Laos during the crisis that erupted in the early 1960s when the Communists, rightists, and neutralists tried to gain military-political advantage in a society badly torn by civil war. In their June 1961 meeting in Vienna Khrushchev and Kennedy agreed that Laos should be neutral. Diplomatically the Soviet Union under Khrushchev supported the neutrality of Laos in the face of determined efforts by the Pathet Lao, supported by Hanoi, to defeat the neutralist and rightist forces. In the period between the Cuban missile crisis and his overthrow Khrushchev actively sought to reach some kind of an accommodation with the United States on a wide range of issues from nuclear weapons to third world insurgencies. He also sought improved relations with Burma, Ceylon, Indonesia, Malaysia, and Thailand, which could have been undermined by a too aggressive Communist insurgency in the Indochinese states. He saw Chinese aggressiveness as a major threat to Soviet Asian interests.

In the mid-1960s the war in Indochina entered a new phase. A combination of factors sucked Moscow and Washington deeper into the quagmire of Vietnam. Under the stepped-up pressure of the Viet Cong guerrillas the government in Vietnam began to lose control over the countryside. In 1963 the repressive President Diem was assassinated with the tacit approval of the United States. President Kennedy before his own assassination had sent 16,500 military advisers to assist South Vietnam. Gradually, but inexorably, U.S. military force in Vietnam increased.

In 1964 there were significant developments in the leadership of the superpowers which in turn had important implications for the war in Vietnam. Khrushchev was overthrown in a coup that made Leonid Brezhnev the General Secretary of the Communist party and Aleksei Kosygin Prime Minister. In the United States Lyndon Johnson defeated his Republican opponent with a campaign that stressed opposition to escalating the U.S. involvement in Vietnam. Yet within a year both governments substantially increased their commitments to their respective sides in the Indochina war. Toward the end of 1964 North Vietnamese Army troops wearing regulation uniforms and carrying full field equipment were reported in the south. Lyndon Johnson came into office determined not to permit the Communists to prevail in Vietnam. On the day after he ordered air strikes against North Vietnam in retaliation for what he claimed was an attack by North Vietnamese PT boats against two U.S. destroyers Johnson declared in a speech at Syracuse University that "The challenge that we face in Southwest Asia today is the same challenge that we have faced with courage and that we have met with strength in Greece, Turkey, in Berlin and Korea. . . ."[22] It was the unanimous view of the Joint Chiefs of Staff "that if we lost South Vietnam we would lose Southeast Asia," and Johnson never doubted it for a moment. In February 1965 the United States began a campaign of sustained air attacks against North Vietnam in response to a Communist attack on U.S. forces in Pleiku. This major escalation of the war took place at the very time Soviet Prime Minister Kosygin was visiting Ho Chi Minh in Hanoi. Washington was concerned that the timing of its attack might damage Soviet prestige and provoke them in giving Hanoi even greater material support.

Washington sought to reassure Moscow of its limited goals in Vietnam and to convince the new leadership in the Kremlin that it had no desire to bring about the destruction of the Communist government in the north. Moscow was either not

persuaded by U.S. assurances or more likely it had come to
the same conclusion that many in Washington had already
reached, namely, that the government in the south was so pre-
carious that collapse was unavoidable. Just as Washington
viewed its involvement in Vietnam as a test of its credibility as
an ally, so unquestionably did Moscow consider its support of
Hanoi a measure of its reliability. And in Moscow's case there
was the added pressure of its rivalry with China for influence
among Asian Communists. Soviet economic and military aid
to Hanoi rose from approximately $40 billion in 1964 to almost
$1 billion annually from 1967 to 1972.[23]

For the United States the measure of its involvement was
the number of U.S. troops sent to fight in Vietnam. When Lyndon Johnson took office there were some 16,000 American
troops there. They were increased to nearly 23,000 by the end
of 1964. In 1965 the number reached 184,000. By the end of
1966 it had jumped to 383,500, rising to 425,000 in 1967. When
President Johnson left office at the end of 1968 U.S. forces
totaled close to 525,000.[24]

The Consequences of the American Defeat
The failure of the United States to prevent the destruction of
South Vietnam by North Vietnam was its most serious defeat
in the third world, and it marked a major turning point in the
larger war with the Soviet Union. Of the five parties involved,
Moscow and Hanoi emerged victorious while Saigon, Washington, and Peking were the losers. Moscow's gains, however,
did not result from a winning strategy. They were more the by-
products of events over which Moscow had as little control as
did Washington. In retrospect one can see that the original
American commitment was a mistake because it was a fight
that the United States could not win. Politically, it could not
win because it was never able to clearly establish that a Communist victory would be a threat to its vital interests. (In reality, the loss of Indochina to communism, while a tragedy for
the people of Indochina, proved to be less damaging to American security than had been imagined.) Militarily, the United

States could not win because the conflict was a guerrilla war that the Americans tried to fight by conventional means. From the beginning, the odds were stacked against stopping Hanoi because the South Vietnamese people themselves were unwilling to risk everything to defend their government. Saigon was a corrupt regime incapable of carrying through the social and economic reforms that would have made South Vietnam worth defending. There were many individuals and groups in South Vietnam who bitterly opposed communism, but as a society the south was too heterogeneous and divided to put up an effective resistance. By contrast, the North Vietnamese were mobilized by a totalitarian regime whose leadership was selfless, dedicated, and ruthless. They were prepared to pay any cost for victory, and the human and material cost they did pay over the several decades of their struggle was substantial. North Vietnam relied on a strategy of psychological attrition, which was superior to the American strategy of physical attrition. The American people were unwilling to fight a protracted war whose outcome appeared to be indecisive. Divisions that developed in American politics over the wisdom of fighting the war were skillfully exacerbated by Hanoi's diplomacy and propaganda.

Politically, the first casualty of the Vietnam war was the Johnson administration. "The Nixon administration," noted Henry Kissinger, "entered office determined to end our involvement in Vietnam."[25] The overriding foreign policy objective of the first Nixon administration was to extricate America from that war without simply abandoning everything that the United States had sought in its defense of South Vietnam. The Republican administration was faced with the prospect of ruinous costs the longer the war endured. In 1968, 14,592 Americans died in combat in Vietnam. The cost of the war in fiscal year 1969 was $30 billion. But how to end it "with honor" as Nixon was determined to do? The answer was a negotiated settlement with Hanoi. But Hanoi stubbornly resisted meaningful talks. Henry Kissinger, Nixon's national security adviser and later secretary of state, thought that the solution might be in Moscow. He believed that since North Vietnam was dependent on Soviet support Moscow was in a position to pressure Hanoi into negotiating a settlement of the conflict.

In order for Moscow to be willing to go along with such an arrangement, however, there had to be some payoff for the Soviet Union, some change in U.S.–Soviet relations. That change took place in the 1970s and it became what we now know as détente. Moscow had its own reasons for wanting to improve relations with Washington. One was its growing schism with China and the need to build a power balance against the day when China might become a genuine adversary. The outbreak of fighting along the Usurri River in March 1969 between Sino-Soviet forces revealed that such a time might not be far in the future. Another factor in the early 1970s was the weakness of the Soviet economy and the Kremlin's desire to expand economic relations with the United States. The reforms of the 1960s — the Liberman reforms — failed to generate economic growth, efficiency, or innovation. Short of radically restructuring the economy, which the conservative Brezhnev was loath to do, Soviet planners were forced to turn to the west for technology to generate growth and food to feed the people. To import technology and grain meant expanded trade with the United States and that in turn involved an improved framework for U.S.–Soviet relations.

Another factor supporting détente was the mutual desire for arms control. In 1970 the Soviet Union pulled alongside the United States in the number of its intercontinental ballistic missiles. Ironically, this growth in Soviet nuclear capability made serious arms control negotiations possible for the first time in the history of the nuclear arms race. The United States was motivated by the desire to curb the headlong Soviet buildup in offensive missiles. Moscow wanted to limit the projected American plan to construct an antiballistic missile defense. There was, in a word, the basis for a mutually beneficial deal. And having achieved nuclear parity Moscow could seriously contemplate an arms control treaty that would not freeze it permanently in an inferior position. Thus it was that, while fighting continued in southeast Asia, the ingredients for a change in the pattern of U.S.–Soviet-Chinese relations were brewing.

Détente Unravels in the Middle East

Détente, however, had a fatal flaw. That flaw was the conflicting views of Moscow and Washington concerning their rivalry in the third world. Nixon and Kissinger expected détente to reduce Soviet-American conflict worldwide, not just on the nuclear or trade issues. Moscow was expected to cooperate with the United States in areas of its vital interests in return for support on issues of concern to the Kremlin. This was the essence of Henry Kissinger's theory of "linkage," which he described in his memoirs as follows:

> *The principle of linkage.* We insisted that progress in super-power relations, to be real, had to be made on a broad front. Events in different parts of the world, in our view, were related to each other; even more so, Soviet conduct in different parts of the world. We proceeded from the premise that to separate issues into distinct compartments would encourage the Soviet leaders to believe that they could use cooperation in one area as a safety valve while striving for unilateral advantages elsewhere.[26]

The Politburo never accepted the concept of linkage. In particular it rejected the interconnection between state-to-state agreements in such fields as arms control and trade and cooperation to diffuse confrontation in the third world. Leonid Brezhnev made the Soviet position explicit when he told the Twenty-fifth Party Congress in 1976 that:

> Some bourgeois leaders affect surprise and raise a howl over the solidarity of Soviet Communists, the Soviet people, with the struggle of other peoples for freedom and progress. This is

either outright naiveté or more likely a deliberate befuddling of minds. It could not be clearer, after all, that détente and peaceful coexistence have to do with interstate relations. This means above all that disputes and conflicts between countries are not to be settled by war, by the use or threat of force. Détente does not in the slightest abolish, nor can it abolish or alter, the laws of the class struggle. . . . We make no secret of the fact that we see détente as the way to create more favourable conditions for peaceful socialist and communist construction.[27]

Thus, no sooner had the ink dried on the several agreements reached in Moscow in the spring of 1972, of which the SALT I agreement was the centerpiece, than fissures began to develop in the newly established détente. First, it was in the Middle East; then it shifted to southeast Asia; then, toward the mid-1970s, to Africa; and finally came the total collapse of détente in Afghanistan at the end of the decade.

One of the several attempts to codify a set of rules to governing U.S.–Soviet relations was an agreement signed on June 23, 1973, "on the prevention of nuclear wars." Article IV of that agreement specified that:

If at any time relations between the Parties or between either Party and other countries appear to involve the risk of a nuclear conflict, or if relations between countries not parties to this Agreement appear to involve the risk of nuclear war between the United States of America and the Union of Soviet Socialist Republics or between either Party and other countries, the United States and the Soviet Union . . . shall immediately enter into urgent consultations with each other and make every effort to avert this risk.[28]

Barely four months after the agreement was signed Egypt attacked Israeli forces along the Suez Canal, exposing the hollowness of that particular agreement and the shallowness of détente in general. On October 6, 1973, Anwar Sadat went to war with Israel in a desperate attempt to recover the territory

Egypt had lost in the June 1967 war. Moscow hardly wanted to see another Arab-Israeli war, but it dutifully fell in line behind the Arab cause. Sadat, who succeeded Nasser after his death in September 1970, had pressed Moscow for greater military support in Egypt's ongoing struggle against Israel. The Kremlin, unsure of Sadat's commitment to the Soviet Union, obtained from Egypt a treaty of friendship and cooperation, which was signed on May 27, 1971. In politically binding Egypt to the Soviet Union Moscow was committing itself more solidly to the military support of a third world country than it had ever done before. Brezhnev, however, was not anxious to encourage Egyptian adventurism and resisted giving the Egyptian leader all the military equipment he sought. Perhaps he sensed in Sadat the unpredictability that was to mark his diplomacy. Certainly, it came as a shock when Sadat unexpectedly announced on July 18, 1972, the expulsion from Egypt of between 15,000 and 20,000 Soviet military personnel including all Soviet pilots. Only the Soviet naval facilities remained more or less in place. Sadat's action was motivated in part by resistance within the Egyptian military to Soviet penetration of the military infrastructure, resentment at the patronizing behavior of Soviet advisers, and by his own deep dislike of communism and the Soviet system. The Egyptian-Soviet relationship in the early 1970s was a good illustration of sharply contrasting personalities and regimes each using the other for its own purposes. Moscow desperately wanted a reconciliation with Cairo and by early 1973 Sadat came to the conclusion that it was in his interest to effect one. Soviet aid was resumed and Sadat went ahead with his planned attack against Israeli fortifications in the Sinai Peninsula.

The October War and Its Aftermath

While not encouraging Egyptian military action in October 1973 Moscow knew in advance of the impending war and not only did nothing to stop it, it actively encouraged other Arab countries to join the fray against Israel once the war began. Egypt's attack was coordinated with a Syrian attack along Israel's northern border. Three days before fighting began Soviet dependents were removed from Syria. A measure of the highly calculated nature of the Soviet game was the fact that Leonid Brezhnev sent Algerian President Boumedienne a message urging Arabs to unite behind the Egyptian-Syrian attack, but the Soviet leader carefully refrained from publishing the letter. (Boumedienne leaked it anyway.) If ever there was a situation called for under Article IV of the Agreement on the Prevention of Nuclear War, this was it. Of course, had Moscow done what it was committed to do under the agreement and consulted with the United States prior to the outbreak of war, the United States would probably have informed Israel and that would have led to an immediate Arab debacle. By encouraging the Arab assault Moscow was violating another of the formal commitments enshrining détente, the Declaration on Basic Principles of Relations between the United States of America and the Union of Soviet Socialist Republics (May 29, 1972). That declaration prohibited "efforts to obtain unilateral advantage at the expense of the other."[29] The October war posed a challenge to the Kremlin. It may well have been a challenge the Kremlin did not seek, but once it had to choose between promoting the Soviet-Arab alliance or détente with the United States, it unequivocally chose the former.

Moscow's tactics during this crisis changed with the circumstances. Initially when the Egyptians were successful in combat the Soviet Union pressed for military victory. On October 10 Moscow started a massive airlift of supplies to the Arabs, which by the end of the month amounted to almost 1,000 plane loads. Only after Israeli counterattacks began to change the military picture did Moscow urge an end to the war. On October 16 Kosygin secretly visited Cairo to work out the provisions of a cease-fire that would be guaranteed by both superpowers. Brezhnev asked Henry Kissinger to come to Moscow to work out the details of a cease-fire agreement, which he did on October 20. The eagerness of Washington and Moscow to end the crisis with a minimum of damage indicated that détente, however flawed, did have some validity.

Israel came close to destroying not only the Egyptian armed forces but also the fragile bonds of cooperation between Moscow and Washington. Toward the end of October Israeli forces smashed through Egyptian lines and appeared ready to encircle and dismantle the main Egyptian Army. Ignoring United Nations calls for a cease-fire Israel seemed determined to achieve a total victory. Another Arab debacle, as in 1967 — even though brought on by themselves — would almost certainly have canceled out any kind of a negotiated Egyptian-Israeli settlement and left the Arabs more dependent than ever on the Soviet Union. This the United States did not want, and so it pressured Israel to show some restraint on the battlefield. Washington, however, was unprepared for the provocative posture taken by Brezhnev who bluntly threatened to intervene directly with Soviet forces and accompanied that threat by placing seven divisions of airborne troops on standby alert. Brezhnev wrote Nixon: "I will say it straight, that if you find it impossible to act together with us in this matter, we should be faced with the necessity urgently to consider the question of taking appropriate steps unilaterally. Israel cannot be allowed to get away with these violations."[30] Nixon replied by placing U.S. military forces on a worldwide alert status. Here was brinkmanship on a grand scale, but both sides responded rationally to defuse the crisis. Moscow dropped its threat to intervene, and the United States pressed Israel to comply with a United Nations-ordered cease-fire. Egypt's Third Army was saved from destruction, and both superpowers could claim some of the credit.

The October war had political and strategic repercussions that few could have imagined when it began. Saudia Arabia, in an attempt to pressure the United States to back away from its support of Israel, initiated an Arab oil boycott. The abrupt halt in the supply of Mideast oil to the west led to a quadrupling of the price of oil with damaging economic consequences for the oil-importing countries. To a degree not previously imagined the vulnerability of the industrialized nations of the world was exposed. Saudia Arabia emerged from the boycott wealthier and more politically powerful than it had ever been. But Saudia Arabia was unable to convert its wealth to political leverage. It could not control the outcome of events in the Middle East, certainly not with regard to the Arab-Israeli conflict. The devastating impact of the oil shortage and price rise stimulated an economic reaction in the industrialized nations — conservation, utilization of other energy sources, and increased oil productivity — that within a decade produced a change in the demand for oil and a political decline of the Organization of Petroleum Exporting Countries (OPEC).

Notwithstanding the adverse effects of the "oil shock" the United States emerged from the October war with more influence in the Arab world than did the Soviet Union. Moscow sought to recover some of its political clout by rebuilding the armed forces of Egypt and Syria. Formerly Soviet prestige was served by the appointment of the Soviet Union to be cochairman (along with the United States) of a Middle East peace conference that opened on December 21, 1973, in Geneva. But the position proved to be meaningless since the conference collapsed before it began. As in 1967, many Arab critics blamed the Soviet Union for its lack of all-out support. Moscow was accused of putting its own priorities ahead of the Arab cause. To some Arabs, the October war revealed anew that concessions from Israel were more likely to come because of political pressure from Washington than because of arms from Moscow.

In addition, American diplomacy had two advantages over the Soviet Union. First, since Moscow broke diplomatic relations with Israel after the 1967 war, only the United States had relations with both sides. The Soviet decision to sever relations with Israel appealed to the hard-line sentiment among the Arabs but at the cost of ruling out the Kremlin as a power broker in the region. Second, Soviet diplomacy suffered from a rigidity and a crudeness that often offended Arabs who were sensitive to the subtle nuances of diplomatic behavior. Because Moscow profited from the continued turmoil in the area it tended to support Arab militants over the moderates. While

Soviet hard-line rhetoric did appeal to the radical Arab governments (Syria, Iraq, and Libya), it did little to facilitate successful negotiations. It was that drawback which ultimately led Sadat to break with Moscow and initiate direct talks with Israel.

The superiority of American diplomacy was best reflected in Henry Kissinger's "shuttle diplomacy." In 1974 and 1975 he succeeded in negotiating two disengagement agreements between Egypt and Israel and one between Syria and Israel. They provided for a pullback of Israeli forces in the Sinai and the return of Egypt's oil wells. Israel and Syria agreed to disengage their military forces in the Golan Heights and permit the presence of United Nations observers to monitor the truce. While small in comparison to the differences between the hostile parties, these agreements were the first significant steps toward even a limited accommodation in over a generation. They laid the basis for the Camp David agreements and the Egyptian-Israeli peace treaty later in the decade. Kissinger's strategy in these negotiations was a carefully crafted step-by-step approach. He was convinced that peace could not be established until the Soviets were eliminated altogether from the region. A major step in that direction was taken on March 15, 1976, when Anwar Sadat unilaterally abrogated the Soviet-Egyptian treaty of friendship and cooperation and then did away with the facilities for the Soviet Navy. Moscow's huge military and economic investment in Egypt went completely down the drain.

By the mid-1970s the Soviet-American rivalry in the third world had become a permanent feature of the Cold War. The collapse of western colonialism created many power vacuums around the globe, providing Moscow with numerous opportunities to shift the geopolitical balance from west to east. Soviet involvement in the third world moved slowly under Stalin, accelerated during Khrushchev's rule, and became consolidated with the Brezhnev administration. The techniques of Soviet involvement included military and economic aid, political sup-

port to friendly governments, and, even in limited circumstances, the use of Soviet military advisers in combat-support
operations.

Characteristics of Soviet and American Third World Activity
Some characteristics of Soviet activity in the third world
should be noted. First, the primary motivation was strategic
and political, not economic or ideological. Moscow sought to
build political relationships with a variety of regimes as long as
they offered the promise of undermining western influence.
While British and French power was waning in Africa, Asia,
and the Middle East, the Soviet Union tried to prevent America from filling the gap. To accomplish this Moscow was prepared to deal with virtually any kind of regime no matter what
its social-political structure or domestic politics. Even governments that repressed Communist parties could be the recipients of Soviet aid and political support. Khrushchev expressed
more concern than Brezhnev about pressuring its third world
allies to pursue a "progressive domestic course," but essentially both leaders thought in terms of the long-term geopolitical advantages of aligning third world countries to the Socialist
camp. Fundamentally, the aim was to weaken the western
powers — most particularly the United States — militarily and
politically.

A second feature of Soviet policy was its caution. Moscow
did not move into a country or region until it was invited, and
almost always great care was given to local concerns and sensitivities. The Soviet Union invested considerable resources in
studying countries and societies about which previously it had
little knowledge or interest. Thus it was possible for the Kremlin to adapt to the unique features of different regions and
countries. Caution was particularly notable in using military
instruments. The U.S.S.R. was careful to avoid committing
itself to military action on behalf of any of its allies or clients.
Before the 1970s Moscow usually avoided sending large quantities of weapons to non-Communist regimes actually engaged
in combat. The Kremlin was even more careful regarding any

direct participation by Soviet personnel in combat or in combat-support positions. It was not until the war of attrition in the Middle East (between Egypt and Israel 1969–1970) that the Soviet Union markedly changed its historic policy of restraint on that score.[31] But even later when it became more adventurous militarily, it went to great lengths to avoid becoming entangled militarily with a western power.

Finally, there is the question of how successful Soviet policy was. As Sadat's expulsion of Soviet advisers — notwithstanding Moscow's huge investment in Egypt — indicates, the U.S.S.R. met with considerable defeats in the third world. Khrushchev encountered domestic opposition because he poured so many resources into regimes that either were overthrown or switched sides. There was no guarantee that Moscow could successfully take advantage of the vast reservoir of antiwestern feeling that accompanied decolonization. The picture was a mixed one: some successes, some failures. Perhaps the Soviet Union's most enduring success was with India, an achievement particularly significant since India was one of the few democracies to emerge from colonialism, and the largest at that. Cuba has been the Soviet Union's most reliable ally in the western hemisphere, though Castro's loyalty has been purchased at a high economic cost. While Soviet fortunes in the Middle East have fluctuated, support for Arab nationalism against Israel has guaranteed Moscow a core of Arab goodwill. And similarly, Moscow's consistent opposition to white-dominated regimes in Africa — notably the Portuguese colonies before their independence, Rhodesia, and South Africa — have guaranteed the Soviet Union widespread sympathy in black Africa.

Overall American policy in the third world was guided by defensive considerations. Consistent with its strategy of containment the United States sought to stop the expansion of Soviet influence in the developing nations. As a general rule Washington was less concerned about the type of government or social structure of a country than it was about its position in the Cold War. Like Moscow, Washington worked closely with democracies or dictatorships. The mentality of the domino theory, or the zero-sum mentality, prevailed in Washington. Fundamentally, the United States was a status quo power facing what it perceived to be a revisionist threat.

The tactics used by the United States were similar to those of its adversary: military and economic aid and political support. Operating from a stronger military position Washington was willing to take greater risks in the period under review than was Moscow. Indeed until the Suez fiasco so were Britain and France. There were numerous examples of western military operations in the third world that the Soviet Union could not have emulated at the time. A particularly popular device in the Eisenhower-Dulles period was the military pact, such as the Baghdad and SEATO treaties. By comparison Moscow relied much less on the multilateral pact, preferring instead to develop ties on a bilateral basis.

In assessing the balance of failures and successes in the third world for America the picture is — as with Russia — mixed. Many of the same factors that made the third world such an intractable environment for the Soviet Union applied equally to the United States, i.e., the impact of indigenous forces on local politics. The west had one advantage unavailable to the Soviet Union and that was a history of involvement and familiarity with many parts of the third world. It knew more about the peoples and cultures of Asia, Africa, Latin America, and the Middle East. But that advantage was more than negated by the legacy of colonialism. The United States had neither the historical involvement nor the colonial legacy of some of its allies. Its wealth and technology gave it some advantage over its rival. However, the 1970s were to witness not only the greatest failure of the United States in the third world, but one of its biggest defeats in the Cold War.

Notes

1. Bruce D. Porter, *The USSR in Third World Conflicts, Soviet Arms and Diplomacy in Local Wars, 1945–1980* (Cambridge, Mass.: Cambridge University Press, 1984), p. 14.

2. See Leo Gruliow, ed., *Current Soviet Policies* (New York: Frederick A. Praeger, 1953), pp. 1–10; Marshall D. Shulman, *Stalin's Foreign Policy Reappraised,* (Cambridge, Mass.: Harvard University Press, 1963), p. 242.

3. Quoted in Stephen T. Hosmer and Thomas W. Wolfe, *Soviet Policy and Practice Toward Third World Conflicts* (Lexington, Mass.: Lexington Books, 1983), p. 4.

4. Adam Ulam, *The Rivals* (New York: the Viking Press, 1971), p. 171.

5. Nikita Khrushchev, *Khrushchev Remembers* (Boston: Little, Brown, 1970), p. 368.

6. John W. Spanier, *The Truman-MacArthur Controversy and the Korean War* (Cambridge, Mass.: Harvard University Press, 1959), pp. 27–28.

7. Quoted in John Lewis Gaddis, *Strategies of Containment, A Critical Appraisal of Postwar American National Security Policy* (London: Oxford University Press, 1982), p. 110.

8. Marshall D. Shulman, *Stalin's Foreign Policy Reappraised* (Cambridge, Mass.: Harvard University Press, 1963), pp. 139–175.

9. Robert C. Tucker, *The Lenin Anthology* (New York: W. W. Norton, 1975), p. 621.

10. Quoted in Rupert Emerson, *From Empire to Nation, The Rise to Self-Assertion of Asian and African Peoples* (Boston: Beacon Press, 1966), p. 364.

11. Leo Gruliow, ed., *Current Soviet Policies II, The Documentary Record of the 20th Party Congress and Its Aftermath* (New York: Frederick A. Praeger, 1957), p. 33.

12. "X" (George Kennan), "The Sources of Soviet Conduct, *Foreign Affairs,* vol. 25, no. 4, July 1947, p. 576.

13. *Khrushchev Remembers,* op. cit., pp. 482–483.

14. Fred Greene, *U.S. Policy and the Security of Asia* (New York: McGraw-Hill, 1968), p. 102.

15. Stephen T. Hosmer and Thomas W. Wolfe, *Soviet Policy and Practice Toward Third World Conflicts* (Lexington, Mass.: Lexington Books, 1983), p. 18.

16. Walter Laqueur, ed., *The Israeli-Arab Reader* (New York: Bantam Books, 1969), p. 187.

17. Charles W. Yost, "The Arab-Israeli War, How It Began," *Foreign Affairs,* vol. 46, no. 2, January 1968, p. 315.

18. Alvin Z. Rubinstein, *Red Star on the Nile, The Soviet-Egyptian*

Influence Relationship since the June War (Princeton, N.J.: Princeton University Press), 1977, p.14.

19.   Ibid., p. 27.

20.   Quoted in Guenter Lewy, *America in Vietnam* (New York, Oxford University Press, 1978), p. 8.

21.   Quoted in John Spanier, *American Foreign Policy since World War II,* 10th ed. (New York: Holt, Rinehart & Winston, 1985), p. 141.

22.   Lyndon Baines Johnson, *The Vantage Point, Perspectives of the Presidency 1963–1969* (New York: Holt, Rinehart & Winston), p. 117.

23.   Alvin Z. Rubinstein, *Soviet Foreign Policy since World War II, Imperial and Global,* 2d ed. (Boston: Little, Brown, 1985), p. 175.

24.   The figures are from Lyndon Johnson, *The Vantage Point,* op. cit., chaps. 6 and 11.

25.   Henry Kissinger, *White House Years* (Boston: Little, Brown, 1979), p. 227.

26.   Ibid., p. 129.

27.   *Documents and Resolutions, 25th Congress of the CPSU* (Moscow: Novosti Press Agency, 1976), p. 39.

28.   *Documents on Disarmament 1973* (Washington, D.C.: United States Arms Control and Disarmament Agency, 1976), p. 284.

29.   *Documents on Disarmament 1972* (Washington, D.C.: United States Arms Control and Disarmament Agency, 1974), p. 238.

30.   Quoted in Joseph L. Nogee and Robert Donaldson, *Soviet Foreign Policy since World War II,* 2d ed. (New York: Pergamon Press, 1984), p. 279.

31.   Bruce Porter, op. cit., p. 1.

Third World Conflict and the Collapse of Détente

Where It Was Played

The decade of the 1970s witnessed a significant shift in United States and Soviet involvement in the third world. Moscow stepped up its interventions in new and unchartered regions while Washington was compelled to reduce its interventionist activities abroad. Moscow's enhanced activity was based in large part on its increased capability to project power beyond the confines of the Soviet bloc. That and the achievement of nuclear parity with the United States gave the leaders in the Kremlin more confidence and more options than ever before.

By contrast, U.S. capacity to project its power abroad was sapped by deep social and political divisions in American society. The Vietnam war generated an antiwar movement that shattered the consensus upon which the policy of containment was based, and the divisions generated by that war were subsequently intensified by the Watergate scandals. These and other domestic conflicts undermined Washington's capacity to exercise a strong foreign policy.

The American Failure in Vietnam

No one understood better than Richard Nixon the debilitating impact of the Vietnam war on American foreign policy. Ending American involvement in Vietnam thus became a priority objective of his administration. But he soon faced the same dilemma that bedeviled his predecessor. As his national security adviser noted:

> For nearly a generation the security and progress of free peoples had depended on confidence in America. We could not simply walk away from an enterprise involving two administrations, five allied countries, and thirty-one thousand dead as if we were switching a television channel.[1]

If the United States hoped to salvage any of its objectives in southeast Asia, there would have to be a negotiated end to the war, not simply an American abandonment of South Vietnam. Operating from the theory of linkage, Nixon and Kissinger signaled the Kremlin that the success of détente required an ending of the war in Vietnam. They urged Moscow to use its influence to get Hanoi to negotiate a settlement. Brezhnev was in fact willing to serve as a conduit between Washington and Hanoi, but he was unwilling to exert pressure on the latter to compromise with the former. Indeed even in the heyday of détente the Soviet leader would not agree to reduce arms supplies to North Vietnam because, argued Brezhnev, that was its obligation as a fraternal ally. To Kissinger's pleading the Soviet leader replied that Hanoi's policies were not subject to Soviet control, an argument that to some extent was valid.

Moscow wanted both détente and a free hand in the third world. Those contradictory goals sometimes obliged the Kremlin to maneuver cautiously between difficult choices, such as in the spring of 1972 shortly before the scheduled Moscow summit. In response to a major North Vietnamese offensive the United States mined the North Vietnam harbor at Haiphong in early May and began a series of heavy bombing raids on Hanoi. It was something of a challenge to Moscow in the face of Nixon's impending visit to Moscow. The question of whether or not to go ahead with the summit was thrashed out in an emergency session of the Politburo which, after acrimonious debate, determined not to cancel the meeting. In fact, during the conference Brezhnev even agreed to send President Nikolay Podgorny to convey new American proposals to the Vietnamese.

Intense negotiations to end the war took place between Le Duc Tho and Henry Kissinger in Paris during the summer of 1972 through the end of January 1973 when a truce was finally signed. That agreement seemed to be a significant victory for the United States inasmuch as Hanoi settled for less than a total victory. The Paris truce agreement provided for an internationally supervised cease-fire, the withdrawal of all U.S. forces from the south, an exchange of prisoners of war, and the creation of political commissions to work out a new constitution and the election of a new government. In Nixon's view this was an "honorable peace," and though there is no

evidence to indicate that Moscow had directly influenced Hanoi's decision to accept the truce, the Nixon administration
was prepared to credit Moscow with exercising a positive
influence.[2]

But if the Soviet Union did in fact assist the United States
in 1972, it was only a tactical move. Moscow's strategic interests lay in the control of all of Indochina by a Communist regime. Shortly after the signing of the Paris agreements the
North Vietnamese began violating them. In March Kissinger
warned Soviet Ambassador Anatoly Dobrynin that a new offensive by Hanoi would have "the profoundest consequences
for US-Soviet relations." In May the U.S. government protested (in vain) against the wholesale illegal infiltration of
North Vietnamese troops into the south. "It was obvious,"
Kissinger lamented in his memoirs, ". . . we could expect little
help from the Soviet quarter."[3] Vietnam was doomed and the
United States could do little more than observe helplessly. The
end came in the spring of 1975 when the collapse of the South
Vietnamese Army led to the Communist occupation of Saigon
(now Ho Chi Minh City) and the forced unification of the country under a Communist government. At the Twenty-fifth Party
Congress the following year Leonid Brezhnev proudly proclaimed that:

> The Soviet people take pride in having rendered considerable
> aid to Vietnam in its struggle against the imperialist invaders.
> Having won independence and national unity at a high price,
> the people of Vietnam are now working arduously to restore
> their country and are building the socialist future. Vietnam's
> victory has opened new horizons for all of southeast Asia. It
> was a glorious victory; and will be inscribed forever in the his-
> tory of the people's struggle for freedom and socialism.[4]

Formal recognition of the Soviet-Vietnamese alliance was
made with the signing of a treaty of friendship and cooperation
between the two states in November 1978. One of the benefits
to Moscow of this alliance was that the the Soviet Navy could

use the giant Cam Ranh naval facility built by the United States.

Soviet Intervention in Africa

The balance of power moved sharply against the United States in the 1970s. A succession of damaging events eroded America's prestige and undermined its capacity to act in world affairs. First there was the oil crisis in 1973, followed by the domestic crisis of Watergate and the resignation of President Nixon. The Vietnam protest movement and the Watergate scandal were particularly damaging because they revealed a badly divided society with a government incapable of taking strong action to protect its global interests. Then came the conquest of South Vietnam, exposing the total failure of American policy in southeast Asia. Later in the decade the fall of the Shah of Iran followed by the seizure of 52 American hostages in Teheran and the bungled U.S. effort to rescue the hostages would bring U.S. prestige and influence in the post–World War II period to an all-time low. As the United States floundered the Soviet Union became bolder, moving actively into a new arena of the third world: central Africa. It is a measure of the overall change in the balance of power that Soviet intervention in Africa was undertaken by a geriatric leadership which on the whole had pursued a relatively cautious foreign policy.

The most aggressive of Soviet interventions were in Angola in 1975–1976 and Ethiopia in 1977–1978. Although motivated by strategic and political considerations, there is no evidence that Moscow was operating from any large strategic plan. The moves into central Africa were the result of opportunities that unexpectedly developed in 1974. On April 25 the Caetano dictatorship in Lisbon was overthrown with dramatic consequences for Portugal's African empire. That same year saw the overthrow of Emperor Haile Selasse in Ethiopia, leading to the emergence of a Marxist government in Addis Ababa. Both coups — led by military forces — opened up unexpected and important opportunities for the Soviet Union, and in both countries Soviet intervention involved the use of Cuban combat troops.

When Portugal decided to pull out of Angola in 1974 there was no political force to replace it. A civil war ensued between three competing insurgent movements each largely ethnic in composition. They were the National Front for the Liberation of Angola (FNLA), the National Union for the Total Independence of Angola (UNITA), and the Popular Movement for the Liberation of Angola (MPLA). The MPLA leadership, headed by Dr. Agostinho Neto, was more urban, intellectual, and socialist than the other two. The Kremlin had longstanding ties with Neto going back to 1964 when Neto visited Moscow and received assurances of armed support.[5] Cuban ties to the MPLA also went back to the mid-1960s. With the government of Angola up for grabs after the Portuguese granted its former colony independence on November 11, 1975, the internal struggle in that central African country became enmeshed in the Cold War as well as the Sino-Soviet rivalry. UNITA, led by Jonas Savimbi, was supported by China for a while and later by South Africa. The FNLA received varied support from Zaire, China, and the United States.

Soviet military support to the MPLA increased substantially in March 1975. That summer Soviet and Cuban personnel began appearing in Angola in small numbers. As the date for independence approached, Cuban forces began to arrive in greater numbers.[6] According to western sources, the MPLA originally requested combat forces from the Soviet Union in the summer of 1975. The Soviets reportedly rejected the request because they feared an American reaction. Instead they advised Neto to ask the Cubans.[7] In January 1975 the United States began giving nonmilitary aid to the FNLA, which escalated into covert military aid when it became apparent that the influx of Soviet military aid was changing the internal military balance among the three liberation movements contending for power. When the Portuguese left Angola on independence day the MPLA was in control of the capital, Luanda, and the oil-rich enclave of Cabinda. Agostinho Neto proclaimed the creation of a People's Republic of Angola, which the Soviet bloc immediately recognized. This was followed by the shipment of tons of sophisticated arms including T54 and T34 tanks. Cuban troops and Soviet arms poured into Angola from the day of its independence through early 1976. An estimated 11,000 Cuban troops were in Angola as of February 1976. While Havana sent troops Moscow provided the bulk of arms, ammunition, and logistical support. In 1976 Cuban forces in Angola peaked at 20,000 (though Fidel Castro claimed that the number was as high as 36,000). These forces achieved their objective. When the conventional fighting ended in February 1976 the MPLA had a decisive advantage over its domestic adversaries.

The Ford administration wanted to give aid to the FNLA and UNITA, but it was prohibited from doing so by the Clark amendment passed by the Congress in January 1976 (that law was repealed in 1985). Undoubtedly the Vietnam experience influenced Congress in its opposition to American involvement in a faraway country deep in Africa. Although Angola was rich in mineral resources many felt that there were insufficient U.S. vital interests in the country to warrant making a commitment. Also, some felt that the alliance of South Africa on the side of Neto's enemies and the support of the MPLA by the Organization of African Unity put U.S. support of the FNLA or UNITA against the tide of African nationalism. Soviet-Cuban intervention in Angola, which was unquestionably a success from the point of view of bringing to power a government favorable to Soviet interests, produced a negative reaction in the United States toward the Soviet Union. Angola turned out to be a large nail in the coffin of détente.

Ethiopia and Somalia

The political revolution taking place in Ethiopia during this period opened up another opportunity for Moscow, but Brezhnev exploited it slowly and carefully. There were several reasons for Moscow's caution. First, the Soviet Union wanted to preserve as much of détente with the United States as possible;

second, Moscow could not know exactly what the outcome would be of the struggle for power within the Provisional Military Administrative Council (known as the Dergue); and third, support for Ethiopia complicated its relationship with Somalia, at the time a Soviet ally.

Although the revolution that dethroned Haile Selassie in September 1974 declared Ethiopia to be a Socialist state, there were sharp disagreements within the Dergue over what domestic and foreign policies to pursue. In short time the government was faced with anarchy at home and hostilities with its neighbors. Relations with the United States deteriorated because of widespread violations of human rights throughout the country. A struggle for power within the Dergue moved the government leftward and resulted in the elimination of prowestern elements. In February 1977 Haile-Mariam Mengistu, a strongly pro-Soviet officer, assumed full control of the government and from that point Moscow replaced Washington as the principal source of its armory.

While Moscow undoubtedly welcomed the political changes taking place in Africa's second largest country it was reluctant to make a full commitment to a state that was drifting toward disintegration and anarchy. The Ethiopian revolution involved nationalization and land reform in its attempt to uproot the old imperial order. Widespread resistance to the revolution developed in the cities and countryside alike. In the province of Eritrea a national liberation movement sought autonomy. Eritrean guerillas — at one time the beneficiaries of Soviet support — could not be suppressed by the Ethiopian Army. Supporting the Eritrean insurgents was the Sudanese government, whose rapidly deteriorating relations with Moscow culminated in May 1977 when it expelled the Soviet military mission from Khartoum. But the most troublesome issues for Moscow were the border tensions with Somalia and the insurgency in the Ethiopian province of the Ogaden.

Until 1977 Somalia was a Russian ally, having signed a treaty of friendship with the Soviet Union in 1974. In return for military assistance Mogadiscio gave Moscow unrestricted access to the Red Sea port of Berbera. The Horn of Africa was critical to the Soviet Union because the Red Sea was the shortest sea route between the Pacific and European ports of the U.S.S.R., and shore-based support in the Horn facilitated the operation of the Soviet Indian Ocean naval forces. Because of the great distances involved the ports in the Horn were vital for provisioning ships and making repairs that cannot be done satisfactorily at sea. Somalia was also important because it was only the second third world country (after Egypt) to allow Russia to use its extensive facilities ashore.[8]

During 1977 Moscow found itself in the uncomfortable position of having to choose between two potential allies. In April the Dergue expelled the U.S. military advisory group and closed down all U.S. military installations in the country. In May Colonel Mengistu made his first trip to Moscow where he succeeded in negotiating a major aid agreement with the Soviet Union. While this was taking place the first contingent of about 50 Cubans arrived in Ethiopia. In July Somalia invaded the Ethiopian province of the Ogaden in an attempt to unite the Somali-speaking people under one government in Mogadiscio. Soviet-made weapons were used in the invasion. Moscow had attempted to prevent this crisis earlier in the year with a proposal for a Marxist state that would unite Ethiopia, Somalia, South Yemen, and Djibouti. In this federation Eritrea and the Ogaden would receive substantial autonomy. Somalia rejected this *pax sovietica* outright.

Before the year ended the new alignment between the countries of the Horn and the superpowers had begun to take shape. In a desperate attempt to get backing from Moscow President Siad Barre visited Moscow in August 1977 but Leonid Brezhnev would not see him. Instead the Kremlin stepped up its military aid to Addis Ababa. In December — following a secret visit by Mengistu to Havana and Moscow — Cuba sent the first contingent of 16,000 combat troops who were used to repel the Somalis from the Ogaden. On November 13 Somalia abrogated its treaty of friendship with the U.S.S.R.

Soviet and Cuban military involvement in Ethiopia continued into 1978. By the end of February Moscow had sent an estimated $850 million worth of arms including about 400 tanks and 50 MIG fighters. Cuban forces with Soviet arms and military advisers succeeded in turning the tide of battle against the Somalis, forcing the invaders to return to their side of the border in March 1978. Those forces were also used to help Addis Ababa in its suppression of the insurgency in Eritrea. In doing this Moscow and Havana were reversing the position toward the Eritrean insurgency that they had taken before Haile Selassie's overthrow. Undoubtedly geopolitical factors played a role in this reversal. Eritrea provided Ethiopia's only opening to the sea without which Ethiopia's strategic value to Moscow would be much less. If Eritrea should succeed in breaking away from Ethiopia, Moscow's access to the valuable ports of Massawa and Assab would be jeopardized. Cuban forces remain in Ethiopia to this day.

Why had the Soviet Union changed sides? As indicated above, it was a choice the Kremlin would have preferred not to make. Ideologically, the revolutionary character of the Ethiopian regime gave it some legitimacy for those to whom such considerations are important. Certainly the comparative size of the two countries — Ethiopia has 10 times Somalia's population — made the newer alliance more significant. Also Ethiopia was more endowed with natural resources than Somalia. Another important factor was the location of the headquarters of the Organization of African Unity in Addis Ababa. The big loss for Moscow was the port of Berbera, but that loss was compensated for by the acquisition of basing rights at the Red Sea ports of Massawa and Assab. With Somalia, Moscow's loss became Washington's gain. Siad Barre switched his allegiance and U.S.–Somali relations became much closer.

Intervention in Afghanistan

Afghanistan was Moscow's third major third-world intervention in the 1970s. Here too the Kremlin responded to events that were originally not of its making, but this time it used its own rather than Cuban forces to do the job. Soviet postwar relations with Afghanistan were generally good. Unlike Pakistan and Iran, Afghanistan was not a party to any anti-Soviet alliance. Though nominally nonaligned, Afghanistan was the recipient of $455 million in military aid between 1955 and 1972. From 1956 to the invasion in 1979 the U.S.S.R. supplied 95 percent of Afghanistan's military equipment. At the time of the invasion there were some 4,500 Soviet military advisers in Afghanistan guiding every phase of its military organization.[9] In the two decades between 1954 and 1975 Afghanistan received $1.263 billion in economic aid, making it one of the largest recipients of Soviet economic assistance. Also, the Soviet Union was Afghanistan's largest trading partner.

During the 1970s the government of Afghanistan underwent several radical changes. King Zahir Shah was overthrown in 1973 in a coup that made his cousin Mohammed Daud the new president. Although Moscow did not engineer Daud's coup it did give it its tacit support, which, according to one authority, was ironic in view of the fact that the period of Zahir Shah's rule was the most trouble-free time in Soviet-Afghan relations.[10] Mohammed Daud initially pursued pro-Soviet policies, but as the years passed he tended to be independent, particularly on foreign policy issues. Internally Daud was opposed by two factions of the Marxist People's Democratic Party of Afghanistan (PDPA) both of whom were bitter rivals. One faction known as the Khalq (masses) was led by Nur Mohammed Taraki and Hafizullah Amin; the other faction, Parcham (flag), was guided by Babrak Karmal. These two wings of the PDPA wanted to transform Afghanistan's traditional society along Marxist-Leninist lines. In April 1978 the Khalq leaders initiated a bloody coup that brought Taraki to power as prime minister. Hafizullah Amin, the reputed strongman of the revolutionists, became deputy prime minister and foreign minister. Because Soviet penetration of the Afghan armed forces was so thorough, there can be little doubt that Moscow was aware of the April coup, but there is no evidence that the coup was planned in Moscow.[11] The Taraki government moved even deeper into the Soviet orbit as evidenced by the signing of a 20-year treaty of friendship and cooperation in December 1978.

Taraki, a fanatical Communist, initiated a series of radical reforms — in social policy, education, and land ownership — which deeply offended large segments of Afghanistan's traditional Islamic tribal society. (Even before these reforms his government lacked legitimacy and a broad base of support.) What began as a trickle of opposition by a few tribesmen grew into a large-scale revolt encompassing a majority of Afghanistan's 28 provinces. Taraki came to be viewed as little more than a Soviet puppet, though in fact Moscow cautioned Taraki to act more slowly in implementing his reforms (as Moscow had cautioned Salvadore Allende in Chile earlier in the decade). The inability of the Afghan Army to stamp out the growing insurgency forced the government to rely more and more on Soviet help. Washington, observing the increasing Soviet involvement in Afghanistan's civil war, warned Moscow against military intervention. Moscow ignored the warning and chose instead not only to increase its delivery of military hardware but to send military personnel to engage the insurgent forces directly in combat.

On September 16, 1979, another coup took place in Kabul with Hafizullah Amin replacing Mohammed Taraki, who was killed. Amin's policies were even more extreme than Taraki's and thus even more objectionable to the Afghan masses. Brezhnev congratulated Amin on his "election," but Moscow was unhappy with the train of events taking place in Kabul. Amin's ruthlessness had brought the whole country up in arms against the regime. The Kremlin decided that a more moderate hand was needed and on December 27, 1979, the Soviet Union moved into Afghanistan with 50,000 troops, had Amin executed, and installed a real puppet, Babrak Karmal, as President.

There were several reasons for the Soviet intervention. The overall consideration was the need to keep Afghanistan in the Soviet bloc. Moscow had concluded by December that as things were going it was only a question of time before the Islamic insurgents would overthrow the government. Hafizullah Amin's fierce pursuit of social change had alienated the bulk of Afghanistan's tribal society. The army, which was the base of his support, was disintegrating under the onslaught of desertions, mutinies, and purges. Compounding these problems was Amin's refusal to accept the Soviet directive to restore order. It was not enough that Kabul be governed by a Communist ideologue; it had to be a Communist regime acceptable to and subservient to Moscow.

The loss of Afghanistan, a state on its southern border, was politically unacceptable to the Brezhnev administration because too much had been invested there — politically, militarily, economically, and in prestige. Afghanistan had been under Communist rule since 1978 and a reversal there would have been a repudiation of the Brezhnev Doctrine, which asserted the responsibility of the Soviet Union to ensure that once a regime went Communist it would remain Communist. But the issue was broader than ideology alone. If Afghanistan had become an Islamic state along with Iran and Pakistan, a large part of Russia's southern border would have been in the hands of regimes sharing a common ideological perspective, one that would have been hostile to the world view of the Soviet Union. Possibly Moscow was worried about the impact of the success of Islamic fundamentalism on the community of 50 million Moslems in Soviet central Asia. Another possible consideration was the geostrategic advantage of having military bases closer to the Indian Ocean. At the least a Soviet-dominated Afghanistan would constitute continuous pressure on Pakistan, an ally of the United States.

There were risks that Moscow was willing to take. One was the opposition of the Moslem states and condemnation by the United Nations General Assembly. Another was the collapse of détente. However, at that point in time there was little that remained of détente. SALT II was already having serious difficulty in the U.S. Senate and Brezhnev may well have concluded that it was a dead treaty. Also, the prospects for a direct U.S. confrontation in Afghanistan was minimal. The United States was deeply mired in the hostage crisis in Iran, and there was little evidence that the Carter administration would or could deploy forces in any form of a challenge. Afghanistan was in Moscow's sphere of influence, and the success of Soviet military action would presumably add to Soviet prestige and the reputation of its military forces.

As it turned out, the intervention in Afghanistan proved to be a tougher operation to complete than to start. The 50,000 original troops soon had to be more than doubled. Within a year the number rose to 110,000 with thousands of reserves available north of the border. As the Afghan Army came close to disintegration the Red Army had to assume the primary responsibility for putting down the guerillas, or mujahadeen. Almost a decade after the invasion, the country is far from pacified. Babrak Karmal and his successor, Najibullah, have failed dismally to establish the authority or legitimacy of their government. Karmal was widely viewed by the public as no more than a Russian stooge and, according to some reports, even by his own father. His inability to unite the factions of the PDPA or to find competent and loyal Afghans to administer the government forced him to rely heavily on the Russians, and real power today in Kabul is wielded from Moscow. In the countryside much of the control of affairs continues to rest with the mujahadeen. Over the past few years there have been negotiations under U.N. auspices to get the Soviet Union to withdraw from the country. Those diplomatic efforts have to date been unsuccessful. At the Twenty-seventh Party Congress in March 1986 Mikhail Gorbachev indicated that the Soviet Union would like to withdraw its forces, but nothing that he said or that Moscow has done points to a withdrawal without assurances that the government in Kabul will remain Communist.

Brezhnev's activism in the third world differed from his predecessor in one very important respect. While Khrushchev was predisposed to back any third world regime, regardless of its domestic orientation and as long as it supported Soviet foreign policy, Brezhnev concentrated Soviet aid on Marxist-Leninist regimes. Brezhnev was no more of an ideologue than Khrushchev — in fact, the evidence shows that in matters of doctrine Khrushchev was much more of a true believer than his successor. But what the Kremlin sought was some assurance that a government would not be an ally one day and an enemy the next. Khrushchev's policies in the third world were criticized for their heavy reliance on "bourgeois nationalist" leaders who often turned out to be unpredictable. Either they proved to be very unreliable, like Toure of Guinea, or they were overthrown by domestic coups like Ben Bella in Algeria and Nkruma of Ghana. What Moscow wanted was the reliability and stability of regimes that were governed by a Leninist party or at the least a one-party regime committed to Marxist principles. There were of course some exceptions to this general rule. For example, Brezhnev supported Anwar Sadat until he reversed Egyptian foreign policy, and Moscow continued its aid to non-Communist "socialist" states such as Iraq, Syria, Algeria, and Libya.

A common element of the MPLA in Angola, the Dergue in Ethiopia, and the PDPA in Afghanistan is that each offered prospects for building a one-party Leninist government at home. Angolan President Agostinho Neto went to Moscow in October 1976 to sign a treaty of friendship and cooperation to guarantee Soviet protection of his Marxist-Leninist regime. Moscow pressed its Ethiopian ally to establish a Communist party which it finally did in 1985 when Mengistu formally set up a one-party state under the control of Ethiopia's Workers' party. Soviet Politburo member Gregory Romanov was present at the Ethiopian National Congress when that step was taken. In Afghanistan, as noted above, the April 1978 coup brought a Marxist-Leninist party to power, so technically the Soviet invasion could be considered as the application of the Brezhnev Doctrine; i.e., the U.S.S.R. has the right to invade Communist states if domestic forces threaten to overthrow a ruling Communist party.

Not all Soviet interventions involved the use of Soviet military forces. Nonmilitary support was given to sustain Communist governments in South Yemen and Cambodia. In June 1978 a coup in South Yemen overthrew a Soviet-leaning leftist government and brought to power a more radical regime dominated by Yemenese Communists. The pattern had some similarity to the April coup in Afghanistan. Moscow quickly endorsed the new regime, which became a member of the Soviet bloc. South Yemen's politics in the 1980s were very volatile with several violent changes of government. These conflicts culminated in a bitter civil war in 1986 but they did not change the Communist character of South Yemen or its strong ties to Moscow.

The Soviet link to Cambodia is a by-product of its alliance with Vietnam. Vietnam joined the Council for Mutual Economic Assistance (CMEA) in June 1978 as a full member and on November 3, 1978, the Soviet Union and Vietnam signed a 25-year treaty of friendship and cooperation. By this time Vietnam and China had become bitter antagonists, and Moscow's alliance with Vietnam was part of its general strategy of containment of China. In the aftermath of the collapse of South Vietnam Cambodia came under the genocidal leadership of the Communist ruler Pol Pot. Pot, a political ally of China, imposed a harsh and destructive regimen on his own people, resulting in the death of several million Cambodians. In January 1979 Vietnam overthrew the government of Pol Pot and established a puppet regime under the leadership of Heng Samrin. Moscow supported the Vietnamese intervention and to this day supports the Heng Samrin regime as the legitimate government of Cambodia. The United States and China are agreed in their condemnation of the Heng Samrin regime although for many years now there has not been a viable alternative. Moscow's endorsement of the Vietnamese invasion has cost it considerable support in the third world because it is such a gross violation of the principle of noninterference in the domestic affairs of states. Even the United Nations is opposed to the government of Heng Samrin and while there has been widespread repugnance of Pol Pot, the United Nations refuses to accept the government of Heng Samrin as the legitimate government of Cambodia.

Losses and Gains in the Middle East

U.S.–Soviet rivalry in the late 1970s shifted back to the Middle East. The latter period of Leonid Brezhnev's rule and most of Jimmy Carter's administration were dominated by Mideast issues. As previously noted, a particular feature of Mideast politics since World War II has been its volatility and unpredictability. The legacy of western colonialism in the region was political instability, coups, and revolutions. Although the dominant conflict in the region was between the Arabs and Israel, the number and variety of hostilities among Arab governments and between Arabs and non-Arabs far exceeded the human and material costs incurred in the conflict with Israel.

Since World War II Moscow and Washington have been engaged in a struggle for influence in the region. In this struggle both sides often found themselves the victims or beneficiaries of events largely beyond their control. As stated elsewhere by one of the authors of this book, "By the 1970s the Middle East with its unstable governments, militancy, and high emotions, and its ability to suck the superpowers into its regional quarrels, increasingly resembled the Balkans at the turn of the century."[12] During the period under review superpower relations with two major Middle East governments changed markedly, one to the disadvantage of Moscow and the other to the disadvantage of the United States. The countries involved were Egypt and Iran.

Egypt Changes Sides

The Carter administration, which came into office in 1977, was determined to make a new effort to bring about peace in the Middle East. It was convinced that the time was ripe to move away from Kissinger's step-by-step approach toward a more comprehensive effort to resolve the root issues of the Arab-Israeli conflict. Basically these issue centered on Israel's security and the disposition of the Palestinians who became refugees as a consequence of the Arab-Israeli wars. Since America had important interests in the Arab world as well as its commitment to Israel's survival, it was clear that the larger interests of the United States would be served by a settlement of the festering conflict. The suspicion in Washington was that Moscow was less committed to a comprehensive settlement because enduring conflict guaranteed Soviet entrée to those states at war with a protégé of the United States. Moscow's practice of supporting the most militant Arab elements — the P.L.O., Syria, Iraq, and Libya — tended to confirm that suspicion. The urgency of American action lay in the vulnerability of Anwar Sadat, the Egyptian leader. He alone among the Arab leaders had indicated a willingness to accept the state of Israel and make peace with it. He thus became increasingly exposed to the extremists in the Arab world. There was the danger that he might be overthrown at home, assassinated, or perhaps even subverted by his former allies.

Initially the Carter strategy differed from that of Kissinger in that the latter sought to exclude the Soviet Union from involvement in negotiations while Carter and Secretary of State Cyrus Vance believed that Moscow might use its influence with the Arab militants and the P.L.O. in a constructive way. Moscow was in fact very sensitive to the question of involvement in Mideast diplomacy. On October 1, 1977, the United States and the Soviet Union issued a joint statement proposing a resumption of the conference on the Middle East in Geneva to be cohosted by the two superpowers. Almost immediately the plan collapsed over the objections of the Israelis and Sadat (and many in the U.S. Congress).

It is generally believed that the reason why Anwar Sadat made his dramatic and historic trip to Jerusalem on November 19, 1977, was to keep the Soviets out of the peace process — in effect initiating a separate Egyptian-Israeli accord. The goodwill generated by Sadat's initiative, however, did not produce the results he expected. For months Egyptian-Israeli talks proceeded inconclusively. Finally in August 1978 President Carter made a dramatic announcement of his own: There would be a summit meeting in September with Anwar Sadat and Menachem Begin at Camp David, Maryland. For 13 days the American president immersed himself in the most intensive negotiations of his presidency. He had one tool that no Soviet leader could ever use, an annotated Bible, which Carter claims was important in his negotiations with Begin.[13] Negotiations were difficult and often emotional. Not until the very end on September 17 was the success of the Camp David negotiations assured. Israel won the major concession of a commitment that within three months a peace treaty between Egypt and Israel would be negotiated. Israel agreed to return the Sinai Peninsula to Egypt. Both sides agreed to undertake serious negotiations toward a settlement of the Palestinian issue. For its part Israel agreed to recognize the "legitimate rights" of the Palestinian people, though it refused to accept the notion of a Palestinian state. In the future negotiations West Bank and Gaza Palestinians would participate, but Israel rejected P.L.O. representation of the Palestinians. Israel agreed to a temporary freeze on settlements on the West Bank and the withdrawal of Israeli settlements from the Sinai.

The only part of the Camp David agreements that bore fruit was the peace treaty signed on March 26, 1979. The efforts to resolve the problems of Israeli occupation of Arab territories and Jerusalem as well as self-determination for the Palestinians failed completely. Israel was a major beneficiary of Camp David because it gained the assurance that Egypt would not make war on the Jewish state. That in itself was a virtual guarantee of Israeli survival because no combinations of Arab states without Egypt could successfully defeat Israel. Jordan, Syria, and Lebanon were too weak.

Sadat's gain was the return of the Sinai including a valuable oil field. But Sadat had taken a risky gamble. In making peace with Israel he alienated Egypt from the mainstream of the Arab world. A group of hard-line Arab states including Syria, Iraq, Libya, and Algeria joined with the P.L.O. to form a "rejectionist front" that opposed negotiations with Israel. Even the moderate states in the Arab world voted to suspend Egypt's membership in the Arab League and several broke diplomatic relations with Egypt. When Sadat was assassinated in October 1981 he had neither succeeded in bridging the differences with Israel over the Palestinians nor with his fellow Arabs because of his commitment to Camp David. But his reversal of Nasser's foreign policy had fundamentally transformed the politics of the Middle East to the benefit of the west.

Notwithstanding the failure to resolve the Palestinian issue, the Camp David accords were a large step forward, and for a period of time contributed toward stability in the region. Egypt's peace with Israel was of great importance in reducing the chances of another war. Not surprisingly the Soviet Union condemned the Camp David accords as a betrayal of the Palestinian cause. Moscow was particularly irritated by the idea that peace in the Middle East could be made without its participation — as it was through the Egyptian-Israeli peace treaty.

Revolution in Iran
While Moscow was forced to watch helplessly as the peace-making efforts of Egypt took place, the United States found itself forced to watch helplessly as its alliance with Iran collapsed in revolution. Iranian-western relations had steadily developed after the overthrow of the Mossadegh government in 1953. With Iranian membership in the Baghdad pact came large amounts of U.S. military and economic aid. The failure of the Baghdad pact in no way undermined U.S.–Iranian relations, which grew to the point that Iran became a pillar of American interests in the Middle East. In January 1979 the Shah of Iran was forced to leave his country as a result of an Islamic revolution which brought to power the bitterly antiwestern Ayatollah Ruhollah Khomeini. Moscow as much as Washington was a helpless onlooker to the revolutionary change taking place, although Moscow may have supported street demonstrations through its control over the Iranian Tudeh (Communist) party. But while the Soviet Union could conceivably benefit by the

fall of the Shah in Iran the United States could only lose, a point the Kremlin understood very well. In the early phase of the Iranian revolution Moscow was concerned that the United States might intervene to crush it. On November 18, 1978, Leonid Brezhnev warned Washington, "It must be made clear that any interference, let alone military intervention in the affairs of Iran — a state which has a common frontier with the Soviet Union — would be regarded by the USSR as a matter affecting its security interests."[14] At the least Moscow could claim that its stand had deterred U.S. intervention.

U.S.–Iranian relations plummeted in November 1979. After the Shah was admitted into the United States for medical treatment, a group of militant students invaded the U.S. embassy, taking some 50 American diplomats as hostages. In open violation of international law the revolutionary government of Iran sanctioned the seizure of the Americans. The endless demonstrations of Iranians around the embassy compounds and the humiliating treatment of the hostages were constant reminders to the American public and the world of the impotency of the U.S. government to rescue its citizens.

In principle the Soviet Union expressed opposition to the seizure of diplomats as hostages, but the general thrust of its propaganda was more to justify than condemn the Iranian action. Moscow concluded that its larger interests would be better served by keeping on good terms with the Iranians than by supporting Washington in this crisis. When the United States organized naval maneuvers in the Arabian Sea as a means of impressing Teheran with its military might, *Pravda* accused the United States of trying to "blackmail" Iran and of committing a "gross violation of international legal norms."[15] Moscow's courtship of Iran has had only a mixed success. Some of the benefits the Soviet Union gained by its generally positive treatment of the Iranian revolution were undone by the attack of Iraq — a Soviet ally — on Iran in the fall of 1980. While Moscow has taken a neutral position in that war the fact that it is a large supplier of Iraqi arms moved Iran to take a critical view of the U.S.S.R.

Leadership Changes in the Kremlin

Soviet-American relations in the 1980s are in transition. As noted above, the competition in the third world was a major cause of the collapse of détente. Another factor influencing the foreign policies of both sides was the emergence of new leaderships in Moscow and Washington. The change in Moscow was prolonged in part because of the lack of a constitutional mechanism for political succession in the Soviet system. There is no constitutional limit to how long a ruler will hold the reigns of power in Moscow. No political leader since the Bolshevik revolution had voluntarily retired from office. Soviet leaders have either been disposed of by coups (Malenkov and Khrushchev, for example) or more typically they have died in office. When he died in November 1982 Brezhnev had ruled for 18 years, longer than any Soviet leader except Stalin. During the last five years of his rule Brezhnev was in his seventies and in poor health. His successor, Yuri Andropov, was a younger man, but he too was in poor health, and he held power less than a year and a half. He died on February 9, 1984. Soviet leadership suffered under the prolonged guidance of elderly hierarchs in poor health. The party leadership understood this but was unable to agree on a younger leader because of sharp divisions within the ruling Politburo. Thus Andropov was succeeded by Konstantin U. Chernenko, a party bureaucrat, 72 years old, and also very frail. He lasted until March 10, 1985, and was replaced by Mikhail Gorbachev, a relative youth in his mid-fifties. The selection of Gorbachev as Secretary-General ended the long succession crisis in Moscow and gave the leadership a new vigor it had lacked for years. No fundamental changes in Soviet third world policies were made during the transitional leadership of Andropov and Chernenko. Their administrations were dominated by other than third world issues. As this is written Gorbachev has been in power several years, but he too has yet to define a new policy toward any of the third world issues over which Moscow and Washington differ. His policies announced at the Twenty-seventh Party Congress in the spring of 1986 were essentially a continuation of his immediate predecessors.

Reagan Activism in the Third World

The election of Ronald Reagan in 1980 marked a significant change in U.S. foreign policy generally and toward the third world in particular. Reagan was committed to building up U.S. military power and asserting a greater American voice in world affairs including a stronger defense of what he considered to be U.S. interests. The result was an increased activism in the third world. He increased U.S. aid to El Salvador in its efforts to defeat a leftist insurgency supported by Nicaragua, Cuba, and the Soviet Union. Increased support was given to the mu-hajadeen fighting Soviet forces in Afghanistan. The three central issues of his administration were U.S. intervention in Lebanon in 1982, the invasion of Grenada in 1983, and support throughout his administration for the contras, who are fighting the Sandinista government in Nicaragua.

American intervention in Lebanon in 1982 was another case where one of the superpowers was sucked into a political and military cauldron over which it had no control. Since 1975 Lebanon had been in the throes of a civil war involving communal forces no one of which was capable of winning. Lebanon's internal problems were complicated by the presence of foreign elements, notably the Syrians and the Palestinians. The Syrians intervened in June 1976 — against Moscow's wishes apparently — to control the Palestinians and to prevent the partition of Lebanon.[16] In June 1982 Israel invaded Lebanon in order to destroy the P.L.O. military capability there. Within days Israeli forces pushed to the outskirts of Beirut where the P.L.O. was headquartered.

Washington and Moscow were both unhappy about the Israeli invasion. President Reagan asked (in vain) the Israelis to withdraw their forces. Moscow bluntly warned Israel that the Middle East was close to its borders and affected its vital interests. But both great powers acted cautiously. Moscow ignored P.L.O. pleas to intervene directly in the fighting. Soviet prestige suffered as a result of the beating that Israel inflicted on Syrian air defenses and the Syrian air force. Moscow agreed to replace Syrian losses but made it clear that its alliance with Syria did not oblige the Soviet Union to protect Syrian forces outside of Syrian territory. A mild crisis in U.S.–Israeli relations developed as Israel laid seige to Beirut and bombed those parts of the city where P.L.O. forces were believed to be located. Inevitably civilian casualties were bound to be high. After intense negotiations between U.S., Israeli, and P.L.O. elements an arrangement was worked out for the lifting of the Israeli seige, the departure of all P.L.O. forces from Beirut, and the creation of a multinational force to help ensure that the evacuation would be done without incident. In August 1982 the first contingent of U.S. Marines arrived in Beirut. Within the 30 days allotted for the presence of U.S. forces the P.L.O. evacuation was completed successfully and the American forces withdrew.

The marines had barely departed when Lebanon was again convulsed in violence. The newly elected president, Bashir Gemayel, leader of the Christian Phalange, was assassinated and shortly thereafter — possibly in revenge — the Phalangists massacred several hundred Palestinians in two of the large camps south of Beirut. Believing that the presence of U.S. forces could help Bashir's successor, Amin Gemayel, to maintain order, President Reagan sent the marines back to Beirut as part of a multinational force on September 20. "We have agreed to form a new multinational force," said Reagan, ". . . with the mission of enabling the Lebanese government to resume full sovereignty over its capital."[17] Little did the American president understand the maelstrom which Beirut had become. At their peak the U.S. Marines numbered about 1,600, and since they were authorized to fight only in self-defense, they were committed to a mission impossible.

During 1983 Beirut disintegrated into virtual anarchy. In April the U.S. embassy was destroyed by a car bomb that cost many lives. While Moslem, Christian, and Druse forces were fighting for power in and around Beirut, intense negotiations were undertaken to bring about the withdrawal of Syrian and Israeli forces. U.S. mediation efforts produced an agreement between Lebanon and Israel, but the failure of Syria to accept its terms ultimately led to its collapse. As fighting intensified in Beirut between forces of the Lebanese Army and Moslem and Druse opponents, the United States found itself drawn in on the side of the government it presumably was attempting to stabilize. In September U.S. naval guns shelled antigovernment positions in the hills around Beirut. What the United States saw as supporting the legitimate government in Lebanon was viewed by antigovernment forces as interference in the country's civil war. On October 23 a devastating blast from another car bomb struck the U.S. marine barracks killing 250 marines. In desperation the United States ordered the battleship *New Jersey* to shell Syrian positions, but that only embittered the many U.S. adversaries in Lebanon. Early in February 1984 the government of Lebanon collapsed under the continuous warfare in the capital and that provided the rationale for the complete withdrawal of U.S. forces. Reagan's initiative was ill-conceived and the best that he could make of the situation was to cut his losses.

Grenada

At about the same time as the catastrophe in Beirut there was a crisis in the Caribbean that gave rise to one of the Reagan administration's most complete successes. The island of Grenada, 80 miles off Venezuela in the Windward Islands, had gone Communist as a result of a coup that replaced Prime Minister Eric Gairey with Maurice Bishop, a Marxist admirer of Fidel Castro. Under Bishop's rule close ties were developed with the Soviet bloc including the announcement of the sale of aluminum ore on a long-term basis to the U.S.S.R. and a five-year-trade agreement between the two countries. Bishop invited Cuban technicians to build a major airport capable of handling jet aircraft. He claimed the purpose was to encourage tourism, but the fear in Washington was that this second airport would be used to service Soviet military aircraft. That suspicion was heightened when Grenada signed a treaty in May 1980 giving the Soviets permission to use the airport to land their long-range reconnaissance planes, the TU-95s.

On October 19, 1983, an event occurred that gave the United States an opportunity to rid the Caribbean of this Marxist thorn in its side. Maurice Bishop and several of his supporters were executed in a struggle with Bernard Coard, a rival for leadership of the leftist New Jewel Movement. Coard was more radical than Bishop and apparently feared that Bishop was seeking to improve relations with Washington. A 16-man military government was set up under the leadership of General Hudson Austin who promptly ordered a curfew and threatened to shoot any violators on sight. Within a week Reagan ordered U.S. military forces to take over the island. He justified the action on the need to protect some 1,000 Americans who were medical students in Grenada plus a request from the Organization of Eastern Caribbean countries, which unanimously asked the United States to intervene in order to protect their security. There was also the argument that Grenada was becoming a Cuban-Soviet base for subversion. On television Reagan proclaimed that "Grenada . . . was a Soviet-Cuban colony being readied as a major military bastion to export terror and undermine democracy."[18]

Domestically the invasion was an overwhelming success, but in the court of world opinion the United States was widely condemned for violating international law, a charge whose validity hung in large part on the true danger posed by the Grenadan government to the American students. The United States was clearly guilty of interfering in the domestic affairs of a sovereign state. On the other hand, in terms of promoting human rights and democracy the U.S. action was justified. Whatever the world may have felt about the presence of American troops in Grenada, there is no doubt that the people of that island overwhelmingly welcomed the Americans as liberators. However, the real party to whom the action was addressed was none of the above. It was the Soviet Union. Reagan's action was intended to tell Moscow that America was willing to use force to defend its interests in the third world.

Central America

Nicaragua has been a more complex and difficult issue. In 1979 the Somoza dictatorship was overthrown by a coalition known as the Sandinista Liberation Front (FSLN). The Sandinistas came into power strongly anti-"Yankee" for a number of reasons. One was the long association between the United States and the hated Somoza family; another was the Marxist beliefs of many of the Sandinista leaders, particularly the Ortega brothers. Unlike many of the Marxist governments in power today the one in Managua came into existence not as the result of a coup but through armed revolution (like Cuba). In Latin America, as elsewhere in the third world, being anti–United States inevitably inclines one toward the Soviet Union. In its first year in power the Sandinistas sent a delegation to establish party ties between the FSLN and the Communist party. In 1981 Nicaragua and the Soviet Union signed an arms agreement providing for Soviet military aid in the form of tanks, small arms, and military vehicles. In 1981–1982 new military arrangements were signed and also a supply of 20,000 metric tons of wheat was sent to Nicaragua.[19] In May 1982 a $166.8 million Soviet aid package was announced. Prior to 1982 much of Moscow's military aid was sent via Algeria. Since then arms shipments have come directly from the Soviet Union, Bulgaria, and other bloc countries. While Moscow has avoided the traditional treaty of friendship and cooperation that link it with some of its other allies, it did sign a cooperation pact with Daniel Ortega in April 1985.[20]

Notwithstanding these Soviet-Nicaraguan ties Moscow's support of the Sandinistas has been cautious and low key. Soviet propaganda embraces the Ortega government as a part of its general line of support to any anti-American movement or government anywhere. But there is evidence that the Soviet Union does recognize the dominant position of the United

States in Central America. For example, in the summer of 1983 U.S. warships halted Soviet freighters bound for Nicaragua in order to prevent arms shipments. Moscow, of course, protested, but it did so very quietly.[21] The Soviet Union is prepared to support leftist movements and governments in Central and South America but not to the point of open confrontation with the United States. It is very unlikely that the Soviet Union would defend Nicaragua if the United States were to take military action there.

Tactically Moscow can operate quietly behind the scenes in Central America because Cuba is available as a substitute. From the beginning of the Nicaraguan revolution the Cubans played an active role providing guidance and large amounts of assistance. The number of Cuban military advisers in Nicaragua is in the thousands and Cuban officers assigned to Sandinista military units reach down to the company level. Daniel Ortega and Fidel Castro are politically close. When Ortega was inaugurated as president of Nicaragua in 1985 Fidel Castro was the only foreign head of state to attend.

U.S. objections to Nicaragua basically fall into two categories: (1) the authoritarian structure that has been created in Nicaragua and (2) the threat of subversion to Central America. Since the revolution the Sandinista regime has steadily worked to build a Leninist structure throughout the country. Opposition and minority groups have been suppressed or eliminated. The press is strictly censored and freedom of speech is curtailed. The only important institution not under Sandinista control today is the Catholic Church, which finds itself increasingly in conflict with the government. Mobs encouraged by the state-controlled media have attacked Catholic priests, and numerous smaller churches have had their property completely confiscated. Sandinista charges that Cardinal Miguel Obando y Bravo, a critic of the regime, preaches "treason" at the pulpit does not bode well for the survival of the Catholic Church in Nicaragua.

From the perspective of American interests, however, it is the issue of subversion in Central America that is deemed to be critical. Today there are leftist movements in El Salvador and Guatemala and much smaller guerrilla movements in Honduras and Costa Rica. Each came into existence as the result of indigenous factors in each country. What concerns the United States is the development of a revolutionary network in Central America with Nicaragua as a central base of support. Cuba may be the guiding director and principal supplier of leftist guerrilla movements in Central America but the focal logistical base of operations is Nicaragua. The country most threatened with insurgency is El Salvador whose Farabundo Marti National Liberation Front has approximately 4,000 fighters backed by several thousand unarmed supporters. Salvadoran guerrillas get considerable support from abroad. Some receive training in Vietnam, Bulgaria, East Germany, or even the Soviet Union.[22] In 1981 the El Salvadoran guerrillas announced a "final offensive" to topple the government. Cuban and Sandinista leaders played an important role in the planning of that offensive but it did not succeed. Although there is disagreement as to the amount of aid being sent to El Salvador via Nicaragua — and in recent years it has apparently dropped off — there is sufficient evidence to establish that Nicaragua has provided military aid to the Farabundo Marti Front. Serial numbers from captured rifles in El Salvador reveal that they were guns left in Vietnam by the United States. For a time the El Salvadoran rebels were allowed to establish propaganda, communications, and logistical offices in Managua. They were asked to leave after the United States invaded Grenada in 1983, though subsequently some have returned.[23]

During the early months of the Reagan administration U.S. economic aid to Nicaragua continued, but relations deteriorated very quickly. There is little doubt that the Reagan administration would like to bring about the downfall of the Sandinistas. Reagan views the establishment of a Communist state in Central America as a long-term threat to U.S. security. Although there have been halfhearted efforts to negotiate the differences between the two countries, it seems clear that the issues are fundamentally nonnegotiable. Increasingly the

United States has relied on military pressure. In April 1984 some Nicaraguan harbors were mined with the aid of the C.I.A. It was an unsuccessful endeavor, widely condemned, and soon abandoned. A more persistent tactic has been to provide aid to contras in their fight against the Sandinistas. Initially the C.I.A. helped the contras clandestinely, but opposition in the U.S. Congress forced the administration to seek public support for its policies. Until late 1986 Congress, reflecting the divisions in American public opinion, was divided on the issue. In 1984 Congress cut off all military aid to the contras but in 1985 and 1986 reversed itself and voted to provide some military and economic aid. The picture changed dramatically in November 1986 when the Reagan administration revealed that funds had been secretly made available to the contras from the sale of U.S. arms to Iran.

Complications of "Irangate"

What became known as the Iranian arms scandal complicated the Nicaraguan policy. Resistance to supporting the contras intensified. For one thing, the fact that the Reagan administration had acted in apparent violation of U.S. law stiffened opposition in Congress to giving aid to the contras. But even more seriously, the state of seige created by the furor over both the covert sale of arms to Iran and the diversion of funds to the contras undermined the credibility of the United States in general and made the pursuit of a coherent foreign policy more difficult than ever.

The Iranian arms scandal was a complex affair that involved many foreign policy strands, a few of which bear directly on the general issue of Soviet-American competition in the third world. A central question is: Why did the United States sell arms to Iran in the first place, to a regime condemned by Washington for its involvement in international terrorism? The rationale given by the American president was important even if other consideration were involved. Ronald Reagan defended the sale of arms to Iran as a means of developing contacts with moderates in that country. The intention was to build a relationship with elements in Iran who might come to power in a post-Khomeini period and who would shift Iranian foreign policy toward a closer relationship with the United States. Iran, it was argued, was geostrategically too vital a nation (because of its size, location, and oil reserves) to fall into the Soviet orbit. In a word, Reagan used the arguments and rhetoric of balance-of-power politics as a justification for his actions.

Such a justification or goal does not in and of itself convert a flawed policy into a sound one. There was widespread doubt that moderate elements even existed in Iran or whether they would be capable of assuming power after the death of the Ayatollah Khomeini. Politics in Teheran were so fluid and volatile that one could not be certain who would ride the crest of Iran's Islamic Revolution. Nor was it ever made clear how the United States could exercise influence in Teheran through the sale of arms. And by secretly trafficking in arms with Iran Washington undermined its credibility with its allies and Mideast friends because the official policy of the United States was to oppose the sale of weapons to terrorist states. But, most damaging of all, was the widespread belief that the objective of the arms sales was really the release of hostages held by pro-Iranian militants in Lebanon. If indeed that was the objective, then the United States was permitting itself to be the object of extortion by the very terrorists it was condemning. For these and other reasons the policy was unquestionably unsound.

Nevertheless, the rationale for that policy — to move Iran into the western orbit — must be taken seriously. It is consistent with the logic of both Soviet and American policy in the third world from the beginning of their competition in the postwar years. Fundamentally, Reagan's actions toward Iran and in Nicaragua were guided by the premise of competition with the Soviet Union, considerations of the balance of power, and a belief that an advance by Moscow in the third world could only be at the expense of U.S. security. Iran was viewed as a potential ally of one side or another. Ultimately, it was expected that Iran — in pursuit of its own national interests — would turn to Moscow or Washington. Nicaragua, though geostrategically less significant, was viewed as already in the enemy camp and therefore to be treated as an enemy. The underlying rationale of Reagan's foreign policy, in the third world as elsewhere, had always been to curb Soviet power and influence.

Competition in the third world thus continues to be a central feature of the Cold War, and in that competition the Soviet Union has shown greater constancy and determination than the United States. During the Vietnam war the American consensus in support of opposing Marxist or pro-soviet governments in the third world began to dissipate. The Carter administration had strong reluctance to intervene abroad. That attitude changed under the Reagan administration, but large segments of the public, Congress, and the media continued to oppose interventionist moves. Since the mid-1970s U.S. policy in the third world, in contrast to Soviet policy, has been erratic, reflecting in part the divisions in the body politic and changes in the balance of domestic political forces. The weakening of the Reagan administration because of the Iranian arms scandal may well have the same impact on American foreign policy as the Nixon administration's paralysis because of Watergate.

Soviet policy is less constrained by domestic political forces. The press, legislative bodies like the Supreme Soviet, and public opinion play a minimal role in foreign relations. But there are constraints. Bureaucratic interests striving for resources as well as the general condition of the economy limit the options available to the men in the Kremlin. Mikhail Gorbachev assumed power over a stagnating and inefficient economy whose reform has been his top domestic priority. Among foreign policy issues the third world has preoccupied Gorbachev less than problems of arms control and east-west relations.

If Gorbachev has inaugurated no new directions in third world policy, he has nevertheless maintained the activism of his predecessors.[24] In Afghanistan the scale of combat operations has intensified; in the Middle East strong military support for Libya's Muammar al Qaddafi and Syria's Hafez Assad — two of the most bitter opponents of U.S. interests in the region — continues unabated; economic ties have been strengthened with antiwestern governments in Africa; arms continue to flow to Nicaragua. Moscow continues its heavy subsidies to particularly important allies such as Cuba, Vietnam, Ethiopia, and Syria. One item of special concern to the United States is Moscow's interest in developing new economic ties with Iran. (It is possible that Reagan's ill-advised attempt to garner influence in Teheran in 1985–1986 was motivated by a desire to preempt Soviet overtures toward Iran.)

Soviet behavior, then, shows continuity over a long period of time. The Soviet Union has proven to be a reliable ally to those with whom it has made commitments. The principal instruments of influence employed by the Kremlin are arms transfers and economic ties. Moscow has consistently moved cautiously, particularly avoiding commitments that would bring it into a military confrontation with the United States. But a central facet of Soviet policy has been to support antiwestern movements and governments in the third world even if that meant straining its relationship with the United States. The Soviet Union has repeatedly avowed its desire for détente — it still does — but not at the expense of its penetration into the third world. It is unwilling to accept the concept of linkage, the idea that superpower tensions are linked to conflicts in the third world. It will not moderate its drive for influence abroad for closer ties with the west. That is the reason why today the third world has become the principal arena of confrontation in the Cold War.

A final question should be considered: How significant is the third world to vital Soviet and American interests? No one can doubt that in the aggregate the third world is important to both sides in terms of trade, raw materials, and access to key transportation routes. Further, it seems clear that almost all the conflicts in the third world are indigenous in nature. They were initially created by local forces, not outside powers. Perhaps the only exception to this was the North Korean invasion of South Korea. In all of the conflicts described here the indigenous conflict became entangled in the struggle by the superpowers for global supremacy.

In and of themselves almost none of these conflicts threatened the vital interests of either the United States or the Soviet Union. If the other rival had not been involved, it would not have significantly mattered to Moscow or Washington which side won. (The survival of Israel would be an exception.) What makes these third world conflicts crucial is the Soviet-American competition to enlist the victor on its side. Thus it would appear that the rivalry in the third world is not the cause of Soviet–American conflict, but rather its symptom. This does not detract from the danger of that rivalry, since there is the ever-present possibility that a third world conflict could escalate into a great power confrontation. It came close to happening in Cuba, Vietnam, and the Middle East. So long as the Soviet Union and the United States are engaged in a struggle for power any arena of conflict contains the possibility of catastrophe.

Notes

1. Henry Kissinger, *The White House Years* (Boston: Little, Brown, 1979), pp. 227–228.
2. See Marvin Kalb and Bernard Kalb, *Kissinger* (New York: Dell, 1975), p. 194; and Tad Szulc, "Behind the Vietnam Cease-Fire Agreement," *Foreign Policy,* no. 15, Summer 1974, p. 23.
3. Henry Kissinger, *Years of Upheaval* (Boston: Little, Brown, 1982), p. 318.
4. Documents and Resolutions, 25th Congress of the CPSU, p. 9. Moscow: Novosti Press Agency, 1976.
5. Arthur Jay Klinghoffer, "The Soviet Union and Angola," in Robert H. Donaldson, ed., *The Soviet Union in the Third World: Successes and Failures* (Boulder, Colo.: Westview Press, 1981), p. 100.

6. See John A. Marcum, "Lessons of Angola," *Foreign Affairs,* vol. 54, no. 3, April 1976, p. 416.

7. Stephen T. Hosmer and Thomas W. Wolfe, *Soviet Policy and Practice Toward Third World Conflicts.* (Lexington, Mass.: D. C. Heath & Co., 1983), p. 81.

8. Richard B. Remnek, "Soviet Policy in the Horn of Africa: The Decision to Intervene," in Robert H. Donaldson, ed., *The Soviet Union in the Third World: Successes and Failures* (Boulder: Westview Press, 1981), p. 129.

9. See Shirin Tahir-Kheli, "The Soviet Union in Afghanistan: Benefits and Costs, in Robert H. Donaldson, ed., *The Soviet Union in the Third World:* Successes and Failures. (Boulder: Westview Press, 1981), p. 219.

10. Ibid., p. 221.

11. Hosmer and Wolfe, p. 111.

12. Spanier, *American Foreign Policy since World War II,* 10th ed. (New York: Holt, Rinehart and Winston, 1985), p. 237.

13. Jimmy Carter, *Keeping Faith, Memoirs of a President* (New York: Bantam Books, 1982), p. 322.

14. Quoted in Joseph L. Nogee and Robert H. Donaldson, *Soviet Foreign Policy Since World War II,* 2d ed. (New York: Pergamon Press, 1984), p. 286.

15. Ibid., p. 287.

16. Carol R. Saivetz and Sylvia Woodby, *Soviet-Third World Relations* (Boulder, Colo.: Westview Press, 1985), p. 63.

17. *The New York Times,* Sept. 21, 1982.

18. *The New York Times,* Oct. 28, 1983.

19. Saivetz and Woodby, op. cit., pp. 87, 112.

20. *The New York Times,* Mar. 23, 1986, Section 4, p. 1.

21. Saivetz and Woodby, op. cit., p. 87.

22. See James LeMoyne, "The Guerrilla Network," *The New York Times Magazine,* April 6, 1986, pp. 18, 20.

23. Ibid., pp. 71, 79.

24. Alvin Z. Rubinstein, "A Third World Policy Waits for Gorbachev," *Orbis,* Summer 1986, pp. 355–364.

Toward an Explanation of the Cold War

Why It Continues

Since its inception the Cold War has gone through many phases. There have been periods of confrontation and high tension, followed by years of relative calm and few crises. The labels "Cold War," "peaceful coexistence," "détente," and "Cold War II" have been applied to the changing phases of what has remained an underlying conflict between the United States and the Soviet Union since 1946. The period following the 1979 collapse of détente is not easily characterized because it is different from all preceding periods and because it contains many contradictory elements. Ronald Reagan, whose policies have been a major factor in shaping U.S.–Soviet relations, has been the dominant political leader of the postdétente period. During the early 1980s Soviet policies were under the tutelage of three elderly, infirm leaders who were unable to establish a clear or consistent strategy. Until Mikhail Gorbachev assumed power in 1985 the dominant influence in Soviet-American relations was the United States under the leadership of Ronald Reagan.

How might the period of the 1980s be characterized? To begin with, there was an increase in tension in U.S.–Soviet relations, partly because of the American president's style and partly because of substantive decisions taken in the capitals of both countries. To a degree unusual in American politics the American president gave vent to a stridently anti-Soviet rhetoric, particularly in his first term. Two of his classic outbursts came at a news conference when he accused Soviet leaders of reserving to themselves "the right to commit any crime, to lie, to cheat . . ." and a speech in which he described Soviet communism as "the focus of evil in the modern world."[1] Reagan was expressing his own revulsion toward the Soviet system in a manner rarely indulged in by western leaders, though unquestionably many in the west, let alone the United States, fully agreed with him. Moscow professed outrage at these expressions but in substance they hardly went beyond the standard fare of official Soviet propaganda.

To what extent did Reagan's rhetoric contribute to the downturn in U.S.–Soviet relations? While it undoubtedly had some impact, the rhetoric alone was not critical. The Soviets are realists who have always been more impressed with actions rather than words. What did concern Moscow were the implications for U.S. policy suggested by Reagan's hard-line rhetoric. In other words, it was the substance of U.S. policy that upset Moscow more than the rhetoric.

Reagan entered office committed to reversing the decline of American power. In his first term he abandoned arms control as a central objective and initiated a buildup of U.S. military forces. A more assertive role in world affairs followed the recovery of some of the self-confidence lost by the United States in the aftermath of the Vietnam war. As Reagan moved into his second term he and his principal advisers were confident that the balance of world power had shifted to the advantage of the United States and that therefore American diplomacy could take a harder line vis à vis the Soviet adversary.

Moscow, of course, rejected the premises upon which U.S. policy were based and doggedly resisted American efforts to operate from a position of strength. The means available to the leaders in the Kremlin were the standard ones: military buildup, intervention abroad, and propaganda. All three instruments were used extensively in the 1980s. But Soviet efforts were undermined by two serious problems, one temporary and the other chronic. The temporary difficulty was the absence of a strong leader until Mikhail Gorbachev took over in March 1985. The other problem was the sluggish Soviet economy, which made it difficult for the Soviet regime to maintain a state of military parity with the United States. Moscow sought to compensate for its political and economic weakness by an intensification of propaganda directed against the United States. The combination of Reagan's rhetoric and Soviet propaganda gave the early 1980s the atmosphere dubbed "Cold War II."

Why the Peace Holds

And yet, in spite of the deterioration in U.S.–Soviet relations in the 1980s, this period was notably lacking in any serious crisis involving the two superpowers. Indeed it is ironic how little confrontation there was between the two countries at a time when rhetoric was heated and military expenditures were rising. There was nothing during the Reagan years comparable to the Berlin crises of the 1940s or 1950s, or the Cuban missile crisis in 1962, or the Middle East crises of 1956, 1967, or 1973, not to mention fighting between American and Communist forces in Korea and Vietnam. Reagan in his second term even negotiated a major arms control treaty with the Soviets.

There are several reasons for this relative lack of violence or threat of violence in superpower relations. First and foremost was the deterrent impact of nuclear weapons. The simple fact was that as inventories of strategic and theater nuclear weapons increased so did the danger of their use. Caution consistently prevailed in Washington and Moscow as both sides recognized the risks that could ensue if a crisis escalated and got out of hand. More effective than crisis management is to avoid becoming involved in a crisis in the first place. Ronald Reagan was never the trigger-happy cowboy portrayed by his critics at home or abroad, nor were the leaders in the Kremlin looking for a fight. One of the fundamental dilemmas faced by those who have argued for the abolition of nuclear weapons is that eliminating the fear of a nuclear holocaust would make war more rational as an instrument of national policy.

Another factor was the growth in U.S. military power, which acted as a constraint on Soviet initiatives. Most of the Soviet-American crises since the second world war developed out of actions initiated by the Soviet Union or one of its allies. A point that will be developed further below is that the United States has pursued essentially a policy of status quo while the Soviet Union has been the revisionist power. Thus, as the balance of power shifted to the west — or was perceived as such — Moscow took special precaution to avoid a confrontation with the United States. Also, it did not hurt the United States to have a leader who had a reputation of spoiling for a fight. It is even conceivable that Soviet caution was in some measure the result of being duped by its own propaganda depicting Reagan as trigger-happy.

A third inducement toward stability between the superpowers was the existence of other issues that distracted each side. For Moscow there were internal and external problems. Afghanistan mired Soviet forces in a continuing, inconclusive war. In 1980–1981 the Soviet Union was preoccupied with the crisis in Poland, which for a time appeared to require Russian intervention to keep a pro-Soviet government in Warsaw. Internally, as noted, the succession problem and the economy preoccupied the rulers in the Kremlin. Early in the Gorbachev administration the Soviet leadership was confronted with the nuclear disaster at Chernobyl, an accident that had much greater economic ramifications than initially acknowledged. The United States too had its economic problems. The first two years of the Reagan administration were burdened by a serious recession. Even after recovery the administration was faced with continuing problems resulting from huge budgetary and balance-of-trade deficits. In foreign policy the major preoccupation was the issue of terrorism and violence emanating from the Middle East. In his first term Reagan became mired down in Lebanon's internal and external wars; in his second term he was faced with the more diffuse issue of terrorism from Libya, Syria, and Iran. Then, as his second term passed the midpoint, his administration got bogged down with the Iranian-Contra arms scandal.

To sum up: Soviet-American relations in the 1980s did not fit a simple pattern. While the conflict has been manifest in an intensification of the arms race and increased propaganda warfare, there have been no military confrontations or even a political crisis that might have given rise to the use or threat of force. But it is clear that the fundamental antagonism that has driven Soviet-American relations since the beginning of the Cold War remains.

Although the term Cold War is often used to describe the period of the 1940s and 1950s, in reality it is a valid label for the entire post–World War II era. Underlying the alternating phases of confrontation and cooperation has been a continuing struggle for power and global influence. The Cold War was cold because it never involved military actions although both countries have been involved in military operations that were a part of that conflict. One could, like the historian John Gaddis, describe the second half of the twentieth century as "the long peace" by emphasizing those factors that have kept the United States and the Soviet Union from engaging in a hot war.[2] After all, war and peace are not absolutely mutually exclusive concepts. We are using the concept of war in its Clauswitzian sense, which views politics and war as closely interrelated. Just as war is a continuation of politics by other means, so can political instruments seek the objectives of war by peaceful means. What determines the warlike character of U.S.–Soviet relations is the incompatibility of their political goals, the sharply contrasting world order each seeks to realize.

We turn now to an explanation for the conflict between the Soviet Union and the United States. What were the basic causes of the conflict, the reasons for the continued hostility, and what would be the conditions to end the belligerency? We propose to identify the general factors that have guided the foreign policies of the two superpowers and in so doing to provide the basis for a theory of the Cold War. The use of the term "theory" may be somewhat presumptuous for an enterprise that only identifies the principal variables involved in Soviet-American relations. Thus at best we are working *toward* a theory of Soviet-American relations.

Three Theories of International Conflict

There is no general theory of international politics on which all or probably even a majority of political scientists are in agreement. There are scores of theories each of which has its advocates.[3] One useful method of classifying these theories is according to the basic unit or structure deemed to be the most important in determining state behavior generally and in particular state behavior that leads to war. Kenneth N. Waltz, in a classic study, identified three basic types of theory to explain war: (1) the individual and human behavior, (2) the internal structure of states, and (3) the anarchy of the international en-

vironment.[4] Later, J. David Singer described two alternative
models, or levels, of analysis that social scientists might use as
a basis for building a theory of international relations. These
were the international system and the nation-state.[5] Drawing
on the insights of these and other political scientists who have
attempted to create a theory for international politics we have
chosen to focus on three distinct levels of analysis which together we believe provide a reasonably complete framework
for analyzing international politics in general and Soviet-American relations in particular.[6] These three levels are (1) the international system, (2) the nation-state, and (3) decision
making.

The international system level encompasses the entire political universe including all the active sovereign states of the
world. It postulates that the behavior of each state influences
the behavior of other states or, more particularly, that the actions of great powers determine the actions or foreign policies
of other great powers. It is the interactive character of the
states or actors that makes it possible to speak of an international system. Historically the international system has
acquired specific characteristics and has produced certain patterns of behavior by the states within this system. Perhaps its
most fundamental feature is its anarchic character. That is,
states are not subject to a higher authority such as a world
government and are thus free to determine whether and when
they will use military force to achieve their goals. One of the
consequences of international anarchy is a generalized insecurity among states, which induces them to enhance their
security by acquiring power. As a means of adapting to the
international system the states of the world have developed a
pattern of behavior commonly referred to as the "balance of
power." The mechanism of the balance of power enhances the
security of states by mobilizing power to counter the threat of
another state's power. Ideally the most perfect and stable condition is when there is an equilibrium of power, but in the real
world that has rarely been atttained.

The nation-state level of analysis seeks to explain the international behavior of the state in terms of its internal characteristics such as its political, economic, or social system. This level of analysis assumes that different types of states behave in different ways and that one can trace the behavior of some states to their internal features. Quite clearly, there are many different and contradictory theories relating behavior to internal characteristics. For example, Woodrow Wilson believed that democratic governments were more peaceful than autocracies, while V. I. Lenin argued that imperialism was an inevitable outgrowth of advanced capitalistic states. Both the international system and the nation-state are abstract conceptions.

The third level of analysis — decision making — focuses on the people who make the decisions on behalf of the state. The argument here is that the individuals who occupy high office in government are the real determinants of foreign policy. Thus the forces controlling the destinies of nations are made up of very subjective and emotional factors. In this kind of analysis the political orientation or ideology of the leaders is important. Also important is the way decision makers perceive the world, themselves, and their adversaries. Reality may be less a factor than the way things *appear* to be by those who wield the levers of power in government. Another consideration in this level of analysis is the impact of a bureaucracy on decision making. Inevitably all regimes have complex bureaucracies that influence the outcome of foreign policy. Even the most absolute leader must rely to some extent on diplomatic, military, scientific, and other institutions for guidance.

We believe that in the absence of a general theory of international relations it is necessary to use several theoretical approaches to explain the general foreign policy tendencies of states. Macropolitical phenomena, such as world war, must examine all three levels of analysis: the international system, the nation-state, and individual decision making. Thus our analysis of the origins, nature, and prospects for the Cold War focuses on three different factors, each reflecting one of the three levels of analysis described above. They are:

1. Geostrategic considerations that derive from the balance
    of power
2. The nature of the Soviet political system
3. Public and elite perceptions of each side

Sources of Soviet-American Conflict: Balance-of-Power
A prerequisite for survival in an anarchic world is to prevent a
great power from acquiring overwhelming power. That is what
the United States did in 1917 and in 1941 when it went to war
to prevent German domination of Europe. It fought to preserve
the balance of power in Europe because Europeans alone were
incapable of doing so. In the past the other great powers kept
the balance in Europe, particularly England as it shifted its
alliances frequently to prevent Spain, France, and then Germany from becoming dominant. Europe became so exhausted
by its wars that by the twentieth century an outside power had
to intervene for the sake of a political balance. It was therefore
the international system itself that sucked America into the
first two world wars. And so it was with the Cold War. For a
third time in less than half a century the United States intervened to prevent European domination by a single great
power, this time the Soviet Union. Only now the stakes were
larger because the balance was global, not continental.

Several factors contributed to the rapidity with which the
United States and the Soviet Union — so recently allies —
became adversaries so quickly. First was the total collapse of
German power. After the Franco-Prussian War in 1870, Germany became the strongest power on the European continent.
In 1945 it was reduced to a political and military zero. Suddenly there was a vacuum in central Europe where previously
a great power had existed. Soviet Russia moved quickly to fill
the vacuum. For a brief period it seemed that Britain (supported by the United States) might constitute a counterforce
to Soviet power, but by 1947 it became apparent that Britain
was no longer a great power.

Second, there was the rapid advance of Soviet power into

eastern and central Europe that began when Stalin established a puppet government in Lublin for Poland and ended with the Soviet-organized coup in Czechoslovakia in February 1948. In just a few years the Soviet Union expanded its empire to include Poland, the eastern zone of Germany (which became the German Democratic Republic in 1949), Czechoslovakia, Hungary, Rumania, and Bulgaria. In addition to control over the governments of eastern Europe the Soviet Union annexed portions of territory that had belonged to Germany, Poland, Czechoslovakia, Rumania, and Finland as well as incorporating Latvia, Estonia, and Lithuania into the U.S.S.R. Within this short period of time 100 million Europeans fell (unwillingly) under the sway of communism.

Third, by the winter of 1947 the ravages caused by World War II revealed the social and economic fragility of the entire continent. Europe was slow to recover economically, and the inability of its governments to meet human needs created widespread social unrest.

A fourth and major factor was that the Soviet Union emerged from the second world war as the strongest military power in Europe. It alone among the victorious allies did not demobilize its armed forces after the surrender of Germany.

There are many problems in using the balance of power both in theory and statecraft.[7] How can one know when a balance is really threatened by the expansionist behavior of another state? What is the proper counterforce to reorder the balance? And what are the consequences of not responding to a particular threat? Was U.S. security really threatened by Soviet domination of eastern Europe and its possible control over western Europe? The central argument made by the Kremlin (and Soviet apologists in the west) was that Soviet expansion was justified by legitimate defensive needs. The eastern European satellites were seen in the east as a buffer against Germany. In view of the terrible costs paid by the Russians for German aggression Moscow had a legitimate right to security guarantees in eastern Europe. This was never questioned by either Churchill or Roosevelt. The difficult question is: How

far can a state expand in the name of security and the legitimate needs of defense?

It was understood by the United States and Great Britain
that the governments of eastern Europe could not be anti-Soviet, as many in the pre–World War II period were. Stalin,
however, in forcibly socializing eastern Europe went far beyond the legitimate needs of Soviet security. Czechoslovakia
is a good case in point: In 1948 the freely elected government
was headed by Premier Klement Gottwald, a Moscow-trained
Communist. Czech policies were clearly pro-Soviet. Yet, because the regime was a parliamentary democracy, not directly
under Moscow's thumb, Stalin ordered the coup that reduced
Czechoslovakia to the status of a satellite. The contention that
the regime must expand in order to protect itself is an old one
in Russian history. To this day the debate continues as to
whether Soviet expansionism is essentially "defensive" or
"aggressive." But in fact the difference is less than the words
themselves would suggest. What is defense to one party is
aggression to another. Russian feelings of vulnerability have
historically been so strong that when the opportunity came,
tsarist and Communist governments alike pushed the nation's
borders as far as they could. There is no limit to how far Moscow might expand in the name of defense. Its appetite for security is insatiable.

The American policy designed to counter Soviet imperialism became known as "containment," largely as a result of
George Kennan's famous article in *Foreign Affairs* in 1947. In
that article Kennan argued that "the main element of any
United States policy toward the Soviet Union must be that of
a long-term, patient but firm and vigilant containment of Russian expansive tendencies." And further, "The Soviet pressure
against the free institutions of the western world is something
that can be contained by the adroit and vigilant application of
counter-force at a series of constantly shifting geographical
and political points, corresponding to the shifts and manoeuvres of Soviet policy. . . ."[8] To put it simply, containment
was the application of balance-of-power politics. Although he

provided the label for U.S. policy during the Cold War Kennan
was not the architect of those policies and in later years he
strongly opposed what he called the militarization of American
policy toward the Soviet Union.[9] Perhaps Kennan's most important contribution to containment was the support he generated for Truman's policies by his articles and public
speeches.[10] While the strategy of containment has changed
over the past four decades the fundamental principles of that
doctrine have remained the cornerstone of U.S. policy toward
the Soviet Union.

During the 1940s and 1950s the principal strategy for maintaining the balance of power was through the formation of alliances. The most important of these was the North Atlantic
Treaty Organization (NATO), which was formed in 1949. No
one can say how far Moscow would have pushed had NATO
not come into existence. Certainly after the formation of
NATO the Soviet momentum in Europe ceased. In retrospect
it seems unlikely that Moscow ever contemplated military action against any state in the alliance. In a variety of different
ways the Soviet Union has sought to break up NATO or to
disassociate Europe from the United States, but it has done
this primarily through political rather than military means. The
only Soviet use of force in Europe after the Berlin blockade
was against its own allies: the East Germans in 1953, the Hun-
garians in 1956, and the Czechs in 1968.

The Chinese revolution in 1949 followed by the formation
of the Sino-Soviet alliance in 1950 was a major blow to U.S.
security. For the first time since the end of the second world
war the prospects seemed real for a united Communist bloc to
dominate the vast Eurasian land mass. The geopolitical nightmare described by Harlford Mackinder as early as 1904
seemed to be a possibility. Mackinder had warned that a great
power in full command of the Heartland — essentially the land
mass of Asia — could dominate the world. He envisioned a
great Heartland power, if it became industrially and militarily
powerful, pressing upon and eventually dominating the several
peninsulas of the World Island. Mackinder had prophesied that

if the World Island were conquered from within the surviving democracies in the world would be doomed.[11]

One does not need to subscribe to Mackinder's grand geopolitical theories to explain the U.S. reaction to the Sino-Soviet alliance. There is no indication that anyone in the State Department or National Security Council did. But it is clear that a monolithic Communist bloc in Eurasia was viewed by Washington as a deadly menace. And North Korea's invasion of South Korea in June 1950 — one of the Heartland's peninsulas — was seen as part of a determined effort to upset the global balance.

After Korea, containment shifted from Europe to Asia. The United States entered into a series of military alliances with Asian powers in an attempt to create a stable balance of power. Two of the alliances were multilateral: ANZUS and SEATO (both defunct today). In addition, bilateral treaties were negotiated with the Philippines, Japan, the Republic of Korea, and the Republic of China. The objectives of these alliances were twofold: (1) to mobilize as much political and military power as possible to contain the Soviet-Chinese bloc and (2) to demarcate the boundaries that presumably divided the two sides.

The use of military alliances to maintain the balance of power has not proven to be effective. One could cite the success of NATO as a contributor to Europe's stability, but it is not at all clear that Europe would *not* have survived without NATO. Moscow was dissuaded from pushing west because of internal problems and the deterrent effect of nuclear weapons, weapons located not in Europe but in the United States and in the oceans adjacent to the Eurasian land mass. The ineffectiveness of alliances was clearly demonstrated with the failure of the prowestern CENTO alliance to stop Soviet penetration of the Middle East and more significantly the failure of SEATO to prevent the collapse of South Vietnam. Indeed Vietnam was a watershed in the U.S. policy of containment. It revealed the obsolescence of traditional balance-of-power techniques in curbing aggression, and it demonstrated that a Communist victory in Vietnam did not substantially undermine U.S. security. The so-called domino theory proved to be invalid.

Nevertheless, the fundamental balance the United States sought to preserve did actually remain intact. It survived because of political and technological changes that evolved during the course of U.S.–Soviet hostilities. One was the Sino-Soviet split, a development over which the United States had virtually no control. In geostrategic terms the Sino-Soviet split was worth a dozen SEATOs. Another development was strategic deterrence. Moscow was constrained by the prospect of nuclear war more than the fear of conventional war. Nuclear weapons have radically altered the techniques of the balance of power. Allies, territory, and resources no longer occupy the major position they once did. The balance of power today increasingly means the balance of strategic nuclear weapons.

Sources of Soviet-American Conflict: Political Culture
The balance of power explains part — but only part — of Soviet-American hostilities. It is central in accounting for the origins of the Cold War, but its explanatory value has lessened as the balance became more stable. Clearly, the first level of analysis alone cannot account for the durability of Soviet-American hostility. For that we must turn to the second and third levels of analysis. We consider now the second level, the internal characteristics of the Soviet regime. We believe that the domestic character of the Soviet regime is a key factor in the perpetuation of the Soviet-American conflict. A variety of factors combine to give Soviet rulers a mindset that views America (and all capitalistic western powers) as enemies and that induces those rulers to act accordingly. The elements in that mindset are many: history, culture, geography, social structure, ideology, and political and economic structure to name the most obvious. A more comprehensive term to describe the impact of these and other elements on the thinking of a state's rulers is "political culture." Political scientists Gabriel Almond and G. Bingham Powell define political culture

as the totality of "attitudes, beliefs, values, and skills that are
current in a population."[12] There are many features of the Soviet political culture that impel the Kremlin to pursue a hostile
and aggressive policy toward the United States. We are not
suggesting that such attitudes constitute the sum totality of the
political culture of the Soviet Union; nor are we denying that
similar elements exist in the political culture of the United
States, although hardly to the same degree. These will be considered later.

Of the several elements that have influenced the political
culture of the Soviet leadership three are particularly crucial.
They can be labeled (1) Russian, (2) Communist, and (3) Soviet. By Russian we refer to the influence of the country's history and culture before the 1917 revolution. The Communist
factor is the impact of doctrine or ideology. By Soviet we mean
the nature of the political and economic system and its role in
setting foreign policy. It is common in some writings to equate
Communist and Soviet. We do not. While there may be some
features of the Soviet regime that resemble Marxism, the system as a whole violates most of Marx's doctrine and stands *sui
generis* as a unique product of the twentieth century.

Many of the features of the U.S.S.R. today have their roots
in Russian history, a point noted by Russian and non-Russian
historians alike. Undoubtedly, the most striking continuity is
the authoritarian character of both the Russian and Soviet regimes. There are many explanations for the autocracy of Russia's past. Arnold Toynbee, the British historian, provides one
with the argument that western aggression made autocracy in
Russia inevitable: He explained it this way:

> The pressure on Russia from the West did not merely estrange
> Russia from the West; it was one of the hard facts of Russian
> life that moved the Russians to submit to the yoke of a new
> native Russian Power at Moscow which, at the price of autoc-
> racy, imposed on Russia the political unity that she now had to
> have if she was to survive. It was no accident that this new-
> fangled autocratic centralizing government of Russia should

have arisen at Moscow; for Moscow stood at the fairway of the easiest line for the invasion of what was left of Russia by a Western aggressor. The Poles in 1610, the French in 1812, the Germans in 1941, all marched this way. Since an early date in the fourteenth century, autocracy and centralization have been the dominant notes of all successive Russian regimes.[13]

Many others go back to the Tatar domination of Russia in the thirteenth and fourteenth centuries. Seweryn Bialer, in his examination of the roots of Soviet foreign policy says, "Russia's exposure to frequent invasions and wars, its relative weakness, its subjugation for many centuries to the Tatars, created in the peoples and especially in its elites and rulers and obsessive security-mindedness."[14] In Russian history the vulnerability of the state to invasion, autocratic rule, and suspicion and hostility toward the outside world were all interconnected. The effect of these forces was to impel the Russian state to expand wherever possible. The Russian historian Vasili Klyuchevski wrote that from the sixteenth century on "the expansion of the state territory, straining beyond measure . . . the resources of the people only bolstered the power of the state without elevating the self-consciousness of the people. . . . The state swelled up, the people grew lean."[15]

Another explanation for Russian expansion is its geographic situation. For all of its vast size the Russian Empire had only limited access to the oceans that serve as the highways for international trade. Russia's economic backwardness was partly due to its inability to compete in trade with the western European states. This explains the military efforts by tsarist rulers like Peter the Great and Catherine the Great to acquire warm water ports. Also, Russia was a state lacking national barriers as a protection against the marauding armies of foreigners. To compensate for its geographic vulnerability the tsars maintained comparatively large land armies. These military forces were used not only for defense but, as Toynbee noted, for the suppression of dissent and opposition at home.

Ideology

A second element comprising the political culture of the U.S.S.R. is Communist ideology. By Communist ideology we refer to what is commonly known as Marxist-Leninist doctrine. Some of the basic ideas that make up that doctrine are the following: (1) societies are divided into classes based on the possession or control of property; (2) under capitalism the exploitation of the working class (the proletariat) by the ruling class (the bourgeosie) is greater than under any other mode of production; (3) the capitalist mode of production contains the seeds of its own destruction, which lead to socialism and the end of the class struggle; and (4) the final phase of capitalism is imperialism, which results in wars between capitalist states and to conflict between capitalism and socialism.[16]

As noted, the Soviet regime bears little resemblance to the socialist utopia anticipated by Marx. That being so, one might question whether Communist ideology has any relevance to Soviet politics at all. We believe that it does, but not as a guide or predictor of specific Soviet behavior or policies. We reject the approach that seeks to explain Soviet behavior on the basis of some statement or textual argument taken from the writings of Marx, Lenin, or any Communist theoretician. For one thing, Communist doctrine is not static. It changes from generation to generation. Since the 1917 revolution Soviet leaders have modified Communist doctrine to suit the needs of the ruling elite internally or the interests of the Soviet state in international politics. For example, there is Lenin's theory of the inevitability of conflict between capitalism and socialism, Stalin's theory of "socialism in one country" and "capitalistic encirclement," Khrushchev's "peaceful coexistence," and the so-called Brezhnev doctrine justifying Soviet intervention in socialist states. That element of the Communist ideology which purports to describe the real world and to formulate policy from that description is constantly changing.

There are, however, some core doctrinal values and ideas that have permeated the thinking of all Soviet leaders and which significantly affected their view of themselves, their enemies, and the world situation. Foremost among these is the

notion that all political activity — domestic as well as international — involves conflict. For Marx the basic social conflict
was the class struggle; for Lenin it was the struggle between
states against what he called imperialism. Both viewed politics
as a bitter struggle that would ultimately be resolved by the
complete victory of one side or the other. Neither Marx nor
Lenin placed a high value on compromise, tolerance, or moderation. It is not surprising, therefore, that both had a profound
contempt for parliamentary democracy, which requires compromise in the enactment of legislation and tolerance of an opposing political party coming to power. Politics for Lenin and
his successors had the characteristics of a war. Indeed Lenin
was a great admirer of the German military strategist Karl von
Clauswitz and cited with approval the famous statement that
war is a continuation of politics by other means. In Communist
slogans to this day policy issues are described by words like
"battle," "struggle," "front," "advance," "retreat" — the
language of war.

Soviet doctrine not only identifies the enemy — capitalism
— but endows it with very specific characteristics. The enemy
is aggressive, determined, and unprincipled. If he has superior
strength, he will use it. If he makes a concession, it is only
because he is forced to do so, not because of compassion,
goodwill, or a sense of fairness. Different states have occupied
the role of principal enemy at different periods of time. In the
interwar period it was Great Britain until the rise of fascism
made Germany enemy number one. After World War II the
United States became the principal adversary. From the Kremlin's perspective the behavior patterns of all these states were
rooted in their social-political system. They could no more
avoid being predatory and pursuing a hostile policy toward the
Soviet Union than could a tiger remove his stripes. Capitalist
states are incapable of being progressive, humanitarian, or
peace-loving. Just the opposite. If the enemy pursues a policy
of moderation, peace, arms reduction, détente, or whatever, it
is because he is compelled to do so by circumstances or, more
likely, by the might of the Soviet Union.

Communist doctrine contains explicit and implicit precepts

regarding the strategy and tactics to pursue in the struggle with the enemy. Basic to Communist strategic thinking is the concept of "correlation of forces," which translates roughly into the overall balance favoring either the Soviet Union or its enemies. If the correlation of forces is favorable, it is incumbent upon Communists to push ahead and maintain pressure on the enemy. On the other hand, when the enemy is stronger it is important to know when to stop and retreat. Communist doctrine advises the strategist to be pragmatic, flexible, and realistic. Compromise may be necessary if the Communist position is not strong enough to prevail; but a compromised position is not viewed as a permanent one. It is an expedient that will endure until the correlation of forces shifts in favor of communism.

Other doctrinal maxims admonish against being provoked by an adversary. One of the greatest tactical sins is to engage an adversary from a position of weakness. Communists are not averse to taking risks, but they do not do so lightly, and when they do they insist that the initiatives be limited and that each step in a progression of steps be controllable. In Communist doctrinal literature there is no premium on martyrdom or fighting a lost cause. If a policy is designed to achieve several objectives and circumstances cause one objective to be too costly to attain, then the doctrine cautions that a lesser goal should be sought. This principle has been described as an "optimizing strategy." These precepts derived from Communist doctrinal literature and public statements have been labeled by Nathan Leites and Alexander George as "the operational code" of Soviet leaders.[17] Elements of that operational code reinforce the traditional Russian perspective of the international environment as populated by hostile forces that must be fought.

Soviet Characteristics

There is a third important ingredient in the political culture of the Soviet Union and that is the Soviet element. Here we refer to the basic features of the Soviet regime and their significance in terms of foreign policy. As noted above, the Soviet regime, while it may share some characteristics with the Russian monarchy (its autocratic character, for example) and while it may conform to some elements of Communist doctrine (its centralization, for example), it is in fact quite different from both. The word "Soviet" itself is not a Communist term. It came into political prominence in 1905 and 1917 to refer to revolutionary groups (councils) who sought to take political power on behalf of the people. After seizing power the Bolsheviks decided to make the "Soviet" the basic unit of state power. The political system we know today as the U.S.S.R. was largely molded during the long rule of Joseph Stalin. It would not be inappropriate to refer to it as a "Stalinist" system even though there have been very significant changes made since Stalin's death, particularly under the leadership of Nikita Khrushchev who replaced the terror with a more liberalized polity. However, neither the liberalization that took place under Khrushchev nor the growth of bureaucratic interests under Brezhnev have altered the fundamentally authoritarian character of the Soviet political system. Nor have Gorbachev's reforms yet made the Soviet system democratic.

All authoritarian regimes are faced with the common problem of dealing with the resentment that results from oppression. One way to overcome such resentment is to resolve domestic problems so successfully that the public is willing to forgo domestic liberty. Another way is to mobilize domestic opinion against external enemies, to deflect hostility, so to speak. This solution tends to propel governments toward aggressive and expansionist foreign policies. Of course, internal opposition to authoritarian regimes varies considerably from society to society, and studies have indicated that the Soviet regime enjoys a widespread acceptance from the Russian population in spite of its authoritarian character.

Nevertheless, every Soviet leader since Lenin showed a strong sense of insecurity. The roots of that insecurity are embedded in the Soviet system. We have referred above to the historical sense of insecurity felt by Russians because of external forces. The Soviet system by its nature adds immensely to that insecurity because it denies its leaders any real sense of legitimacy. Legitimacy establishes the rights of those who hold power to govern and contributes toward popular acceptance of the rulers' programs. It can be established in many ways. The tsars ruled by divine right. In kingdoms governed by royal families legitimacy is established by blood lines. Constitutional regimes provide various methods by which leadership is legitimately selected. With democratic governments the legitimacy of the leaders follows from popular election. But the Soviet system lacks an established method for the selection of its leaders. The structure controlling the system is the Communist party, which bases its claim to rule on the assertion that it is the vanguard of the working class and that it possesses a unique ability to know what is best for the working class. At the core of this ideological claim is the belief that history ordains the rule of the Communist party. The problem with relying on Communist doctrine for legitimacy is that history has failed to sustain the claims of Soviet theorists and as a consequence belief in that doctrine has eroded and with it the legitimacy of the Communist party and its rulers.

Soviet history and politics are permeated with countless myths that are widely understood to be fictions, some more so abroad than internally. Among these historical myths are the contentions that the Bolshevik revolution was a workers' revolution; that the purpose of allied intervention in Russia was to crush Bolshevism; that leading members of the old Bolsheviks betrayed the revolution; that collectivization of agriculture was achieved voluntarily; that the Soviet Union had no responsibility for World War II; and that the Red Army alone defeated Nazi Germany. However, it is the myths that pertain to the political system that more directly bear on the issue of the legitimacy of Soviet leaders. The distinctly Soviet myths include the claims that the Soviet Union is a democracy; that there is a monolithic unity among the Soviet people and between the people and the government; that national antagonism (including anti-Semitism) no longer exist in the U.S.S.R.; that the Union Republics are sovereign (and presumably free, if they so chose, to become independent states); that the Supreme Soviet legislates; that political power resides in the structure of the Soviets; that elections are meaningful; that the Communist party knows better than anyone what the interests of the people are and strives always to achieve them; and that the leader (while alive) is always right. The falsity of these and countless other myths that make up the fabric of Soviet political culture breeds cynicism and discontent. And it undermines the sense of legitimacy of those who rule in the Soviet Union.

Psychologically one method of dealing with an unpleasant reality is denial. The political equivalent of denial is propaganda and disinformation. Thus one of the striking features of the Soviet regime is its reliance on propaganda to control its own population and influence opinion abroad. The Soviet regime cannot be open with its neighbors because it is not honest with its own subjects. Obviously, not all government communiqués or public speeches are dishonest. Sometimes the truth is not damaging. But Soviet practice is to calculate what the impact of any public statement might be and to craft that statement to serve the authority (and legitimacy) of the leadership whether the statement is true, partially true, or outright false. One cannot exaggerate the central element that propaganda plays in the Soviet system and in its foreign relations. We believe that the practice of deception is endemic in the Soviet system. George Kennan in the 1970s described this behavior as follows:

> There are deeply-rooted traits in Soviet psychology — some of old-Russian origin, some of more recent Soviet provenance. . . . Chief among these, in my opinion, are the congenital disregard of the truth, the addiction to propagandistic exaggeration, distortion, and falsehood, the habitual foulness of mouth in official utterance. So pernicious has been the effect of 50 years of cynicism about the role of objective truth in political statements that one begins to wonder whether these Soviet leaders have not destroyed in themselves the power to distinguish truth from falsehood.[18]

He saw this practice of dissimulation as an obstacle to close or even normal relations between the Soviet Union and the United States. We believe an even more fundamental problem is connected with this Soviet practice, and that is the lack of a common basis or standard for determining what is true from what is false. Not only is trust and goodwill undermined, but also the capacity to communicate.

Two crises in the post-Brezhnev period illustrate the depth and persistence of Soviet insecurity and inability to acknowledge fault or imperfection. Both were tragedies involving the death of many civilians. One was the shooting down of a commercial Korean airliner (KAL 007) that strayed over Soviet territory on September 1, 1983. The plane was a Boeing 747 with 269 passengers all of whom perished. What is significant about this event is not whether the Soviet air defense personnel knew they were shooting down a civilian aircraft at the time or whether the airplane had deliberately or inadvertently crossed into Soviet territory. The important thing was the Soviet reaction and response to what was revealed to be a major tragedy. The first report from Tass was to deny that the plane had been shot down.[19] The Kremlin then blamed the United States for the disaster. In the face of worldwide (though by no means universal) condemnation, the Soviet Union went to great lengths to argue that the aircraft was a spy plane. On September 9 an unprecedented two-hour press conference was held in Moscow presided over by Marshall Nikolai Ogarkov, then Chief of the Soviet General Staff. He described the incident as a "provocation perpetrated by the US special services. . . . It has been proved irrefutably that the intrusion of the South Korean airline's plane into Soviet airspace was a deliberate, carefully planned intelligence operation."[20] In short, Soviet authorities could not admit to having made a blunder in shooting down a commercial airplane because that would have been an acknowledgment of weakness, incompetence, or guilt on their part; so they placed the entire blame on the United States and Japan. Ogarkov insisted under questioning: "We have nothing to apologize for."[21]

A tragedy of a different sort took place in the early hours of April 26, 1986 when an explosion in a nuclear reactor at the Chernobyl station in the Ukraine about 80 miles north of Kiev led to a discharge of lethal amounts of radiation across the western portions of the U.S.S.R. and then into eastern and western Europe. Before it was brought under control the Chernobyl reactor spewed more radiation into the atmosphere than was released from the bombs dropped on Hiroshima and Nagasaki.[22] The issue of concern here is not the cause of the accident, the safety of Soviet nuclear reactor design, or the quality of Soviet technology. Our focus is on the way the Soviet leadership responded to the disaster. To begin with, they failed to provide any warning to potential victims of nuclear radiation either inside or outside of their border. Their initial reaction was a kind of denial which took the form of silence in the media. In fact, the first public reports that a radiation problem existed came from Swedish authorities who detected unusually high levels of radiation over Sweden and who when they called Moscow were told that nothing was amiss. Moscow claims that it did not know about the nature of the accident until April 28 (a day and a half after it happened). It is difficult to believe this could be so in a highly centralized system such as exists in the U.S.S.R. Indeed it is virtually certain that the Kremlin knew otherwise. Subsequently, the Soviets themselves acknowledged that military helicopters began dropping materials to douse the fire in the reactor as early as April 27.[23] When denial became impossible, information was released but in a minimal and fragmentary manner that grossly distorted the real situation. On April 30 *Pravda* made the false claim that "the radiation situation at the power station and in the adjacent locality has stabilized."[24] At that very time, according to information given to Harrison Salisbury by an associate of Mikhail Gorbachev, the Politburo was unsure when, how, or whether the nuclear disaster could be brought under control.[25] The situation was not "stabilized" as the Kremlin well knew.

Gorbachev's handling of the Chernobyl crisis reveals that the patterns of secrecy, duplicity, and manipulation that have been a part of the Soviet political culture have not changed. The impact of political culture goes beyond the influence of a single leader or one administration. Gorbachev was hailed as the harbinger of a "new politics" in the U.S.S.R. On taking power he promised a new policy of openness ("glasnost") in the Soviet media and public affairs, but when the pressure was on he reverted to the Soviet form. Nowhere was this more evident than in his first televised address to the Soviet public after Chernobyl. His accounting of the event was vague and revealed no new information. He stressed that everything possible was being done to minimize the consequences of the incident. But the striking feature of his speech was the attack he made on the western powers for criticizing the failure of Soviet authorities to release information to those who needed it in a timely fashion. He accused the U.S. news media of committing "lies — very shameless and malignant lies," of engaging in an "immoral campaign" to "defame the Soviet Union." "Speaking frankly," he said, "certain Western politicians were pursuing some very definite goals: to close off possibilities for putting international relations on an even keel, to sow new seeds of distrust and suspicion of the socialist countries."[26] In a word, Gorbachev was pursuing exactly the same tactic that Andropov had used with the KAL 007 incident: to divert responsibility and blame from themselves by making accusations against outside forces.

The characteristics we have described — suspicion, hostility, inability to accept blame or responsibility for their actions, unwillingness to acknowledge a flaw in their system, or not admitting that the highest authority can make a mistake — are the product of the interaction of Russian (traditional), Communist (ideological), and Soviet (authoritarian) forces. We have chosen to call this the political culture of the U.S.S.R. Some have used other labels — mindset, national character, national style — but whatever the label, this endemic way of thinking and acting has contributed substantially to the perpetuation of Soviet-American hostilities.

This is not to deny the seriousness and importance of Gorbachev's policies identified under the labels "openness," "restructuring," and "new thinking." They represent a determination to rid Soviet society of the inefficient, corrupt, and demeaning practices that have accumulated under Communist rule. Gorbachev's Politburo has given freedom to scores of political dissidents; it has widened the arena of artistic and cultural expression; the press is freer to report national disasters and social disorders; and jamming of foreign broadcasts into the Soviet Union has been reduced. Gorbachev has also introduced democratic practices in the selection of local officials and he has opened up incentives for individual initiative by legalizing small private enterprises and encouraging practices that permit laborers to benefit more from their labor. Collectively Gorbachev's reforms will unquestionably improve the quality of life for many Soviet citizens. They even give the appearance of moving Soviet society toward western norms.

But "glasnost" does not represent a fundamental change either in the structure of Soviet governance or the intellectual or philosophical norms that underlie that structure. It must be understood for what it is: an effort to make the existing system more efficient, more productive and tolerable to the growing Soviet middle class. It is not a repudiation of Leninism or an abandonment of the one-party dictatorship that came into existence after the Bolshevik revolution. The press, which reveals more than it did previously, is still subject to official censorship. Limited elections have not eliminated the "nomenklatura" system by which important positions in Soviet society are filled by party authority. Laws that prohibited criticism of the Soviet system or its leaders and legalized the arrest of dissidents are still on the books. Literary freedom may be extended to permit the publication of Boris Pasternak's *Dr. Zhivago* — but not of Aleksandr Solzhenitsyn's *Gulag Archapelago*. If the Voice of America is no longer jammed, Radio Liberty is. The limited scope of free enterprise in the U.S.S.R. does nothing to change the mechanism of centralized control of the economy by the party bureaucracy. To this point all of Gorbachev's reforms have modified but not dismantled the Stalinist apparatus.

Sources of Soviet-American Conflict: Perceptions

Finally, we consider the impact of the third level of analysis, the decision-making level, on Soviet-American relations. This level involves the actions of individual political leaders and the factors that influence those decisions. There is obviously some overlapping between the second and third levels because quite clearly political culture as well as conceptions of the balance of power influence the behavior of individual leaders in government. The aspect of the decision-making level that we focus on is the impact of perception on leaders. This is a more transient and changeable factor than political culture, but it can, particularly in crisis, be just as strong a determinant.[27] How policy makers perceive themselves and the outside world may be more important than reality.

Seweryn Bialer, in a recent examination of U.S.–Soviet relations, concluded that "Misperceptions and false analogies account for at least part of the stalemate and spirit of confrontation that have dominated Soviet-American relations in the 1980's".[28] While it would be erroneous to consider misperception to be the core of Soviet-American differences, there is little doubt that the devil image that each side has of the other has exacerbated and at times magnified those differences. Once public opinion in the United States was mobilized behind Truman's efforts to contain Stalin's aggression, it became difficult for the passions against communism to be cooled when Soviet foreign policy changed. The phenomenon of "McCarthyism" is evidence of the distortion of reality that an obsession with anticommunism can lead to.

In retrospect we can see that many American policies in the struggle with the Soviet Union were based on erroneous perceptions, inaccurate information, or false assumptions. As examples we could mention the erroneous belief that U.S. policies made possible the Communist revolution in China; that the Sino-Soviet alliance constituted a monolithic bloc; that Soviet success in launching its Sputnik meant that the United States had fallen behind in science and technology; the bomber and missile gaps of the 1960s; and the failure to understand the nature of guerrilla warfare in Vietnam. In general the tendency has been for Americans to exaggerate the strength of Soviet power and to impute to every Soviet action a malign intention. As a result of these misperceptions the United States has often overreacted to Soviet moves and at times failed to take advantage of opportunities to negotiate some of the differences between the two countries.

Above we examined the Soviet political culture as a contributor to hostile relations with America. We did not suggest that the political culture of the United States has had a similar effect because we do not believe it is a significant factor in the Cold War. Nevertheless, we believe the long years of American anti-Sovietism have bred an instinctive distrust and hostility toward the Soviet Union that has exacerbated the real differences between the two sides. To a degree, hostility toward Russia has become a habit. According to Stephen Cohen, the American public in the Reagan years was in the grip of "Sovietophobia," which he defined as an "exaggerated fear of the Soviet threat."[29] Public hostility toward the U.S.S.R. has gone through periods of greater and lesser intensity. Sovietophobia, as described by Cohen, began in the late 1970s.

Aside from the fluctuations in American public opinion there is an enduring anti-Sovietism in government, the media, and academia that has many of the characteristics of an ideology. Admittedly in the United States we are talking about only a minority. The anti-Soviet ideologist refuses to acknowledge that the Soviet Union has changed considerably since the demise of Joseph Stalin. Those holding an implacable view of Russia refuse to see any basis for agreement or compromise with the leaders in the Kremlin. They oppose all arms control agreements, any trade or cultural exchanges, or any measures of cooperation. We are not suggesting that arms control or trade will bridge the chasm that differentiates the two socie-

ties, but simply that a segment of U.S. opinion refuses to consider these issues on their merit or concede that some agreements with the Soviets may also benefit the United States.
Opinion polls support our contention that this rigid, hard-line
view is held by only a minority.

Part of the crisis in U.S.–Soviet relations in the 1980s stems
precisely from the tendency of elites in both countries to exaggerate the capabilities and evil intentions of the other side.
The Reagan administration included a number of individuals
with just such a view of the Soviet Union. Strobe Talbott
provides a detailed account of how key members of the Reagan administration opposed (in his first term) any serious
negotiations toward arms control. He notes, "Some officials
questioned the desirability of any agreement that entailed accommodation with America's principal adversary and limitation of America's military options. It forced to keep up the
appearance of playing the old arms-control game, they believed, the U.S. would do best with gambits at the negotiating
table that would lead to a diplomatic stalemate."[30]

Misperception, of course, operates on both sides. Soviet
leaders have notoriously misunderstood the intentions of U.S.
leaders just as they have been baffled by the dynamics of
American society. This has been particularly true of the Kremlin's understanding of the Reagan administration. A high-level
K.G.B. defector informed the British that Soviet leaders believed that President Reagan intended at the opportune time to
order an attack against the Soviet Union or one of its close
allies, perhaps Cuba.[31] An associate of Mikhail Gorbachev told
Harrison Salisbury that in the early stages of the Chernobyl
crisis the Soviet leadership feared that the United States might
seize the opportunity for an anti-Soviet maneuver.[32]

The forces, then, that pit America and Russia against each
other are multiple and enduring. At one level it is a struggle of
one great power to change the global balance and of another
to preserve the status quo. At another level it is the suspicion
and aggressiveness deeply rooted in the Soviet culture. And at
yet a different level it is the misunderstanding of individual

elites of what the other side is doing or intends to do. The Cold War between America and Russia will not end quickly. Nor does it seem likely that either side will emerge a clear victor in the near future. The conflict will end when conditions permit a radical change of outlook in the Soviet Union. Such a change could be facilitated by the pressures for modernization and economic development in the U.S.S.R. For the United States and the west the fundamental challenge is to remain strong without being provocative. The Soviet sense of insecurity cannot be the basis for U.S. policy, though U.S. actions must be careful to avoid challenging legitimate Soviet interests. But equally the United States must defend its interests and values.

The greatest threat to the security of both states lies in a nuclear war, which neither side desires. We do not foresee the Cold War taking the form of a military clash between the superpowers, because we believe that nuclear deterrence works. Until a better technique is developed, deterrence is the strongest guarantee of nuclear peace. But even deterrence cannot be taken for granted. Overriding their deep antagonism the United States and the Soviet Union have a powerful interest in making deterrence as stable as is humanly possible. There is good reason to believe that both sides understand this imperative of the twentieth century.

Notes

1. *The New York Times,* January 30, 1981, p. A10 and March 9, 1983, p. A1.
2. John Lewis Gaddis, "The Long Peace: Elements of Stability in the Postwar International System," *International Security,* vol. 10, no. 4, Spring 1986.
3. One of the best surveys of international relations theories is James E. Dougherty and Robert L. Pfaltzgraff, Jr., *Contending Theories of International Relations, A Comprehensive Survey,* 2d ed. (New York: Harper & Row, 1981).
4. Kenneth N. Waltz, *Man, the State and War, a Theoretical Analysis* (New York: Columbia University Press, 1959).

5. See J. David Singer, "The Level-of-Analysis Problem in International Relations," *World Politics,* October 1961.

6. This three-tiered framework was devised by John Spanier and is developed further in *Games Nations Play,* 6th ed. (Washington, D.C.: Congressional Quarterly, 1987), pp. 22–52.

7. See Inis Claude, Jr., *Power and International Relations* (New York: Random House, 1962), pp. 11–93. Kenneth Waltz has written, "If there is any distinctively political theory of international politics, balance-of-power theory is it. And yet one cannot find a statement of the theory that is generally accepted." Quoted in R. Harrison Wagner, "The Theory of Games and the Balance of Power," *World Politics,* vol. 38, no. 4, July 1986, p. 546.

8. George F. Kennan, "The Sources of Soviet Conduct," *Foreign Affairs,* vol. 25, no. 4, July 1947, pp. 576–577.

9. See "Mr. X Revisited, An Interview with George F. Kennan," in Charles Gati, ed., *Caging the Bear* (New York: Bobbs-Merrill, 1974), pp. 33–34.

10. See David Mayers, "Containment and the Primacy of Diplomacy: George Kennan's Views 1947–1948," *International Security,* vol. 11, no. 1, Summer 1986, p. 124; and Charles Gati, "Mr. X Reexamined: The Meaning of Containment," in *Caging the Bear,* op. cit., p. 4.

11. See Halford J. Mackinder, *Democratic Ideal and Reality* (New York: W. W. Norton, 1962).

12. This definition is taken from Frederick A. Barghoorn and Thomas Remington, *Politics USSR,* 3d ed. (Boston: Little, Brown, 1986), p. 20.

13. Arnold Toynbee, *Civilization on Trial and the World and the West* (New York: Meridian Books, 1958), p. 238.

14. Seweryn Bialer, *The Soviet Paradox, External Expansion, Internal Decline* (New York: Alfred A. Knopf, 1986), p. 259.

15. Quoted in Barghoorn and Remington, op. cit., pp. 2–3.

16. Three books by Alfred G. Meyer contain useful summaries and analyses of Communist doctrine. They are *Marxism, the Unity of Theory and Practice* (Cambridge, Mass.: Harvard University Press, 1954); *Leninism* (Cambridge, Mass.: Harvard University Press, 1957); and *Communism,* 3d ed. (New York: Random House, 1967).

17. See Alexander L. George, "The Operational Code: A Neglected

Approach to the Study of Political Leaders and Decision-Making," in Erik P. Hoffmann and Frederick J. Fleron, Jr., eds. *The Conduct of Soviet Foreign Policy* (Chicago: Aldine & Atherton, 1971), pp. 165–190.

18. "Mr. X Revisited," op. cit., p. 32.

19. The denial was implicit, not explicit. On September 2, the day after the event, Tass reported: "The air defense fighters that were sent up to meet the intruder-plane attempted to provide assistance by escorting it to the nearest airfield. However, the intruder-plane failed to respond to the Soviet fighters' signals and warnings and continued its flight toward the Sea of Japan." See *The Current Digest of the Soviet Press*, vol. 35, no. 35, September 28, 1983, p. 1. Recent evidence indicates that the Soviet action was a blunder. See *The New York Times*, August 24, 1986, p. A1.

20. *Current Digest of the Soviet Press*, vol. 35, no. 6, October 5, 1983, p. 1.

21. Ibid., p. 5. The best account of the KAL 007 flight is Alexander Dallin, *Black Box* (Berkeley: University of California Press), 1985.

22. The Soviet Union acknowledges that 3.5 percent of the radioactive material in the reactor got into the atmosphere which western experts calculated exceeded the radioactivity from the bombs dropped on Japan. See *The New York Times*, August 22, 1986, p. 4.

23. *The New York Times*, August 22, 1986, p. 4.

24. *Current Digest of the Soviet Press*, vol. 38, no. 16, May 21, 1986, p. 1.

25. Harrison Salisbury, "Gorbachev's Dilemma," *The New York Times Magazine*, July 26, 1986, p. 25.

26. *Current Digest of the Soviet Press*, vol. 38, no. 20, July 18, 1986, p. 19.

27. A particularly thorough analysis of the role of perception and the consequences of misperception in international politics is Robert Jervis, *Perception and Misperception in International Politics* (Princeton, N.J.: Princeton University Press, 1976). An application of many of Jervis' ideas to the early period of the Cold War is Deborah Larson, *Origins of Containment, a Psychological Explanation* (Princeton, N.J.: Princeton University Press, 1986).

28. Bialer, op. cit., p. 361.
29. Stephen F. Cohen, *Sovieticus, American Perceptions and Soviet Realities* (New York: W. W. Norton, 1986), p. 17.
30. Strobe Talbott, *Deadly Gambits* (New York: Alfred A. Knopf), 1984, p. xii.
31. The defector was Oleg G. Gordiyevsky. See *The New York Times,* August 9, 1986, p. 1.
32. Salisbury, op. cit., p. 25.

Bibliography

Acheson, Dean: *Present at the Creation*. New York: W. W. Norton, 1969.

Adler, Selig: *The Isolationist Impulse*. New York: Abelard-Schuman, 1957.

Almond, Gabriel: *The American People and Foreign Policy*. New York: Frederick A. Praeger, 1960.

Alperovitz, Gar: *Atomic Diplomacy*, rev. ed. New York: Penguin, 1985.

Ambrose, Stephen E.: *Rise to Globalism*, 4th ed. New York: Penguin, 1985.

Aron, Raymond: *The Great Debate*. New York: Anchor Books, 1965.

Ball, Desmond: "Can Nuclear War Be Controlled?", *Adelphi Papers*. London: International Institute for Strategic Studies, 1981.

———— and Richelsen, Jeffrey, eds.: *Strategic Nuclear Targeting*. Ithaca, N.Y.: Cornell University Press, 1986.

Barnet, Richard: *The Alliance — America, Europe, Japan*. New York: Simon & Schuster, 1983.

Bell, Coral: *The Diplomacy of Detente*. New York: St. Martin's Press, 1977.

Bialer, Seweryn: *The Soviet Paradox, External Expansion, Internal Decline*. New York: Alfred A. Knopf, 1986.

Blair, Bruce G.: *Strategic Command and Control*. Washington, D.C.: The Brookings Institution, 1985.

Blechman, Barry M., ed.: *Rethinking the U.S. Strategic Posture*. Cambridge, Mass.: Ballinger, 1982.

Blechman, Barry M. and Kaplan, Stephen S.: *Force without*

War, U.S. Armed Forces as a Political Instrument. Washington, D.C.: The Brookings Institution, 1978.

Bohlen, Charles E.: *Witness to History, 1929–1969.* New York: W. W. Norton, 1973.

Borisov, O. B. and Koloskov, B. T.: *Sino-Soviet Relations.* Moscow: Progress Publishers, 1975.

Bracken, Paul: *The Command and Control of Nuclear Forces.* New Haven, Conn.: Yale University Press, 1983.

Bradsher, Henry S.: *Afghanistan and the Soviet Union.* Durham, N.C.: Duke University Press, 1983.

Brzezinski, Zbigniew: *The Soviet Bloc,* rev. ed. Cambridge, Mass.: Harvard University Press, 1971.

————: *Game Plan.* Boston: The Atlantic Monthly Press, 1986.

————: *Power and Principle.* New York: Farrar, Straus, & Giroux, 1983.

Brodie, Bernard: *Strategy in the Missile Age.* Princeton, N.J.: Princeton University Press, 1959.

Brown, Harold: *Thinking about National Security.* Boulder, Colo.: Westview Press, 1983.

Brown, Seyom: *The Faces of Power.* New York: Columbia University Press, 1983.

Bull, Hedley: *The Control of the Arms Race,* 2d ed. New York: Frederick A. Praeger, 1962.

Caldwell, Dan, ed.: *Soviet International Behavior and U.S. Policy Options.* Lexington, Mass.: Lexington Books, 1985.

Carter, Jimmy: *Keeping Faith, Memoirs of a President.* New York: Bantam Books, 1982.

Churchill, Winston S.: *The Second World War,* 6 vols. Boston: Houghton Mifflin, 1948–1953.

Clemens, Diane Shaver: *Yalta.* London: Oxford University Press, 1970.

Clubb, O. Edmund: *China and Russia.* New York: Columbia University Press, 1971.

Cohen, Stephen F.: *Sovieticus, American Perceptions and Soviet Reality.* New York: W. W. Norton, 1986.

Cohen, Warren I.: *America's Response to China,* 2d ed. New York: John Wiley, 1980.

Dallek, Robert: *The American Style of Foreign Policy.* New York: Alfred A. Knopf, 1983.

Dallin, David: *Soviet Foreign Policy after Stalin*. Philadelphia: Lippincott, 1961.

Daniels, Robert V.: *Russia, the Roots of Confrontation*. Cambridge, Mass.: Harvard University Press, 1985.

DePorte, A. W.: *Europe between the Superpowers*. New Haven, Conn.: Yale University Press, 1979.

Destler, I. M., Gelb, Leslie, and Lake, Anthony: *Our Own Worst Enemy*. New York: Simon & Schuster, 1984.

Dinerstein, Herbert: *The Making of a Missile Crisis*. Baltimore: The Johns Hopkins Press, 1976.

————: *War and the Soviet Union*, rev. ed. New York: Frederick A. Praeger, 1962.

Djilas, Milovan: *Conversations with Stalin*. New York: Harcourt, Brace and World, 1962.

Donaldson, Robert H. ed.: *The Soviet Union in the Third World: Success and Failures*. Boulder, Colo.: Westview Press, 1981.

Douglas, Joseph D., Jr. and Hoeber, Amoretta: *Soviet Strategy for Nuclear War*. Stanford, Calif.: Hoover Institution Press, 1979.

Edmonds, Robin: *Soviet Foreign Policy, the Brezhnev Years*. New York: Oxford University Press, 1983.

Eisenhower, David: *Eisenhower at War*. New York: Random House, 1986.

Eisenhower, Dwight: *Crusade in Europe*. New York: Doubleday, 1959.

Ehrlich, Paul, Sagan, Carl, et al.: *The Cold and the Dark*. New York: W. W. Norton, 1984.

Emerson, Rupert: *From Empire to Nation, The Rise to Self-Assertion of Asian and African Peoples*. Boston: Beacon Press, 1966.

Enthoven, Alain C. and Smith, K. Wayne: *How Much is Enough?*. New York: Harper Colophon, 1972.

Feis, Herbert: *The China Tangle*. Princeton, N.J.: Princeton University Press, 1972.

Feis, Herbert: *From Trust to Terror, the Onset of the Cold War, 1945–1950*. New York: W. W. Norton, 1970.

Feis, Herbert: *Churchill, Roosevelt, Stalin*. Princeton, N.J.: Princeton University Press, 1957.

Floyd, David: *Mao against Khrushchev*. New York: Frederick A. Praeger, 1963.

Ford, Daniel: *The Button*. New York: Simon & Schuster, 1985.

Freedman, Lawrence: *The Evolution of Nuclear Strategy*. New York: St. Martin's Press, 1983.

Freedman, Robert O.: *Soviet Policy toward the Middle East since 1970*, rev. ed. New York: Frederick A. Praeger, 1978.

Gaddis, John Lewis: *The United States and the Origins of the Cold War*. New York: Columbia University Press, 1972.

———: *Strategies of Containment*. New York: Oxford University Press, 1982.

Gardner, Lloyd C.: *Architects of Illusion*. Chicago: Quadrangle Books, 1974.

———: *A Covenant with Power*. New York: Oxford University Press, 1984.

Garthoff, Raymond: *Soviet Strategy in the Nuclear Age*. New York: Frederick A. Praeger, 1958.

———: *Detente and Confrontation*. Washington, D.C.: The Brookings Institution, 1985.

Gati, Charles, ed.: *Caging the Bear, Containment and the Cold War*. Indianapolis: The Bobbs-Merrill Co., 1974.

Gelb, Leslie and Betts, Richard K.: *The Irony of Vietnam*. Washington, D.C.: The Brookings Institution, 1979.

George, Alexander and Smoke, Richard: *Deterrence in American Foreign Policy*. New York: Columbia University Press, 1974.

George, Alexander, ed.: *Managing US-Soviet Rivalry*. Boulder, Colo.: Westview Press, 1983.

Greene, Fred: *U.S. Policy and the Security of Asia*. New York: McGraw-Hill, 1968.

Gromyko, A. A. and Ponomarev, B. N., eds.: *Soviet Foreign Policy, 1917–1945*. Moscow: Progress Publishers, 1981.

———: *Soviet Foreign Policy, 1945–1980*. Moscow: Progress Publishers, 1981.

Haig, Alexander: *Caveat*. New York: Macmillan, 1984.

Halberstam, David: *The Best and the Brightest*. New York: Random House, 1969.

Halle, Louis: *The Cold War as History*. New York: Harper & Row, 1967.

Hammond, Thomas T.: *Red Flag over Afghanistan, the Communist Coup, the Soviet Invasion, and the Consequences*. Boulder, Colo.: Westview, 1984.

Hannes, Adomeit: *Soviet Risk-Taking and Crisis Behavior.* Boston: Allen & Unwin, 1982.

The Harvard Nuclear Study Group: *Living with Nuclear Weapons.* New York: Bantam Books, 1983.

Herken, Gregg: *Counsels of War.* New York: Alfred A. Knopf, 1985.

Herring, George C. Jr.: *Aid to Russia 1941–1946, Strategy, Diplomacy, the Origins of the Cold War.* New York: Columbia University Press, 1973.

————: *America's Longest War.* New York: John Wiley, 1979.

Hoffmann, Stanley: *Primacy or World Order.* New York: McGraw-Hill, 1978.

Holloway, David: *The Soviet Union and the Arms Race,* 2d. ed. New Haven, Conn.: Yale University Press, 1984.

Hooper, Townsend: *The Limits of Intervention.* New York: David MacKay, 1969.

————: *The Devil and John Foster Dulles.* Boston: Atlantic Monthly Press, 1973.

Hough, Jerry F.: *The Struggle for the Third World, Soviet Debates and American Options.* Washington: The Brookings Institution, 1986.

Hosmer, Stephen T. and Wolfe, Thomas W.: *Soviet Policy and Practice toward Third World Conflicts.* Lexington, Mass.: Lexington Books, 1983.

Johnson, Lyndon B.: *The Vantage Point, Perspective of the Presidency 1963–1969.* New York: Holt, Rinehart & Winston, 1971.

Jones, Joseph M.: *The Fifteen Weeks.* New York: The Viking Press, 1955.

Kahan, Jerome: *Security in the Nuclear Age.* Washington, D.C.: The Brookings Institution, 1975.

Kalb, Marvin and Kalb, Bernard: *Kissinger.* New York: Dell, 1975.

Kaplan, Fred: *The Wizards of Armageddon.* New York: Simon & Schuster, 1983.

Kaplan, Stephen S.: *Diplomacy of Power, Soviet Armed Forces as a Political Instrument.* Washington, D.C.: The Brookings Institution, 1981.

Karnow, Stanley C.: *Vietnam.* New York: The Viking Press, 1983.

Katz, Mark N.: *The Third World in Soviet Military Thought.* Baltimore: The Johns Hopkins Press, 1982.

Kennan, George: *Russia and the West under Lenin and Stalin.* Boston: Little, Brown, 1961.

―――: *American Diplomacy, 1900–1950.* Chicago: The University of Chicago Press, 1951.

Khrushchev, Nikita S.: *Khrushchev Remembers.* Boston: Little, Brown, 1970.

―――: *Khrushchev Remembers, The Last Testament.* Boston: Little, Brown, 1974.

Kissinger, Henry A.: *The White House Years.* Boston: Little, Brown, 1979.

―――: *The Years of Upheaval.* Boston: Little, Brown, 1982.

―――: *The Troubled Partnership.* New York: Anchor Books, 1965.

Krepon, Richard: *Strategic Stalemate.* New York: St. Martin's Press, 1985.

Kuniholm, Bruce: *The Origins of the Cold War in the Near East.* Princeton, N.J.: Princeton University Press, 1980.

Laird, Robbin F. and Herspring, Dale R.: *The Soviet Union and Strategic Arms.* Boulder, Colo.: Westview Press, 1984.

Larson, Deborah W.: *Origins of Containment.* Princeton, N.J.: Princeton University Press, 1985.

Lebow, Richard Ned: *Between Peace and War.* Baltimore: Johns Hopkins Press, 1981.

Leebaert, Derek, ed.: *Soviet Military Thinking.* Boston: Allen & Unwin, 1981.

Lefeber, Walter: *Inevitable Revolutions.* New York: W. W. Norton, 1984.

―――: *America, Russia and the Cold War, 1945–1980,* 3d. ed. New York: John Wiley, 1981.

Lenczowski, John: *Soviet Perceptions of U.S. Foreign Policy.* Ithaca, N.Y.: Cornell University Press, 1984.

Levine, Robert A.: *The Arms Debate.* Cambridge, Mass.: Harvard University Press, 1963.

Lewy, Gunter: *America in Vietnam.* New York: Oxford University Press, 1978.

Lomperis, Timothy J.: *The War Everyone Lost — and Won.* Washington, D.C.: Congressional Quarterly, 1987.

Mackintosh, J. M.: *Strategy and Tactics of Soviet Foreign Policy.* London: Oxford University Press, 1962.

Maddox, Robert J.: *The New Left and the Origins of the Cold War*. Princeton, N.J.: Princeton University Press, 1973.

Mandelbaum, Michael: *The Nuclear Question*. Cambridge, England: Cambridge University Press, 1979.

Martin, Herz: *Beginnings of the Cold War*. Bloomington: Indiana University Press, 1966.

Mastny, Vojtech: *Russia's Road to the Cold War*. New York: Columbia University Press, 1979.

McGuire, Michael: *Military Objectives in Soviet Foreign Policy*. Washington, D.C.: The Brookings Institution, 1987.

McNamara, Robert: *Blundering into Disaster*. New York: Pantheon, 1986.

McNeill, William H.: *America, Britain and Russia*. New York: Oxford University Press, 1953.

Menon, Rajan: *Soviet Power and the Third World*. New Haven, Conn.: Yale University Press, 1986.

Mitchell, R. Judson: *Ideology of a Superpower: Contemporary Soviet Doctrine on International Relations*. Stanford, Calif.: Hoover Institution Press, 1982.

Morgenthau, Hans J.: *In Defense of the National Interest*. New York: Alfred A. Knopf, 1951.

National Conference of Catholic Bishops. *The Challenge of Peace*. Washington, D.C.: United States Catholic Conference, 1983.

Newhouse, John: *Cold Dawn*. New York: Holt, Rinehart, & Winston, 1973.

Nixon, Richard M.: *The Memoirs of Richard Nixon*. New York: Grosset & Dunlap, 1978.

Nogee, Joseph L. and Donaldson, Robert H.: *Soviet Foreign Policy since World War II*, 2d ed. New York: Pergamon, 1984.

North, Robert C.: *Moscow and Chinese Communists*. Stanford, Calif.: Stanford University Press, 1965.

Nye, Joseph S. Jr.: *The Making of America's Soviet Policy*. New Haven, Conn.: Yale University Press, 1984.

Office of Technology Assessment: *The Effects of Nuclear War*. Washington, D.C.: U.S. Government Printing Office, 1979.

Osgood, Robert E.: *Ideals and Self-Interest in America's Foreign Relations*. Chicago: The University of Chicago Press, 1963.

————: *NATO*. Chicago: The University of Chicago Press, 1962.

Palmer, Norman: *Strategic Weapons,* rev. ed. New York: Crane Russak, 1982.

Papp, Daniel S.: *Soviet Perceptions of the Developing World in the 1980's: The Ideological Basis.* Lexington, Mass.: Lexington Books, 1985.

Parmet, Herbert S.: *Eisenhower and the American Crusade.* New York: Macmillan, 1972.

Paterson, Thomas G.: *On Every Front.* New York: W. W. Norton, 1979.

Payne, Keith B.: *Strategic Defense.* Lanham, Md.: Hamilton Press, 1986.

Pierre, Andrew J., ed.: *Nuclear Weapons in Europe.* New York: Council on Foreign Relations, 1984.

Pipes, Richard: *Survival Is Not Enough.* New York: Simon & Schuster, 1984.

Porter, Bruce D.: *The USSR in Third World Conflicts, Soviet Arms and Diplomacy in Local Wars, 1945–1980.* Cambridge, Mass.: Cambridge University Press, 1984.

Quester, George H.: *The Future of Nuclear Deterrence.* Lexington, Mass.: Lexington Books, 1986.

The Report of the President's National Bipartisan Commission on Central America (also known as the *Kissinger Report*). New York: Macmillan, 1984.

Rubinstein, Alvin Z.: *Red Star on the Nile, The Soviet-Egyptian Influence Relationship since the June War.* Princeton, N.J.: Princeton University Press, 1977.

————: *Soviet Foreign Policy since World War II,* 2d ed. Boston: Little, Brown, 1985.

Saivetz, Carol R. and Woodby, Sylvia: *Soviet-Third World Relations.* Boulder, Colo.: Westview Press, 1985.

Schell, Jonathan: *The Fate of the Earth.* New York: Avon Books, 1982.

Schelling, Thomas C. and Halperin, Morton H.: *Strategy and Arms Control.* New York: Twentieth Century Fund, 1961.

Schwartz, David N.: *NATO's Nuclear Dilemma.* Washington, D.C.: The Brookings Institution, 1983.

Sherwood, Robert E.: *Roosevelt and Hopkins.* New York: Bantam Books, 1950.

Seton-Watson, Hugh: *The East European Revolution*. New York: Frederick A. Praeger, 1961.

Shirley, Christian: *Nicaragua*. New York: Random House, 1985.

Shulman, Marshall D.: *Stalin's Foreign Policy Reappraised*. Cambridge, Mass.: Harvard University Press, 1963.

Sick, Gary: *All Fall Down*. New York: Random House, 1985.

Sigal, Leon N.: *Nuclear Forces in Europe*. Washington, D.C.: The Brookings Institution, 1984.

Smith, Gaddis: *American Diplomacy during the Second World War*. New York: John Wiley, 1966.

Smoke, Richard: *National Security and the Nuclear Dilemma*, 2d ed. New York: Random House, 1987.

Spanier, John: *American Foreign Policy since World War II*, 11th ed. Washington, D.C.: Congressional Quarterly, 1988.

————: *The Truman-MacArthur Controversy and the Korean War*, rev. ed. New York: W. W. Norton, 1965.

Stares, Paul B.: *The Militarization of Space*. Ithaca, N.Y.: Cornell University Press, 1986.

Spiegel, Steven L.: *The Other Arab-Israeli Conflict*. Chicago: University of Chicago Press, 1985.

Talbott, Strobe: *End Game*. New York: Harper & Row, 1979.

————: *Deadly Gambits*. New York: Alfred A. Knopf, 1984.

————: *The Russians and Reagan*. New York: Vintage Books, 1984.

———— and Mandelbaum, Michael: *Reagan and Gorbachev*. New York: Vintage Books, 1987.

Taubman, William: *Stalin's American Policy*. New York: W. W. Norton, 1982.

Treverton, Gregory F.: *Making the Alliance Work*. Ithaca, N.Y.: Cornell University Press, 1986.

Tsou, Tang: *America's Failure in China, 1941–1950*, 2 vols. Chicago: Phoenix Books, 1963.

Tucker, Robert W. and Wrigley, Lindley, eds.: *The Atlantic Alliance and Its Critics*. New York: Frederick A. Praeger, 1983.

Tucker, Robert W.: *The Radical Left and American Foreign Policy*. Baltimore, Md.: The Johns Hopkins Press, 1971.

————: *The Nuclear Debate*. New York: Holmes & Meier, 1985.

Ulam, Adam: *Dangerous Relations — The Soviet Union in World Politics, 1970–1980.* New York: Oxford University Press, 1983.

————: *The Rivals.* New York: The Viking Press, 1971.

————: *Expansion and Coexistence,* 2d ed. New York: Frederick A. Praeger, 1974.

Union of Concerned Scientists: *Why Space Weapons Can't Protect Us.* New York: Vintage Specials, 1984.

Valkenier, Elizabeth K.: *The Soviet Union and the Third World, an Economic Bind.* New York: Frederick A. Praeger, 1985.

Volgyes, Ivan: *Politics in Eastern Europe.* Chicago: The Dorsey Press, 1986.

Wheeler-Bennett and Nicholls, Anthony: *The Semblance of Peace, The Political Settlement after the Second World War.* New York: St. Martin's Press, 1972.

Williams, William Appleman: *The Tragedy of American Diplomacy,* 2d ed. New York: Delta, 1972.

Whiting, Allen S.: *China Crosses the Yalu, The Decision to Enter the Korean War.* Stanford, Calif.: Stanford University Press, 1960.

Wolfe, Thomas W.: *Soviet Power and Europe, 1945–1970.* Baltimore, Md.: The Johns Hopkins Press, 1970.

————: *The SALT Experience.* Cambridge, Mass.: Ballinger, 1979.

Yergin, Daniel: *Shattered Peace.* Boston: Houghton Mifflin, 1977.

Zagoria, Donald: *The Sino-Soviet Conflict, 1956–1961.* Princeton, N.J.: Princeton University Press, 1962.

Zimmerman, William: *Soviet Perspectives on International Relations, 1956–1957.* Princeton, N.J.: Princeton University Press, 1969.

Index